HAWKINS OF PLYMOUTH

SIR JOHN HAWKINS, aged 58
From the portrait now in the possession of the Corporation of Plymouth

HAWKINS OF PLYMOUTH

A new history of Sir John Hawkins and
of the other members of his family
prominent in Tudor England

BY

JAMES A. WILLIAMSON

SECOND EDITION
WITH SEVENTEEN ILLUSTRATIONS

BARNES & NOBLE, INC · NEW YORK

PUBLISHERS · BOOKSELLERS · SINCE 1873

FIRST PUBLISHED 1949
SECOND EDITION 1969

61.249

REPRODUCED PHOTOLITHO IN GREAT BRITAIN

PREFACE

This book records the history of the Hawkins family in Tudor England. Although Sir John Hawkins is its chief subject, his father William Hawkins, his brother, also William Hawkins, and his son Sir Richard Hawkins, were all prominent in the story of the time, and their careers are here narrated.

Twenty-two years ago I wrote a life of Sir John Hawkins which the Clarendon Press published and which is now out of print. It was based on a research as comprehensive as I was then able to make it. Since that time, much new material has become available to amplify parts of the story, and my own judgements and outlook have naturally altered in the course of years. I have therefore not revised the former book, but have written an entirely new one. It is relieved of some of the documents and critical arguments of its predecessor, which is available to students in libraries, and in general it omits footnote references to facts which are documented in the older book. It does, however, give references to facts which are based on the new material.

Much of this new evidence is from Spanish sources, consisting of documents edited by Miss I. A. Wright and published by the Hakluyt Society from the Archives of the Indies. Here we have depositions of witnesses and dispatches from officials on the trading operations of John Hawkins in the Spanish colonies. While furnishing many new details and infusing a human element, sometimes amusing, into the transactions, they corroborate broadly the impressions derived from English sources and render possible an estimate, based on the testimony of both sides, of the characters of John Hawkins and the men with whom he dealt.

No less important for another purpose, that of understanding Hawkins's conduct of the expeditions and the way of life of English sailors, and the large part which religious belief played in it, is the evidence that has been collected by Mr. G. R. G. Conway from the records of the Inquisition in Mexico. The Inquisitors tried a number of Hawkins's men who were captured in 1568, and kept full records of their interrogations. The questioning dealt chiefly, but not exclusively, with religious practice, and the statements elicited add colour to the picture of the time. Mr. Conway's

v

transcripts are yet unpublished. I owe him my sincere thanks for his generous sharing of information of which only he had knowledge.

To the Delegates of the Clarendon Press I am especially grateful for their resignation of any rights in the older work which might stand in the way of its successor, and for their release of the blocks of the illustrations which, with three exceptions, are the same in both books.

April 19, 1949   J. A. WILLIAMSON

PREFACE TO THE SECOND EDITION

I have taken the opportunity to make a number of corrections kindly furnished or suggested by my critics. Among them are those on John Hawkins's proceedings in the Canary Islands. These are drawn from the researches made in the records of the Canarian Inquisition by Señor A. Rumeu de Armas, whose book (see p. 40 fn.) is a full description of the western voyages based mainly on the Spanish documents.

1951   J. A. WILLIAMSON

PORTRAITS OF SIR JOHN HAWKINS

FIVE portraits or supposed portraits of Sir John Hawkins are reproduced in this book, and of them only two have hitherto been at all well known. They are: the painting showing Hawkins in 1591 (frontispiece), formerly in the possession of members of the Hawkins family and now in that of the Corporation of Plymouth; and the print (p. 256) from Holland's *Herwologia*, 1620, taken most likely from a painting now unknown. The first, the Plymouth portrait, is probably the best-authenticated that we possess. The name is not inscribed on it, but it carries the arms that John Hawkins alone was entitled to bear in 1591, and its statement of his age, 58, is corroborated by other evidence. The *Herwologia* print is recognizably a picture of the same man, and bears his name, and also a motto 'Advauncement by dilligence', which he may well have adopted.

I owe to the kindness of Mr. A. M. Hind, formerly Keeper of Prints and Drawings at the British Museum, the knowledge of another print (p. 173), which is of the same general type, but which has not previously been reproduced. It is from Holland's *Bazileiwologia*, 1618, a rarer work than the *Herwologia*, and one of which the British Museum Library does not possess a copy.

The remaining two portraits are paintings now in the National Maritime Museum. One is known as the Hope portrait (p. 128), bought for the Museum at a sale in 1938. It has no authentication as a portrait of Hawkins, and was indeed thought by its former owners to be a portrait of Drake. A comparison with established portraits of Drake renders that supposition hardly tenable. On the other hand, this portrait bears a facial resemblance to those of Hawkins already mentioned, most strong perhaps to the Plymouth portrait, if we can imagine at an earlier period of his life the man there depicted. The late Sir Geoffrey Callender, who was then Director of the National Maritime Museum, was struck by the resemblance to Hawkins and acquired the portrait on the strength of it. I think it is at least a good possibility.

The last of our portraits (p. 316) was long in the Sir John Hawkins Hospital at Chatham and has recently been acquired by

the Museum. It is well-authenticated in the sense that it has been
in the possession of the Hospital from an eaily but not precisely
known date and has been generally accepted as genuine. Its inscription gives the date 1581 and the age of the subject as 44, and,
in different lettering, 'Sʳ John Hawkins'. The age is incorrect for
Hawkins, who was 48–9 in 1581, while the name cannot have
been inscribed at that time, since Hawkins was not knighted until
1588. These inaccuracies, while arousing doubt, are not fatal to
the acceptance of the portrait. My own strongest doubt arises
from the face depicted. It does not look like the man who appears
in the Plymouth painting and the prints. If it is meant to be that
man, the artist was so unsuccessful that his rendering is not a like-
ness. However, this is only my opinion; and the portrait is reproduced in order that others may form theirs. For facilities and advice
in reproducing the two portraits from the National Maritime
Museum, my warm thanks are due to the director and his assistants.

CONTENTS

ILLUSTRATIONS

BOOK I
THE MERCHANT ADVENTURER

I

THE ATLANTIC

In the sixteenth century, when modern England began to take shape under the influence of the Renaissance and the Reformation, three generations of the Hawkins family made their mark upon the history of their country. Their enterprises were maritime, conducted from the port of Plymouth, and nearly all within the bounds of the Atlantic Ocean, which was the area of special appeal to the adventurous men of business as contrasted with the explorers and projectors who sought northern passages to Asia. The Atlantic that attracted them was already, in the middle years of Henry VIII, a finite ocean with a farther shore. Beyond that, Europe had much to learn of it, and knowledge was yearly expanding. In the decades of the thirties and forties a sea-going merchant of Plymouth could hear of great news coming in, some of it public, some mysterious and hard to come by. Historical periods are never exactly alike, but sometimes there are illustrative resemblances. There is one between the sixteenth century and the nineteenth. An engineer or a manufacturer of 1840, when railways and steamers and the electric telegraph were new, found himself in a world of expanding opportunity, the fruition, as it seemed to him, of an industrial development rapidly quickening. Just so the merchant adventurer of 1540 saw the geographical expansion of the Renaissance, and heard the call of the Indies and the challenge of discoveries still to make. In both ages the adventurous and forward-looking men were dominant, and in Tudor times they worked amid perils and personal sufferings of which their Victorian counterparts read only in books. The resemblance there breaks into difference, the difference between the heroes of Samuel Smiles and those of Richard Hakluyt.

It will be useful therefore to begin with a survey of Atlantic possibilities as they appeared in the 1530's when William Hawkins was the leading merchant of Plymouth, and his sons William and

John were young. Both the eastern and western fringes of the ocean concerned him and many of his fellow countrymen; and indeed their geographical outlook was more immediately upon seas and oceans than upon kingdoms and continents. The facts were collectively known in Europe at the time and could have been gathered by a diligent inquirer, although it is unlikely that many individuals had a general grasp of them all.

Portugal had discovered and still controlled the trade of the West African coast, which was very valuable from Cape Verde to the equator and rather less so from there to the southwards. Near Cape Verde the intractable Berber peoples gave place to the true negroes, and the coastline southwards to Sierra Leone formed the most prolific slaving territory yet exploited. The Portuguese indeed took slaves wherever potential slaves were to be found, and large numbers were shipped from all parts of the negro coast; but those of Cape Verde were reckoned the best and commanded the highest prices. From Sierra Leone south-east to Cape Palmas stretched the coast of Malagueta, known to the English as the Grain Coast and roughly covered by the modern Liberia. Here the chief attraction was the so-called malaguette pepper, not a true pepper but a pungent spice or 'hot fruit', which commanded its price in a Europe that lived for most of the year on salt and semi-putrid food. 'Guinea grains' were good merchandise in the fifteen thirties and Englishmen meditated other ways of acquiring them than buying from the Portuguese. The thousand miles from Cape Verde to Cape Palmas constituted Upper Guinea, with an easy outward voyage and a practicable return. It yielded more than slaves and pepper. In its river-mouths the factors collected vegetable products, ivory, and a little gold. Out in the ocean lay the Cape Verde Islands, of which the chief was Santiago. The islands contained a Portuguese colony which made its living by collecting the wares of Upper Guinea and shipping them to Europe.

Beyond Cape Palmas the coast was called Lower Guinea, and ran eastward for a thousand miles to the mouths of the Niger and the Bight of Biafara. The Guinea current runs eastward with it, and so does the prevailing wind. It was therefore easy to follow the coast outwards, but hard to return. The skilled navigator worked southwards to the equator, where a favourable current could be found, although the calms often caused westing into the open Atlantic to be very slow. Much of the mortality in Lower Guinea voyages occurred during the fatal protraction of the homeward passage. But Lower Guinea was worth the risk. In it was the Gold Coast, where the negroes would trade paying quantities of dust; and farther on, the kingdom of Benin on the Niger, where a true pepper grew, as valuable in Europe as that of the east. The Portuguese spoke of the gold as coming from a mine, and named their castle on the coast St. George of the Mine.[1] In fact there were no mines. The gold was dust, which the natives obtained by washing the alluvium of river courses. Long before the Portuguese reached Africa the gold came to Europe by overland trade routes. The small quantities irregularly available in Upper Guinea were provided by branches of these routes. Confusion was caused in the mid-sixteenth century by the invasion of the Sumbas, a fighting people who ravaged Africa from east to west. The Portuguese had once had a fortified post in Benin, but by this period they had abandoned it on account of the unhealthy climate. Farther south, the islands of San Thome, Principe and Fernando Po, close to the equator, plantations and slaving bases, complete the list of their tropical African possessions of the early period. Angola was a later development, supplying labour to the later development of Brazil.[2]

Portugal claimed the monopoly of exploiting the African coast by virtue of papal grant, prior discovery and an assertion of effective occupation. The last mentioned was not true as it concerned Upper Guinea and of limited truth for Lower Guinea. In that region there was no Portuguese occupation of Benin, but only mercantile visits to the independent negro inhabitants. On the Gold Coast the fortress of Elmina was permanently held by a garrison and governed by an officer of the crown. There was another fort also farther west at Axim. In the middle of the sixteenth century that

[1] São Jorge da Mina, but the form Elmina has prevailed.
[2] For information on Guinea in the sixteenth century see J. W. Blake, *European Beginnings in West Africa*, London, 1937, and *Europeans in West Africa*, 2 vols., Hakluyt Society, 1942.

was all, but towards its close a third post was established at Accra. These stations by no means dominated the thousand miles of coast. Hostile witnesses said that their influence extended no farther than the range of their guns. The native chiefs commonly considered themselves independent. They traded freely with interlopers in defiance of Portuguese instructions, and they misgoverned their subjects in the established African fashion without any Portuguese interference. Some of them professed a skin-deep Christianity and understood a few words of Portuguese.

In Upper Guinea there were no fortified stations and no government officials. The trade in slaves, malaguette pepper and the other commodities was carried on by factors resident in the numerous river mouths of the coast. The factors were Portuguese, half-breeds, or Jews, with occasional Spaniards and Italians. Most of them were men with a past, bankrupts or criminals, cut off from civilization, and living the life of the natives; and there were not many of them. They could not be considered as constituting a Portuguese occupation. On the test question of trade their actions belied the Portuguese claim, for they often supplied slaves and commodities to trespassers on the monopoly. The monopoly itself belonged to the crown of Portugal, and in spite of some pretences to the propagation of Christianity it was treated mainly as a producer of revenue. For this purpose the right to trade for given periods on specified sections of the coast was farmed to contractors, who paid a lump sum and made what they could of it. They were the employers of the factors who so often let them down, and in theory the sole dealers with the negro kings of the Gold Coast and Benin.

When it was first realized about the middle of the fifteenth century that Portugal had discovered something valuable in Guinea, there was a period of trespass and infringement by Castilians, Flemings, and probably some Englishmen. In the 1480's Portugal countered the threat by a treaty with Castile, by diplomatic protests to England, and by merciless severity to the intruders captured on the coast. Thenceforward for half a century the Portuguese exploited their monopoly in peace. Meanwhile the Spaniards were discovering great and rich lands in the West. After a brief phase of tension and jealousy Spain and Portugal came together, drew the meridian of partition between their respective areas in the Atlantic, and consistently backed one another in maintaining the two monopolies against all other challengers. The Portuguese government attempted a policy of secrecy about Guinea. The chronicles of the discovery were altered, maps and charts suppressed, and all who had been in Africa forbidden to reveal any information to foreigners. Such a policy, enforced by spying and despotic arrests, defeated its own object, for it caused men who had served their country overseas to feel that they were suspected when they came home. Accordingly many fled in fear of their lives, and throughout the sixteenth century there were well-informed Portuguese renegades in France and England, making their living by placing their knowledge at the disposal of foreign interlopers. From about 1530 a new wave of trespassers, English and French, passed along the Guinea coasts, and the long seclusion of the monopoly was broken, never to be restored.

These transactions, which all parties tried to keep secret, have left little or nothing in the form of detailed narrative, and for the most part only summaries and allusions in the official documents that have survived. French records are probably fuller than English, but difficulties of access have prevented research in soi e which might be valuable. English state papers for the first half of the Tudor period are almost a blank on the subject of Portugal. The fact that a Portuguese nobleman fled to England under an assumed name and tried to inspire a trespassing expedition to Guinea, and that Henry VII put him in the Tower, has left not a trace in English records. But all such things were known at the time to interested parties, better known than they can ever be to us. The English merchant traded at Antwerp, where he saw merchandise that spoke for itself. For Portugal made Antwerp her staple for sales in northern Europe, and sent thither shiploads of Guinea commodities, together with sugar from the San Thome plantations, and spices from the Far East. The same Englishman no doubt had his connections in Portugal, although in that land of suspicion he might not learn much about the origin of the goods. But he would also do business in Rouen and the new port of

Havre de Grace, and there he might see charts drawn by refugee pilots who had served in Guinea and might meet Frenchmen also who had trespassed on the monopoly in Guinea and Brazil alike. Before Henry VIII's reign ended there were Englishmen who had the same experience, and to whom there was little mystery about the African coast and its products.

Brazil may be mentioned as a pendant to Guinea, for it constituted another Portuguese claim to a long trading coast. Brazil fell to Portugal by the decision to draw the line of demarcation between her monopoly and that of Spain; and its discovery took place in 1500, some years after the drawing of the line. For the first thirty years there was no more Portuguese occupation than in Upper Guinea, but simply the purchase from unsubdued natives of the brazil wood or dyewood which gave the country its name. The French quickly began interloping, for dyestuffs were valuable. After a generation of protest and sporadic fighting on the coast, Portugal reluctantly adopted the policy of fortified stations, with permanent garrisons. Round them grew a few plantation settlements deriving slave labour from Africa; but the development was inconsiderable in the first part of the century, when Brazil, like Upper Guinea, was anybody's trading ground.

The same germinative period brought great news from the farther West, where Spain was expanding her own monopoly. We know curiously little about Englishmen in Portugal at this time, but a good deal about Englishmen in Spain. Their trade was mainly in Andalusia, where some resided in Seville, the head city for all the official business of the Spanish Indies. The passage up river to Seville was difficult for the greater ships, and merchandise was dealt with at San Lucar, lower down, and also at Cadiz, whose importance grew with the century. San Lucar was the chief resort of the English merchants, where they were recognized as a regulated company, and had their own church of St. George. Here, along with Londoners and Southampton men, were merchants of Bristol and the west country. Some were resident, some came and went, and among those we may perhaps count the Plymouth Hawkinses; for, as will be shown, they had an early Spanish connection.

Thus there was in south-west Spain an important English colony, which stood well with the Spanish government while the Anglo-Spanish alliance endured. These Englishmen were allowed to take part in trade with the Spanish empire in the West, their goods being shipped from Seville and crossing the Atlantic under the Spanish flag in the regular colonial convoys. As early as 1526 (and perhaps earlier) there were Englishmen in the Indies. In the year named the Thornes of Bristol had a factor named Tyson in Hispaniola. Somewhat later we hear of Englishmen in Mexico, and by 1550 there were a number of them, mainly engaged in trade, but also serving the Spanish government in various capacities. Spain never made an attempt to keep her Indies secret. She gloried in her conquests and allowed historians to write freely of them. Until the reign of Charles V was well advanced her monopoly seemed secure. Charles was not only King of Spain but German Emperor, and he allowed his Germans and Flemings to go westwards like his English allies. So long as they sailed under his flag and were sound on his religion they might go.

There was no great secrecy even about voyages of discovery. A Bristol man accompanied Magellan in his voyage westward through his Straits to the Spice Islands, but unfortunately he died while crossing the Pacific. Two Englishmen sailed with Sebastian Cabot, Pilot-Major of Spain, in 1526, on the expedition which explored the River Plate and made a distant reconnaissance of the trans-continental route to Peru.[1] These men were Roger Barlow, a Bristol merchant, and Henry Latimer, a pilot, and they were planted in the expedition to learn all they could at an expense of 1,400 ducats invested by Robert Thorne, their backer. There was no concealment about it, and when Cabot sent home a report of his doings he sent Barlow with it, and Barlow was personally presented to the Emperor. Englishmen of the second quarter of the sixteenth century who belonged to mercantile and shipping circles could hear of all the great deeds that were done in the

[1] The expedition was publicly designed for the Spice Islands, but Cabot diverted it to South American exploration without incurring the displeasure of the Emperor.

Spanish West and could get accurate information about its trading conditions.

And what they heard in the twenties, thirties and forties was exciting. In the 1520's America began to show itself in a new light. After Columbus there had been a disappointing period in which the great new continent appeared only as a barrier on the road to Asia, which had been Columbus's goal. Spanish explorers tried to find a strait whereby to pass the barrier, but failed. Farther north the English tried, in the cold seas to the north of Newfoundland, and also failed. Not until 1522 was it known that Magellan had found a strait in the south and had actually reached the Far East by a western voyage. The news meant little to the Spaniards of the Caribbean, the colonists planted by Columbus. They had settled in Cuba, Hispaniola, Jamaica and Puerto Rico. They had almost exterminated the inoffensive natives and had almost collected the scanty stock of gold. As adventurers they seemed to have no future, and as colonists they were hampered by lack of labour. Slaves of some sort were their necessity, and to obtain them they raided the neighbouring islands and the Tierra Firme, or Main Land to the southward, the Caribbean coast of South America. But none of the natives made good slaves. The Caribs of the Lesser Antilles and the Guiana Coast were so cruel and recalcitrant that they had to be left alone, and thus preserved their national life for another two centuries. The others, in descending order of spirit from the warriors of Tierra Firme, who gave more trouble than they were worth, to the poor innocents of the Bahamas, who made no resistance and died of broken hearts, were all a bad economic investment. The solution of the labour problem was in the African negroes, who lived for the most part under tyrannies of such terror and brutality in their own homes that they did not take hardly the exchange into servitude to white men. Negroes, however, were not carried to America until about 1510, and it was several years after that before the movement became extensive.

Meanwhile, almost suddenly, the situation changed, and the depressed Antillean colonies became bases for adventurers animated by the prospect of unlimited conquest. Expeditions seeking a westward outlet from the Caribbean came upon a new kind of native, organized, disciplined and rich, inhabiting the coast-lands of the Gulf of Mexico; and soon obtained intelligence of the Aztec overlords in the interior, and the great emperor in the city on the lake. Hernan Cortes and a following of Cuban colonists forsook their Cuban prospects and answered the call. With his march into Mexico in 1519 the great age of the Conquistadores began, a quarter of a century in which Spaniards dared and endured and achieved to an intenser degree than any other men until the great wars of our time.[1]

The decade of the 1520's is the period in which Europe heard of the conquest of Mexico and riches far greater than any so far obtained in the Antilles. France heard of it and was at the same time at war with Charles V. French privateers looked out for returning treasure-ships, and scored an early success by capturing a consignment of rich stuff despatched by Cortes to his sovereign. Jean Ango of Dieppe became a name of note in the next twenty years, a great organizing shipowner whose captains seemed always to meet the right Spanish ship at the expected place, and whose success was undoubtedly based on a sound system of acquiring information. England heard of it also. Thomas Tyson, the Bristol man in Santo Domingo, is sufficient guarantee of that, even if there were no others like him. And indeed, the mariners of that time were international, as they have been ever since. Wherever we have details of crews and officers we come upon men serving out of their proper nation, Frenchmen and Flemings in English ships, Flemings, Germans and Englishmen in Spanish, and so forth; which makes it obvious that nothing of importance could happen in the Atlantic world which would not come to the notice of a collector of maritime news. How a merchant could inform himself on matters in which there was some motive for secrecy is illustrated by some letters of Christoval de Haro to Charles V.[2] At the Emperor's request, Haro sent a man to get news of French

[1] A concise account of the conquests is in R. B. Merriman, *Rise of the Spanish Empire*, Vol. III, Ch. xxvii–xxx, New York, 1925. For a more extended and very well written account see F. A. Kirkpatrick, *The Spanish Conquistadores*, 2nd edn., London, 1946.

[2] Printed in H. P. Biggar, *Documents relating to Cartier and Roberval*, Ottawa, 1930, *passim*.

ocean voyages in 1541. This man made a tour of the ports from Bordeaux to Dieppe and reported a variety of expeditions preparing for Guinea, Brazil and Canada. His method was simply to frequent waterside taverns and talk to sailors, most of whom in those garrulous days were prepared to converse as carelessly as he desired.

If Mexico astonished Europe the sensation was outdone by Peru in the following decade. The discovery of Peru was the natural outcome of the earlier expeditions along the Main and the Atlantic side of Central America, which culminated in 1513 when Balboa crossed the Isthmus and discovered the South Sea. The search for a central strait did not yield one, but the Isthmus of Panama, narrowing to fifty miles, afforded a practicable access to what lay beyond. In less than ten years the Panama Spaniards heard of the great empire of the Incas in Peru, and while Cortes was rounding off the dominion of New Spain to the northward the preliminary probings southward from the Gulf of Panama were taking place. They were difficult and protracted, and Peru had not been reached when Sebastian Cabot entered the basin of the River Plate and learned that contact with the great empire was possible from that direction. Cabot, however, was four years absent, and when he returned it was to find that Pizarro of Panama had come to Spain and received the Emperor's support for the push down the west coast. After ten years on the approaches, the Spaniards entered and conquered in a few months. The accumulated wealth which they found was staggering even to minds attuned to wonder by the tale of Mexico. Peru produced far more hoarded gold. Its extensions, from Quito in the north to Chile in the south, continued for years to excite hopes of equally rich strikes, while the Eldorado legend of a last hidden refuge of Inca wealth long remained an incentive to adventure.

The fifteen thirties resounded with the gold of Peru, and when the gold hoard was all gathered in, leaving scattered placer mining to continue the supply, the discovery of the Potosi silver mine in 1545, literally a mountain of silver, enabled Peru to remain the world's chief treasure ground. In Mexico also silver mining proved permanent when the gold had been skimmed off, but

Mexican silver, like the Mexican gold, was less great than Peruvian. The gold when in Mexico and Peru had served for a royal hoard and for the making of objects of art and religion. It would appear that much the same uses awaited it when it was transferred to Europe. It was extremely convenient as hoarded wealth, but too precious to use as wealth in circulation. In that capacity the silver was a much greater factor in history. From the late forties onward the silver stream had important effects on European life, raising prices, stimulating enterprise, breaking down stagnant social and economic arrangements; and then reached out to larger consequences in vitalizing the trade with Asia which was to be the complement of emigration to America in producing the industrial revolution and the mechanized world.

England in the mid-sixteenth century had no prescience of long-term developments, but was affected by the early results of the flow of precious metals. Prices rose and trade was unsettled, with enrichment for some and impoverishment for others, and in effect a small-scale social and economic revolution. Its most important feature, in the historical perspective, was to let loose energies in independent enterprise which had previously been canalized in predetermined grooves. The first half of the Tudor period had been the age of the regulated companies. The second half was to be more characteristically the age of joint-stock syndicates and individuals playing a lone hand. To the men of the time it was all action and excitement and 'Faites vos jeux!' To us it has a wistful appeal as the growth of liberty whose death we witness.

As the thirties passed into the forties the news was of the conquest of a third treasure state in the high plateau which now forms the centre of the republic of Colombia. The conquerors called it New Granada and founded a capital at Santa Fé de Bogotá. The approach had been made almost simultaneously by three mutually independent expeditions, striking north from Peru, west from the Orinoco and south from the Main. This last push under Jimenez de Quesada beat the others by a small margin, a result of some importance to future English proceedings, since it ensured that the communications of New Granada should be through the Spanish Main, and led to the foundation of Cartagena as the coastal port for the purpose.

The Spanish Main, so celebrated in romantic literature, was not the most desirable region of the Spanish empire. It had been visited first for discovery and then for slave-raiding, which had blighted the prospects of steady-going colonization. True settlement made hardly any progress until the second quarter of the century, when the half-dozen seaports became centres of struggling plantations. There was potential wealth, small supplies of alluvial gold almost everywhere, pearls at one point on the Venezuelan coast, hides as cattle multiplied, and sugar where hands could be found to grow it. Labour was the difficulty. The Indians of the Main refused to be slaves and inhumanely killed their hunters with poisoned arrows. The Main cried out for negroes. With them it might become a valuable all-round tropical colony of the kind which Spaniards were fitted to develop. Without them it could hope for little. The supply from West Africa, filtered through a mesh of bureaucracy and controlled at source by monopolists who had no wish to cheapen the commodity, was never liberal. To the judgment of a clear-thinking man of business it was apparent that a freer trade in slaves would make a better Spanish Main.

If there was stagnation on the Main there was regression in the Antillean islands. The four greater islands had been colonized. The Caribbees, the crescent of smaller islands from Puerto Rico south to Trinidad, were left to the Caribs, who fought like devils and ate their prisoners. The Bahamas, the original discovery of Columbus, were emptied by slave hunters and left derelict. In the four big islands the Indians were shared among the colonists in the relationship of feudal serfs to lords of manors. But a feudal aristocracy did not take root, for the serfs did not play their part. They simply died out, and by 1520 there were not many left. Here also the negro was needed, and was not available in sufficient numbers to make a real tropical colony. Gold mining ceased in Hispaniola, for without plentiful Indian labour the returns were so small as to be profitless. Sugar planting made small headway. Ultimately the cattle ranch, with hides for export, collected by a few half-bred nondescripts, was the economic destiny of the islands which had entranced Columbus as the most favoured scene on earth. Even so there remained large areas in them unused and void of people.[1] Two cities of first-rate importance remained amid the decay, Santo Domingo in Hispaniola, and Havana in northern Cuba. The first-named had been the capital and official headquarters of the colonies in the early days before the Mexican extension. It did not keep its hold on that extension, which became the Viceroyalty of New Spain. But it did keep authority (subject to the Viceroy) over the settlements on the Main which slowly grew there after the slave-raiding period. Santo Domingo therefore remained a place of government expressive of the wealth accumulated by the official class. Havana flourished also for a purely external reason. It was the chosen harbour of concentration and departure for Europe of all the shipping, whether from the Main, the Isthmus or New Spain. Concentration and ultimately sailing in strict convoy were necessitated by the long wars between Spain and France and the growing tendency of French seamen to disregard the nominal peace of the intervening periods.

Northward of the Caribbean the Atlantic, save at one point, was undeveloped and unattractive to the merchant, athough full of promise to discoverers and geographical speculators. Florida had been explored by Spaniards, who found no temptation to settle in it. The present east coast of the United States had been examined by various expeditions in search of a strait leading to the Pacific. But surveys of a very long coastline conducted in a few weeks had produced no accurate knowledge, not even a certainty that the strait did not exist. Until the end of the century this remained the least known part of the Atlantic. By contrast the waters surrounding Newfoundland were visited by thousands of men every summer in exploitation of the cod fishery which John Cabot had first discovered. Frenchmen, Spaniards, Portuguese and English all took part, and long before 1550 'Newland fish'

[1] John Sparke, who was probably in Hispaniola with John Hawkins in 1563, said that the great island contained only thirteen villages in addition to its capital, Santo Domingo.

was an important article of English diet. Yet these thousands of annual visitors were there for the sole purpose of catching fish, and they made hardly any contribution to the geographical exploration of the region. The geographers did not even learn from them whether Newfoundland was part of the continent, a large island, or an archipelago of small ones, and all three interpretations are to be found in maps of the period. A full generation elapsed before the French, who were in early days the most active of the fishermen, became familiar with the Gulf of St. Lawrence, which they called the Grand Bay. Jacques Cartier was the first to push up to the sites of Quebec and Montreal in the fifteen thirties.

North of Newfoundland there was repellent actuality and a glowing promise, the promise of the strait leading to the Pacific and eastern Asia. There was scarcely a decade in the century in which some expedition was not dispatched or projected for the Northern Passage—North-West, North, or North-East—and a large proportion of the attempts were English. They were part of the Tudor ambition to open a direct trade with Asia, a no less formative movement than that of intruding upon the monopolies of America and Africa.

The island groups of the eastern Atlantic have an importance of their own in a survey of the mid-Tudor possibilities. The Cape Verde group, already mentioned, were essentially a part of Upper Guinea, but the others fall into a different category. The Canaries, Madeira and the Azores had all been discovered in the more liberal early fifteenth century, before the idea of rigid monopoly had become firmly established. Madeira and the Azores became Portuguese settlement colonies, which were not barred to the merchants of other countries. The Azores, in particular, had direct and regular contact with England early in the Tudor period. The Canaries, after French adventurers had failed to subdue them, were in dispute between Castile and Portugal, but were recognized as Spanish by the treaty of 1479 and have remained so ever since. At that date their aboriginal Guanche inhabitants were in possession. The Spanish conquest, island after island, took several years, and resulted in the extermination of the Guanches and the colonization of the soil by sugar-planting and

THE GREAT OCEAN SEA, AS DRAWN BY JOHN ROTZ IN 1542

Royal MSS. 20 E ix.

wine-producing white men. English trade was active from the outset and was never forbidden by Spain. More than that, a number of English adventurers took part in the conquest and settled down with grants of land as Spanish subjects.[1] We may regard 1490 as a central date in the extended process, and it follows that the second generation of these English settlers was still active in the mid-Tudor period. Their existence is interesting and may well have been important in some of the transactions with which this book will deal.

Such was the Atlantic, 'the Great Ocean Sea' of a contemporary geographer, as it appeared to the Plymouth Hawkinses. We have now to take a view of the family and some of its early proceedings.

[1] *A Brief Summe of Geographie*, ed. E. G. R. Taylor, Hakluyt Society, 1932. p. xxi.

II

HAWKINS OF PLYMOUTH

Late in the fifteenth century a certain John Hawkins of Tavistock married Joan, daughter of William Amydas of Launceston. Their son, born between 1490 and 1500 and probably not their only child, was William Hawkins, who became a merchant of Plymouth and the first of three generations prominent in the history of the Tudor period. The name of Hawkins occurs frequently in the records of the time. There were landowning Hawkinses in Kent, and mercantile Hawkinses in London and Bristol, but there is no demonstrable relationship between these families and the Plymouth group with whom this book is concerned. In Plymouth the customs ledger shows activity by a merchant named William Hawkins in 1497–8. There was probably some connection between him and John Hawkins of Tavistock, but its nature is not apparent. Meanwhile the historical William Hawkins was growing up. He was appointed Receiver or Treasurer to the Corporation of Plymouth for the year 1524–5, and at the same time Collector of the subsidy for the county of Devon. He was then thirty years of age, more or less, and thenceforward his career is traceable with increasing certainty.

In 1527 there is a record of a town emergency in which Hawkins played his part. An Italian ship came into the harbour pursued by French pirates. Plymouth was not rigid in its views on such transactions, provided that they took place at a respectful distance; but on this occasion the pirates threatened to attack their quarry in the port, where the townsmen were determined to preserve the peace. Their resolute attitude was sufficient, and the French withdrew. William Hawkins soon afterwards contributed to the defences by selling the corporation two brass guns for £24, and 196 lb. of powder at 6d. a pound. In the same year Hawkins was defendant in a legal action sufficiently important to come before the Court of Common Pleas at Westminster. He, with

James Horsewell, Peter Grisling and three others, were accused of beating and wounding John Jurdon of Plymouth to the danger of his life. No evidence or decision on the charge is recorded, and the matter is worth notice only because it introduces the names of Horsewell and Grisling, the one a lifelong ally of Hawkins, the other shortly to appear as a persistent enemy. The politics of Plymouth were tempestuous and its manners as rough as was usual in seaports. The affair of 1527 was only the first of several in which the family were to be concerned.

In the meanwhile Hawkins had married Joan Trelawny and had become the father of a family. His elder son William was born about 1519, and John, the younger, in 1532. There were no other sons who lived to grow up, if we may believe a statement by one who knew them, that John was the only brother of William. But there was a daughter who probably married a member of the Horsewell family. The evidence is the existence of a youth named Paul Horsewell who sailed with John Hawkins on his third West Indian voyage and was known as Hawkins's nephew. He could only have been so if his mother was a sister of Hawkins. Very few parish records of the early Tudor period have been preserved, and we have none that contain the baptisms and marriages of the Hawkinses. The first William Hawkins's date of birth is merely conjectural. That of his son William rests on a statement that in 1579 he was about sixty years of age. John's date, 1532, is fairly well established by two mutually but not quite exactly corroborative testimonies, the inscription on his monument in St. Dunstan's-in-the-East in the City of London, and the inscription on the portrait which forms the frontispiece of this book. The monument (destroyed in the Great Fire) said that he was sixty-three when he died in 1595. The portrait states that he was fifty-eight in 1591. Here it may be as well to set forth the sixteenth century members of the family in tabular form (see page 20).

All the Hawkinses here recorded spelt the name as Hawkyns. Richard Hakluyt and nearly all subsequent historians have rendered it Hawkins. That spelling, although inexact, must be regarded as established, and it would be pedantic at this late date to seek to alter it.

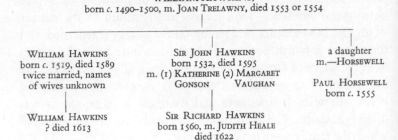

WILLIAM HAWKINS,
born *c.* 1490–1500, m. JOAN TRELAWNY, died 1553 or 1554

WILLIAM HAWKINS born *c.* 1519, died 1589 twice married, names of wives unknown	SIR JOHN HAWKINS born 1532, died 1595 m. (1) KATHERINE (2) MARGARET GONSON VAUGHAN	a daughter m.—HORSEWELL PAUL HORSEWELL born *c.* 1555
WILLIAM HAWKINS ? died 1613	SIR RICHARD HAWKINS born 1560, m. JUDITH HEALE died 1622	

William Hawkins was Mayor of Plymouth in 1532–3. In the ensuing years the town was disturbed by rival factions and by a prolonged dispute with the borough of Saltash over the exercise of jurisdiction in the waters of Plymouth Sound, 'the haven and its members'. The details are for the most part preserved in some recorded proceedings in the Star Chamber, but the story is not entirely clear. It seems, however, that Peter Grisling, who lived sometimes in Plymouth and sometimes in Saltash, was searcher of the port, or, as we should now put it, the chief customs officer. It was a government appointment without salary, the holder re-couping himself by charging fees to each ship searched. It is easy to imagine how a stringent performance of the search and exaction of the fees would arouse the resentment of merchants and shipowners in days when a certain laxity was normal. Hawkins and his allies, James Horsewell and John Elyot, both shipowners, complained that Grisling made the office of searcher his sole means of livelihood and exercised it with rapacity and extortion. Religious bitterness also had its part in the affair, as may be inferred from the record that Grisling called Horsewell 'a naughty heretic knave'. This was in 1535–6, when Horsewell had become Mayor of Plymouth, and when also Thomas Cromwell and Henry VIII were setting about the dissolution of the monasteries. Given the temper and the suspicions of the time, it was a dangerous thing for Grisling to say. His opponents affected toleration by answering that they considered the statement malicious but not treasonable, the words having been spoken in fury and drink. The Privy Council summoned both parties to London and enjoined moderation, after which all returned to Plymouth together, apparently reconciled.

Grisling then suggested that Hawkins and Elyot should use their influence to get him a seat in the Plymouth Council. They gave a tepid promise to try, but after six weeks there had been no success. Grisling, who had been living in Plymouth, returned to Saltash in a bad temper. Then, in the autumn of 1536, Horsewell's mayoralty ended, and Thomas Bull, one of Grisling's friends, succeeded him. The result verged on civil war. Bull and his party denounced Horsewell to the Privy Council and got him banished from the town for a year and a day. Hawkins, Horsewell and Elyot countered by calling a town meeting, which disregarded the banishment and appointed Horsewell Town Clerk, whilst Hawkins gave vent to 'divers slanderous words'. Bull and Grisling reported the matter to the Lord Privy Seal (Thomas Cromwell), who ordered that the Hawkins party should be expelled from the Town Council. But Hawkins was still unsubdued and claimed an investigation of the whole dispute. Cromwell appointed Sir Piers Edgecumbe and three other county magnates to perform the task. This commission heard the case for two days and reported in Hawkins's favour, adding that Grisling's conduct had been intolerable. Bull and Hawkins then agreed to live in peace according to the ancient customs of the town.

Peace appears to have been restored in Plymouth, and the contest became one between Plymouth and Saltash. Just when Grisling's power in Plymouth declined with the decision above noted and with the end of Bull's mayoralty, Grisling himself became Mayor of Saltash, for the year 1537–8. He had now two means of annoying and humiliating the Plymouth shipowners, first by his continued extortion as searcher, and second by exploiting an ancient privilege of Saltash. That borough, as the senior port within the Sound, claimed to levy dues on all the rest, and also to compel the attendance of all shipowners at a court for the purpose of enforcing regulations. Presumably these rights had been allowed to sleep and were now revived in full harshness by Grisling. He levelled his gun principally at Hawkins and swore by blood and wounds that no ship or goods of his enemy should pass but he would levy on them. Hawkins refused time after time to attend the Saltash court, which sentenced him to fine after fine until the accumulated total was £80, not a penny of which did he pay.

Plymouth backed Hawkins as its champion and in 1538 again elected him Mayor and his friend Horsewell Town Clerk. From this strong position Hawkins brought a suit against Grisling and Saltash in the Star Chamber. The above story has been drawn from the pleadings in the case, but the record of the decision is missing. There can be little doubt, however, that the victory went to Hawkins, for he and his party were thenceforward dominant in Plymouth and in favour with the King's government. In 1539, while still Mayor and Town Clerk, Hawkins and Horsewell were chosen members for Plymouth in the Parliament which passed the Act of the Six Articles and witnessed the end of the remaining monasteries.

Plymouth's share in the dissolution had been accomplished in the previous year, when its small house of the Grey Friars had been abolished in September.[1] Hawkins and Horsewell valued and sold the effects, of which the most considerable were pieces of silver plate weighing 73 ounces and fetching £12. It seems possible that this was a low price paid by the Corporation, for a few years later it sent Hawkins to London to sell some former church plate, and he obtained £41 for it.

The foregoing records are not entirely insignificant. They do give some impression of the sort of society that inhabited Plymouth and many another English town, and of the sort of men who led it. They were headstrong and turbulent, with an instinct of liberty that made them speak boldly even to such higher powers as Henry VIII and his Lord Privy Seal. The law was much in their thoughts, but it was their weapon rather than their curb. The Tudor man of action decided on his course and then sought law to strengthen him. He was not happy without it, and he seldom failed to find it. We shall meet with the process again and again in the Hawkins story. These men served their town and their

[1] Mr. C. W. Bracken's *History of Plymouth*, Plymouth, 1931, shows that there were other establishments and mentions of White and Black Friars, but the subject is still obscure. The dissolution evidence relates clearly to the Grey Friars.

country without pay, but not without reward. Hardly any offices were paid. The reward lay in position, prestige and influence. It was worth while to be a ruling man in such a society, vexatious often, and sometimes dangerous, but better than being ruled by rough customers like Grisling and William Hawkins. It was a bracing age, and turned out self-reliant men, ready to take initiative and responsibility.

Before leaving municipal affairs, let us look at their Plymouth. We can reconstruct its aspect fairly well, for there is in the Cotton manuscripts a great rolled map and survey of the south-west coast on a scale of about an inch to the mile, made in the early 1540's to show the coast defences in preparation for the approaching French war. Every seaport, large and small, is noted, the houses and forts set in their landscapes in delicately drawn birdseye views, and Plymouth and its district are included. The relevant portion is here reproduced, but on a scale that is regrettably small: the illustration covers 24 square inches, while the same region in the original has an area of about 350 square inches.

Two great ships are seen sailing up the Sound, leaving the Mewstone to starboard and Rame Head to port. There was no breakwater (a nineteenth century improvement), and the Sound itself was not a secure anchorage. The ship reaching its northern end passes St. Nicholas Island (now Drake's Island) and makes for the Cattewater. This was the outer roadstead of Plymouth harbour, the inner being formed by Sutton Pool, round which were grouped the houses of the town. The Plymouth of that day covered only a small part of the modern city, from the White Friars to St. Andrews Church and a little beyond. The Hawkinses lived in Kinterbury Street, in the south-western quarter. The street existed until recently, although its Tudor houses had long disappeared. German bombers destroyed many of their modern successors, and post-war planners have obliterated most of the street itself. A large castle with four towers, of which only a fragment now remains, stood on the rising ground at the west side of the entrance to Sutton Pool, and there was a square fort commanding the mouth of the Cattewater, and nearly on the site of the present Citadel. The Hoe was edged with batteries facing southward, but there were no houses there or on the slope behind it. Stonehouse was a separate place, with fields between it and Plymouth. The Mill Bay, west of the Hoe, had the corn mills built across its narrow entrance, the basin serving as a head of tidewater which turned the wheels as it flowed out. To the westward the map shows Mount Edgecumbe with its fenced deer-park; Saltash, named simply Aysshe; and the country and coastline, somewhat out of scale, to Liskeard and Looe. The portlet on the extreme western edge of the illustration is Polperro. Looe, which even then had its bridge, when most estuaries were merely crossed by ferry, is described as 'a tyde haven drye at halfe ebbe', which it still is; and the purpose of the map, a survey of Home Guard possibilities, is indicated by the further statement that there is 'good landynge before the towne'. Fifteen forty and nineteen forty!

Local politics were not the main activity of William Hawkins. They were forced on him as an element of his career as a merchant, on the principle that such a man had either to rule or be ruled by a rival. The local boss and the successful trader are but two aspects of the same character. Faction fights secured his position in Plymouth, but commerce made his place in English history. The place amounts to this, that he was a pioneer of oceanic enterprise, the first regular transatlantic trader in our record.

The customs ledgers of the last years of Henry VIII show William Hawkins exporting cloth and tin to the ports of western Europe, and importing a variety of goods, the salt of Rochelle, wines of Bordeaux, Portugal and Spain, sugar and pepper probably from Portugal, olive oil most likely and soap certainly from Spain, 'Newland fish' perhaps direct from the Banks but more probably bought from French middlemen. The ledgers list the goods but not the countries from which they came. But it is very probable that some of the sugar and wines were brought from the Canaries. Those islands were regarded by Spain as part of her European dominion and were as freely open to foreigners as Seville or San Lucar. Hakluyt records that John Hawkins traded with the Canaries in his younger days, and the Plymouth port books show a regular traffic by Hawkins and others; but the port books were first kept in the 1560's, and are not a testimony to the 30's and 40's.

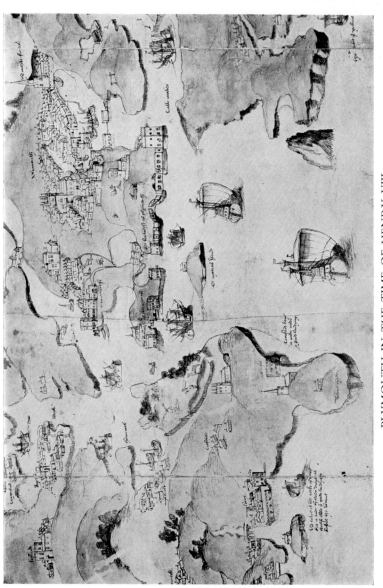

PLYMOUTH IN THE TIME OF HENRY VIII

From Cotton MSS., Aug. I. i. 38

Whether or not William Hawkins had a Canary trade in those
years, his European connections were sufficient to enable him to
learn the Atlantic possibilities. Spain, as we have seen, made little
secret of her western empire. Portugal tried to be very secret
about Brazil and Africa, but her renegades betrayed her. Hawkins
could have found them in the French ports which he frequented,
and the French themselves had long been attacking both monopolies. English historians have generally passed over the fact that
the French seamen were a generation before us in defying the
papal bulls, opening the ocean routes and prising open the sealed
areas. But it is none the less true, and the Elizabethan achievement,
the basis of European freedom, would have been more difficult
but for the antecedent efforts of the French.

A French ship from Honfleur reached the Brazilian coast in 1504,
only four years after the Portuguese discovery. French traders
followed, and established their business in spite of Portuguese
hostility. The Portuguese, who had hoped to monopolize the
Brazil trade without expenditure on armaments, found themselves obliged to fight, and grew extremely indignant. In 1523
John III of Portugal ordered his subjects to sink any Frenchmen
caught on the coast. But the French were able to take care of
themselves. In 1530 they plundered the new Portuguese settlement of Pernambuco. At the same time they began to take a
greater interest in West Africa, and their Guinea voyages formed
a business parallel to and connected with that of Brazil.

It should be noted that, just as there were two Guinea coasts
divided by Cape Palmas, so there were two Brazil coasts divided
by Cape San Roque. One trended north-westwards towards the
Caribbean. It included the delta of the Amazon. Beyond that lay
Guiana, then known as the Cannibal Coast, and often loosely
thought of as part of Brazil. Portuguese settlement, hardly begun
in 1530, spread very slowly westward from Cape San Roque
and did not reach the Amazon until the following century.
Neither Portuguese nor Spaniards had any interests in Guiana,
and Spanish settlement on the Orinoco began only at the end of
the sixteenth century. The true Spanish Main lay west of the
Orinoco. This northerly Brazil and Guiana coast lay mainly in the

belt of the north-east trades, and was subject to an ocean current flowing from east to west and continuing as the Caribbean current along the Spanish Main. It was therefore usual, and often necessary, for ships visiting northern Brazil to pass on into the Caribbean and out by the Florida Channel in order to sail back to Europe. In other words, the northern Brazil trade led to raids in the Spanish Indies. In the 1530's the French were engaged in both. The other Brazil coast led southwards from Cape San Roque, through and beyond the tropical latitudes towards the Spanish discovery of the River Plate. It was on this south Brazilian coast that the greatest trading activity prevailed in the early days. Here the Portuguese were obliged to establish bases for their coastal forces, first at Pernambuco, then at Bahia, and later at Rio de Janeiro; and from these fortified stations their true colonization slowly spread. Pernambuco, close to the angle of the two coasts, long remained the strategic key to Brazil. In 1530 the Portuguese occupation was so thin as to be hardly discernible. The native peoples were independent, and the whole country lay open to all comers.

William Hawkins of Plymouth, visiting the French and Spanish ports, and perhaps the Portuguese, had obtained early information of these possibilities. He had heard of the malaguette pepper from the Upper Guinea coast, and of ivory and occasional gold dust to be had there. As for the other country, the Portuguese had first named it the Land of Holy Cross, and then, more descriptively, the Land of Parrots. But by now it was the Land of Brazil; for brazil was an old word that meant dyewood, of which the clothmakers could never get enough; and the dyewood from the Land of Brazil was an excellent species worth anything up to £10 a ton in the English market. In 1530 Hawkins ventured a combined Guinea and Brazil expedition. The details, such as they are, were narrated fifty years afterwards to Richard Hakluyt by John Hawkins, whose boyhood memories retained the family tradition on the subject. Perhaps he told Hakluyt all he knew, perhaps not. He was commonly reticent on his own past adventures, and may have seen no reason to be expansive about his father's. But there is no other evidence about the opening voyages, and we have to make the best of the tale as we know it.

Hawkins, then, fitted out his ship *Paul*, of 250 tons, and sailed to the River of Sestos in Upper Guinea, in the part which is now Liberia. This was the centre of the malaguette pepper coast, and Hawkins probably laded that commodity, although Hakluyt mentions only that he obtained ivory and other goods. From the River of Sestos Hawkins crossed the Atlantic to Brazil, where he laded the local produce and thence returned to England. Hakluyt says nothing whatever about the Portuguese, and we are left to guess whether Hawkins dodged them or fought them. Neither is there anything about the French, although it is very likely that Hawkins obtained his preliminary information from them. To sail to the River of Sestos and pick up Guinea grains, he must have known where it was and how one approached it. The same considerations applied to the Brazilian destination, wherever that may have been. We are left to imagine how all was done, with some guidance from what we know to have happened in other adventures. When, for example, John Hawkins in the next generation began trading with the West Indies, he was careful to provide himself with foreign pilots who knew the way. His father in the 1530's must equally have had a pilot for Guinea and Brazil. It is almost certain that his pilot was a Frenchman or a Portuguese renegade enlisted in France. We are not told where in Brazil Hawkins did his business; but since there is no reason to suppose that he went on to the Caribbean, it is probable that he sailed to the east coast of Brazil, not far south from Pernambuco. There, near Bahia, other Englishmen are known to have collected Brazil wood a few years later, and Hawkins may have led the way.

Since he had this information about Brazil and could make a profitable voyage there, it may be asked why he could not have made the equally easy voyage, with very likely more profit, to the Spanish West Indies, where the French in his day were beginning to raid and plunder with lucrative results. The answer is political. The French were, more often than not, at war with Spain. The English were Spain's allies against the French. Trespass on Portugal's claimed but really unoccupied preserves caused little embarrassment to the English government. Trespass in the Spanish West would have aroused complaints which Henry VIII and his

ministers could not afford to disregard. Later on, as we shall
see, a man who tried it found himself in an English jail for
piracy. William Hawkins was already in touch with government and wished to stand well with it. A Caribbean adventure
would have been undesirable. Throughout the century all the
Hawkinses planned their business in close accord with the political
situation.

The omission of the French and Portuguese from the Hakluyt
account leaves the story less than half told. William Hawkins
reached the coast of Brazil during a period of violent activity. In
the 1520's the French established their trade in many places, making
friends with the Indians, and planting factors to dwell permanently among them. The coastal tribes were fighting men and
cannibals, and so well did the French handle them that they made
a clear and reliable distinction between the two white peoples; for
it is on record that French residents were safe among them, while
Portuguese were eaten. In 1526-7 the Portuguese took the offensive. They sank French ships, burned settlements and ravaged the
tribes who favoured the French. In 1530 Francis I issued letters of
reprisal to Jean Ango and other merchants concerned. He revoked
them next year, but it made little difference and the war went on.
In 1531 the Mediterranean French took part and an expedition
from Marseilles stormed the new Portuguese fort at Pernambuco
and built a French fort near by. Before they could be reinforced
the French had to surrender to a new Portuguese armament.
Farther south the Portuguese established a permanent occupation
at São Vicente, near the modern Santos. The great intervening
stretch of coast was still open to the intruders, and a steady French
trade and quasi-occupation continued for many years, to culmi-
nate with Villegagnon's colony at Rio de Janeiro in 1555-9.[1] Not a
hint of all this is conveyed by Hakluyt's story of William Hawkins,
who is represented as adventuring in a vacuum.

In 1531 William Hawkins made a second voyage to Guinea

[1] The story of the French in Brazil has been compiled by the research of French
and Portuguese historians, whose results are drawn together in the first volume
of Ch. A. Julien's *Histoire de l'expansion et de la colonisation françaises*, Paris, 1948,
Ch. iv.

and Brazil, presumably to the same localities. On this occasion he grew so friendly with a Brazilian chief that the savage consented to take passage to England. In pledge for his good treatment Hawkins left an English volunteer, one Martin Cockeram of Plymouth, to live among the natives until the ship returned. It was a risk, but Cockeram thought it well taken for the reward, twelve months of lordly ease in place of two toilsome ocean passages, all hard work and short commons. What domestic arrangements were made for Cockeram among the tribe, the record states not, but no doubt there were some. Hawkins brought the heathen king to England and took him up to court for introduction to the Defender of the Faith. It was a good move, bringing Hawkins into contact with his sovereign, and obtaining recognition of the new Brazil trade, on which henceforward there could lie no imputation of the clandestine. Henry VIII was greatly interested in his royal brother, who had 'in his cheeks holes made according to their savage manner, and therein small bones were planted an inch out from the said holes, which in his own country was reputed for a great bravery. He had also another hole in his nether lip, wherein was set a precious stone about the bigness of a pease. All his apparel, behaviour and gesture were very strange to the beholders.' They gave him a good time and honourably sent him back with William Hawkins on the voyage of 1532.

In that year, the year in which John Hawkins was born with ocean venture in his blood, the *Paul* sailed south and west for the third time. On the voyage the Brazilian chief died, 'by change of air and alteration of diet', it was surmised. Most of these children of the forest did very shortly die when they were brought to the germ-ridden cities of Europe. There were fears lest the chief's death should endanger the life of Martin Cockeram. But the Indians were so impressed with Hawkins's fair dealing that they believed his word and restored the hostage without demur. Cockeram had filled in his time by acting as factor for the collection of a cargo, and the *Paul* departed fully laden with 'the commodities of the country', which meant, principally, Brazil wood. Martin Cockeram lived half a century thereafter. Kingsley makes him the aged man who talked with the captains on Plymouth Hoe as the Armada drew near; which is legitimate fiction. A friend of the present author used to say that he was the wild-looking mariner yarning to the boys in Millais' picture 'The Boyhood of Raleigh'. That is at least artistic truth.

The narrative furnished by John Hawkins carries the Brazil story no later than the voyage of 1532, which may have been the last in which his father personally sailed. He certainly could not have gone again in the following year, for, as we have seen, he was Mayor of Plymouth for 1532-3 (October to October). For the two-and-a-half years that followed the end of the mayoralty we have no clue to William Hawkins's whereabouts. He may possibly have made more voyages to Brazil. He certainly was sending ships there, even if he did not go himself, as may be inferred from a letter which he wrote to Thomas Cromwell in 1536. In that letter he remarked that he had already ventured ship and goods to seek for the commodities of strange countries, and had had a safe return. One of his pilots, however, had 'miscarried by the way', which means without much doubt that he had lost his ship. All things considered, the letter continues, the writer is emboldened to propose an extension of the business. For this purpose he asks Cromwell to forward his suit to the King for the loan of £2,000, four brass guns, and a last of powder, all on good security. The money is to be used for the operation of three or four ships in the seven years following. 'And I doubt me not,' concludes Hawkins, 'but in the mean time to do such feats of merchandise that it shall be to the King's great advantage in His Grace's custom, and to your good lordship's honour for your help and furtherance herein.'

This letter gives evidence of a continuance of the Guinea and Brazil trade and a hope of expanding it. Whether Hawkins obtained his loan we do not know, but the trade certainly did go on. The Brazil wood furnished dyes for the most expensive kinds of cloth, and was therefore in demand by the makers of superfine stuff in Florence and the other Italian cities. English customs records show a considerable export of Brazil wood to the Mediterranean. One of the exporters was Nicholas Thorne of Bristol, whose ship *Saviour* was run in Thomas Cromwell's interests and was partly owned by the minister. It is probable therefore that Hawkins and Cromwell had a closer mutual interest based on Brazil wood than appears in the letter quoted above. All such letters were made as uninformative as possible to any third parties into whose hands they might fall.

The Southampton merchants followed Hawkins's lead in trading with Brazil. We have no narratives of their proceedings, but only a few isolated facts which Hakluyt collected fifty years afterwards from the descendants of the men concerned. The earliest date mentioned is 1538 and the latest 1542, but the lack of further information does not prove that business was not going on before and after those years. Robert Reneger and Thomas Borey were wealthy Southampton men who habitually sent ships to Brazil. So also was John Pudsey, who built a fort on the Brazilian coast in 1542 near Bahia. The trade was evidently expanding. The French of the Norman seaports were still actively engaged. On Portuguese protests, the King of France forbade the traffic in 1538, but he soon changed his mind and connived at it. Envoys from Portugal were suing vainly for it to be stopped in 1541. In the same year the English Brazil traders were causing anxiety to the Spanish ambassador in England, who feared a consequent intrusion in the West Indies. There is one known instance of a voyage financed by an Anglo-French syndicate. Two ships, the *Saviour* and the *Wolf*, sailed from Dieppe in 1539 and returned to Rye in Sussex with cargoes from Brazil. If this was the English *Saviour* in which Thomas Cromwell was interested, the record brings him personally into the trade and fits well with his ultimate support of Hawkins in the local dissensions of Plymouth.

The other Brazil voyage, to northern Brazil and on by Guiana to the Caribbean, was practised by the French, and there is one recorded English example of it. The *Barbara* of London, commanded by John Phillips, sailed from Portsmouth in March, 1540. Phillips made straight for Brazil without touching in Guinea on the way. He arrived early in May, and had some trade and fighting with the natives. He then sailed on into the Caribbean and came to the south coast of Hispaniola. Here he behaved as a pirate by capturing a Spanish ship laden with hides and sugar. His reason seems to have been that his own vessel was leaking badly and he wanted a new one. Phillips abandoned his own ship, renamed the prize the *Barbara*, and sailed home in her, having set the Spaniards ashore in Hispaniola. The new *Barbara* was back at Dartmouth in August, her crew having done all these things in six months. John Phillips was arrested for piracy on the complaint of the Spanish ambassador, but the result of his trial is unknown. No one, so far as we know, was ever arrested on the complaints of the Portuguese.

It seems reasonably clear that William Hawkins carried on his tropical trade all through the fifteen thirties. There are unfortunately no Plymouth customs ledgers surviving for most of those years, and the material for the story is lamentably weak in the matter of commodities, prices and profits. At length, however, we find the customs records preserved for the years 1539–40 and 1540–1, each book running from September for twelve months; and here at last we have an official view of a voyage of the famous *Paul* of Plymouth to Guinea and Brazil. On February 25, 1540, the *Paul* left Plymouth, her master being John Landy.[1] In her William Hawkins, the sole shipper, laded 940 hatchets, 940 combs, and 375 knives; 5 cwt. copper and 5 cwt. lead made up into manelios or arm-rings; 10 cwt. copper and 10 cwt. lead in the lump; three pieces of woollen cloth, and nineteen dozen nightcaps. This was the whole cargo, valued at £23 15s. 0d. and paying duties of £1 7s. 3d. The combs, knives and hatchets passed simply as 30 cwt. of iron worth £3 15s. 0d., and were not assessed at their value as manufactured goods. This is incidentally a light on the struggle between the shipowners and the searcher. In the days when Grisling had been searcher of the port it is improbable that Hawkins would have got away with such low valuations.

On October 20 the *Paul* entered Plymouth again, having been absent eight months. From Guinea she brought 'one dosen olyfantes tethe', twelve tusks making up a hundredweight of

---

[1] It is possible that Landy was a French pilot engaged for the tropical voyage. Soon after her return, the *Paul* is shown by the customs ledger to have been engaged in European trade, but Landy was not in command.

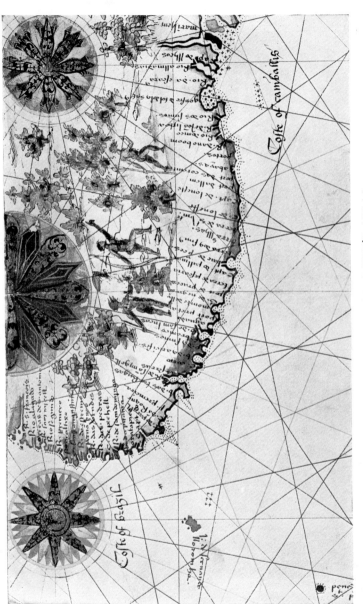

NORTHERN BRAZIL, FROM ROTZ'S ATLAS, 1542
Note that the south point of the map is at the top.
Royal MSS. 20 E ix

ivory; and from Brazil 92 tons of Brazil wood. The whole cargo
was valued at £615 and paid duty of £30 15s. od. So far as it goes,
this represents a very handsome profit; and it probably went
farther. For Upper Guinea produced malaguette pepper, of which
there is no mention. The *Paul*, moreover, was a ship of 250 tons,
yet brought home ostensibly only 92 tons of cargo. It may be
suggested that the remaining tonnage was filled with pepper, and
that the persons who had passed out the knives and hatchets as
pig iron were quite equal to passing in the pepper as ship's
victuals. Hawkins may have got some gold in Guinea, but of this
one could expect to find no trace in the customs account.

The above are the last records of the early trade with Guinea and
Brazil. The years 1540 for Plymouth and 1542 for Southampton
are the latest dates we have, after which oblivion covers all. But it
will have been observed that our knowledge rests on evidence
haphazardly preserved, fragmentary and precarious. The trade
also is going strong when we lose sight of it, promising rather
to expand than to diminish. Yet more, we have plenty of evidence
that the French continued their trade, and their circumstances
were similar to those of the English. On the whole it is unsafe to
presume from the silence of the records that the English Guinea and
Brazil trade ceased in the early forties. We have on the other hand
no proof that it went on. In 1543 England was involved in a war
with Scotland and France which took a serious turn and called for
a concentration of sea power to foil invasion. The diversion of
shipping may be the factor that stopped the Brazil trade.

The war became active in 1544 with Henry VIII's invasion of
France and capture of Boulogne. Then in September his ally
Charles V made a separate peace at Crespy and left him isolated.
Henry had in the previous years used the wealth confiscated from
the Church to rebuild the Navy and fortify the coast. He had no
regular army. German captains would contract to bring bodies of
arquebusiers into service if there was money to pay them; but
not more than a few hundred men could be expected from this
source. The defence of the realm lay in the county militias,
mustering under their lords-lieutenants when the alarm should be
given. The coastal forts and batteries were constructed by the

government and manned by the local people when the enemy drew near. Francis I of France could command large bodies of experienced troops. So long as he was at war with Charles V he had to dispose them on all his frontiers, Spanish, Italian, German and Flemish. The Peace of Crespy enabled him to concentrate them against England. The oceanic energy of France during his reign had built up a sea power fit to challenge that of England. There were fine French ships of war and plenty of seamen. All this pointed to the invasion of England as the event of 1545. It was a serious crisis.

Hawkins at Plymouth, where he was deputy-mayor in 1544, the Mayor being James Horsewell, did various local work for the government. In September he, with Horsewell and Elyot, received a commission to annoy the King's enemies with four, six or eight barks at their own charges, and power to impress men and take up victuals and munitions. This commission, or 'letters of marque', constitutes the entry of the Hawkins family into the business of privateering, which was hardly to cease for the rest of the century. Here it may be remarked that the word privateer is used in this book because it best describes the status of the men concerned. It was not in use in the Tudor period, when the privateers were known as freebooters, or simply as men-of-war, both terms which have now acquired other meanings.

The privateers licensed by Henry VIII inflicted great damage upon French commerce with great profit to themselves. The Peace of Crespy made the Emperor's subjects, Spaniards, Flemings and Germans, into neutrals. They began to carry French goods, claiming that the neutral flag covered them. The English contended that French goods were lawful prize wherever found, and even that the neutral ship carrying them was liable to capture. Action on this doctrine incensed the Spaniards and others. Charles V arrested all English goods in Flanders and suspended English trade with his dominions. There was even a possibility that he might declare war, in which case the invasion and overthrow of England looked certain. The English government, which had let loose the privateers, was now obliged to disavow some of their actions.

One of William Hawkins's ships took a Spanish vessel, whose cargo he asserted was French, falsely represented as Spanish. The owner, a certain Juan Quintana Dueñas, complained to the English government. It was in the summer of 1545, French invasion imminent, the Emperor's attitude uncertain, the situation critical. Robert Reneger of Southampton had recently captured a rich Spanish prize, about which the most indignant protests were being raised. Hawkins's affair had to be taken seriously. The Privy Council heard his explanation and remitted the case to the Admiralty Court, which seems to have decided against him. Characteristically, he had not waited for the end of the trial to sell the goods out of the prize. The adverse decision therefore revealed him as guilty of contempt. He was summoned to Portsmouth, where the King and Privy Council had taken station to counter the invasion, and committed to prison until he should have made restitution to Quintana Dueñas. The curious thing about this case is that William Hawkins was in the right, although he himself did not know it. For French documents show that Quintana Dueñas, who did much business at Rouen and had a French wife there, had become a naturalized Frenchman some years previously. Hawkins had lawfully taken his ship, and he had regained her by colossal impudence. All this was part of the privateering game. Business was so brisk in these war years that there was little time for any but the roughest justice. Hawkins had a privateer called the *Mary Figge*, which almost got him into prison again by capturing some Flemish goods which he could not substantiate as lawful prize; and in 1546 he was again in trouble for the capture of a Breton vessel just after peace had been signed.

There was a good deal of partnership and mutual support among the privateers, and in this matter it is notable that one of Hawkins's associates was Thomas Wyndham, a naval officer who served in the King's regular forces and also equipped private ships of war. Wyndham's ships took more than one richly laden Portuguese vessel bringing tropical produce up channel to the staple at Antwerp. He no doubt interrogated his prisoners, and he could have learned something of Guinea from his ally William

Hawkins. It is not surprising therefore that in the years to come it was Wyndham who revived the African trade and led the first English expedition to the Gold Coast.

Going to prison was not discreditable to a public man in the sixteenth century, and in the case of William Hawkins it did not lower him in the estimation of those who sent him there. They knew that it was only a gesture demanded by the higher politics for the satisfaction of the Emperor. The war ended in 1546, and Henry VIII died in the following January. Later in 1547 the Protector Somerset called a Parliament, in which Hawkins was again one of the members for Plymouth. The town paid him £14 for his expenses in representing it. Now that Henry was dead the French were unlikely to acquiesce in the English retention of his conquest of Boulogne, and warlike preparations were still necessary. William Hawkins played his part by improving the fortifications of Plymouth and collecting victuals for the fleet. This was in 1549, and the victuals were taken and consumed by the rebels in the 'Prayer Book Rebellion' of that year. Both Cornwall and Devon revolted against Cranmer's new prayer book, and there was serious fighting round Exeter before order was restored. The rebels entered Plymouth, but the castle held out for the government. We have no record of William Hawkins. With his official connections he is almost certain to have been on the side of authority. He was evidently not a rigid Catholic of the old school which disapproved of Henry's reformation. Whether he was an ardent Protestant may be doubted. He was probably one of the great majority to whom the abolition of papal jurisdiction and the secularization of church property were commendable, while innovations in ritual were not.

William Hawkins was now growing old. He was not a member of the Parliament of 1552, which may indicate his disapproval of Northumberland's ultra-Protestant policy. But inferences of that sort are only guess-work when we know so little. The omission of Hawkins may have been due to pressure of business or ill health. In 1553 Mary Tudor came to the throne and executed Northumberland. A new Parliament met at the close of the year to undo many of the religious changes of the past decades; and in this

Parliament old Hawkins again sat for Plymouth. It was his last public service. Whether he died in London or came back to his home we do not know. A document of February 8, 1554, alludes to him as recently dead. He was a man of his time, a rough, hard hitting, coarse-tongued time, the parent of the Elizabethan age, but different in quality as March from midsummer. Englishmen believed in themselves and took their risks, as individuals and as a nation. How few there were of them for the proud game they played—some three to four millions facing the sixteen millions of France with a hostile Scotland harrying their rear. Their quality carried them through, free men, free spoken, free living, contemptuous of officialdom, revering no man but their great free-thinking King. Him they trusted, and he did not fail them. William Hawkins was one of these men through and through. The King knew him personally and esteemed him 'for his wisdom, valour, experience and skill in sea causes'. He left a tradition after him. For the rest of the great period he was 'old Master William Hawkins', one of the chief sea captains of the west country.

William Hawkins the second was about thirty-five when his father died. We know virtually nothing of him up to that date. After it he appears continually in two of his father's characters, those of the merchant-shipowner and the local magnate of Plymouth—he was Mayor in 1588, Plymouth's most important year in the century. In all probability he had served in his father's Brazil voyages, and at the age of eleven may even have sailed on the first of them. Boys did go to sea at that age. The great Admiral de Ruyter in the next century made his first ocean voyage at the age of ten. However that may have been, William Hawkins seems to have stayed mainly at home after becoming the head of the family. He is known to have led two ocean expeditions, and may have led more; but, apart from them, nearly every notice we have of him shows him in or near Plymouth, of which he was three times mayor. William Hawkins the second is characteristically the Plymouth magnate, local office-holder, leading ship-owner, supporter of the Crown and servant of its administration, link with the foreign Protestants in the wars of religion, and the brain and director of the west-country efforts in the irregular

Channel warfare that preceded by twenty years the formal outbreak with Spain.

John Hawkins was twenty-one or two years old when his
father died. His youth fell in the last years of Henry VIII and the
troubled time of Edward VI. He was a boy of fifteen when Henry
died, and a young man of twenty-one when Queen Mary came in.
The outlook and interests that formed him were those of the
merchant-shipowners who put Plymouth on the map as the home
port of adventurers and made it the forward base of the Navy in
the new oceanic operations which distinguish the Tudor century.
John Hawkins was at first his brother's partner in the shipping
business. They remained in association and mutual loyal support as
long as they both lived; and when William died at the age of
seventy, John wrote an epitaph in which sincere affection is
obvious. But at some date the formal partnership was severed, and
the firm became two separate business entities, each nevertheless
continuing to invest in the ventures of the other. It is not clear
when this took place. All we have is an allusion by John Hawkins
to winding-up the firm, and to the fact that his share of the
capital was £10,000. It may have been when John went to London
about 1560 to seek support for his West Indian project. Ten
thousand pounds was a goodly sum in the sixteenth century, and
its young possessor was a man of wealth. The fact that he had not
much increased it after a lifetime of hard and successful work is
some indication of his quality as a public servant; for John
Hawkins in his later years was to labour more for the state than
for himself, and the state was never liberal of reward.

Throughout life John Hawkins was much more a man of the
sea and of ships than his brother. He was a sea-captain, skilled to
conduct a difficult voyage, and also a shipmaster conversant with
every detail of the handling and running of a ship. It is clear
that he had ships and squadrons in the hollow of his hand. In
crisis of storm or battle this mastery made him the leader that all
looked to. There is no doubt that he loved the sea, in the sense
that he was happier there than ashore. In difficult land employments he was sometimes querulous and pessimistic. Amid the
perennial difficulties and anxieties of the sea he was cheery and

radiant of well-being. To his last years he seized every chance of getting afloat, and fretted when chances were denied him.

If John Hawkins was a seaman, with all the meaning which that simple word contains, he was also much beside. And here his upbringing comes into the account. We must imagine that vanished house in Kinterbury Street and the life lived in it. We can the better do so because there are such houses surviving in our English towns, built by the prosperous burghers of Tudor England. There these men and their families lived, well provided and well served, entertaining their merchant friends and their land-owning cousins—for they were generally connected with the gentry, and Joan Amydas, the mother of old William Hawkins was of a Cornish landed family—talking of sea business and county business, the news from foreign parts, and affairs of state. The boys grew up listening and learning and acquiring a point of view and a standard of judgement at an early age. They had also books. A man like William Hawkins would see that his sons were educated, and we know in fact that he did. For John Hawkins wrote the letters of a cultivated man in the spelling and hand of one who had been effectively to school. What school is not known, perhaps that of a chantry priest who taught the boys of Plymouth. But taught he had been, and if he went early to sea he took with him that which ensured that he would not be an ignorant seaman. He was, as we shall find, genial, wary and alert, a good mixer, a man with a charm of manner who made friends, with common sense and give-and-take the basis of his dealings; and in the background he kept things of which he did not talk, the hidden springs of his actions. He liked good clothes, too, the fine material and brilliant colouring which then cost so much, and the golden chains and buttons that a man of spirit loved to flaunt. He was once, to his own undoing, mistaken for Sir Christopher Hatton, the greatest dandy of the court.

All these are the externals of a character bred in the home of 'one of the principal sea captains in the west parts of England'. Outside was the unruly Plymouth of slums, mobs and riots, in which even a well-balanced man might have to use his fists or his weapon at slight notice. The young Hawkinses did not shirk that side of life. They were men of the world in all its aspects. By the time he was twenty John had killed a man, one White, a barber of Plymouth, and was adjudged by the coroner to be guiltless of felony, having struck the man 'because he could not avoid him'. We can, if we like, imagine the affair, and probably get it all wrong. A killing, even in a Tudor seaport, was a serious matter, and old William Hawkins took no chances. He got the coroner's verdict translated into a royal pardon for his son duly inscribed on the patent roll, a process for which heavy fees were payable to the officials who served the Lord Chancellor.

During the reign of Mary the brothers worked together from their Plymouth headquarters. William was clearly there, as the local records prove, in 1555, 1557 and 1558, in the last of which years he was elected a privy councillor of the borough. John at the same time became a common councillor, but he put in some of his time at sea or in foreign countries. For we know, by his own statement to Richard Hakluyt, that he made several voyages to the Canary Islands, and the period up to 1561 is the only time in which he can have done so. Recent Spanish research shows him to have been known at Teneriffe before 1560, and in that year he came there again in the ship *Peter*. He sold cloth and bought sugar, and attended the Catholic church at Teneriffe.[1] The Canaries were legally part of Spain and by treaty free to English traders. Hawkins in after years displayed a familiar knowledge of the island anchorages. In 1556 he was in France for some time trying to obtain restitution of a ship captured by the firm during the previous war. When this prize had since gone into a French port she had been seized and detained by her original owners. Whether John Hawkins succeeded does not appear, but it is characteristic of his methods, to be exemplified in many greater matters, that he introduced himself to the French ambassador in England and the English ambassador in France and induced both to favour his suit. He never missed a chance of making the personal acquaintance of a man in high politics. His French connection was soon to be interrupted by war, the disastrous war of

[1] A. Rumeu de Armas, *Los Viajes de John Hawkins a America*, Seville, 1947(8), pp. 71–7.

Philip and Mary against Henry II of France, in which the Duke of Guise took Calais while the too-religious Queen was unable to turn out a fleet to save it. As before, the Hawkinses engaged in Channel privateering with general success and an occasional setback in the Admiralty Court. William Hawkins in one case tripped over the question of neutral rights, just as his father had done, and completed the parallel by selling the spoil in anticipation of the judgement.

Mention of Philip of Spain introduces an obscure matter which may have had a considerable effect on the career of John Hawkins. Negotiations for Philip's marriage with Mary Tudor were carried on in 1554–5 while he himself remained in Spain. Some of the emissaries travelled through Plymouth, utilizing the services of its leading firm of shipowners. There was here an opportunity for acquaintance with highly placed Spaniards, but John Hawkins did not stop at that. A Spaniard who knew him asserted in after years that when Philip landed in England he conferred a knighthood on Hawkins for some special service rendered.[1] Philip landed at Southampton after suffering bad weather on the voyage from Spain. Was Hawkins an officer of the royal convoy, and did he perform some feat of seamanship for the safeguarding of one to whom he persistently referred at a later stage as 'my old master'? The knighthood is of course an exaggeration, for John Hawkins was indubitably knighted thirty-three years later for service against King Philip. But it seems possible that he did attract the favour of the king at a time when it was not discreditable to do so. Philip came in peace in 1555 to marry the Queen of England and confirm an Anglo-Spanish alliance that had already stood for more than half a century.

A year later the Queen died, and a new age opened for England and her seamen.

[1] This statement was made by the pilot Juanes de Urquiza. It occurs in a document in the Archives of the Indies cited by Miss I. A. Wright in *Spanish Documents concerning English Voyages to the Caribbean*, Hakluyt Society, 1929, p. 79 n.

III

THE FIRST SLAVING VOYAGE

To the modern mind a slaving voyage is an incongruous opening to the career of one who was to prove himself among the most honest, unselfish and public-spirited men of his time. In the sixteenth century there was not the least incongruity about it. No one saw anything wrong in the slave trade. Certainly John Hawkins, who was sensitive to his good name, was not ashamed of it, or he would not have adopted the new crest of the 'demi-Moor proper, bound'. He saw the bloody and capricious tyrannies to which the negroes were subject in Africa, he knew that some negroes voluntarily gave themselves to the slavers in order to escape, and he knew also that negroes were valuable enough in the western colonies to ensure from their owners treatment which must have seemed quite decent to the poor souls themselves. That would have been his answer if anyone had argued about it. But no one did. Much morality is relevant to time and place. What is wrong to-day was right yesterday. England before Wilberforce accepted slaving with an easy mind. After Wilberforce she rejected it as mortal sin. Those who would reply that wrong is always wrong and that no explanation can exonerate the early slavers may be invited to consider the further proposition that some things which are right to-day may be wrong to-morrow, and almost certainly will be. While John Hawkins was gaining his knowledge of the Canary Islands, Thomas Wyndham, a friend of his father's, was opening new branches of the African trade. This time the initiative did not proceed from the west country. Wyndham was a Norfolk man, and his financial backers were a group of London merchants. They were men already engaged in the Spanish trade, with its extension to the Canaries, which gave them an outlook on Africa. Some of them may have been trading in Morocco as early as 1548.[1] The more

[1] Blake, *Europeans in West Africa*, II, pp. 302-3.

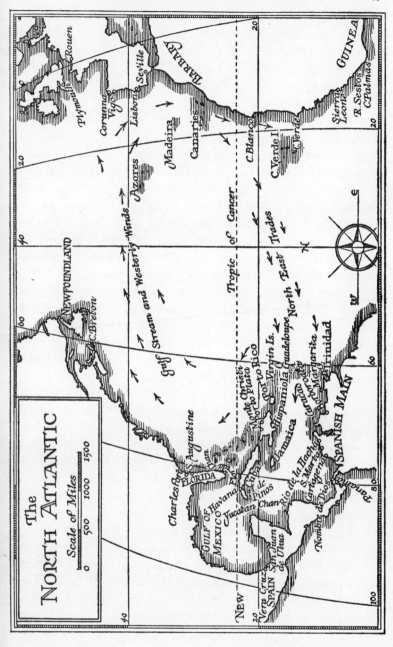

The
NORTH ATLANTIC

Scale of Miles
0   500   1000 1500

closely one comes to grips with the details of the English expansion the more important appears the English colony in Spain, dug in and protected there by the policy of Anglo-Spanish alliance pursued by Henry VII and Henry VIII. Some of these men lived so long in Spain as to become in effect Spaniards. They had their counterparts in Spaniards long settled in England. The Castlyns of London, a merchant family prominent for three generations in these affairs, may have been, by their name, of Spanish origin; for 'Castlyn', also spelt 'Castelin', looks suspiciously like 'Castilian'. Wyndham and his partners fitted out two ships[1] in 1551 and made a voyage from England to the Atlantic coast of Morocco. He opened a trade at Santa Cruz, the modern Agadir, and obtained cargoes chiefly of sugar and dates. In 1552 he repeated the venture, and thenceforward the Barbary trade was established. In the sixteenth century sugar was always scarce. The Barbary traders obtained it from its producers where previously England had paid a profit to Portuguese middlemen. The Portuguese were much annoyed, but dissembled their reasons. Instead they denounced the English for impiety in selling arms to the infidel and Hebrew bibles to the Jews of Morocco. The trade remained in the hands of the Londoners, who after twenty years were doing greater business in Barbary than in Portugal itself.

Wyndham himself went on to another innovation. In 1553, with the guidance of two Portuguese renegades, he led the first English expedition to the Gold Coast and Benin. Old William Hawkins had traded with Upper Guinea, and, so far as is known, the English had never before rounded Cape Palmas and passed on to Lower Guinea. Most of the pioneers, including Wyndham, died of the coast fevers; but the survivors, less than one-third of the company that had sailed from England, brought home gold, pepper and ivory to a notable amount. In the view of the London syndicate the profits outweighed the losses, and this trade also was established. Numbers of English ships went year after year to the Gold Coast in spite of Portuguese efforts to stop them. Those efforts included a strong protest in 1555, resulting in prohibition of the trade by Philip and Mary; three protesting embassies in the

[1] Blake, *Europeans in West Africa*, II, p. 272.

early years of Elizabeth; and the patrolling of the Guinea coast by
armed squadrons which became increasingly bold in attacking
the interlopers. It was all in vain. Queen Mary might forbid the
trade, but her officials from the Lord Admiral downwards connived at it.[1] Queen Elizabeth refused to forbid it on the ground
that the Portuguese occupation was not effective and that Guinea
was a country of independent peoples with whom anyone might
trade. Sir William Cecil at the same time made occasion to remark to the Spanish ambassador that England did not recognize
the distribution of territories by papal grants. By the opening of
the Elizabethan period it was English doctrine and established
practice that West Africa was free to all.

The same could not be argued of the other side of the Atlantic.
In the Spanish dominions there were empty spaces but there was
also much more occupation than in Africa. By the standards of the
time the occupation was effective, as even the English admitted.
Elizabeth's Privy Council did once attempt to challenge it by
asking the Spanish ambassador to specify the places of which
his master claimed the monopoly. He answered, 'All the West
India, continent and islands,' and after some haggling they gave
way.

The weakness of the Spanish Empire was not lack of occupation but lack of defence. It was surprising after the Franco-
Spanish wars had been going on for a generation, but so it was.
Three or four Caribbean seaports, including Santo Domingo and
Cartagena, were fortified; and there were a few soldiers maintained chiefly to keep the subject-peoples in order. But there was
no Caribbean fleet nor even a service of small armed patrols. On
the Pacific coast, as Drake found to his profit, there was not a gun
on board the Spanish ships. The Pacific, however, was not within
range of the French. The Caribbean was. After intercepting its
shipping nearer home in the 'twenties, they entered it in the
'thirties, and from then onwards their plundering raids scarcely
ceased. In the 'fifties there was no pretence of observing treaties
signed between the respective governments, for religion had

[1] After the formal issue of her prohibition, a ship of the Navy was chartered
by the traders.

embittered the question. Radical and revolutionary Calvinism had entered France, whose Huguenots were showing ever less respect for their Catholic monarchs. The seamen of the Norman ports, notably of Dieppe and Rouen, were mostly Huguenots. Westward lay the Breton coast, where they remained Catholics; but southward on the Bay of Biscay was La Rochelle, the greatest stronghold of Protestantism. The Calvinist Frenchmen ranged the Caribbean under leaders like François Le Clerc (Jambe-de-bois), Jacques de Sores and Jean Bontemps. They captured and burnt the colonial seaports almost at their pleasure, and took a great deal of booty from coastal shipping.

In peace or war in Europe there was 'no peace beyond the line'. The phrase is often quoted by people who do not explain what line they mean. The tropic of Cancer will not by itself answer the question, neither will the line of demarcation. 'Line' is in fact a misquotation, which should be 'lines'. The 'lines of amity' were verbally agreed upon by the French and Spanish negotiators of the Peace of Cateau Cambrésis in 1559. They were to be the tropic of Cancer *and* the prime meridian passing through Ferro in the Canaries. On the European side of both lines the treaty was to be binding; west and south of them its breach was to be disregarded.[1] The agreement was a belated recognition of what had long been the practice. It amounted to a disclaimer by the French government of responsibility for its seamen's doings beyond the lines, coupled with an admission that the Spaniards could do whatever seemed good to them in resisting the intrusion.

By 1560, therefore, the French were the recognized enemies of the Spanish western empire. They had already captured, sacked and abandoned in ruins Cartagena, Santa Marta (twice), Havana, Santiago de Cuba and many smaller seaports. The officials and inhabitants of these places wrote vehement prayers to Spain for armed defence. They got little satisfaction. The European wars of Charles V and Philip II absorbed more revenue than their European provinces produced, and every ducat of the surplus

[1] On this matter see Blake, *European Beginnings in West Africa*, p. 160. The treaty is in F. G. Davenport, *European Treaties bearing on the History of the United States*, Washington, 1917, Vol. I, pp. 219–21.

wealth of the Indies was needed for the Spanish treasury. There was nothing to spare for the defence of those who produced the wealth. They were pardonably dissatisfied. It was no light matter, but too often a passage of horror, for a small Catholic settlement to be raided by a crew of corsairs who were also fanatical Calvinists.

On the sea the heavy losses of Spanish merchantmen had compelled the adoption of a convoy system. It was gradually evolved under Charles V and standardized by Philip II. At the beginning of his reign all the western trade was concentrated in two annual fleets, the *flota* and the *galeones*. The *flota* sailed from Spain to the Greater Antilles and Mexico, some of its vessels stopping at places like Santo Domingo on the way, but the majority going on to San Juan de Ulua on the Gulf of Mexico in order to receive the treasure and commodities of New Spain. There was no attempt to return the same year, but all the units of the fleet were due to re-assemble at Havana in the following spring and thence sail for Spain in company. The *galeones* similarly served the Spanish Main, but did not detach vessels to all the minor ports. Almost the whole fleet went on to Nombre de Dios on the north side of the Isthmus of Panama, there to pick up the treasure from Peru, brought up the Pacific coast to Panama and carried across the Isthmus. The Main itself had a fair amount of treasure and merchandise to contribute to the *galeones*, and in anticipation of their arrival this stuff was concentrated at Cartagena and Nombre de Dios by unconvoyed local shipping. The *galeones*, like the *flota*, made Havana the port of departure for the homeward voyage to Spain, and when possible the two fleets returned together as one great convoy. At the opening of Philip's reign it was a regulation that each fleet should be convoyed by a fighting galleon of 36 guns, unencumbered with merchandise; and in later years there were generally two fighting ships with each fleet, detailed from a special force known as the Galleons of the Indian Guard. The convoy system entailed slow voyages, prolonged halts, excessive expenditure on wages and victuals, and a struggle to get things done under the paralysing control of a bureaucratic hierarchy, an 'overhead' which had also to be carried by the trader. All this made freights and insurance unnaturally high and the cost of goods received by the colonists from Spain unbearably dear. In addition, every penny spent on the armed defence of the fleets was recovered by imposts on the trade. If the colonial trade could have been conducted by free shipping unfettered of control, the prosperity and value of the colonies would have been immensely greater. The French menace was, so far, the only reason why the trade should not be normally so conducted. The Spanish colonists were vividly conscious of these considerations, and so were many people in Spain.

Meanwhile John Hawkins was making his voyages to the Canary Islands and collecting information. He was known as an honest dealer and made many friends among the people, one being an influential man named Pedro de Ponte dwelling in Teneriffe. De Ponte, of Genoese descent, belonged to one of the great Canarian families.[1] His association with Hawkins was the hinge upon which the new Atlantic ventures were to turn. From him and others Hawkins obtained details of the commercial position in the colonies and of the slave trade on the African coast, together with promises of aid in entering into the trade himself. Señor Rumeu de Armas thinks it possible that this arrangement was made during Hawkins's visit in 1560, but more probably in a subsequent one in the following year.

The present writer believes that Hawkins had more than this in mind from the outset, but that will appear as the tale unfolds. For these further purposes it was necessary to be closely in touch with the English government and to secure more powerful backing than Plymouth could provide. Hawkins therefore moved to London, where he kept a house in the City for the rest of his life. He did not cease to be a Plymouth man. He was often in the town, particularly during the early 1570's. His son Richard speaks of 'the love and zeal which I, my father and predecessors have ever borne to that place [Plymouth] as to our natural and mother town'. The London move probably took place about 1559, when

---

[1] More than a century afterwards, in 1699, William Dampier met the Governor of the Canary Islands. His name was 'Don Pedro de Ponto', and he was a native of Teneriffe, probably a descendant of Hawkins's friend.

John Hawkins married Katherine Gonson, daughter of Benjamin Gonson, the Treasurer of the Navy. Their only child Richard was born in the following year.

In London Hawkins gained the support of a syndicate or partnership which included Gonson, his father-in-law; William Winter, Surveyor of the Navy and Master of the Ordnance; Sir Lionel Ducket and Sir Thomas Lodge, City magnates; and others. Three of these men are known to have engaged in the Gold Coast trade which continued side by side with Hawkins's slaving, and there is no foundation for the statement that the slaving prejudiced the gold trade by antagonizing the negroes. The gold came from Lower Guinea, while Hawkins took his slaves in Upper Guinea, and there was a thousand miles between the two scenes of operations. The syndicate put up the money for Hawkins to make a modest preliminary venture with 260 tons of shipping and a hundred men. On the face of it there was no need for him to resort to London for these facilities. He and his brother could have found the capital, the ships were already in their possession, and Plymouth could have furnished the mariners, as indeed it did. Old William Hawkins had operated the 250-ton *Paul* at his own sole adventure. It is clear that this first voyage was for gaining experience before the syndicate should proceed to greater things.

With the *Salomon*, the *Swallow* and the *Jonas*, and possibly another vessel unnamed, Hawkins sailed from Plymouth in October, 1562 with Thomas Hampton as his second in command. He went first to Teneriffe to meet Pedro de Ponte, who was apprised of the undertaking and had ready to join Hawkins a pilot named Juan Martinez of Cadiz, who knew the West Indian navigation. De Ponte had also written to friends in Hispaniola to sound them on their willingness to trade with Hawkins, who was able to go forward in the knowledge that he and his wares would be welcome. Hawkins had English manufactures in his ships, but slaves from Upper Guinea formed an essential part of the plan, since they were the commodity most in demand in the west. Before the end of the year he was on the coast, which he followed as far south as Sierra Leone.

E

Hakluyt's account,[1] furnished long afterwards by Hawkins, says that 300 negroes were taken, partly by the sword and partly by other means, together with other merchandise yielded by the country. When this record was prepared for the press in 1588–9, the national circumstances had entirely changed, and neither Hakluyt nor Hawkins could have been desirous of raking up old matters distasteful to the Portuguese. Drake was at that very juncture leading an expedition designed to stir up the Portuguese as allies of England against Spain. Hence the Hakluyt account passes easily over the African proceedings and says not a word about the Portuguese. The Portuguese at the time, however, had a great deal to say for themselves, and sent in a thumping bill of complaints against Hawkins. They said that in the River Caces he took a ship belonging to Blasius de Veiga, of Santiago in the Cape Verdes, which ship contained 200 negroes and other goods to the value of 15,000 ducats: 'and the said Blasius and his sailors and other Portuguese, overwhelmed with many insults and tortures, and despoiled of their goods, were cast out upon the bank of the River Mitombi in Sierra Leone'. Next, he took two ships in the Mitombi, together containing more than 140 negroes, with ivory and wax and other things, to a total value of 8,000 ducats; farther on, a fourth ship with 70 negroes and other stuff worth 3,000 ducats; a fifth, with many negroes, worth more than 6,000 ducats, the owner and crew subjected to 'many blows and torments'; and lastly, at Sierra Leone, a great ship belonging to the contractors for the trade with 500 negroes and worth an unspecified number of ducats: totals, ships 6, negroes over 900, ducats over 32,000. If it is true, as the Portuguese asserted, that Hawkins had four ships of his own, he must have sent one of them direct to England with the ivory and other commodities. They said

---

[1] The principal authorities for this voyage are: the narrative furnished by Sir John Hawkins and printed in Hakluyt's *Principal Navigations*; Public Record Office, S.P. Foreign, Eliz. Vol. 99, a Latin MS. book containing the Portuguese version of the African transactions; and I. A. Wright, *Spanish Documents Concerning English Voyages to the Caribbean*, 1527–1568, Hakluyt Society, 1929, consisting of translations of documents selected by Miss Wright from the Archives of the Indies at Seville. This work will henceforward be cited as *Caribbean Documents*.

further that he retained the last great ship taken at Sierra Leone and carried her with him across the Atlantic. This seems to have been true if for 'retained' we read 'chartered', as will be explained in due course.

Portuguese complaints of the above type form a recurring chorus to all the slaving voyages. It may be well therefore to take a critical view of the first set. The witnesses to the allegations were the factors maintained by the Portuguese in the river-ports and the owners of the local shipping which collected wares from the factors and concentrated the cargoes at Santiago for shipment to Europe. Only one ship, it will be noticed, belonged to the contractors in Portugal. The factors and the Santiagians were a shady collection of broken men and half-breeds from whom no great honesty was to be expected. They were quite capable of selling their goods to Hawkins and afterwards alleging that he had overcome them by violence, a certain quota of symbolic 'blows and insults' having been thrown in *pro forma*. On this first occasion we have no evidence that this was so, but on later occasions we have, and so it is fair to make an assumption. The ships, except the last, were evidently restored to their owners—if they were ever really captured—for if they had been destroyed the fact would certainly have been mentioned. Then again, no one was killed. We are asked to believe that six ships, including one large one capable of holding 500 negroes, were violently taken without a life being lost. It must have been a gentlemanly piece of piracy. On the whole it looks much more like trade, which one side had afterwards to disguise for fear of retribution from its own rulers. The arm of the King of Portugal was long, and his justice merciless. Those who had traded with interlopers had to swear themselves out of an awkward scrape. The total number of negroes obtained by Hawkins is given by him as at least 300, and by the Portuguese as many more than 900. A Spanish observer on the other side of the ocean put it at 400, which may be about right. They were not all obtained from the Portuguese. Hawkins implies that he captured some himself, as he certainly did in subsequent voyages.

With his three Plymouth ships and the Portuguese slave-ship

he stood out to sea and picked up the north-east trades. His objective was the island of Hispaniola, where the city of Santo Domingo was the seat of government for the islands and the Spanish Main. If there was to be any objection to his trade, Hispaniola was the place where it was likely to be most strongly expressed; and if he could get himself accepted there he had less opposition to expect anywhere else. A group of officials and planters at Santo Domingo were awaiting him. The city itself was too public a place for the prospective business. It had been arranged therefore, through Pedro de Ponte at Teneriffe, that he should sail to the partially deserted north coast of the island, where a few plantations were interspersed with large areas of waste. Here were the minor seaports of Isabella, Puerto de Plata, and Monte Christi. Guided by the pilot from Seville, Hawkins entered the first of these in April, 1563. He began to sell negroes and English merchandise to the planters, and afterwards moved along the coast to Puerto de Plata and Monte Christi.

If the officials at Santo Domingo had taken no action they could not have justified themselves to the home government. They accordingly despatched seventy men under a temporary captain named Lorenzo Bernaldez to arrest or destroy the intruders. Bernaldez was a lawyer and a converted Jew. It is clear that he acted collusively with Hawkins and that those who sent him expected him to do so. But there were feuds among the Santo Domingo officials, and another lawyer named Echegoyan, who hated Bernaldez, wrote to Spain in order to expose him. In fact all who were implicated seem afterwards to have written to Philip II denouncing the rest.

Bernaldez told a tale of having captured two Englishmen and of having compelled Hawkins to give him more than a hundred negroes for their ransom; and said that then, in order to get rid of Hawkins, he had given him leave to sell his remaining negroes and depart. The hundred negroes were re-sold to the planters, and look like Bernaldez' own speculation. He was very lucky if he got them as ransom for two prisoners. The license to trade was also a fact. It was legally worthless, as both its giver and receiver well knew; for Bernaldez worded it as given only so far as he was authorized to do so, which was not at all. But Hawkins had a purpose in collecting such permits, of which this was the first of several. They were useful in the diplomatic arguments arising from his undertaking. There were no cash transactions, for coined money was scarce in the Indies. All was done by barter and by bills on Seville. Hawkins paid the proper customs dues by giving negroes at a valuation and also by handing over a caravel. It is not clear what vessel this was.

As there was no money, the whole success of the voyage depended on the colonial produce brought back to England. The Spanish accounts say that Hawkins received some gold. In general, gold-seeking in Hispaniola had ceased by this time, but there may still have been a little available here and there. He does not mention gold, but says that he had pearls, ginger, sugar and hides. The great days of West Indian sugar were in the future, and no large amount was produced at this time. Hides were the only really plentiful product of the Spanish islands. They must have formed the bulkiest part of the lading.

Hawkins laded not only his English ships but two others. One was a caravel owned in Hispaniola by some people named Martinez, perhaps related to Juan Martinez, his pilot. This vessel was hired by Hawkins, who put Thomas Hampton in command and despatched him for Seville of all places. The other was the Portuguese ship which he was alleged to have stolen from Guinea. He placed some hides and sugar in her and despatched her also for Seville under her own captain and crew and without an Englishman on board. This is sufficient proof that the vessel was not a pirate's prize for, if she had been, Hawkins was virtually giving her back, with some goods of his into the bargain. He was confident of the goodwill of the Portuguese crew, but he made a mistake, for they carried the ship into Lisbon, where the cargo was seized by the farmers of the Guinea trade in pursuance of the highly coloured charges they were making against him. It looks as though Hawkins himself was genuinely unconscious of having committed any offences in Guinea.

The Spanish caravel duly reached San Lucar (for Seville), her cargo consigned to Hugh Tipton, one of the most important

English merchants in the city. It did not arrive in the name of Hawkins, but in that of a Spaniard who acted as intermediary. There could, however, have been no serious intention of concealment, since the caravel's crew would have known all the facts and talked about them. Here again, Hawkins was unlucky, for the Licentiate Echegoyan had written so vehemently, not only to the King but to the Casa de Contratacion at Seville, that the home authorities had to take notice. The result was that the goods were seized and Tipton arrested for receiving them. Hampton would also have been imprisoned, but he was warned in time and escaped to England.

The two lost cargoes were the least valuable proceeds of the voyage. With the more important stuff Hawkins made a good passage to England, which he reached some time in August, 1563. There is evidence in the Canary archives that some English ships visited Teneriffe in June 1563, and Señor Rumeu de Armas suggests[1] that 'with sufficient probability' they may have been Hawkins's fleet on the homeward voyage. But the documents do not mention him by name, and he would have been off the usual course. The visitors may well have been some of the pirates who haunted the island groups at this period. Hampton met his commander with the story of the Seville seizure. Hawkins at once travelled to London and induced the government to take up his case.

If we take the history of these voyages at its face value, as most have done, and do not probe beneath the ostensible, the conduct of Hawkins in consigning two cargoes to Seville is hard to explain save as the action of a fool. For, as Miss I. A. Wright has made clear,[2] he had broken three of the most important Spanish laws governing the Indies trade. First, as a foreigner he had travelled to the Indies without the royal licence to do so. Second, he had traded there without the necessary additional royal licence. Third, he had carried thither goods which had not been manifested at Seville. Every merchant doing business with Spain or the Canaries knew of these laws, and Hawkins can have been no exception. He

---

[1] *Op. cit.*, pp. 121–6.   [2] *Caribbean Documents*, p. 8.

had broken them openly and without attempt at concealment. A clandestine trader would have conducted the voyage differently The Hispaniola part of it would have been a hole-and-corner affair, obscurely managed on smuggling lines, and probably no one but the participants would ever have heard of it. There are indications, in fact, that Portuguese slave-smugglers were working in this way. Hawkins, however, not only breaks the law openly, with the undeniable knowledge and even the attested consent of the colonial officials, but then sends the proceeds to Seville, the headquarters of the colonial administration. There can be only one explanation, that he believed that his proceedings might be allowed by the supreme authority and was prepared to play for that high stake.

IV

THE QUEEN'S VENTURE

In his first voyage Hawkins had proved that a triangular trade between England, Africa and the Spanish colonies was practicable. In Africa he had acted well within the scope of declared English policy, which regarded the Guinea coast as an autonomous region free to trade with all comers. If the King of Portugal really exercised authority over the negroes, Elizabeth said, he could settle his complaint by forbidding them to trade with the English; but since the people were willing and able to trade she would not order her subjects to forgo the natural liberty of merchants. In the West, Hawkins had demonstrated that the colonists and the officials desired his goods which, with his uncontrolled shipping and expert management, he could sell at lower prices than those charged by the merchants of Seville. And in England, in spite of the loss of two cargoes, the venture showed a profit which was to cause a great expansion of the financial support at its command.

The two lost cargoes moved Hawkins to two different lines of action. One, it will be remembered, had been seized in Lisbon, the other in Seville. On the first, he took action in the Admiralty Court, making a formal statement of complaint against the Portuguese authorities and the farmers of the slave trade. Since these persons were without the jurisdiction he obtained no redress. He probably did not expect it, but the process was useful as a counter to the complaints that the Portuguese were making against him, and also as giving ground for any subsequent issue of letters of reprisal which he might be able to obtain from his own government.

He evidently regarded the Seville seizure as much more important. The whole incident makes it clear that he expected the Spanish laws which he had infringed to be dispensed with so far as they referred to him. When Thomas Hampton met him with the news of the seizure he went at once to London and put the matter before the Queen's ministers. By the 8th of September 1563, he had already secured their support. This was quick work. It may indicate that the voyage was not a business newly introduced to their consideration, but one of which they already had cognizance. However that may have been, the Queen sent two letters, one to Sir Thomas Challoner her ambassador in Spain, the other to King Philip himself, recommending Hawkins's cause. Hawkins himself intended to go to plead in person. There is some evidence that he did so. Hugh Tipton, by that time released from arrest, wrote to Challoner from Seville on December 8: 'In one with this I do write unto Master Hawkins, who I think is with your lordship ere this day'; which shows that Tipton believed Hawkins to be in Spain. On the other hand Challoner wrote to Hawkins in July 1564: 'So in mine opinion ye did well not to come hither yourself'; which is good evidence against the visit. If not in person, Hawkins acted by deputy, and failed in his suit. His confiscated cargo was not restored.

All this activity of great persons was somewhat excessive in relation to a caravel's lading of hides. There was more in it than that. Hawkins and the Queen were working to get his trade recognized as legitimate. The whole transaction of sending this cargo to Seville was probably intended to serve as a test case. If the cargo had not been arrested, it would have formed a precedent. Since it was arrested, it supported an argument. And what, on the English side, that argument was, we unhappily do not know. On the Spanish side it was of course that the law had been broken and must be vindicated. In 1489 Henry VII and the Spanish sovereigns had signed the Treaty of Medina del Campo, whereby either party agreed to allow trade in all their dominions by the subjects of the other. The treaty was still in force, and under it the English were duly permitted to trade in the Canary Islands. It had been framed three years before the first voyage of Columbus, so that American dominions were not in the mind of either signatory. Whether 'all the dominions' meant only those existing in 1489 or included those subsequently acquired might have provided a pretty controversy such as sixteenth-century diplomats loved. But there is no evidence that the question was raised, no mention anywhere of the treaty of 1489. If the English had appealed to it there would probably be some allusion to the fact. It is possible that such an appeal was already ruled out. When Columbus discovered the Antilles (supposed to be tropical Asia) for Castile, and Cabot discovered the New Found Land (supposed to be Cathay) for England, either government began to issue patents and other documents reserving the respective discoveries for its own subjects, and barring foreigners. It may then have been agreed that the Treaty of Medina del Campo should not apply to trans-atlantic possessions. No such agreement is on record, but the diplomatic records of the 1490's have mostly perished. Anyhow, it is fairly clear that Elizabeth did not appeal to the treaty in 1563.

What consideration she did advance can only be guessed. The significant and also puzzling circumstance is the confidence of Hawkins that he had a case and that the Spanish government would listen to it. He was already in a position above that of an ordinary merchant. His queen was writing letters on his personal behalf, and we have the probability that he was personally known to Philip. He consulted ambassadors as a matter of course. Even at this early stage of his adventure, it was an affair not only of trade but of high politics, an aspect which the Queen was about to make still more evident. All this considered, there must have been some English *quid pro quo* to be offered for the relaxation of the Spanish colonial laws, and we have to make an effort to penetrate its nature. A survey of the international circumstances of the 1560's will assist.

For the first ten years of Elizabeth's reign the old relationship of the European powers, established since the beginning of the century, appeared to hold good. France, central, military, maritime and populous, seemed rich and strong and ever ready to aggrandize herself by filching her neighbours' territory. Her neighbours were for the most part the countries that made up the empire of Charles V, who died in the year after Elizabeth's accession. His Spanish, Netherland and Italian possessions had already been transferred to his son Philip, and his German overlordship, carrying the imperial title, went to his brother Ferdinand.

The seventeen provinces of the Netherlands, alive with manufacture, commerce and shipping, were the richest tract in Europe, and the old emperor had held that their continued attachment to Spain was essential to the well-being of that kingdom. But France lay between the Netherlands and Spain. Their natural line of communication was through the Channel, and maritime France held one of its shores. Alliance with England was therefore indispensable to the anti-French combination, for English sea power alone could prevent its Channel artery from being cut. The alliance was also necessary to England, for it promoted her economic well-being. The Netherlands ranked first and Spain second among the markets for her exported cloth, and she had to be on good political terms with her best customers. The alliance was therefore based on powerful and permanent interests on either side, and it endured until other interests arose to overthrow them. Charles V hoped that he had made it indissoluble when he married his son Philip to Mary Tudor; but that bond expired with the queen in 1558.

If Spain had a British supporter in England, France had one in Scotland. The Franco-Scottish alliance was ancient and enduring. The Scots were few in numbers, but their fighting power was high. It contained, in the technical sense, a considerable part of the men, wealth and shipping which England could mobilize for war. Meanwhile she faced southwards with the rest against a France that had four times her population and her natural wealth and a sea power at least equal to her own. The statesmanship of Henry VIII worked hard to liquidate the Scottish menace. There was only one way of doing it, promotion of mutual interests and ultimate union on equal terms. Henry made some headway with the problem. After his death the Protector Somerset threw away his work. He won the tactical victory of Pinkie and suffered strategical defeat when the Scots sent their girl-queen Mary Stuart to be brought up in France and ultimately to marry the French king's son. Never had the Franco-Scottish alliance appeared so firmly knit as after Somerset's campaign; and never did it promise such dire results to England as when Elizabeth ascended the throne with a questionable title, an empty treasury, and a defeated army and navy. For Mary Stuart, Queen of Scots and Dauphiness of France, claimed the crown of England by virtue of her descent from a Tudor princess who had married James IV. It looked as though Mary might win, for England was in a bad state. Misgovernment by rogues and fanatics had demoralized the people. Most men doubted, grumbled and shirked. Yet we in our time may take courage from that old crisis; for it was the prelude to the great Elizabethan age.

The Spanish attitude in all this is what concerns our story. Philip saw that it was essential to preserve the English alliance, although he disliked being allied to the heretic that Elizabeth speedily showed herself to be. For a year or two he and his ambassadors strove to bully her into submission to the Church of Rome. They genuinely believed that she would lose her throne if she did not conform. Therein lay their danger. For her supplanter in a Catholic revolution would be Mary Stuart backed by the might of France. And then France, England and Scotland would be a solid block, the Channel closed, the Netherlands cut off from Spain and conquered by the French, the hegemony of Europe transferred from the house of Hapsburg to the house of Valois, and France a radiant sun surrounded by satellites, of whom proud Castile might in her turn be one. A grim prospect. The Spaniards who hated the English heretics could not lift a finger against them, and might even be compelled to draw sword in their defence. The alliance had to go on.

In the next ten years Philip was to be delivered from that predicament by the failure of the Valois house to breed a man. Henry II, its last able king, was killed by accident in 1559. His sons, Francis II, Charles IX and Henry III, following in succession and dying without issue, were degenerates who allowed the monarchy to collapse and France to sink into civil war. Gradually these things became evident, and Philip slowly realized that France was ceasing to be dangerous and that Mary Stuart, from being his peril, might become his instrument. With that realization was to come the end of the English alliance. When Hawkins began his voyages there was as yet no inkling of it. Meanwhile Protestantism was rising like a salt tide, to submerge the older politics and align Europe in the new pattern that coincided also with the oceanic period of her development. Scotland established her Calvinism in 1560. France had her first religious war in 1562–3. The Netherlands were already uneasy.

Such was the general outlook in 1564. We turn to some particular circumstances in the West. The French attacks on Philip's Caribbean coasts were scarcely intermitted by the peace of 1559, which was no peace beyond the lines. So continuous and widespread were they that in any Spanish seacoast settlement the sight of white sails on the horizon was a portent of evil like the Norse raven flying inland over Saxon England. The sails were probably French, and the settlers hurried off their women and their treasures into the interior while yet there was time. The Frenchmen took unconvoyed ships and sacked the ports, but the slow system of the *flota* and the *galeones* averted the major disaster of the oss of a whole year's consignment of treasure. Then in 1562 began a new French enterprise that threatened the plate fleets themselves. Jean Ribault, a Huguenot captain, led a party of French colonists to the North American continent and settled them at Charlesfort in 32° N, on the Atlantic coast of the base of the Florida peninsula. Florida had long been reputed rich in the precious metals, although Spanish exploring expeditions had come to grief there. The French reported gold and silver in the hands of the natives and had good hopes of reaching the golden city of Cibola, the North American counterpart of Manoa in the South, and, like it, completely fictitious. The enterprise made a considerable stir, and some expected it to produce treasure on the scale of Mexico and Peru. Any strengthening of France, such as this would entail, would imperil both England and Spain. If there was gold in Florida they had a common interest in eliminating the French. Spain had a further interest of her own. The north-east trades and the Caribbean current prevented shipping from sailing eastwards in West Indian latitudes. The plate fleets entered the Caribbean from the east, but had to go out by the Florida Channel at the north-west corner of the sea. The Gulf Stream and the winds kept them near the Florida coast until they could strike across the Atlantic homewards in the belt of the westerlies. A French base in Florida threatened to cut the treasure route. It was the greatest peril that had yet menaced the Spanish West.

After planting the colony Ribault returned to France to organize further emigration. He found the first civil war in progress and took part in the defence of Dieppe by the Huguenots. When the place fell in October 1562 he escaped to England. The result of the civil war, substantially a victory for the Catholics, caused Ribault, an ardent Protestant, to seek English aid for the continuance of the Florida project. In 1563 he published in English a *Relation* of the advantages of Florida, and the English government began to regard him as a man who might be useful. Meanwhile the French colonists gave it up and came home, as early colonists so frequently did unless continuously fed from the mother country. Before their arrival the English government had agreed to maintain Florida as an Anglo-Huguenot concern and had appointed a Devonshire man, Thomas Stukeley, to collaborate with Ribault in its management. Stukeley was a bad choice, an untrustworthy fellow who did not honestly mean to devote himself to the colony, but preferred privateering in the Channel. He used the colonial job as a pretext to get ships for his Channel purposes, and revealed the Florida plans to the Spanish ambassador. Few such things escaped Sir William Cecil, the Queen's Secretary of State, and before long Stukeley was removed from the Florida business. The delay, however, deprived the English of control. Early in 1564 René de Laudonnière sailed from Havre as the servant of the French crown and replanted the colony. Ribault left England in order to join the new venture. Florida, which might have been made an English colony, was now to be purely French and to enrich the government which still recognized Mary Stuart as lawful Queen of England. French Florida, as we shall see, became one of the objectives of the new expedition which John Hawkins began to fit out in the summer of 1564.

Before describing that expedition we must consider one more of the attendant circumstances in order to attain a just appreciation of the balance of events. Between the seamen and merchants of England and of Spain there was already deep hostility and a sense of intolerable wrong. It arose from the depredations of English pirates who based themselves on the Irish ports and haunted the Spanish coast and the Channel approaches. It arose equally from the cruelty and rapacity of the Inquisition, which burnt English sailors and seized their masters' goods. It was intensified by the English support of the Huguenots in the religious war of 1563-4. England was at war with the French monarchy, and English privateers lawfully took French ships. The French merchants then traded under neutral flags, and the privateers refused to agree that the flag covered the goods. They held, on the contrary, that the detection of enemy goods rendered the neutral ship herself a lawful prize. This infuriated all Spaniards from the King downwards, and was probably the chief reason that Hawkins lost his West Indian cargoes in Spain. The state of the European seas in the 1560's is graphically described in Chapter XII of Froude's *Reign of Elizabeth*.

The first voyage had been promoted by senior citizens of London and officers of the Navy Board. The list of adventurers in the second voyage is more impressive. It included, as before, Benjamin Gonson and William Winter from the Navy Board, with Sir William Garrard, Sir William Chester and Edward Castlyn from the City; but in addition there was a court and ministerial interest represented by the names of Sir William Cecil, Lord Robert Dudley (made Earl of Leicester in the summer of '64), the Earl of Pembroke, and Lord Clinton, the Lord Admiral. These names are from a list dated March 3. Cecil afterwards told the Spanish ambassador that he had not been an investor, but at least the three noblemen were, as appears from subsequent documents. Thus, even if we omit Cecil, three of the Queen's Privy Councillors were engaged in the venture, while Cecil had a good deal to do with its management and supervision.

Nor was this all. The Queen herself joined the undertaking and allowed it the use, on charter, of one of the large ships of her Navy. The chartering alone does not prove much, save that the venture had the royal approval. For the Queen had already chartered ships to the gold traders in Lower Guinea, who certainly had her good will, but were private merchants and not in any special sense her servants. But the Queen's participation in the second Hawkins expedition was of a different kind. She summoned Hawkins to a personal interview and gave him her instructions, she authorized him to describe his squadron as her ships and to offer to do service with them to the interests of King Philip, and she commanded him to sail not only under the Cross of St. George but under her own royal standard by way of making clear to the Spaniards in the West that the Queen of England's Navy was in their waters.[1] John Hawkins sailed in 1564 as the Queen's officer. He stated this clearly in a document written in February 1577, wherein he dated his entry into her service from 'thirteen years past'. Hawkins was still a merchant adventurer as well as a naval commander. Trade was the basis of the political objects which the Queen had in mind, and she herself was an investor to the extent of the £2,000 at which her ship was valued for the purposes of the accounts. But those who hold that the voyage was a trading expedition and nothing more can only do so by ignoring the facts given above about the Queen's position and the status of Hawkins as her officer. If she had merely wished to put a ship of the Navy to profitable use she could have done so, as in the gold trade, by simply chartering it to the adventurers without assuming any personal control of their expedition. And if, moreover, great lords and privy councillors desired a flutter in the gold trade, they took it without letting their names appear in the directors' lists, which, for African voyages pure and simple, include no one of higher rank than City knights and gentlemen of the Navy Board. The noble members of the Hawkins syndicate place it in a different category.

What then was the Queen's purpose? Financial gain? Hardly. In spite of all that has been said about her meanness and money-grubbing, she was not an irresponsible fool to encumber her tortuous foreign policy with yet another complication for the sake of a profit on two thousand pounds. Her parsimony, in fact, is entirely misconceived by those who regard it as a personal foible.

[1] The evidence for the royal standard relates to the third Hawkins voyage, that of 1567. On that expedition he used it habitually. His position as the Queen's officer leading the Queen's fleet was the same in 1564 and 1567, and we are justified in assuming that the royal standard was used on the former occasion also.

It was not as an individual that she saved revenue and cut expenditure, but as the embodiment of the nation, doing all she could to spare her people's pockets. The profits earned by a queen's ship on a trading voyage were never touched by the Queen herself. They were paid to the Treasurer of the Navy and lightened *pro tanto* his expenditure of the taxpayer's money. Would that our modern rulers knew her parsimony, the faithfulness of a great lady entrusted with a great estate. She contributed a ship because this was her expedition, but her motive could not have been trading profit. Was it then to annoy Philip by breaking his laws, not only by conniving at her subjects doing it, but by taking part, ostentatiously, herself? Read the details of the early years of her reign, as they are amply set forth in the pages of Froude, and that view will not be tenable. Elizabeth was beset with enemies, practised upon by hostile diplomatists, bled by military campaigns demanding taxation from a miserable people, faced with reconciling her Catholics and Protestants, as ready for mutual murder as Moslems and Hindus to-day, tortured with anxieties, she and her Secretary Cecil, as rulers are apt to be when the national existence is at stake. She was obliged to do many things that annoyed the King of Spain. She was not likely to annoy him gratuitously. Yet she sent her officer, her ships and her royal standard into the prohibited West. We have no state paper, commission or letter of instructions that gives us the reason. It can only be inferred ; and the inference, if it is to be provisionally accepted, must not be at variance with any of the established facts.

At first sight the Florida colony looks like a sufficient explanation. English statesmen were really concerned about the supposed wealth of Florida and the possibility of its use to finance French military adventures. Hawkins was ordered by the Queen to go to Florida and find out how things stood, and he provided himself with a pilot from Dieppe who knew the coast. But Florida cannot be the whole answer to the question, since it could have been reached without entering Spanish waters at all. Moreover, there was to be another voyage in 1567 with the same royal commands, royal standards and royal ships, when the Florida business was dead and buried.

We have to look elsewhere than Florida for illumination of the Queen's intrusion into the Caribbean. In the present writer's opinion the following suggestion agrees with the known facts up to 1564 and receives support from recorded transactions subsequent to that date. It may serve as a working hypothesis. No other has been advanced save that illicit trade was the sole incentive; and that is inadequate. The motive, then, of the Queen, her councillors and John Hawkins was the strengthening of the somewhat dilapidated Anglo-Spanish alliance by the creation of a new mutual interest. Hawkins and his associates were to supply slaves and English merchandise to the colonies, and might even become the concessionaires of a slaving monopoly, such as Spain was already accustomed to grant to foreigners like the Genoese financiers. For this concession the English would pay, not in financial services, but in naval. The colonies were being severely damaged by the French, Spain appeared unable to defend them, so why not let English ships and seamen do it? The Queen's ships and the Queen's flag were an offer, Hawkins's cheap negroes were an inducement, Hawkins's honest, non-predatory conduct was a guarantee. It was surely common sense to close with it. A precedent existed for supposing that Spain would at least discuss the proposition. In 1544 Charles V, negotiating the Treaty of Crespy with Francis I, had agreed to a clause whereby the French were permitted to trade in the West Indies. Not twenty years had elapsed, and it is quite possible that Elizabeth's advisers knew of the Emperor's concession. The concession indeed never became operative owing to protests raised in the Council of the Indies against ratification of the clause.[1] But the transaction does show that the monopoly was not sacrosanct to Charles V; and Philip II had yet to make it clear that his view was more extreme. Admission of the English promised mutual advantage. A firm alliance would have ensued. Spain would have had her empire defended, its trade increased, and its expenditure reduced. England would have expanded her sea power and her trade, while in Europe she would have been strong against the French and Mary Stuart.

[1] See Davenport's *Treaties*, I, p. 209: and C. A. Julien, *Histoire de l' expansion et de la colonisation françaises,* Paris, 1948, I, pp. 170–1.

John Hawkins, the author of the plan, would have grown great as merchant and admiral, the trusted servant of two sovereigns.

It was not to be. Religion was the difficulty. Philip employed Italian admirals to contract for supplying fleets of galleys to fight the Turk, but he could not bring himself to employ English seamen to fight the French. He had been enjoined by his father to preserve the English alliance and withstand heresy. The alliance might be preserved without American concessions, while heretics must positively not be permitted to enter the colonies. Catholic Englishmen might trade with the West from Seville, but Protestant Englishmen must not do so from Plymouth. Philip sent an ambassador to speak his mind on this matter to Elizabeth, and strict orders to his colonies not to trade with the English. Many Spaniards in the colonies meant to disobey him, and perhaps some in Spain took the decision lightly. To begin with total rejection of a proposal on which one is actually disposed to negotiate is a common diplomatic procedure. Philip's prohibition did not impress either Spaniards or English as irrevocable.

Such is the provisional inference. But one would give much for a report of the interview between Hawkins and the Queen at Enfield in the autumn of 1564, or for minutes of the consultations with Cecil which undoubtedly preceded it.

V

THE SECOND VOYAGE

In these days when a servant of the state must not make profits from activity in private business, and much less from his share in any dealing in which the state itself is involved, it is difficult to realize the position of public servants in the Tudor period. There were then no formal rules and there was no unwritten code against their making money out of the public affairs which it was their duty to administer, and also out of private business carried on side by side with their public duties. Not only were there no rules against this, but they were expected to do it, since the practice saved direct government expenditure on the salaries which it would otherwise have been necessary to pay to them. The able man served the state without pay and served himself by using his official position to his own advantage. So John Hawkins sailed in 1564 as the Queen's naval officer, unpaid, and also as the merchant adventurer which had been his only status in the previous expedition. He was thirty-two years old and had in front of him a career in the public service of more than thirty years' duration.

The fleet which he commanded consisted of the *Jesus of Lubeck*, of the Royal Navy, and three Plymouth ships belonging to the Hawkinses. A description of the *Jesus* is necessary to an understanding of some of the events of the following four years. The ship's characteristics had a great influence on Hawkins's fortunes while in command of her, and undoubtedly helped to form the views on constructional policy which he was to bring long afterwards to his administration of the Navy. The *Jesus* was of 700 tons, one of the largest ships in the fleet, but she was rotten from prolonged neglect during the bad period of Edward VI and Mary. She had been purchased by Henry VIII from the Hanseatic League in 1545, when she may have been nearly new. So bad was her condition at the opening of Elizabeth's reign that she was condemned as beyond repair, although subsequently reprieved. It

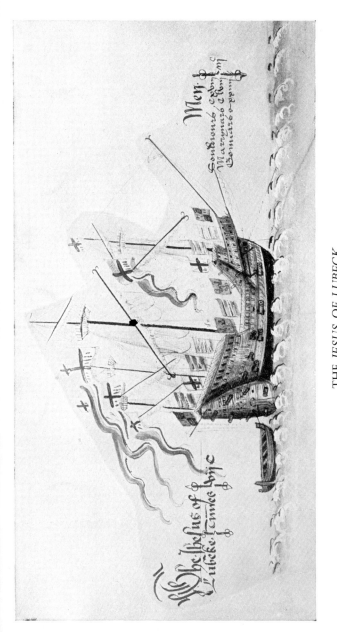

THE *JESUS OF LUBECK*

From Anthony's Roll, Pepys MSS., Magdalene College, Cambridge

THE SECOND VOYAGE

is often said that the old-time wooden ships were long-lived and durable. That is not true of the majority of the Tudor ships of which we have record; and one reason was that many of them were not built of seasoned timber. When the construction of a great ship was decided upon, the officers concerned searched the forests for suitable oaks for the job. The trees may have been already felled and seasoned, but sometimes they were felled and used forthwith. It is evident that some vessels, particularly those built in time of war, began to rot from the day they were launched. The remedy was constant vigilance and the removal and replacement of affected planks and timbers. This was so badly neglected during the eleven corrupt years between Henry VIII and Elizabeth that the effective fleet almost ceased to exist. The *Jesus* was one of the victims, and her condition was exceedingly decrepit when she was sent on ocean voyages with Hawkins.

We have a drawing of the *Jesus* as she was in 1545, preserved among the Pepysian MSS. at Magdalene College, Cambridge. It shows her to have been a great ship of the type regarded as capital in the Channel wars of the mid-century, with lofty poop and forecastle and probably a beam very broad in proportion to the ship's length in order to provide the necessary stability. The high superstructures were for defence against boarding. Poop and forecastle were separate fortresses, and boarders could enter only in the waist, which was a trap between cross-fires. A few great guns were carried low on the broadside, medium guns appear above them, and in the superstructures there were a number of small pieces mounted on swivels, and firing hail shot and dice shot at point-blank range. The drawing is superficial and impressionistic, but it does give some facts about the rig. There were four masts. The fore and main carried each a course and a topsail, the mizzen and bonaventure mizzen each a single lateen sail. The accompanying inscription says that three hundred men formed the crew for war service. Hawkins did not place anything like that number in the ship. This kind of 'high-charged' ship had inherent disadvantages, some of which will appear in the course of the narrative. Experience imbued Hawkins with a hearty dislike of the type, and moved him in after years to equip the Navy with something very different when he came into control of building policy.

While the *Jesus* was fitted out in the Medway, Hawkins equipped three ships at Plymouth: the *Salomon* of 130 tons, which he had used in the first voyage; the *Tiger* of 50 tons, a small but well-armed vessel which had been employed in Channel privateering; and the *Swallow* of 30 tons, not the same as the ship of that name which had sailed on the first voyage. For the 910 tons of shipping there were crews amounting to 150 men, of whom 80 went in the *Jesus*. Landsmen in the expedition numbered another 20, comprising gentlemen adventurers and their servants. It is always interesting to observe the proportion of seamen to tonnage in the records of Tudor expeditions. John Hawkins generally employed fewer men than did his contemporaries. On this occasion his proportion was one man to six tons. Unlike the other sea-captains of his time, he gave much thought to problems of health. For this reason he avoided overcrowding, which was the enemy of cleanliness. As he rule he lost few men by sickness. Others were wont to embark with excessive numbers to allow for casualties, which in due course they suffered. When the Navy was mobilized for war, much heavier crews were thought essential, in the early part of the century at the rate of one man to one-and-a-half tons. The result was rapid exhaustion of victuals and terrible epidemics of typhus and other deadly ills, which almost invariably swept away the crews after they had been a few weeks on board.

There is no full list of the officers and gentlemen who accompanied Hawkins. Among the names which we have are those of John Sparke, George Fitzwilliam and Anthony Parkhurst. Sparke had most likely sailed in the first expedition and is the author of the detailed account which forms our main authority for the second.[1] Fitzwilliam was a trusted adherent of Hawkins and may have played an important part in the underground history of the

---

[1] Sparke's account is printed in Hakluyt's *Principal Navigations*. The Portuguese complaints are in P.R.O., S.P.For., Eliz., Vol. 99 and Vol. 95 pp. 242–67. Miss Wright's *Caribbean Documents* contain much new matter from the Spanish side. John Sparke was afterwards Mayor of Plymouth in 1583–4 and 1591–2.

undertaking, for he had a footing in Spain by kinship to Jane Dormer, the English wife of the Duke of Feria, one of Philip's senior ministers. Parkhurst also came from Spain to join the expedition. What he had been doing in that country is not clear, but he came over in the summer with a recommendation to Hawkins from Sir Thomas Challoner, the English ambassador.

Hawkins sailed from Plymouth on October 18, 1564. At sea he fell in with some ships from London going to the gold trade of Lower Guinea, and they continued more or less in his company to the African coast. A head wind caused him to stop for five days at Ferrol in north-western Spain. If the local authorities guessed his destination, they made no move to interfere, and indeed could not, since the *Jesus* was the Queen of England's ship and Hawkins her officer. At Ferrol Hawkins issued routine sailing orders for the voyage and appointed Teneriffe as the next rendezvous in case of dispersal by bad weather. His instructions ended with the oft-quoted words: 'Serve God daily, love one another, preserve your victuals, beware of fire, and keep good company'. Changes in our language have tended to obscure the fact that the above are not pious exhortations but tersely worded orders. The five orders consist of three words each, a model for bureaucrats. The first means that all hands are to attend daily prayers; the second, avoid dissension and quarrelling; and the last, that all the ships are to sail as closely together as possible. We have an account of the daily prayers in a statement made years afterwards by one of Hawkins's men under examination in the Inquisition.[1] He said:

In the flagship of the said John Hawkins . . . every morning and evening the master took a book in English, like those which the clergy had in England, and went to the mainmast, where all the sailors, soldiers [and the] captain knelt on the deck, and all attended under pain of twenty-four hours in irons. And all being on their knees, the said master . . . recited the Lord's prayer and the creed, word for word, and then made the same prayers which . . . are made in England. Also [the witness] said that in the

[1] *Trial of Miles Phillips*, Mexican National Archives, *Inquisition Records*, Vol. 54, evidence of William Collins, pp. 12-13 of transcript by Mr. G. R. G. Conway.

same manner the said master read the epistle of St. Paul and a gospel . . . and that was done in all the ships of the said fleet of John Hawkins, and in others.

The call at Teneriffe was necessary for consultation with Pedro de Ponte. He had undoubtedly been collecting information from the West and would be able to send thither notice that Hawkins might be expected. Sparke's account gives no details of the conference, but its general purport must have been to arrange at what places the expedition should trade. Guzman de Silva, the new Spanish ambassador in England, reported afterwards, 'if it were not for these Spaniards helping them in the islands, these expeditions would never have commenced'.

From Teneriffe the expedition sailed to Cape Blanco, on the African coast, where the Portuguese had a fishery. Hawkins obtained some fish, but the natives of this part were not merchantable, being tawny Moors and not negroes. He went on to Cape Verde, where the true negroes were to be found. However, the gold-trading squadron bound for Lower Guinea passed along the coast in advance of him, and some of its men told the negroes that he was coming for slaves, with the result that he captured none. There is no reason to regard this as deliberate hostility on the part of the gold traders, some of whose merchant adventurers were also members of the Hawkins syndicates.

Sparke gives an interesting account of the natives of the coast. The goodly men dwelling about Cape Verde were the Leophares and the Jaloffes, kindly in their ways and accustomed to trading with the French. A Frenchman who had been shipwrecked was living contentedly among them. He was offered a passage in Hawkins's fleet, but was half minded to refuse it, and yielded only to the persuasion of some of his countrymen on board the ships. The French, then as since, got on well with the African peoples, but it is not true that they took no part in the slave trade; for Spanish documents reveal French slavers in the West Indies at this time. It was the method rather than the principle of slaving that alienated the Africans. Indiscriminate raiding and capture by armed parties naturally aroused fierce resistance, but the tribes

were often at war and were quite ready to sell their prisoners to
the slavers. It was the common punishment also, as Sparke records,
for offenders against tribal laws to be sold to the white men. From
this arose the system which became standard in later times,
whereby the coast tribes acted as agents for the supply of slaves,
whom they obtained by raiding in the interior. South of the
Jaloffes were the Sapies, who inhabited the main coast and the
off-lying islands of the Bissagos and Los groups. They had been
over-run and partly enslaved by the people whom Sparke calls
the Samboses from beyond Sierra Leone. These are evidently the
conquering Sumbas who were then penetrating West Africa
from the interior. Sparke says that they were cannibals and sold
slaves to the Portuguese.

In mid-December Hawkins moved on to the island of Sambula,
where he captured a number of Sapies who were themselves
slaves to the Sumbas. He then moved over to the mainland and
anchored at the mouth of the River Callousas. He left the two
large ships at the entrance and went twenty leagues up with the
smaller vessels, to a point where the Portuguese were to be found,
'and dispatched his business, and so returned with two caravels,
loaden with negroes'. This is Sparke's indefinite mode of statement, and it leaves us in doubt whether the transaction was trade
or piracy. The Portuguese account, which we shall have to
consider, is positive that it was piracy. Sparke nowhere makes any
defence to such a charge, and the reason is that it did not occur to
him that the charge could be brought. For him all the proceedings
were lawful and justifiable. Certainly the next thing he records is
voluntary collaboration by the Portuguese with Hawkins. They
told him of a town called Bymba which he might attack on the
way back to the great ships, and they themselves guided him to it.
The attempt failed badly. Hawkins took forty of his men and
some Portuguese and entered the place. Most of the men scattered
to search the houses for the gold which their guides assured them
was there. The negroes rallied, fell upon the stragglers, and drove
them back with heavy punishment to the boats. Hawkins kept a
dozen men together and averted a massacre of the whole party.
Seven of the English were killed, including Field, the captain of

the *Salomon*, and twenty-seven wounded, and only ten negroes were taken. Sparke was struck with Hawkins's self-command and concern for his men, and notes it in words which are similar to those used by other observers on later occasions: 'Thus we returned back somewhat discomforted, although the Captain in a singular wise manner carried himself, with countenance very cheerful outwardly, as though he did little weigh the death of his men, although his heart inwardly was broken in pieces for it.' The assumed cheerfulness, the account continues, was for Portuguese observation. The grief was genuine enough, as we know by much other evidence. No captain was more a father to his men than John Hawkins.

The next anchorage was at Taggarin, in the Sierra Leone region, at the mouth of the River Caceroes. As before, the two large ships remained outside while the two barks, the *Tiger* and the *Swallow*, went in, together with the large boats or pinnaces of the *Jesus* and *Salomon*. In five days the small craft, 'having dispatched their business,' returned to Taggarin. In the light of the subsequent Portuguese complaint, the phrase may be read as covering the acquisition of more negroes, some of whom had been collected for the contractors who legitimately supplied Spain with slaves. But the contractors were far away, and the Portuguese on the spot were faced by a masterful man who was determined to have the goods and would pay fair prices for them. They took his money and subsequently cleared themselves by some thorough-going lies. Little else could be expected of the exiles and broken men who were sent to maintain 'the dominion of the King of Portugal' in tropical Africa.

Their depositions, as on the previous occasion, are collected in books of complaint sent to the English government. We need not repeat them in detail. Their sum is that Hawkins took by force sixteen or seventeen Portuguese ships, with 600 negroes, much ivory, and some gold, the total damage being 48,000 ducats; and all without anyone being killed. We have to place what construction we can upon it, noting meanwhile that the Spanish ambassador de Silva, a witness hostile to the English, made enquiries about the African transactions and sent a brief account to Spain. He said that Hawkins traded with the Portuguese, not that he fought with them, and that the Portuguese aided him in attacking negro settlements. De Silva collected these facts in England after the expedition came home, and if there had been any consciousness of piracy among the English crews he would probably have picked up the scent.

The Portuguese depositions contain something else, of considerable interest to one of our present enquiries. One of the deponents said 'that he heard the English shout loudly to him that the contract belonged neither to the King of Portugal nor to the contractors, but to the realm of England and John Hawkins'. It was evidently common knowledge in the expedition that the English government and the Hawkins syndicate were expecting to be the concessionaires of the slaving contract. That must be the meaning of *tractatio*, the Latin word employed in the document.

On January 29, 1565, Hawkins sailed from Sierra Leone with all his ships and four or five hundred negroes. It took him eighteen days to work clear of the coast into the trade wind belt, but then all went well, and he reached Dominica on March 9. The island was one of the Carib preserves which the Spaniards had learned to respect, but Hawkins was lucky enough to fill his water casks without fighting. Not two months before, says Sparke, a Spanish caravel had come there to water. The cannibals stole up by night and cut the cable so that the ship drove ashore, when her crew were killed and eaten.

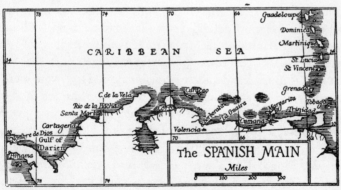

From Dominica Hawkins sailed to Margarita, which he reached on March 16. The island lay off the eastern end of the Spanish Main, and derived its name from a pearl fishery discovered by the pioneers and continuing to give a diminished yield. The alcalde of the small Spanish community was civil and provided victuals, but the governor refused to speak with Hawkins or to give him licence to trade. He was in fact the first Spanish officer so far encountered who took the King's orders seriously; and in this second voyage he was to be the only one. The trade possible at Margarita does not seem to have been worth much, and it was in another respect that the governor seriously disobliged Hawkins, by preventing a Spanish pilot from sailing with him. Hawkins had never been on the Main or in the Caribbean, and he relied on the pilot's services. The want of them caused loss of time and of trade. The disapproving governor sent word at once to Santo Domingo that Hawkins was on the coast. The audiencia duly warned all the ports as far west as Cartagena and Nombre de Dios not to have any dealings with him. It is unlikely that this did Hawkins any harm. For the corrupt gang at Santo Domingo already knew that he was coming, and their warning no doubt served as a notification to their friends on the Main to concert measures for opening trade when he should appear.

He made Cumaná his first landfall on the Main, and watered the ships at the Indian settlement of Santa Fé. Sparke, the narrator, gives many details of the Indians and their customs, of their powerful arrow poisons, and of the foodstuffs obtainable. Among them, maize and potatoes were both novelties to him: 'these potatoes be the most delicate roots that may be eaten, and do far exceed our parsnips or carrots.' The Indians were probably Arawaks, for Sparke describes the Caribs encountered farther along the coast as much less desirable acquaintances. They were wont to lure white men by showing gold, and then to capture and eat them.

The expedition sailed westwards, with Hawkins in a pinnace close inshore, and the large ships farther out. He reached Borburata, the first important settlement, on April 3. The governor here was Alonso Bernaldez, nephew of Lorenzo Bernaldez of Santo Domingo, and Hawkins was provided with a letter of introduction from the uncle. He must have obtained it two years before when in Hispaniola, unless it had been sent to the care of Pedro de Ponte at Teneriffe. In either case it gives the impression that the Hawkins ventures were long planned and carefully worked out. The governor was absent at Coro, but travelled to Borburata as soon as he heard that the English had arrived.

Meanwhile the general public of Borburata, knowing nothing of Hawkins, observed the approach of a powerful squadron and concluded it to be French. There was a panic and a rush out of town while yet there should be time. The ships came to anchor and Hawkins landed with a Spaniard as interpreter. This Spaniard, Cristobal de Llerena, was a colonist and merchant of Jamaica whom Hawkins had rescued from captivity among the negroes of Guinea. What he had been doing there is not explained, perhaps engaging in some unlicenced slaving. Hawkins and Llerena found the governor's lieutenant and told him that the purpose of the English was peaceful and mercantile. Hawkins said that the fleet belonged to the Queen of England and that he was sailing under her orders; and that he himself was a man of good standing and in a special sense a servant of King Philip. 'I am a great servitor,' he said, 'of the majesty of King Philip, whom I served when he was king of England'. He asked the lieutenant for licence to sell negroes and other merchandise and undertook to pay the proper duties on the trade. He added that if the licence were not granted he would do the best he could for himself without it. He handed the letter of introduction to the lieutenant for transmission to Bernaldez. It was evidently useful as an identification, a guarantee that they were dealing with the right man.[1] There can be little doubt that Alonso Bernaldez had been notified of the whole affair by his uncle, who would hardly have given Hawkins the letter without advising his nephew of it.

The governor's lieutenant answered that he had no power to give licence for trade and that it was contrary to the law, and that it would be ten days before he could receive an answer from his superior at Coro. In the meantime he would furnish victuals to the English. He wrote to Coro asking Bernaldez to come at once and take charge of the matter. He said that the inhabitants desired to

---

[1] These and other details, statements and incidents not included in Sparkes' account are drawn from Miss Wright's *Caribbean Documents*, Nos. 9–11, pp. 76–83.

trade, being much in need of the wares which Hawkins brought, and that 'the royal revenues would be augmented and the country bene-fited, for this captain promises to please everybody'. Bernaldez set out for Borburata fully intending to come to terms with Hawkins.

Before his arrival Hawkins had concluded that the ten days delay would be an unnecessary waste of time and had opened a new negotiation with the lieutenant. This resulted in a permission to sell some sickly negroes who were likely to die if they were not landed; but no brisk trade was done before the governor's arrival, because prospective buyers were afraid that their negroes might after all be confiscated. As soon as Bernaldez reached Borburata, Hawkins made a formal request for leave to trade, setting forth the arguments in favour of it, and threatening the use of force if it should not be granted. All the circumstances, and the records of what took place at other ports, indicate that the threat was collusive, being required by the governor as an excuse to the King for yielding. In conversation with a Spaniard, Hawkins played the same part: 'he [Hawkins] asked deponent if the governor was of a mind to grant the licence, and when deponent replied that he did not know, the Englishman grew violent and swore an oath that he was a great servitor of King Philip, our master, and that if the permit were not given him, from here down the coast he would not leave a thing standing, that he would do all the damage he could, and that we were not to think he was a corsair thief,' and a good deal more to the same effect. All this was useful to the governor and was duly recorded for trans-mission to Spain. Juan Pacheco, the witness quoted, added his own opinion that Hawkins could inflict sufficient damage to compel the abandonment of Borburata, and that Valencia (inland from it) would then be in danger from Indian attacks. The Indians had killed many Spaniards and were always seeking to co-operate with the French when they drew near the port: 'and he considers that God, Our Lord, and his royal majesty will be better served by granting the said licence than by ruining the people of this city and Valencia, and risking the safety of the whole province and the entire coast'.[1]

[1] *Caribbean Documents*, pp. 80–1.

As the whole story of his expeditions proves, Hawkins did not in fact mean to do any damage, neither were his Spanish associates telling the truth when they professed belief that he would. It was make-believe to serve the Spaniards as an excuse for disobedience. The colonists were in no happy position between the Indians and the French. Their efforts to make a prosperous plantation were hampered by shortage of labour and infrequency of communication with the mother country. They did not view the English in the same perspective as did their king. He was dominated by the fear of heresy and would rather have no subjects than reign over heretics. They were dominated by fear of poverty and would rather buy slaves of heretics than go without. We should do wrong to visualize the governors and officials as the species of uniformed excellencies who rule our tropical possessions to-day. The sixteenth-century governor was poorly paid and made his living from the job only by dint of a reasonable amount of corruption. He was nearly always a planter himself, and was hard put to it to maintain prestige and authority over his fellow-planters. His military force consisted solely of the planters in arms, and he therefore had no means of coercing them. He was almost obliged to swim with the tide. This is to speak of the smaller settlements such as those along the Main. Wherever there were troops at the governor's disposal his position was much stronger.

After mature consideration Alonso Bernaldez, nephew of the able lawyer of Santo Domingo, granted Hawkins the licence, and business began in earnest. Next day, however, there was a hitch. The incident which it occasioned is recorded both by John Sparke and by a Spanish witness whose testimony has been recovered from the archives of the Indies; and on all essential points they corroborate one another. This is some indication that Sparke may be held trustworthy on matters in which there is no corroboration. Hawkins was willing to pay the ordinary 7½ per cent duty which was levied on all merchandize entering the Indies. The officials demanded in addition a slave fee of 30 ducats a head, to be paid by the vendor. Since the fixed maximum price of a slave was 100 ducats, this impost was probably more than the trade could endure, although it seems to have been levied on the recognized contractors for slaves. Hawkins refused to pay, exhibited considerable anger and tore up the governor's licence, and landed an armed party of a hundred men in order to 'displease' the Spaniards. Bernaldez hastened to submit, even with abjectness, and gave two hostages for the observance of the conditions. Whether this was more collusion or a genuine dispute is not apparent. It may be noted that the colonists as well as Hawkins were the gainers by the decision not to add thirty per cent to the costs.

Thenceforward all went smoothly. Hawkins sold as many of his wares as the colony could buy, the Spaniards revelled in his black market, and their governor plunged to the neck in the business and hoped for the best. Towards the end of April the French captain Jean Bontemps came in with the *Dragon Vert* of Havre. He had been in Guinea and had been driven off the Gold Coast by the Portuguese galleys. He had then crossed the Atlantic to sell 'such wares as he had'. Sparke, the authority for the incident, does not say whether they included slaves. The French usually plundered where they could. It may be inferred that Bontemps made no move to do so, and it is certain that Hawkins would not have allowed it. It was an illustration of his offer to serve the King of Spain in the Indies. The night before he left, a Carib raiding party tried to break into the town. The Spaniards beat them off and captured one of their leaders, who for his pains 'had a stake thrust through his fundament'. Such was life at Borburata.

Hawkins quitted the place on May 4, after spending a profitable month. His next port, if it can be so called, was the island of Curaçao, where the ships rode in the open sea and several times dragged anchors and had to make sail. The attraction was that Curacao was a great cattle ranch, where Hawkins not only filled his beef casks but laded hides. The prices obtainable in England made them a profitable cargo. He left on the 15th and sailed westwards past Cabo de la Vela to Rio de la Hacha, the centre of an important settlement with pearl fishing as well as gold mining to recommend it. Such places were always ready to lay out some of their wealth in negro slaves.

The chief Spanish officer at Rio de la Hacha was not styled the governor but the King's treasurer, and his name was Miguel de

Castellanos. Some time before the arrival of the English, he received the warning and prohibition of trade with them sent out by the audiencia of Santo Domingo. He prudently sent away to safe places inland all the gold and pearls and the women of Rio de la Hacha, leaving nothing of value to attract attack. This was the routine proceeding when the French were expected, and Castellanos had as yet no experience of dealing with the English. Hawkins had conference with him and demanded leave to' trade, showing at the same time a certificate of good conduct which he had obtained from the governor of Borburata. The treasurer replied that he had been expressly forbidden to trade. Hawkins then threatened to use force, whereupon the treasurer and his officers gave in and granted the licence.

So much is stated by Sparke, the English narrator. One of the newly recovered Spanish documents gives some illuminating additional information.[1] It says that as soon as Hawkins entered the port and made it known that he had slaves and merchandize to sell, the inhabitants immediately began to deal with him. He announced that he came as the King's servitor and a friend of peace, and would do no harm. He showed the gold obtained at Borburata together with certificates that it was the fruit of honest trade. The leading men of Rio de la Hacha were satisfied, but there was the matter of the royal prohibition. They therefore agreed that their treasurer should speak privately to Hawkins and suggest to him 'that he should threaten and feign to intend to burn the houses of the town or settlement, in order that they might take various depositions of witnesses and prove that they were forced to trade with him'. Accordingly, the treasurer and other persons conferred with Hawkins and came to the above arrangement with him. The collusive threat of violence, therefore, was by this Spanish testimony initiated from the Spanish side. The similarity of the technique at Borburata and at Rio de la Hacha might even suggest a common origin, at Santo Domingo. The employment of a caravel at the King's expense to carry warning that Hawkins was approaching undoubtedly afforded the conspirators there (the elder Bernaldez and his friends) an opportunity

[1] *Caribbean Documents*, pp. 87–91.

to send instructions on the best means of dealing with him. Can we wonder that Hawkins played his part? The Victorian writers,[1] prejudiced against him on account of the slave trade, and knowing only the story as told from on board his own ship, disbelieved it freely, and accused him of falsehood and high-handedness. The Spanish evidence vindicates him and exposes the conditions on which he could do business with some slippery double-dealers. He took these people as he found them and does not come dishonourably out of the story.

As at Borburata, there was a hitch after the trade had been agreed on in principle. This time it was due to the grasping attitude of Castellanos and his friends. The Spanish document states that they were determined to make money in spite of the King. They tried also to do it in spite of John Hawkins, telling him that they would pay for a slave no more than half as much as he had received at Borburata. Hawkins replied that this was cutting his throat, and lost no time in landing with a hundred armed men and some pieces of ordnance. Rio de la Hacha turned out 150 foot and thirty horse. But the artillery was too much for them. As soon as a gun was fired, all the Spanish foot fell flat on the earth, which was not in those days accounted good military conduct; while the horse gave ground and consulted what they should do. The result was a flag of truce and more negotiation. Hawkins and Castellanos again conversed privately, and the English demands were agreed to, with some hostages thrown in to ensure punctual performance.

Trade continued for a fortnight, during which time, according to the Spanish evidence, the treasurer and inhabitants of Rio de la Hacha bought three hundred negroes and much merchandize, wines, flour and biscuit, cloth, linens and ready-made clothing, and many other things. Something like a department store was set up in the town, to which everyone resorted. Not only this, but Hawkins booked orders for negroes and other goods to be brought on a subsequent voyage. He received in payment a quantity of gold and silver in the lump and also of worked precious metals. The account further states that the inhabitants

[1] Particularly Froude and Sir John Laughton, author of the article on Hawkins in the *Dictionary of National Biography*.

did business with the English peaceably and quietly, and visited their ships freely and safely. Details such as these, collected by the Spanish authorities, help us to realize, as the more summary English accounts do not, how little of a corsair Hawkins was, and how beneficial his enterprise could be to Engand and Spain alike. Philip's colonies were bleeding for want of defence and starving for lack of trade. Here was the offer of both, had he the sense to see it.

Just before Hawkins left he had a last brush with the treasurer, who had quietly called in some reinforcements and field-guns from neighbouring places and now declined to pay a debt due to Hawkins from the governor of Borburata. Sparke says that Castellanos meditated a surprise attack on the English, but this did not come off. Hawkins, 'standing in doubt of their courtesy,' landed his usual armed party and 'cleared all things between the treasurer and him', without, however, obtaining payment of the Borburata debt. He received from the treasurer's own hand a testimonial to his good behaviour and civilly took his leave and departed; after which the treasurer and his associates began to take the depositions of numerous witnesses in their defence, to be produced in the event of trouble from higher authority.

Hawkins had now sold all his wares. His return cargo was rich but small, and he had room to stow hides to the value of £2,000, for which purpose he steered for Hispaniola. He had not previously sailed across the Caribbean and was not informed of the strength of the current which flows through it from east to west. Instead of reaching Hispaniola he was carried so far westward as to sight the south coast of Jamaica, where cloudy weather delayed a proper identification. The only man in the expedition who had been there before was the Spaniard Llerena who had been rescued in Guinea. His home was in Jamaica, and he was so over-joyed to see it that he threw away his old clothes and dressed in his best. But he proved a useless pilot, and was unable to point out a habitation or a landing-place. Meanwhile wind and current were carrying the ships westwards, and the outcome was that Hawkins was set to leeward of Jamaica with no chance to return. He lost the prospect of a cargo of hides, while Llerena was carried back in his Sunday best to England.

The lack of a pilot was a serious disability as Hawkins coasted southern Cuba with its shoals and islets. He rounded the western end and tried for Havana on the north coast, the port of assembly of the plate fleets bound for Europe. Here again there was a confusion of landmarks, and a certain hill was falsely identified as being eastward of Havana when in fact it was to the westward. Hawkins turned away before the wind only to find that the scent was false. He had lost so much ground that there was no time to beat back again. He had to visit Florida before going home, and to Florida he sailed, leaving Havana unattempted. What he would have done there can only be guessed. De Silva, the Spanish ambassador, said afterwards that he was looking for a treasure-ship. That was untrue, as the whole record demonstrates, and the object was most likely hides.

Hawkins had a pilot for the Florida coast, a Frenchman whom he had enlisted for the purpose. He made a thorough examination from Cape Sable up the Atlantic shore to the latitude of $30\frac{1}{2}°$ N., where he found René de Laudonnière established at Fort Caroline near the River of May. Laudonnière had reached the place in June 1564 with two hundred men. The French were soon on bad terms with the Indians, and short of food. Like most of the early colonists they were not prepared to till, but thought of themselves as a garrison entitled to be victualled from without. Some of them grew discontented and went off to plunder the Spaniards in the Caribbean. After an early success they were overthrown, and only a few got back to Fort Caroline. The gold and silver of Florida, of which the world had heard so much, proved disappointing. The Indians were in possession of some gold, but it was not native to the country, having been obtained from Spanish ships wrecked in the Florida Channel. By the date of Hawkins's visit, July 1565, the French were disillusioned and starving, and anxious to go home. Laudonnière alone was determined to remain. He knew the strategical importance of Florida as a menace to the Spanish treasure-route, and he counted on receiving supplies and new men from France.

These circumstances were soon clear to Hawkins, who displayed sympathy and friendliness to the French. His business, of course, was to aid them to evacuate Florida, since their presence there was

distasteful to the English government and a serious threat to the
King of Spain whom he was eager to serve. He accordingly
offered them a passage home, promising to land them in France
before entering an English port. If Laudonnière had agreed, the
prospects of Spanish recognition for Hawkins in the Indies would
have been greatly improved. But Laudonnière would not quit his
post. He politely refused the offer and decided to hold on in the
hope of relief. Hawkins swallowed his disappointment and behaved
with the generosity which was part of his character. He sold
Laudonnière a fifty-ton ship (presumably the *Tiger*), twenty
barrels of meal, six pipes of beans, and other victuals. The sale was
really a gift, for payment was by a bill that was never discharged.
Laudonnière himself put this on record, adding that John
Hawkins 'has won the reputation of a good and charitable man,
deserving to be esteemed as much of us all as if he had saved all our
lives'. It was an incident honourable to both.

The foodstuffs had not been spared out of abundance, and
Hawkins was left ill supplied for the homeward voyage. He sailed
northwards along the American coast to the Newfoundland bank,
where he revictualled by catching cod and buying from the
fishermen. It was now late in August, and the westerlies were fair
for the run to England. On September 20, 1565, the squadron
arrived at Padstow on the north coast of Cornwall. It had lost
twenty men in the course of the voyage, of whom we know seven
to have been killed on one occasion in Guinea. This leaves about a
dozen as the maximum number who can have died of disease, and
is an excellent record for a tropical voyage at a time when a large
mortality was usual. John Hawkins is the only captain of his
generation who is recorded to have shown any interest in hygiene.

Sparke says nothing of the condition of the *Jesus of Lubeck* at the
end of the voyage, but it may be inferred that she was seriously
strained and leaking. Repairs were necessary before she could put
to sea again, and it was not possible to sail her round the Land's
End and up Channel to Chatham until the following spring. The
repairs bill came to £500, a quarter of the total value at which the
ship stood in the syndicate's accounts. The charter-party or
agreement for the use of the *Jesus* by the syndicate has not been

preserved, but such documents do exist for the employment of
various ships of the Navy by the Guinea adventurers of this
decade. In broad principle the terms were standardized and
undoubtedly applied to the *Jesus* in this voyage and in the
subsequent one of 1567–8. The Queen supplied the ship, fitted out
and fully equipped by a given date. The syndicate found and paid
the crew, and provided the victuals. At the end of the voyage a
proportion of the profit was due to the Treasurer of the Navy. A
final proviso was important: the Queen bore the adventure,
which means the risk of loss, of the ship for the voyage; but, if the
ship came home, it was to be repaired and handed back in good
condition at the expense of the syndicate as a whole. Thus, if
Hawkins had lost the *Jesus* in this voyage, the loss would have
fallen wholly on the Queen; but, as it was, the expense of making
good the damages fell on the syndicate, of which the Queen was
one member among several. This point will be seen to be of great
importance in a decision which Hawkins was destined to make
three years later.

John Hawkins had a little son growing up in these years, and the
boy had sharp ears for tales of his father's prowess. Among his
memories was one of the *Jesus* being set on fire by some careless-
ness in the gunners' room. The ship would have been burnt
without redemption if Hawkins had not taken the proper action.
He ordered the scuppers to be stopped and the pumps manned.
The water pouring on the deck was prevented from flowing
overboard, and was soon several inches deep; and thus with
scoops and swabs it was directed down the hatchway upon the
fire. Sparke's observations on the potato have been noted.
Another feature of his account forms probably the first English
mention of tobacco. He describes how the natives of Florida use
'a kind of herb dried', and a cane with an earthen cup at the end;
and with this apparatus and the aid of fire they suck in the smoke
of the herb. It satisfies their hunger and voids phlegm from the
stomach, 'and this all the Frenchmen used for this purpose.' The
continental Indians were pipe smokers in contrast with the cigar
smoking which the Spaniards had observed in the Antilles.

VI

LOVELL'S VOYAGE

Immediately on reaching Padstow, Hawkins wrote to the Queen to announce his safe arrival and to notify her that the voyage had been satisfactory. No prudent man put into such a letter any more information than was unavoidable, since it might fall into the wrong hands, and the customary technique was to communicate by reference to what was already known between the parties. So Hawkins goes into no detail: 'Your majesty's commandment at my departing from your grace at Enfield I have accomplished, so as I doubt not but it shall be found honourable to your highness, for I have always been a help to all Spaniards and Portugals that have come in my way without any harm or prejudice by me offered to any of them, although many times in this tract they have been under my power. I have also discovered the coast of Florida in those parts where there is thought to be great wealth.'[1]

There is little to be learned from this save the certainty that it was the Queen's policy that Hawkins should be of service to Spaniards in the Indies. The sentence on Florida is a model of discretion, making no reference to the French and hinting only by the turn of a phrase that no great wealth had been found.

The voyage as a whole had yielded a good profit, if we may judge by the apparent satisfaction of the investors. There are no details available, but de Silva reported to Philip that the dividend was 60 per cent. The joint-stock syndicates of this period were in the habit of winding up the entire stock at the close of each voyage and returning principal as well as interest to the members. The only concern then operating in England with a permanent joint-stock in the modern manner was the Muscovy Company. The Queen herself seems to have been well pleased with Hawkins, and granted him a coat of arms to celebrate his achievement. Its specification is: sable, on a point wavy a lion passant or; in chief

[1] Letter printed in Froude's *History* (Everyman edition), II, p. 217 n.

three bezants; for a crest, a demi-Moor proper bound in a cord. Sir William Cecil and the Earl of Leicester made the formal recommendation, and the draft in the College of Arms is corrected in Cecil's hand. This discounts Froude's fervent statement on the shareholders' list: 'Cecil alone, ever honourable, ever loathing cruelty and unrighteousness, though pressed to join with the rest, refused, "having no liking for such proceedings."' There is evidence that Cecil may have been a shareholder, and his own word to the contrary was passed only to the Spanish ambassador, thus ranking merely as a diplomatic falsehood. As for dishonour, cruelty and unrighteousness, there is no scrap of evidence that Cecil or any of his fellow-countrymen applied such terms to the slave trade. Cecil was indeed an honourable man, as was Hawkins, by the standards of the reign of Queen Elizabeth, which were not those of the reign of Queen Victoria.[1]

In spite of the calculations of English statesmen and Spanish officials, Philip meant what he said in prohibiting trade by foreigners in the Caribbean. It is possible that his determination was not fixed at the time when the Hawkins voyages began, since the Queen and Hawkins alike had evidently grounds for expecting his compliance. But by 1565 he had made up his mind not only to exclude the English, however well they might behave, but to deal with the French, whose Florida settlement had already shown its possibilities in the premature incursion of Laudonnière's men into the Caribbean. The king was greatly annoyed when he heard of the doings at Borburata and Rio de la Hacha. From the former place he had Alonzo Bernaldez brought to Spain a prisoner

---

[1] I mean no disrespect to Froude, whose humble admirer I am. But genius may have its blind spots, and one such was Froude's view of Hawkins. It was due to two causes. When Froude was working on his great history there were slaves in the United States, the French and Spanish colonies, and Brazil; and illicit slave-ships were still carrying their cargoes across the Atlantic with greater cruelty than in the days of the legalized trade. For humane men this was a thing to be fought and destroyed. Their souls were in the battle, and they could take no cool and comparative view, as we can now that it is long finished. Froude approached Hawkins with a prejudice creditable to himself. His other disability was that more than half the present evidence was unknown in his time. The record is incomplete now, and was fragmentary then; and prejudice misconstrued it.

to answer for his conduct. Castellanos at Rio de la Hacha, who had kept up more appearance of resistance to Hawkins, was not immediately deprived of his post, but the threat hung over him; for the leading men of the place were required to answer some straightly worded questions whose clear implication was that the treasurer had betrayed his duty. These officials had a worrying life between the Indians and the French, and now between John Hawkins and their own sovereign.

With regard to Florida, Philip had taken decisive action before Hawkins appeared there, and the settlement at Fort Caroline was under the shadow of the sword at the moment of Laudonnière's refusal of the passage home offered him by Hawkins. In the previous March (1565) Philip had appointed Pedro Menéndez de Avilés, a distinguished captain, to lead an expedition of 500 men to colonize Florida after exterminating the French. Menéndez had sailed on this mission when Hawkins arrived at Fort Caroline. Another Florida expedition was also crossing the ocean at the same time, in the shape of French reinforcements under Jean Ribault, sent by Admiral Coligny to succour the hard pressed Laudonnière. Ribault arrived first, at the end of August, just as Laudonnière was yielding to the clamour of his men to be taken home. Supplies and new men put heart into the French, and it seemed that the colony was saved. A week later Spanish ships were seen. Ribault took the best of the men and went out in chase of them, not knowing the true strength and position of the enemy. The truth was that Menéndez had landed at St. Augustine, some forty miles south of Fort Caroline, and that the ships descried were making a reconnaissance of the French. Menéndez lost no time. He marched northwards in strength, took Fort Caroline by a night attack, and killed most of its defenders. Then he heard that Ribault's ships had been scattered by storms and driven ashore. He found the Frenchmen in two separate parties. They were stranded and starving and in no condition to fight. He refused to promise them their lives, and they surrendered at discretion. Menéndez then killed them all except ten who satisfied him that they were Catholics. There was a last remnant who were rounded up at a later date. Menéndez spared their lives on surrender. But in the main the end of Florida was in massacre. A great occasion was made of it, with jubilation in Spain and execration in France; and three years afterwards a flying raid of Frenchmen carried out a counter-massacre on the new Spanish St. Augustine. On a general view it should be admitted that the French had initiated these western wars and that Menéndez' severity was effective; for there were no more French colonies for the rest of the century.[1] Ribault was killed in the massacre, and Laudonniere was one of the few who escaped to tell the tale.

This was the first victory of the Spaniards over the French intruders since the intrusion had begun with the Hapsburg-Valois wars. The wars were now recommencing as Catholic-Protestant, the French seamen were mostly Huguenots, the Dutch Calvinists were soon to join them, and the English were to be fully involved. But little of this was evident to the men of the middle sixties. To them the old political lay-out of Europe was still valid, and they thought in terms of Hapsburg versus Valois and of the Anglo-Spanish alliance. Nevertheless the Florida affair, of which the news became public early in 1566, must have been a blow to Hawkins, for it showed that Philip was capable, if goaded, of defending his western interests. But the effort might not be sustained—in fact it was not—and Hawkins went on with his plans.

Don Guzman de Silva, the Spanish ambassador in England at this time, was primarily concerned with the great affairs of European politics, and especially with Scotland, where the reckless proceedings of Mary Stuart were ripening to her ruin. But he had also been definitely instructed by Philip to take up the matter of Hawkins's trade and to try to induce the Queen to stop it. De Silva was a good ambassador who knew how to maintain his master's interests without infuriating those who were opposed to them. When he had to make a demand he made it coolly and clearly, showing comprehension of the contrary view, and not losing his temper at a rebuff. His friendly and sympathetic manner enabled him to say hard things to the Queen and her ministers and remain on good terms with them; and altogether

---

[1] As a French historian put it: 'Menéndez avait achevé sa tâche. La Floride française avait vécu.'

his mission forms a cheerful passage in the otherwise depressing story of the Spanish envoys to Elizabeth.

When Hawkins arrived in London in the autumn of 1565, de Silva sought his acquaintance and asked him to dinner. It was no more the done thing then than now for an ambassador to dine with a pirate; and the incident shows that however much the Spanish officials might write down Hawkins as a *corsario*, they knew very well that he was an honest man and entitled to honourable treatment. De Silva had already been at pains to gather information about the recent voyage and had sent a brief account of it to Spain. He must have learned the names of some of the highly placed members of the syndicate, but it is curious that he betrays no knowledge, even in his letters to Philip, of the connection of the Queen with the venture. He now wished to know Hawkins personally in order to judge of his character and fathom his intentions. Hawkins on his side was eager to open a new approach to the heart of Spain. He had always been a collector of ambassadors, and this one promised to be especially useful. They met as equals, conversed freely and with seeming frankness, and parted with civility. Although Hawkins is reported to have employed an interpreter in important dealings on the Main, some of the documents give the impression that he spoke Spanish. Probably de Silva had some knowledge of English. The interview would have been worth hearing. At its close Hawkins, who with all his pleasing speech and charm of manner had told the ambassador nothing that he did not already know, went away well pleased to have made a new contact. De Silva, impressed with the ability of the Englishman, sat down to write in a dispatch: 'This needs decisive action. I could complain to the Queen, but would first like any information you may have from the places visited. . . . It may be best to dissemble so as to capture and castigate him on the next voyage.'

After a visit to Plymouth, Hawkins was again in London early in 1566, and remained there for some months. He dined again with de Silva, and other interviews followed. Hawkins spoke of the cargo of hides confiscated in Spain and asked the ambassador to help him obtain restitution. He produced the licences which had been given him by colonial officials, as evidence of his honest dealings, and declared that he would not go again to the Caribbean without the King's permission. De Silva did not believe it, and suggested to Philip that it was advisable 'to get this man out of the country, so that he may not teach others, for they have good ships and are greedy folk with more liberty than is good for them'. From this arose the proposition that Hawkins should serve the King with armed ships against the Turks in the Mediterranean. It was what Hawkins desired above all things. He knew that he and his English crews, with the formidable little ships that Channel privateering had evolved, would do better service than the King was getting from his Italian galley-masters. He would be able to impress Philip not only with his fighting value but with his integrity. The recognized position in the Caribbean would surely follow.

This, in de Silva's report to the King, is the first categorical mention of Hawkins's desire to serve with armed forces in return for commercial privileges. Hitherto he has been seen in the West offering to do the King service, but the nature of the service has been unspecified; although it must have been obvious enough to the oft-raided West Indians. Now we have it in clear terms. Whether de Silva sincerely thought that the King would agree we cannot tell. Perhaps he was only dissembling. In any case the King did not agree. He did not say so, but merely kept silence. The months passed with the two men talking hopefully in London and not a word vouchsafed from Madrid. By August there was no longer a hope for that year, although Hawkins told the ambassador that when the weather grew too bad for the Turkish galleys to remain at sea the English ships could still cruise for merchant prizes in the Levant. Galleys were brittle craft, less seaworthy than sailing ships. Philip had no doubt taken his time to ponder, as he always did, and had then decided unfavourably. Italian contractor-admirals for squadrons of galleys were one thing. A compact English fleet under a man of commanding ability would be another. The first did not always beat the Turk, but they gave no anxiety to their employer. The second might be altogether too successful. England was not yet a power in the

Mediterranean. It would be as unwise to attract her thither as to the Caribbean. Such, probably, was the royal line of thought, and silence was its only expression.

Hawkins was not taken in, nor beguiled into wasting a season. He had not staked all on the King's compliance. The negotiation which was never concluded gave him the opportunity to equip some ships, supposedly for Philip's service, but equally for the tropical voyage which was best commenced in the autumn. So was initiated the expedition which forms the main subject of this chapter.

In the summer of 1566 three ships, the *Paul*, *Salomon* and *Pasco*, totalling about 350 tons, were fitted out at Plymouth, together with the *Swallow*, which was destined for a somewhat different purpose. The ships belonged to the Hawkins brothers. Whether John Hawkins purposed to command them is not clear. In the event he did not, and they sailed under Captain John Lovell. Hawkins may have decided that negotiations with Spain, if not service in the Mediterranean, would occupy his attention, and that he could entrust the Caribbean business to a deputy. There was no ship of the Queen's, and the modest scale of the preparations resembles rather the first voyage of John Hawkins than the second. The purpose was to deliver slaves and merchandise at places on the Main where Hawkins had booked orders in 1565. We know from the record of a subsequent lawsuit that there were other investors besides Hawkins, but we have no list for this voyage. It may be reasonably assumed that the same great persons had a hand in it as on the previous occasion, and that Cecil and the Queen, if not participators, at least knew what was intended.

De Silva knew of the preparations and was led to believe that the ships were for Philip's service against the Turk. We have no right to accuse Hawkins of duplicity. Very likely they were for that purpose, which was changed only when Philip withheld his consent. In August, at any rate, de Silva wrote that Hawkins was sincerely anxious to serve the King and was not intending to trade in the Indies. It turned out, however, that Hawkins was both; and in October de Silva had certain information that a West Indian voyage was intended. He complained to the Queen, who was quite ready to engage in an argument about the justification of Caribbean voyages. It was not what de Silva wanted, but rather a prompt prohibition, for the season for sailing had arrived. The Queen referred him to Cecil, who summoned the adventurers and interrogated them on their intentions, while the Privy Council chopped words with the ambassador on his master's claim to monopoly. All this was to give Hawkins a chance to cut the knot by getting his ships to sea before a decision had been reached. Perhaps they were not ready, but more probably he was unwilling. He had always a liking for legality, even though the law had to be stretched taut. The ships did not stir, and the Council called him up from Plymouth to give an account of himself. When we remember that this voyage was one of a series, and that the Queen and members of her Privy Council had been adventurers in its predecessor, we can realize that all this apparent need for information was simply play-acting. The Council solemnly examined Hawkins, and Hawkins declared that he was not going to King Philip's Indies nor would send his ships there. The Council then sent him along to the Court of Admiralty to execute a bond for £500 to that effect, the money to be forfeited if the conditions were transgressed. All was now in order, de Silva wrote that he was satisfied, and Philip instructed him to thank the Queen.

On November 9, 1566, the four ships sailed for Guinea under the command of John Lovell, the *Swallow* to return direct with commodities, the other three to make the round voyage to the Spanish Main. Hawkins duly stayed behind. As for the three ships, they may no longer have been his. His brother William, who had given no bond, was possibly their legal owner by the date of sailing. The quibble is frequently met with in contemporary trials in the Admiralty Court. In any case the bond itself was not for a crippling sum, about the price of a score of negroes, and its forfeiture would have been no great matter.

Lovell is stated in a Spanish document to have been a kinsman of Hawkins, and in another, to have traded in the Canaries and spoken blasphemously of religion, but nothing else is known of him apart from the record of this voyage. Thomas Hampton accompanied him as a merchant, and James Hampton went as master of the *Paul*. James Ranse, who afterwards played a part in Drake's Nombre de Dios raid, was master of the *Salomon*. Young Francis Drake himself, then aged about twenty-three or four, was also a member of the company, going westward for the first time. His achievements in the expedition are unknown, save one, the conversion of a Welshman to Protestantism. The man in question, Michael Morgan, was taken prisoner on a later occasion and examined in the Inquisition of Mexico; and there he confessed that he had become a heretic by the persuasion of his shipmate Francis Drake.[1] The name at that time conveyed nothing to the Inquisitors, but they were to hear it again.

As Lovell was going to places in the Indies where he was expected, he omitted Hawkins's customary call for liaison at Teneriffe, and sailed straight to Cape Verde. There he comes within the compass of the Portuguese books of complaint, which are the sole testimony to his doings in Guinea. They assert that he came late in the year to Cape Verde with four ships, and there took a Portuguese vessel with negroes, wax, ivory and other stuff. That is the only transaction recorded on the mainland coast, and the scene shifts to the Cape Verde Islands. In February 1567 Lovell was close to Santiago, the capital of the group, where he captured a ship with a rich lading of sugar and negroes; and not only that, but he killed some of her crew. Also in sight of Santiago he took a Lisbon ship bound for Brazil; and off the Island of Maio he took two other prizes. The totals of ducats claimed as damages are all given as before, but are not worth quoting. The story as a whole is a variation from the Hawkins procedure. The reason may be that Portugal now had armed ships on the Upper Guinea coast. There were some in the autumn of 1565, for they sank a vessel sent out by William and George Winter of the Navy Board. A year later they may have been the reason for Lovell's withdrawal to the islands. The fact that some Portuguese were killed in his transactions there is also in contrast with previous happenings. Irregular trade was breaking down into irregular war.

[1] The trial of Michael Morgan alias Morgan Tillert, copied by G. R. G. Conway from the records of the Inquisition in the Mexican National Archives.

It seems clear that Lovell sent the *Swallow* home with the commodities, since only the three other ships are recorded to have gone to the West Indies.[1] Spanish documents give varying numbers, and are unreliable because they count every vessel seen separately as a 'ship', even were it only a ship's boat. One witness indeed credits Lovell with 'a large fleet of English galleons and ships'. Lovell, following in Hawkins's track, visited Margarita, Borburata and Rio de la Hacha. Nothing is on record of the Margarita visit, and not much of that to Borburata.[2] There, however, we do hear of an artless development of trading technique. As usual the governor, a new man, had issued a prohibition. Thereupon Lovell's men captured two Spanish merchants, who were careless enough to be caught with 1,500 pesos in their pockets. A little while afterwards Lovell released them, but instead of giving their money back he bestowed on them twenty-six negroes. The English ships brought also provisions and manufactured goods. The official report continues: 'The colonists' needs are great and neither penalties nor punishments suffice to prevent them from buying secretly what they want. In fact they make their purchases, but nothing can be learned of them, for they buy at night and cover each other, and no measures suffice to prevent it. . . . This jurisdiction would not suffer as it does for lack of necessary articles if your majesty would deign to order that when the *galeones* pass to Tierra Firme a ship should call here to supply the colony.'

In 1565 the Frenchman Jean Bontemps had seen Hawkins trading at Borburata. He had since gone in for slaving himself and had sold negroes on the Main in 1566. He was now repeating the venture, and arrived at Borburata at about the same time as Lovell. Both squadrons went westwards along the coast, and Bontemps reached Rio de la Hacha ten days in advance of the English. The Spaniards of Rio de la Hacha, according to their own account, showed a bold front and beat off every attempt of the Frenchman to land, whereupon he took himself off and found

---

[1] High Court of Admiralty, Libels, 3/39. Nos. 22, 101.
[2] The Spanish evidence for the voyage is in Miss Wright's *Caribbean Documents*.

easier game at Santa Marta. They had heard from him of Lovell's
approach, and when the Englishman appeared they surpassed
themselves in heroism in order to defeat him. The story can only
be told in their own words:

Sacred Catholic Royal Majesty,
  Since we understand that because of your majesty's benevolence
and clemency, happy events which befall your majesty's servants
and vassals will afford your majesty pleasure, we have determined
to render your majesty a brief and succinct account of the
victories which in this current year of '67 we in this little city
have won over two very large corsair armadas, one French and
the other English. If, compared with the glorious achievements of
your majesty's captains in Italy, Flanders, Barbary and other parts
of the world, these victories of ours seem a little or a worthless
thing, we entreat your majesty to consider that in its own way
black jet is as fine as precious carbuncle, and if yonder others
achieve great victories, they possess also a corresponding equipment of very good arms, very experienced soldiers and very
excellent officers, and what is more important still, they have
nearer at hand the good fortune of Caesar, while this city,
although rich and a source of much profit to the royal treasury
because of the pearl fisheries carried on here, is nevertheless so
small that its residents and transients together are not usually more
than sixty men, inexperienced and lacking many arms, and what
is worse, far outside your majesty's thoughts. Therefore if these
have undertaken and accomplished a worthy deed, their success
must be attributed solely to God, the victor in battles, and to the
skill of our captain-general, and to the desire which he and this
city have always had to serve your majesty.
  Coming now to the narration of the event, [details follow of the
visit of Jean Bontemps].
  We might have anticipated a period of quiet, the French having
departed, had not they themselves told us of another armada,
English, which was on this coast and would soon reach this city.
Instead of resting we returned to labour, keeping watch every
night, until on the eve of Pentecost we saw the said English
armada appear off this city. The second day of Pentecost [Whit-
monday] it entered and anchored in the harbour of this city.
  That same day, in pacific attitude, there came to speak with our

general one John Lovell, general of the said English, who made
the identical proposal the French general had made. Our general
returned him the same reply he had given the Frenchman, and
so dismissed the Englishman, who went back to his ships, where
he remained six days without daring to attempt anything further.
During this period he sometimes came, and sometimes sent to land,
to persuade our general to trade, and also to discover the strength
of the city, whether he could storm it, and when he saw that he
could not damage it because of the great precautions our general
had taken on every hand, driven thereto by the hunger and thirst
he was suffering, Lovell landed ninety or ninety-two slaves on the
other side of the river from this city. No one could prevent his
doing this; and that same night he sailed away in very great
desperation and grief.

All envy aside, this preparation against corsairs, the country's
successful defence against their attempt to land, and their shame-
ful retreat, must be attributed to the spirit and foresight of our
captain-general, who furnished arms to the majority of the soldiers,
fortified the place with bastions, led the people, arrayed them in
military formation, and provided against every contingency. In
effect he was to this city another Horatius, and if to the man who
saved a city the ancient Romans gave a civic palm, then, because
he has so many times defended this city, it is just and reasonable
that to our general your majesty should grant, not civic palms,
since this is no longer customary, but those honours with which
your majesty with lavish hand rewards those who serve loyally.

The Horatius in question was Miguel de Castellanos, and the
above letter was signed by his brother.[1] We are left to imagine its
effect on his Sacred Catholic Majesty, who toiled daily at his
desk reading multitudes of such effusions, and whose practised eye
would have seen that Rio de la Hacha had been getting negroes
from the English again and that Castellanos was pulling off another
audacious bluff. The concluding paragraphs may have evoked a
weary smile, for the letter goes on to beg that the ninety negroes
may be divided among the inhabitants—'we have earned this by
our courage'—and that the city may be relieved of the extortion
of certain judges sent from Santo Domingo 'at the very moment
we were fighting off this corsair, casting our lives upon the table

_____
[1] *Caribbean Documents*, pp. 95–100.

every moment, and enduring a thousand calamities'. These judges, it seems, were investigating the visit of Hawkins in '65, and were empowered to collect their fees from such as they found guilty. Even loyal and suffering Rio de la Hacha had to protest against such a method of justice.

On that coast there was no lack of meat and water, and scarcity could not have been the reason why Lovell landed the negroes. He had been in daily communication with the treasurer, and the landing must have been the result of a collusive arrangement. But Lovell was too unwary to cope with the Spaniard, who kept the negroes and tricked him out of payment. This was stated by John Hawkins in a letter which he had occasion to write to Castellanos twelve months later: 'My ships which I sent hither the last year with negroes and other merchandise, you being the chief cause, came all in a [misfortune?], which being reparted among divers adventurers, my loss was the more tolerable; and I cannot lay the fault so much the less upon you that I blame not much more the simpleness of my deputies, who knew not how to handle these matters. The negroes they left here behind them I understand are sold and the money to the King's use, and therefore I will not demand it of you.' So it seems that the Hachians, for all their reckless courage, did not get the negroes gratis.

From Rio de la Hacha, according to the Spanish reports, Lovell sailed to Hispaniola, as Hawkins had tried to do in 1565. Lovell reached some point on its coast, and was alleged to have done great damage. He was no doubt seeking primarily for hides, and can have been in no sweet temper on the score of the ninety negroes. But we have no details. The expedition returned safely to Plymouth at the beginning of September 1567. It had not been a great success, but may not have been financially disastrous.

VII

THE THIRD VOYAGE:
PLYMOUTH TO SIERRA LEONE

Among the Portuguese renegades of the 1560's were two who bore a part in the setting forth of Hawkins's third tropical expedition. They were Antonio Luis, who had been a merchant trading in Guinea, perhaps one of the Guinea factors who had covertly sold goods to the English; and Andre Homem, who was perhaps a pilot and one of a family known for its cartographical skill and information. The same man is, however, found calling himself Gaspar Caldeira, and it is uncertain whether that or Homem was his true name. Here he will be referred to as Andre Homem. These two Portuguese declared that they had a secret of great wealth for sale. In a part of Africa, they said, unoccupied by Portugal, there was an immensely rich gold mine within twenty leagues of a good harbour. The annual output would be worth at least £300,000. The land also was fertile and fit for colonists, produced dyewoods, and would produce sugar. It was Florida over again, or rather a rival to Florida, for the story was first told before the wealth of Florida had been disproved. The atmosphere of greed and mutual jealousy among the governments of western Europe which the Florida venture had generated was suitable for the launching of another such proposition, in some respects even more attractive. The two Portuguese seized the chance. Whether they were pure impostors, or whether they really knew something and persuaded themselves of more than they knew, we cannot tell. They never gave their discovery an even approximate location, save that it was in Africa. Contemporaries spoke of Guinea, the Congo outlet, and Mozambique, while a modern writer has even suggested the Transvaal and Rhodesia. It is anybody's guess and has never, in the terms of their description, been discovered.

Luis and Homem first offered their project to the King of Spain, who sent them in 1565 (the first date we have in the story) a safe-conduct to come and explain themselves. It seems that they did not go, and no doubt they were wise to think better of it, for Philip might have handed them across the frontier to the mercies of their own outraged sovereign. They went instead to France, where they gained the support of a young nobleman of Guienne, Pierre Bertrand de Monluc. He and his friends, with some English associates, fitted out an expedition of 750 men conveyed in French and English ships. Monluc had the countenance of Admiral Coligny, whose motive was probably that of establishing a base for the interception of the spice trade as well as the collection of treasure.[1] The leaders kept the destination secret, and an accident of war frustrated the whole adventure. For Monluc chose to stop at Madeira on his way south for the ostensible purpose of filling his water casks. The batteries of Funchal fired on him, and he landed to assault the town. The French took Funchal but lost Monluc, who was killed in the onset. No one else knew whither the expedition was bound save Luis and Homem, and they either kept silence or were distrusted by the surviving officers. The expedition accordingly returned to France with the plunder of Madeira.

Luis and Homem next came to England in the spring of 1567, and introduced themselves to William Winter, of the Navy Board. They told him some of the facts narrated above, and he thought the affair sufficiently important to be revealed to the Queen. She was not incredulous, or perhaps may have seen, like Coligny, that the scheme might support an ulterior purpose. She turned it over to the syndicate which was directing the operations of John Hawkins. Exactly how the syndicate or Hawkins himself received the scheme, and what part it played in the preparation of his third westward voyage, cannot be conclusively stated. The alternatives are that the promoters, or some of them, believed in it and based their plans upon it, or that they did not believe in it, but found it a convenient cover for their real design. On the whole, the present writer thinks the latter explanation the more probable

[1] See C. A. Julien, *Histoire de l'expansion et de la colonisation françaises*, I, p. 264.

as concerns the syndicate, and almost certain as concerns Hawkins; but the facts must speak for themselves.

There can be little doubt that if Luis and Homem had never been heard of, Hawkins would have prepared an expedition this year. He had stayed in England in 1566 in order to negotiate with de Silva, and through him with Philip II, and the negotiation had been inconclusive. He had kept the trade warm by sending out Lovell with an expedition on a minor scale. Lovell had not yet returned, but Hawkins certainly had news of his fortunes in Guinea and perhaps, by way of Teneriffe, of his earlier doings on the Main. It was natural that Hawkins should go himself in 1567 in order to make up for the partial loss of the previous season.

As has been noted, the capital stock in these ventures was wound up and distributed at the end of each voyage, and there is no certainty that the membership of the new syndicate would be the same as that of its predecessor. We have no list for the voyage of 1567, but from various sources we have the names of some certain and some probable members. First, the Queen was a stockholder, by the contribution this time of two ships of the Navy. De Silva reported to his master that some members of the Privy Council held shares. We find throughout the preparations Sir William Cecil taking an active interest, almost to the extent of being managing director, while Clinton, the Lord Admiral, is also consulted. These two are fairly certain, while if de Silva's 'some members' means more than two, Leicester is a probable and Pembroke a possible, both of them having subscribed to the second voyage. Among the merchants we know that Sir William Garrard, Sir Lionel Ducket and Rowland Heyward, all of the City of London, belonged to the syndicate, as also did John and William Hawkins. Winter certainly, and Benjamin Gonson possibly, represented the Navy Board. The complete list would be fuller, but what we have is sufficient to show that the expedition was prepared by the Queen and her trusted men and was as truly an act of state as were any of the joint-stock expeditions that carried on the oceanic war with Spain in later years. Hawkins was again to be the Queen's officer and to sail under the royal standard in command of the Queen's ships.

There was of course no advertisement of the intention, and de Silva first became aware of it at the end of May, when he learned that two of the Queen's ships were being fitted out for Hawkins in the Medway. He probably did not know at this date that Lovell had gone to the Caribbean, and so may have believed that his protest of 1566 had been effective. He went again to the Queen for an assurance that there would be no trespass on the Spanish monopoly. She and Cecil readily gave the assurance, saying that the expedition was bound for Elmina to exact reparation for the sinking of Winter's ship *Mary Fortune* on the Guinea coast in the previous season. Elizabeth and Cecil may have believed that Africa was to be the only destination, but they accompanied their declaration with a piece of make-believe. For Elizabeth summoned 'the merchants' and made them swear in her presence that Hawkins was not going to the Spanish West; as if she, being one of the syndicate, did not know as well as they did where he was going. De Silva remained suspicious until he heard about the project of Luis and Homem, which was no doubt purposely allowed to come to his ears. This seemed to show that the voyage was for a new purpose, against which it could be no business of his to protest. Yet there were indications to the contrary. The ships were now brought round from Chatham to the Thames, and after receiving their guns from the Tower armouries proceeded to lade large quantities of beans. This was a bad sign, for beans were the staple food for slaves on the middle passage. A similar indication was the lading of fine cloths and linens which Spanish planters would buy, but which were unsuited to the cruder taste of the Gold Coast. Again de Silva went to the Queen, and received the same assurance, while Cecil standing by (not Froude's Cecil, surely) confirmed it with a great oath. It was desirable not to allow suspicion to mount to ultimatum-point, and so more talk was released of the Luis and Homem eldorado and the dazzling fortune expected from it. De Silva grudgingly accepted it and ceased to give trouble. He was no fool, but he had other important affairs to negotiate and could not make himself obnoxious on anything short of certainty.

The African gold mine was obviously valuable, if not in one

sense then in another. A piece of evidence at the end of June has some bearing on it. It is a document signed by Hawkins and furnishing a list of ordnance, powder and other stores to be provided from the Tower for equipping a fort in Guinea, 'if there shall be need of fortification.' It is conceivable that the paper was written in order to provide some leaky tub at the Tower with material for de Silva's edification. However, on the face of it this is evidence for the genuineness of the African project. At the end of July Hawkins sailed with the ships for Plymouth, while some other members of the expedition went down by road. Suspicion, protest and intrigue were by no means ended, as the events of the next two months were to show.

The Queen's ships were the *Jesus* of 700 tons, which Hawkins had commanded in the second voyage, and the *Minion*, which had more than once been chartered by the gold traders but had never yet crossed the Atlantic. Some particulars of the *Jesus* have already been given. The *Minion* was of 300 tons, and had been built for Henry VIII about 1536. She was a high charged ship like the *Jesus*, and like her also had suffered from neglect; for early in the Queen's reign it was declared that her upper works were 'spent and rotten'. For war service her allotted crew was 220 men, a far greater number than Hawkins thought fit for a tropical voyage. At Plymouth the two Queen's ships joined those furnished by the Hawkins brothers. They were the *William and John*, of 150 tons; the *Swallow*, 100; the *Judith*, 50; and the *Angel*, 33. Many lists of ships with tonnage stated are on record for the Tudor period, and it is often found that if the same ship is mentioned on different occasions it is with variations of the tonnage figure. The tonnage in fact was not arrived at by exact measurement, but was an estimate of the number of wine-tuns which could be stowed in the hold; and the estimates were sometimes conservative and sometimes liberal in accordance with the standpoint of the estimator, who might be paying for tonnage or being paid for it. We have therefore to regard the figures given for Hawkins's fleet as approximations. Such as they are, they amount to 1,333 tons. The total number of all ranks in the companies we know exactly: 408 persons, or one man to 3¼ tons. It was a higher proportion than in the second voyage.

More is known about the officers and men in this expedition than in its predecessors. This is because the issue was unfortunate, and a considerable number became prisoners of the Spaniards and ultimately of the Inquisition, a court which kept records that have survived to be scrutinized in our own time. The course of the voyage itself is also much more fully described in surviving narratives, which mention many of the participants.[1] The officers included Thomas Hampton and Francis Drake, who had both been out with Lovell and arrived home in time to join Hawkins; but Lovell himself was not included. Others were William Clarke, a London merchant, James Ranse, afterwards to co-operate in Drake's exploit at Nombre de Dios, George Fitzwilliam, a confidential servant of Hawkins, John Varney, gentleman adventurer, Captain Edward Dudley, a soldier, and Robert Barrett of Saltash, master of the *Jesus* and cousin of Drake. The names of three other gentlemen are imperfectly recorded: Fowler (Christian name unknown); Guillermo de Oclando, so called in Spanish documents, who may have been William Okeland or Oakland; and Valentine Verd, whose surname in English may have been Bird or Green, or

---

[1] The narratives are: *A True Declaration of the troublesome Voyage of Mr. John Hawkins to the Parts of Guinea and the West Indies in the years of our Lord 1567 and 1568*, the official narrative by Hawkins himself, published in 1569, and reprinted by Hakluyt; *A Discourse written by one Miles Philips*, in Hakluyt; *The Rare Travels of Job Hortop*, independently published in 1591, and reprinted by Hakluyt; a much longer and more detailed account by an unnamed officer of the *Jesus*, in British Museum, Cotton MSS., Otho E viii, ff. 17–41b, a manuscript unfortunately mutilated in many passages, printed in *Sir John Hawkins*, 1927; and Robert Barrett's deposition in Miss Wright's *Caribbean Documents*, pp. 153–60. Spanish documents are numerous, many being in *Caribbean Documents*, and others, including an important letter by Juan de Ubilla, in two articles by Professor Michael Lewis in *The Mariner's Mirror*, July, 1936 and July, 1937. Portuguese evidence is in the MSS. cited for the Second Voyage. The trials of Hawkins's men in the Mexican Inquisition have been found and transcribed from the Mexican archives by Mr. G. R. G. Conway, who summarized the facts in *An Englishman and the Mexican Inquisition*, Mexico, 1927, Appendix III, and who brought to light Ubilla's letter mentioned above. A valuable recension of Spanish evidence is by C. Sanz Arizmendi in *Boletin del Instituto de Estudios Americanistas*, Seville, 1913–14, p. 55. Numerous other references to authorities will be found in *Sir John Hawkins*, 1927, *passim*.

even something beyond guessing, for Spanish scribes were very wild in their rendering of English names. Finally, there was a nephew of John Hawkins on board, Paul Hawkins or Horsewell, who has been mentioned in an earlier chapter. Thomas Hampton was captain of the *Minion*. Drake began the voyage on board the *Jesus*, although he afterwards had command of another ship. The Mexican Inquisitors were afterwards told that Harry Newman, Francis Drake (who married Mary Newman after the voyage), and Nicholas Antony sailed in the *Jesus*, and were great Lutherans, who spoke much against the Roman Church and argued for Protestant doctrines. Fitzwilliam and Dudley also sailed in the *Jesus*. Two humbler members of the expedition, Miles Phillips, a boy aged about thirteen in 1567, and Job Hortop, a gunner, escaped after many years of captivity with the Spaniards and came home to write accounts of their adventures; while David Ingram, a seaman, also came home with a yarn which few believed in his time or have since. Others will be mentioned as the story unfolds. Many belonged to the West Country, but the *Jesus* and the *Minion* had come to Plymouth with skeleton crews recruited in London; and there were Frenchmen, Irishmen and Dutchmen, the usual cosmopolitan gathering.

Ocean winds and tropical seasons, both in Guinea and the West, made early autumn the best time for departure, and Hawkins had some weeks at Plymouth in which to complete his victualling and crews. His ships lay in the Cattewater, the nearest deep anchorage to the town as it then stood. Towards the end of August a squadron of seven armed ships under Spanish colours sailed into Plymouth Sound. They had come from the Spanish Netherlands, under the command of a Flemish admiral, the Baron de Wachen, known to the English as the Lord of Camphyre [Campveere]. De Wachen was ostensibly cruising to meet Philip II on a passage which the king might be making to the Netherlands, and afterwards declared that he was driven into Plymouth by bad weather. For purposes of refuge, Plymouth Sound offered a variety of good anchorages, but de Wachen made straight for the narrow Cattewater. He saw the two Queen's ships there, and the other vessels of Hawkins's expedition, and he refrained from making the customary salute by dipping flags and lowering topsails. The salute was so well established for ships entering a foreign port that its omission was something more than arrogance, it was a declaration of hostile intent.

Hawkins saw Spanish flags approaching, and they found him on board his flagship, ready and alert. He knew that Spain had protested about his expedition and had been fobbed off with assurances that carried no conviction. He was convinced that the strangers meant to attack him and destroy his project at the start. We may agree with Hawkins that de Wachen did intend just that. A month before sailing he might expect to find the English unready for action, officers and men ashore, guns not cleared, no one in command. He might anchor close among them, trump up a quarrel, and burn them where they lay. A diplomatic argument would follow, with plenty of hard swearing about who began it; but the object would be achieved, in that no Hawkins expedition would sail that year. So de Wachen came on, trailing his coat, and prepared to anchor in the Cattewater. John Hawkins surprised him. He opened fire from the *Jesus* and the *Minion*, and continued to fire until the salute was hastily made and de Wachen changed course and came to an anchor north of St. Nicholas Island, the present Drake's Island.[1] Hawkins's offering was not merely ceremonial shots across the bows, but hits upon the hull of the leading adversary which left no doubt about the state of preparedness prevailing in the Cattewater.

De Wachen sent an indignant message to the Mayor of Plymouth, declaring that he had been fired on, he knew not why, by ships, he knew not whose. It was of course untrue. Coming from Flanders, he knew quite well that Hawkins had taken the *Jesus* and the *Minion* to Plymouth; and even had he not known, those vessels were unmistakably of the Navy, high-charged and heavily armed, such as no merchant built. Their flags proclaimed them the Queen's, and their commander's action showed how foolish it had

[1] This is the substance of the account given in the Cotton MS. story of the voyage. The wind seems to have been from south-west, since it is stated that after being fired at, de Wachen 'loofed' towards the island.

been to refuse the honour due to her. The Mayor referred the complaint to John Hawkins, whom in due course another messenger approached. Hawkins received him as the Queen's officer, pacing the deck in state before an armed guard. The Fleming did his errand civilly, speaking of stress of weather, port of refuge, friendly country, and inexplicable bad treatment therein: 'Right worshipful sir, the Lord of Camphyre, my master, general of this fleet, who to-day through foul weather at sea came into this port, being, as he is, a subject unto the King of Spain, with whom your prince hath amity, marvelleth why you should either shoot at his ships or forbid him this place where you ride....' Hawkins answered that as general of the Queen's ships in the Cattewater he must enforce the respect that was her due, and that he would have no neighbours who should so stubbornly refuse it: 'Therefore the Lord of Camphyre should consider that though there is great friendship between them and us, the haven which he entered was the Queen's, the ships that rid therein hers also, that any stranger ought to be obedient in such case to this prince, and not seem to enter after such manner.' Conceiving the matter thus cleared up, Hawkins followed his answer with a present of poultry and London beer, for which de Wachen returned courteous thanks. He nevertheless wrote to de Silva and urged him to complain about Hawkins to the English queen. Elizabeth may have been secretly pleased, but thought fit to appear uncomprehending. She sent through Cecil a reproof to the man of action, who remarked, 'I had rather Her Highness found fault with me for keeping her ships and people to her honour, than to lose them to the glory of others;' and on this philosophic acceptance the incident ended.

Spaniards and Flemings were still to be a worry to Hawkins. There was a Spanish ship in the Cattewater having on board some Flemish prisoners condemned to the galleys. One afternoon masked men surprised the Spanish crew and released the prisoners. De Wachen at once asserted that Hawkins and the English had done this, although Hawkins denied knowing anything about it and suggested that de Wachen's own Flemings were the more likely culprits. But de Wachen's business was to create distrust between Hawkins and the government. He complained bitterly in London and obtained some apparent credence. At length he rid Plymouth of his presence by putting to sea towards the end of September. His mission throughout had been to delay the expedition. His ostensible business of meeting Philip II at sea was fictitious. Philip did not make the voyage and did not mean to.

A final incident now stirred up more reprimand and recrimination. Luis and Homem, the Portuguese guides to the gold mine, had come down to Plymouth with some London merchants and had been living in the town, well supplied with money and drink. On September 16 they disappeared, and it was found that they had escaped in a small vessel to France. Hawkins had not believed in them and was glad that they had gone. Their flight made it obvious that they were impostors, for they had such an expedition and such a commander at the service of their plan as they could never hope for elsewhere; and the only inference must be that they did not know the way to the gold mine and preferred the exposure to come before they should be at sea without means of escape. Hawkins at once sat down and wrote to the Queen:

My sovereign good Lady and Mistress,
/ Your Highness may be advised that this day, being the xvith of September, the Portingals who should have directed us this pretended enterprise have fled, and as I have certain understanding taken passage into France, having no cause, for that they had of me better entertainment than appertained to such mean persons, and an army prepared sufficient to do any reasonable enterprise; but it appeared that they could by no means perform their large promises, and so having gleaned a piece of money to our merchants are fled to deceive some other. And although this enterprise cannot take effect (which I think God hath provided for the best) I do ascertain Your Highness that I have provision sufficient and an able army to defend our charge and to bring home (with God's help) forty thousand marks gains without the offence of the least of any of Your Highness' allies or friends. It shall be no dishonour unto Your Highness that your own servant and subject shall in such an extremity convert such an enterprise and turn it both to Your Highness' honour and to the benefit of your whole realm.

Which I will not enterprise without Your Highness' consent, but am ready to do what service by Your Majesty shall be commanded; yet to show Your Highness the truth, I should be undone if Your Majesty should stay the voyage, whereunto I hope Your Highness will have some regard. The voyage I pretend is to lade negroes in Guinea and sell them in the West Indies in truck of gold, pearls and emeralds, whereof I doubt not to bring home great abundance for the contentation of Your Highness and to the relief of a number of worthy servitors ready now for this pretended voyage, which otherwise would shortly be driven to great misery and ready to commit any folly. Thus I, having advertised Your Highness the state of this matter, do most humbly pray Your Highness to signify your pleasure by this bearer, which I shall most willingly accomplish.

From Plymouth the xvith day of September, 1567,

Your Highness' most humble servant,

JOHN HAWKYNS.

The bearer was probably George Fitzwilliam, for the answer reached Plymouth by his hand a few days later. The answer was from Cecil, but was written on the Queen's instructions: 'The Queen's Majesty,' says the best account of the voyage, 'gave new commandments that our general should, seeing the Portugals were gone, make his voyage towards Guinea, and there making slaves negroes, with them to sail over from that coast to the West or Spanish Indies, as he had heretofore done in other voyages.' The Lord Admiral had also been consulted. He said that he had foreseen that the Portuguese might run away and had warned Hawkins to keep stricter watch on them; but now that they were gone he approved of the altered destination of the voyage. Cecil concurred, and reprimanded Hawkins for negligent keeping of the guides. Cecil was a clear thinker, yet it seemed not to occur to him, as it did to Hawkins, that their flight was itself a proof that the gold hunt was a fool's errand. Were the Queen's councillors merely simulating displeasure? Had they genuinely entertained the treasure hunt? The questions are open. Hawkins at any rate was ready for the customary slaving expedition, and could not have been without long preparation.

On September 28 he wrote Cecil a justification of his actions.

He repudiated the blame for letting the Portuguese escape, saying that he never had charge of them, and that they had been committed to some of the merchants' factors. About firing on de Wachen, he would not have done it if the Flemish ships had anchored at a distance; but they came pressing into the Cattewater and would have been 'proud neighbours'. He denied any part in releasing the prisoners from the Spanish ship. 'That I have always,' he concluded, 'desired the name of an orderly person and have always hated folly, my doings before this have been a witness, and now are.' It was true, as his record indeed bears witness; too true, as the coming voyage was to illustrate; for a day was to come on which less scruple, less consciousness of his obligation as the Queen's officer, might have saved disaster.

The expedition was ready for sea. In the two months at Plymouth, as one of its members afterwards deposed to the Inquisitors, Hawkins regularly assembled the crews for service in the church, presumably St. Andrew's, which has seen many such gatherings. He sailed with his six ships and four hundred men on the second of October, 1567. About seventy of those men were destined to return.

The squadron left Plymouth with a fair wind, but ran into a gale when four days out. The *Jesus of Lubeck*, rottener than ever after her previous tropical voyage, gave a display of her quality which frightened her company, and rehearsed the part she was later to play in bringing the expedition to its crisis. She was, in her commander's words, so weak that she was not able to endure the wind or the sea. The excessively high-charged type, with lofty forecastle and towering poop, was liable to strain in heavy weather when in the best condition, because these top-weights acquired great momentum as the ship rolled and plunged, and caused the planks and timbers below them to 'work' and to 'spew out' the caulking that kept the seams watertight. Ships of this kind had not been designed for the ocean, but for summer campaigns in home waters where they could find shelter if the weather grew bad. The *Jesus* in an Atlantic gale was out of her element, and she was far gone in senile decay. 'The weather,' says the Cotton narrator, 'was very extreme and brought the *Jesus* in such case that she opened in the stern aft, and leaks broke up in divers places in her, but where she opened in the stern the leak was so great that into one place there was thrust 15 pieces of baize to stop the place.' Hawkins, he continues, knew more than he wished the company to know of the weakness of the ship and had kept his knowledge to himself. But now he expected her to founder and saw no hope but in prayer. He called the crew together and composedly told them that the ship was sinking and that he therefore 'desired them to pray unto almighty God that he would take us to his mercy. His countenance never showed his sorrow, but his words pierced the hearts of all his company, and it seemed unto them that death had summoned them when they heard him recite the aforesaid words, for they knew such words could not issue out from so invincible a mind without great cause. There was not one that could refrain his eyes from tears, the which when our general saw he began to enter in prayer and besought them to pray with him, the while indeed he letted not with great travail to search the ship fore and aft for her leaks. Thus we passed the 4th day at the mercy of God.'

The gale blew itself out, and the old ship, her gaping seams stuffed with cloth from the cargo, remained afloat. The wind came fair out of the north, and Hawkins went forward undismayed. The squadron had been scattered, and only the *Angel* remained in company. But that did not greatly matter. The first rendezvous had been fixed at Teneriffe, and thither the six vessels made their several ways.

At Teneriffe Hawkins anchored in the roadstead of Santa Cruz, the *Judith* having joined him on the way. None of the English accounts says anything of Pedro de Ponte, but Canarian records show that he and Hawkins had an interview. De Ponte was already under the unfavourable notice of the authorities, who were also keeping watch on Hawkins.[1] They tried with a civil invitation to lure him on shore, but he refused. Then at nightfall the Spanish ships in the road, lying between the *Jesus* and the castle's guns, quietly shifted their position. Hawkins noted it, and next morning he was out of range, anchored again and sending boats to the beach

[1] Rumeu de Armas, op. cit., pp. 208–19.

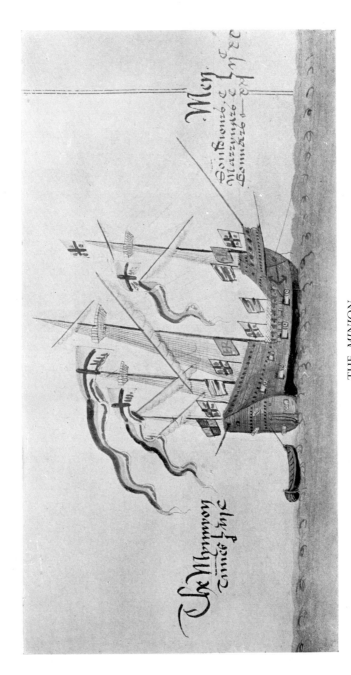

THE *MINION*

From Anthony's Roll, Pepys MSS., Magdalene College, Cambridge

for water. The Spaniards, who had meant to open fire at dawn and sink him, could hardly conceal their discomfiture. Hawkins refused to take offence, and fired a salute as he sailed away for Gomera, where he had learned that the other ships had arrived. The Teneriffe incident, coming after that of de Wachen, must have shown him that the Spanish government had made up its mind; and that, far from getting any permission to trade, he was to be treated as an enemy and destroyed if occasion served. Yet he judged that one more trading tour was possible, and continued, when he reached the West, to play the old part of King Philip's servant and the friend of all Spaniards. The outcome was to show that his judgement was correct, and that his error lay in going to sea once too often in the *Jesus*. She was to be the crazy villain of the tragedy.

More than one incident has already been narrated in which Hawkins displayed coolness and self-mastery. The men of that time were in general far more emotional than are we. They laughed, cheered, wept or lost their tempers on occasions when the modern Englishman remains stolid. A commander who could coolly tell his men bad news acquired an unusual hold over them. Hawkins added to this a sympathy and capacity for friendship which showed that his composure was self-discipline and not heartlessness. One of his crew, William Collins, has told how, when a man was sick and likely to die, Hawkins or the captain would go to him and pray with him, ask him about his wife, and take any statement he could make 'for discharge of his conscience'. He inspired affection as well as respect, and his men were his devoted servants. An event which took place at Teneriffe is illustrative. Two officers of the *Jesus*, George Fitzwilliam and Edward Dudley, quarrelled and agreed to go ashore and fight. Hawkins heard of it and forbade them. Dudley was excited and insubordinate. His words provoked Hawkins to strike him. Dudley drew sword on his commander, who drew in self-defence, and both were slightly hurt before men parted them. All were so incensed against Dudley that he was in danger of being killed out of hand. Hawkins told them not to harm him, but to iron him and bring him formally to judgement. It seems that in a case of this sort, where the facts were not disputed, there was no need of a court-martial; not even the prisoner claimed one. The matter went direct to judgement by the commanding officer. Dudley admitted his offence and threw himself on the mercy of his commander. He had done that, he said, for which he would have hanged any of his men who had done it to him. Hawkins answered that he could forgive the personal injury with all his heart, but the offence was against the Queen. The ships were hers, and the delinquent had committed an act of mutiny in the presence of the Spanish enemy. Therefore he must be summarily punished. With that Hawkins sent for a loaded arquebus, and all the company supposed that Dudley was to be shot then and there. The men who had clamoured to kill him now interceded with tears for his life. After much entreaty Hawkins pardoned him, and declared that the incident was to be forgotten as if it had never been. Dudley was his man thenceforward and Hawkins was his friend.

It is significant that Hawkins used the phrase of being 'in the midst of our enemies the Spaniards' before the Teneriffe authorities had attempted the little trick which ended the English stay in their roadstead. He knew already that it would be war with King Philip's officers if they saw any chance of overcoming him.

From the Canaries the squadron made for the African coast at Cape Blanco, where the Portuguese had a fishery. A French force had passed plundering down the coast shortly before, and many of the fishermen had deserted their ships and sought refuge on shore. Hawkins found three caravels abandoned. By the law of the sea (or his view of it) they were his. He took the best caravel along with him to serve as a pinnace, and released the others on promise of a nominal ransom by their masters, who came forward to claim them before he left. About November 26 he arrived at Cape Verde, where slave hunting might begin. Hawkins anchored by night and at once landed with 200 men to surprise a village before daybreak. Edward Dudley went with him, but they received a rough welcome. The negroes turned out in force and shot poisoned arrows. Very few were taken, and a number of the English were wounded, of whom eight died from the poison. Hawkins and Dudley received arrow wounds but escaped. Job Hortop says that one of the negroes gave Hawkins the antidote.

The slaving coast was from Cape Verde to Sierra Leone. Beyond that it was inadvisable to go because of the difficulty of getting clear of the Guinea current and making westing out into the ocean. The gold traders incurred this risk and often suffered badly enough, but they did not encumber themselves with slaves. Hawkins's expeditions never went beyond Sierra Leone. On this last occasion he visited all the important river mouths and had more fighting than trade with the Portuguese whom he found there. The Portuguese government in fact was beginning to make its prohibition effective upon its own subjects, as that of Spain was determined to do in the West.

Soon after leaving Cape Verde, Hawkins sighted six sail of the Frenchmen of whom he had learned at Cape Blanco. One of the French commanders was named Bland (the contemporary English version, but the name may have been Planes). This Captain Bland was in a captured Portuguese caravel. He had a fighting crew and no trading goods, so that his employment was obvious. The Cotton narrator says: 'Our general took her and her captain and all her men to go with him in the voyage.' Hortop says that Captain Drake was made captain of the caravel, in a context which indicates Bland's caravel. But Hortop wrote from memory long afterwards and can be convicted of several inaccuracies. It is possible that it was the other Portuguese caravel, acquired at Cape Blanco, that was entrusted to Drake, and that Captain Bland willingly threw in his lot with Hawkins and was never deprived of his ship. He was certainly in command of the caravel, named the *Grace of God*, at the crisis of the voyage ten months later. He and his crew then fought gallantly, and it is unlikely that they were serving under compulsion. They would have had many opportunities to part company had they wished to. Before the two squadrons parted, another of the Frenchmen asked to be allowed to join Hawkins, and was duly taken into his company, raising his numbers to nine sail.

The expedition worked southwards, trying the successive river-mouths to see what trade they would afford. The Cotton MS. gives the only detailed and systematic account of the business, but is defective in many places, and has in some lost a considerable

part of its substance. Consequently it is not possible to establish a
certain record of events, although the general procedure is
evident. The large ships were unable to enter the rivers, owing to
lack of depth on the bars. They accordingly anchored off, while
strong parties went in with the small craft, usually under the
command of Robert Barrett, the master of the *Jesus*. Hawkins had
lost some of his ships' boats in the gale soon after leaving Plymouth, and it was with the river work in view that he recruited
the Frenchmen and acquired the abandoned caravel at Cape
Blanco. He still needed small craft, and in the Rio Grande, soon
after leaving Cape Verde, he bought another Portuguese vessel
described as a bark.[1] The fact that he bought her contributes to his
vindication against the general charge of piracy which the
Portuguese brought against him on this occasion, as on the
previous voyages.

The situation on the Guinea coast was nevertheless hardening.
The Portuguese government was establishing its authority over
its distant subjects, who were no longer able to disobey and lie
their way out of the difficulty. An English ship had been sunk on
the coast in the previous season, and another captured. Hawkins
himself found that the Portuguese factors and shipmasters were
unwilling to trade and serious in their resistance. An Inquisition
witness stated that on one occasion Hawkins subjected three captured Portuguese to the *tormento de cordel*, a cord tightened round
the head, but that when they yielded their negroes he rewarded
them with merchandise.[2] In four of the rivers Barrett found
caravels laden with or awaiting negroes and merchandise. He
tried to parley and persuade, but was not listened to, and could
only obtain what he wanted by capturing the ships and driving
the crews ashore. On every occasion, however, it is claimed by
the Cotton narrator that Hawkins found means of paying fairly
for the goods he had taken. In one river Barrett landed,
contrary to Hawkins's orders, and attempted to take a negro
town, and suffered a damaging repulse. In another, a boat was
sunk by a hippopotamus, an affair of which Hortop gives some
lively details. Hortop was always interested in the more out-

[1] See the Cotton narrative, ff. 24, 29, 38b.   [2] Trial of Phillips, p. 25.

rageous kinds of beasts and reptiles, and his stock of anecdotes would have made him a good showman. At an island, probably one of the Los Islands, a likely young negro surrendered to the English, explaining that he had been too friendly with the chief's wife and preferred slavery to more unpleasant consequences. Altogether the tour of the coast yielded a poor result, about 150 negroes, with whom it seemed hardly worth while to cross the Atlantic. The Portuguese bill of complaint includes nine ships taken, worth 41,000 ducats, and plunder on shore to the extent of 30,000. The amounts look inflated, and against them stands the English claim to have paid for everything. We have no means of deciding between them. It is certain that some of the fighting was not of the sham description, and there were casualties on both sides.

Having arrived at the Taggarin River in Sierra Leone, Hawkins took counsel with his officers on the advisability of going on to the Gold Coast and trying for treasure, since one hundred and fifty negroes were insufficient for a lucrative trade in the West. So far as is known, no intruders had yet reached the Gold Coast in anything like the strength which Hawkins possessed, and he might have been able to overwhelm the defences of Elmina. It was not, however, the voyage on which he had set his mind. While he was debating, a message arrived from the king of Sierra Leone and another chief who were jointly besieging a town named Conga. They asked him to assist and promised him the prisoners. Success would enable him to cross the Atlantic, and he accepted the invitation. The fact that he considered a sufficiency of slaves essential to justify the westward passage shows that he really was an honest trader in the Spanish Indies and that the Spanish authorities were untruthful in describing him as a corsair.

Conga was a town of 8,000 inhabitants, walled with great logs bound together with withes. Hawkins first sent up Robert Barrett with about a hundred men, who suffered twenty casualties in two days and made no progress. Hawkins then went himself with all his available force, and arranged that his native allies should attack from the land side and he from the river frontage. For some time the defence continued stout, and

Hawkins was losing men and unable to break through. At length his guns made a breach, and he then ordered that they should be loaded with 'fire works' and aimed at the houses. Soon the reed huts were well alight, and the defenders became unsteady. Led by Hawkins, the English sailors charged through the breach and drove the negroes through the blazing town, while the allies burst in from the other side and completed the rout. Much of the town was destroyed and many of its people killed. The victorious negroes indulged in a cannibal banquet in the ruins, while Hawkins withdrew his men outside. He had lost eight or nine killed and many wounded. During the night his negro allies marched away. They had massacred most of the townspeople, but spared him 260 prisoners. These, with a few taken by himself, made up his total to nearly 500, and the voyage as he had planned it was saved. Yet it had been a gruelling business all the way from Cape Verde, with negroes hardly won at high cost in sickness and fighting casualties. The voyage had not the air of go-ahead adventure noticeable in its predecessors. It was from the outset 'troublesome'.

On February 7, 1568, Hawkins sailed westwards. He had with him according to the Cotton narrator ten ships, comprising the six English vessels with which he had left Plymouth, the caravel found abandoned at Cape Blanco, the caravel *Grace of God* belonging to Captain Bland, the other Frenchman (names of ship and captain unknown), and lastly the small bark bought from the Portuguese at Rio Grande. It is worth noting that the number was ten, explicitly listed as above in the Cotton MS., because the fact has a bearing on the ships present at the battle of San Juan de Ulua and helps to clear up some obscurities in the accounts of that action. Hitherto it has been supposed that Hawkins left Africa with eight or nine ships.

VIII

THE THIRD VOYAGE:
THE SPANISH MAIN

The middle passage, from Africa to the Indies, moved with the stickiness that had characterized the voyage from the beginning. It endured for over seven weeks as compared with the five-and-a-half of the second voyage, which had itself been reckoned slow. There were probably losses among the slaves and among the English crews, although the only death of which we have record is that of Captain Edward Dudley. Hortop briefly notes that event, but says not a word about the scene at Teneriffe. Miles Phillips also does not mention it, and Hawkins naturally omitted it from his published account of the voyage. But for the Cotton narrative, a systematic record not intended for publication, we should know nothing about it.

Hawkins reached Dominica at the end of March, watered there, and went on to Margarita. There was a small settlement of Spaniards in the port town of Cubagua, which the French had raided time and again. As the English approached in the evening they saw the Spaniards running out of the town. Although it was almost dark by the time he had brought up, Hawkins sent in a message without waiting for morning. 'In the shutting of night' his boat approached the shore. Spaniards on horseback called out to ask who the newcomers were. 'Englishmen,' answered someone in Spanish, 'we are Englishmen, and the worshipful Master John Hawkins is our general. We have a letter from him to your governor.' Dark though it was, the Spaniards were reassured. Juan Haquines was a name they knew, and it did not mean sack and massacre.

The letter ran as follows:

Worshipful,

I have touched in your island only to the intent to refresh my men with fresh victuals, which for my money or wares you shall sell me, meaning to stay only but five or six days here at the furthest. In the which time you may assure yourself and so all others that by me or any of mine there shall no damage be done to any man, the which also the Queen's Majesty of England, my mistress, at my departure out of England commanded me to have great care of, and to serve with my Navy the King's Majesty of Spain, my old master, if in places where I came, any of his stood in need.

There are several of these letters from Hawkins or from Spanish governors in reply, embodied in the Cotton manuscript. The originals were in Spanish, but the Spanish text is not preserved and the translation is that of the Cotton author. He did not transcribe the addresses or subscriptions of the letters.

Three years earlier the governor of Margarita had been disobliging, but now he was complaisant. He wrote cordially to Hawkins and furnished him with what he required. There was entertainment by both parties, and the governor showed Hawkins the damage done to the town by the latest French raid, some six months before. It was no doubt the factor that promoted civility. Hawkins expressed indignation because the French had burnt the church, and said that he would not have churches touched or damaged. Later, when some of his men robbed a church at Rio de la Hacha, he made them give up the plunder and restored it to its owners. After nine days the English sailed for Borburata, in the province of Venezuela.

Borburata was the first of several difficult places which called for all the tact and determination, the man-mastership, of Hawkins. Alonzo Bernaldez, the governor who had traded with him in '65, had been sent home for trial, and the province was now under his successor Pedro Ponce de Leon, specially appointed to enforce the King's orders. The prospect of amicable trade must have looked hopeless. In the event, Hawkins stayed for two months at Borburata, on good terms with the governor and all his subjects, to whom he sold many negroes and much English merchandise.

When he arrived, the governor was up country at Santiago de Leon. Hawkins at once sent him the following letter:

Worshipful,
This voyage on the which I am was ordered by the Queen's

Majesty of England, my mistress, another way and not to these parts, and the charges being made in England, before I set sail the pretence was forcibly overturned. Therefore I am commanded by the Queen's Majesty my mistress to seek here another traffic with the wares which I already had and negroes which I should procure in Guinea, to lighten the great charges hazarded in the setting out of this navy. I know the King of Spain, your master, unto whom also I have been a servant, and am commanded by the Queen my mistress to serve with my navy as need requireth, hath forbidden that you should give licence for any stranger to traffic. I will not therefore request any such thing at your hand, but that you will licence me to sell sixty negroes only and a parcel of my wares, which in all is but little, for the payment of the soldiers I have in my ships. In this you shall not break the commandment of your prince, but do him good service and avoid divers inconveniences which happen oftentimes through being too precise in observing precepts without consideration. If you may, I most instantly desire you that you will take the pains to come hither, that I might confer with you myself. Truly it would be liefer to me than 10,000 ducats. If you come you shall not find me ingrateful not count your travail lost.

Two points should be noted in the above: first, that Hawkins now admitted that he knew of the King's prohibition of trade; and second, that he was still putting forward his and the Queen's offer of armed service in return for concessions. With the French raiders more rampant than ever, as we know from Spanish dispatches that they were, Hawkins's peaceful doings and his offer of defence must still have made a strong appeal. Had he not two French crews, tamed and well-conducted, in his present fleet? Had not Jean Bontemps behaved correctly when he had entered Borburata on the occasion of Hawkins's previous visit? These were the public grounds on which Hawkins could urge the governor not to be 'too precise in observing precepts'. The private lure of financial gain was also present, and Ponce de Leon, although he had condemned his predecessor, and may not have been personally corrupt, was obliged to connive at it.

While awaiting the governor's answer Hawkins behaved as if in any place of regular trade, setting up booths on shore for the sale of merchandise, and filling his casks and collecting supplies. Borburata was the port of the larger inland settlement of Valencia, where also a market existed for English goods. The chief authority at Valencia was its bishop, concerning whom Hawkins had acquired some information. Addressing him as 'Right reverend father in God', he wrote asking to be supplied with a hundred oxen and mentioning that he had negroes and English wares to dispose of. He also asked the bishop to use influence with the governor for the opening of trade and invited him to visit the English ships. Some Spanish bishops would no doubt have reacted stiffly, but not so he of Valencia. He replied graciously, promising to intercede with the governor and admitting that the whole colony desired to trade. Age and sickness and unwillingness to compromise himself prevented him, however, from visiting Hawkins in person. Hawkins responded with 'divers presents' and could thenceforward count the bishop among his friends.

After a fortnight Ponce de Leon's answer came to Borburata, a refusal to permit trade, expressed in the most deferential language: 'Right worshipful, Your arrival here, seeing that I cannot show you any pleasure, is unto me a great grief, considering your merits,' and so forth. Some of the bishop's townsmen, anticipating an acquiescence, had come down to the port, but hearing that trade was denied, turned homewards again. They let Hawkins know that if he would send an armed party to capture them at Valencia and compel them to buy negroes, all could be colourably arranged. Accordingly Robert Barrett set off with sixty men, including Job Hortop, and marched up to Valencia. On second thoughts, however, the Valencians judged it too risky. They and their bishop evacuated the town on Barrett's approach, and all that the English had for their long march was a stock of refreshments left for them in the bishop's house. Hortop collected information on the deceitful ways of tigers which lurked in the woods, and was impressed by a two-headed serpent, 'a monstrous venomous worm,' which Barrett slew with his sword.

We do not know the further dealings between Hawkins and the governor, but it is evident that they came to some arrangement, and that if the governor did not formally permit trade he at least did nothing to prevent it. The large ships stayed until early June, cleaning and refitting and 'selling every day some wares'. English cloth and linen were among the goods and there were no disputes or resorts to force as on the previous occasion three years before.[1] The Spaniards of Borburata were content. They were in contact with the great world which often forgot them, buying labour and decent clothes, selling their gold for something real. So long as the Queen's ships with their far-ranging culverins dominated the anchorage there was surcease from fear of the French by sea and the Caribs by land. Borburata was sorry when Haquines made sail. He had already sent forward the smaller ships to Coro for minor trade, and to Curacao for supplies of beef and mutton. On the previous voyage he had taken the *Jesus* to Curaçao and had found the anchorage precarious. This time he had been careful to provide enough auxiliary vessels for such tasks. He still had with him all the ten ships with which he left Africa. How greatly this business would have grown if Philip II had been more in sympathy with his colonists.

The next port of call for the whole fleet was Rio de la Hacha, where a considerable trade was to be had. The King's treasurer, Miguel de Castellanos, still bore rule there. Hawkins had found him difficult in '65, and Lovell had found him impossible in '67. It remained to be seen how Hawkins would fare with him now. But first Drake came along the coast in advance of his commander with the *Judith* and the *Angel*. Drake, as we have seen, had been placed in charge of one of the caravels, and this is our first intimation that he was in command of the *Judith*, in which vessel he remained to the end of the voyage. Drake was well pleased to come again to Rio de la Hacha under a commander who meant business, for he was one of Lovell's crew with a score to settle with the treasurer. He stood close in and demanded leave to fill his casks. The treasurer opened fire. Drake replied with two shots through his adversary's house and then anchored out of range. There he waited five days for the fleet to come up, improving the occasion by chasing a caravel which came from Santo Domingo. The caravel's captain made for the shore, and

<hr>

[1] Robert Barrett's deposition, in *Caribbean Documents*, p. 156.

Drake followed and cut him out under the fire, so Hortop said, of two hundred Spanish arquebusiers. Hawkins arrived to hear of hostilities sufficient to damage all the prospects of trade, but he did not let them worry him. He knew his treasurer. He also knew the arquebusiers, and he did not think that the opposition would prove insuperable.

Castellanos we have already seen as a truculent egoist incapable of fair give-and-take. In 1565 he had been willing to trade with the English on terms which would have given him all the profit. Two years later he had outwitted Lovell and got his negroes for nothing, and had been able at the same time to claim the King's favour for patriotic endeavour. Now he had decided that patriotic loyalty was his game and that the English trade was no way to advancement in the royal service. He had fortified Rio de la Hacha with field-works defending the town's landing-place and the approaches along the shore. He had armed his colonists, of whom there were really about a hundred, as attested by mutually independent witnesses, aided by negro slaves and Indians. He had even a troop of horse, twenty strong, and probably not to be despised, for the colonial horsemen were accustomed to killing wild cattle with the lance. With these forces he might hope to defend his town against the larger numbers that Hawkins could land, on one condition, that the forces would fight. That was the weak point, for the forces consisted of Spanish planters who would rather buy negroes than repel their vendors. The English leader was perfectly aware of it.

Hawkins opened with a letter to the treasurer, alluding to the bad treatment of Lovell and demanding leave to trade: 'This I desire now, that you will give me licence to sell sixty negroes only, towards the payment of my soldiers, to help to lighten the charges of this voyage, which was appointed to be made other ways and to none of these parts. If you see in the morning armed men aland, let it nothing trouble you, for as you shall command they shall return aboard again. Shewing me this pleasure, you shall command anything I have.' The treasurer answered that he was armed and ready for Hawkins, whose soldiers should buy their wages dear if they set foot ashore in Rio de la Hacha.

Next morning Hawkins landed with Robert Barrett and about two hundred men, at a point some two miles from the town. With them was a friendly Spaniard from Borburata, who had already bought some slaves and was interested in the further fortunes of the trade. Hawkins sent him with a message to the treasurer, who repeated his refusal to allow any trade. Marching towards the town, the invaders came to a work described as a bulwark commanding the road. It was, however, close to the sea, and the English, with guns mounted in their large boats and pinnaces, made it untenable. This means that the Spaniards could not occupy it without some personal risk, the risk alone being the deterrent; for they had no actual casualties in the whole affair. Outside the bulwark were deployed ninety[1] arquebusiers with an ensign displayed, while the treasurer hovered in the distance with the mounted troop. Hawkins led his men against the arquebusiers, who fired a volley at too great a range and fled without staying to reload. The volley killed two of the English but did not stop them, and a race for the town, distant about a mile and a half, resulted in a win for the English sailors. They shouldered the running Spaniards off the road into the woods, and chased the horse through the town and out the other side.

So was Rio de la Hacha captured, not on this occasion by any collusive sham-fighting. It is fair to give the townsmen's account of it.[2] Two of them reported to the King how Hawkins landed with 600 men, his ships and pinnaces firing many guns, for which reason Miguel de Castellanos was unable to prevent them from landing. Undismayed, however:

He went out to encounter them with as many as sixty men, whom he had succeeded in assembling, and with this, the small force he had, he offered as fine and valorous a defence as has ever been made in these Indies, and killed more than thirty of the enemy. He rendered such signal service that all were astonished at his great valour (both his adversaries and his countrymen), for certainly it was a business that to-day, on looking back at it,

[1] Hortop again says 200. The 90 is from the Cotton author, obviously more reliable.
[2] *Caribbean Documents*, pp. 116–19.

fills with fright those who were present and those who hear it related. In good order he withdrew with this small force without losing a man, whereas truly it seemed incredible that any should have escaped, and the English general took the town.

The town was devoid of valuables and people, for all had been removed six miles inland at the first sight of strange ships. The pursuit having halted, the treasurer collected his men and sent in a defiance, saying that he would die in the field before he would give licence to trade. Hawkins sent the Borburata Spaniard to threaten that the town would be fired if its inhabitants refused to trade. The treasurer retorted that he would see 'all the India afire' without yielding. Some of the sailors must have overheard these messages, for they began setting fire to the houses without waiting for orders. Hawkins stopped it as soon as he could, but about twenty houses were burnt. The treasurer observed the blaze, and sent a new message to say that the fire pleased him, for the King would build his colonists a new town better than the old. It was unwise of him to send unnecessary messengers under flags of truce, since it gave Hawkins a chance to make touch with the planters. On this occasion the flag was accompanied by several Spaniards anxious to see if their houses were among those burnt. Hawkins answered the message by telling these men that the treasurer would make his profit at their expense, out of the money the King might allow for rebuilding. He himself, he promised them, would pay for the damage done as soon as he got leave to trade. The planters went back discontented with the treasurer. The next move was that Hawkins led out a party, but what it did is not evident owing to a hiatus in the Cotton manuscript. It came back with a captured ensign. Three years afterwards the College of Arms made an alteration to Hawkins's arms, and the grant mentioned that he had captured Rio de la Hacha and brought away the ensign of Miguel de Castellanos in 1568.[1]

A deadlock followed, with the English holding the town, and the Spaniards encamped somewhere in the countryside. It was probably only a matter of time before a revolt would overthrow the authority of Castellanos. The end was precipitated by one of

[1] John Prince, *Worthies of Devon*, 1810 ed., p. 472.

his negro slaves, who deserted to the English and offered, as the price of his liberty, to lead them to the place where the treasure of Rio de la Hacha was concealed. That night Hawkins sent a strong party with the negro as guide. They found the stuff and also captured a Spaniard, who told Hawkins that all hated the treasurer and desired peace and trade. Hawkins went out himself, had the treasure loaded in carts and sent his latest prisoner to Castellanos to tell him in the presence of others that the booty would be taken on board the ships in default of the opening of trade. Some of the treasure was the King's, but some was private property. Its owners rushed at the treasurer and demanded that he should negotiate with Hawkins. Castellanos was cornered and submitted after a furious outburst, in the course of which he said a remarkable thing: 'There is not one of you that knoweth John Hawkins. He is such a man as that any man talking with him hath no power to deny him anything he doth request. This hath made me hitherto to be careful to well keep myself far from him, and not any villainy that I know in him, but great nobility; and so do not desire me to do no such thing, for therein ye shall be in danger to prefer his desire before the commandment of my master the King.' This is the Cotton author's version of the Spanish that must have come to him by hearsay. We are justified in believing that the treasurer did speak to this effect. It is a striking piece of evidence about John Hawkins.

The two men had their interview, talking in private for an hour. All was arranged as Hawkins desired. The treasurer agreed to give 4,000 gold *pesos* from the King's chest for sixty negroes, and 1,000 *pesos* of his own for another twenty, after which the trade should be open to all.[1] It may seem that Castellanos was putting his head in the noose by this brazen employment of the King's money, but he had his way out, as will appear. As soon as general business was open, the planters bought 150 negroes and quantities of English goods. Hawkins and the treasurer were now ostentatiously friendly and exchanged costly presents. Hawkins gave his former enemy a velvet cloak with gold buttons, which Castellanos answered with 'a woman's girdle of large pearls, a

[1] Barrett's deposition, in *Caribbean Documents*. p. 157.

very rich thing'. Robert Barrett saw it on board the *Jesus*.[1] We may be certain that it came home from the wreck of the voyage to gladden the eye of Katherine Hawkins—or perhaps the Queen's. Traffic continued for some time, the expedition remaining nearly a month at Rio de la Hacha. Hortop studied the habits of alligators, and assisted in catching one with a dog as live bait on a hook and chain. The skin was cleaned and stuffed, but he records that it did not reach England. About the beginning of July the fleet moved on.

The treasurer had a difficult account to square with authority. When he had made terms with Hawkins he did not announce the fact until another meeting of the planters had applied further tumultuous pressure to him. He had thus plenty of witnesses that he had acted under duress from both sides in giving licence to trade. In due course he explained to the King.[2] He gave much the same account of the fighting as his two townsmen did, writing on the same date. After the capture of the town, he continued, Hawkins burned two-thirds of it. Then the runaway negro, with a mulatto, revealed the hiding-place of the treasure. Hawkins seized the treasure, together with some poor and sick people and some women, who were at the place. The English not only seized the property but threatened that in default of ransom they would kill these poor people. In order to prevent such grievous cruelty, Castellanos said that he paid 4,000 gold *pesos* as ransom for the people and also for what remained of the town, 'including its holy church.' When the 4,000 *pesos* were paid, the enemy released the prisoners. They did not, however, restore the seized property, but carried it off. Before they sailed, they thrust ashore a number of negroes whom they could not feed. Some were children under six, and some were old men and women over a hundred. They said that these negroes were in recompense for the damage done to the town. They were now being sold to the planters who, however, demanded them for nothing because of the damage. His majesty is asked to decide. All hope that his majesty will provide a naval force to defend this coast.

Thus did Castellanos account for the King's gold *pesos* and the negroes bought with them. Once again Rio de la Hacha had

---

[1] Barrett's deposition.   [2] *Caribbean Documents*, pp. 120–3.

THE HOPE PORTRAIT
Now in the National Maritime Museum, Greenwich
For discussion of authenticity, see Note on Portraits, pp. vii-viii

obtained its slaves from the English. The first time it paid for them, the second time it had them at Lovell's expense, the third at the King's. The treasurer and his colleagues seem to have got away with it. A colonial empire in which the governor of a settlement could write such a letter of impudent fraud to his sovereign was evidently in a primitive stage. Or perhaps it is only the details and the phrases that give the impression of remoteness; perhaps it is true that, however the mode and the cant may vary, a government that supervises and prohibits its subjects as though they were school-children will always evoke the same sort of loyalty as the Spanish colonists displayed to Philip II.

Hawkins sailed on westwards until he came to Santa Marta, a settlement of forty-five houses, smaller than Rio de la Hacha, but reasonably rich, and more than once a victim of the French freebooters. The business here was quite simple. Arriving on the evening of July 10, Hawkins at once sent in a letter, to which he received a friendly answer. Next morning he went ashore for a private talk with the governor, who was quite amenable, having no force to be otherwise. In return for his complaisance, the governor asked Hawkins to go through all the motions of capturing the place by force; and Hawkins returned to his ship to organize the attack. His official landing was in full armour at the head of his men, with covering fire from the guns of the fleet. The bombardment demolished an old house, previously selected, and did no other damage nor caused any personal injury. Hawkins marched without opposition to the market place, where a messenger told him that the governor awaited him in the out-skirts. There, before witnesses, the governor told Hawkins that if he burned the town he must carry away the inhabitants in his ships, for they could not stay among thousands of hostile Indians. Having made this point, with witnesses to testify to it, the governor had obviously no option but to grant the English leave to trade. No one else made any objection, and all proceeded merrily thenceforward, with banquets and friendly traffic, sale of more than a hundred negroes and some English wares, and collection of fresh victuals for the fleet. After a pleasant sojourn Hawkins set sail for Cartagena.

The above is from the Cotton account. The *Caribbean Docu-ments* contain no Spanish dispatches on the Santa Marta proceed-ings, although one can imagine how the governor described them. Hawkins did not mention his visit in the published story of the voyage. Hortop remembered very little save that two of the company killed 'a monstrous adder, going towards his cave with a coney in his mouth: his body was as big as any man's thigh, and seven foot long: upon his tail he had sixteen knots, every one as big as a great walnut, which they say do show his age: his colour was green and yellow.'

Cartagena presented a different problem from those offered by the other places visited by Hawkins. It was regularly fortified, with something more than makeshift earthworks; its position was such as to offer all the tactical advantages to its defenders; and they numbered, by the English estimation, 500 Spanish foot together with horsemen, negroes and 6,000 armed Indians. Hawkins had by this time 370 men in his fleet, and he had to admit that any attempt to take the place by force would be 'a mere folly'. He opened with a letter to Martin de las Alas, the governor, asking for victuals for the homeward voyage; and he told the messenger to notify privily the governor and his colleagues that presents were awaiting them. The governor was both able and determined to do his duty. He consented to read the letter after first refusing to receive it. He answered that he counted as the King's enemy any stranger asking leave to trade and that he would not allow victualling or any other intercourse.

The city had two waterfronts, one on the open sea, the other on a lagoon to which the entrance was a mile-and-a-half south-east of the buildings. Hawkins at his first approach led his fleet in line ahead past the sea front, firing as he did so a thunderous salute. He then turned into the lagoon and brought his ships within range of the defences on the sheltered side. He had over half-a-hundred negroes left and probably some other goods, and it is evident that he greatly desired to trade. He tested the defences by ordering the *Minion* to open fire. The town replied shot for shot, neither received any damage, and both shortly ceased fire. Meanwhile the pinnaces were searching the great lagoon and its islands for anything which might enable Hawkins to apply the screw. All they found was a stock of wines and other refreshments on an island used as a pleasure-garden. A landing was evidently not feasible. Eighteen years later Drake was destined to capture the place whose strength he was now assessing, but with a force five or six times as great as that of Hawkins. There was nothing for it but to withdraw, and Hawkins put a good face on it by saying that their trade was so nearly finished that it was not worth while to take risks. He wrote again to the governor, calling shame on him for refusing victuals, 'a thing not denied unto infidels.' He found a servant of the man who owned the wines on the island, and with his consent took them in exchange for English goods to his satisfaction. He then sailed out of the harbour and was kept at anchor outside by a two days' calm.

Here he reduced the fleet from ten sail to eight. One of the Frenchmen (not Captain Bland) who had joined him at Cape Verde now desired to dissolve partnership. Hawkins squared accounts and bade him farewell. He went off on a West Indian venture of his own and was subsequently taken by the Spaniards.[1] The Portuguese bark acquired in the Rio Grande was no longer required now that trading was finished, and was condemned as unseaworthy. Hawkins took the men and gear out of her and sank her. Then, with his own original six ships, the caravel from Cape Blanco, and Bland's caravel, he set sail on his homeward voyage, not meaning to call at any other port in the Indies. It was the end of July, and the hurricane season was setting in. The sooner that elderly invalid the *Jesus of Lubeck* could be got clear of the Caribbean the better.

[1] *Caribbean Documents*, p. 19, fn. 4.

IX

SAN JUAN DE ULUA

The ensuing months witnessed the climax and disaster of John Hawkins's earlier career. He was thirty-six years old, and for the last six of those years had been commanding expeditions and conducting negotiations with the great. The unrecorded time from youth to thirty had played its part in shaping him. He was now formed and matured, his character graved by experience, and not sapped by too easy success. Throughout life, indeed, he never suffered that misfortune, never found success easy. Character, said the astrologers, is destiny. It was so in the closing scenes of this expedition, destiny with all the inevitability of classic tragedy. A man more supple than John Hawkins would have come off better—and smaller.

The expedition left Cartagena with enough victuals for a favourable passage home. With luck two months would have brought England in sight, and there was food and water for that. If the voyage looked like outrunning the supplies, there was the chance of picking up more at the Newfoundland fishery, where the fishers from the West Country stayed at least until the end of August. The luck, however, was steadily and malignantly adverse from the beginning. Three weeks after leaving Cartagena the fleet was still in the Caribbean, approaching the western end of Cuba with the intention of passing out through the Florida channel. At that point, about the middle of August, heavy weather came on. It was not a hurricane, for the ships retained some power of manoeuvre, but it was sufficiently extreme to come near to ending the *Jesus of Lubeck*. She was obliged to turn and run before the wind. The others conformed, except the *William and John*, which continued to sail to windward and was not seen again. She made a lone passage home. This reduced Hawkins's numbers to seven sail.

The plight of the *Jesus* is described by the Cotton author, who was on board:

The *Jesus* was brought in such case that she was not able to bear the sea longer, for in her stern on either side of the sternpost the planks did open and shut with every sea, the seas ... without number and the leaks so big as the thickness of a man's arm, the living fish did swim upon the ballast as in the sea. Our general, seeing this, did his utmost to stop her leaks, as divers times before he had ... about her. And truly, without his great experience had been, we had been sunk in the sea in her within six days after we came out of England, and escaping that, yet she had never been able to have been brought hither but by his industry, the which his trouble and care he had of her may be thought to be because she was the Queen's Majesty's ship and that she should not perish under his hand. But all that he might do now would not help, but that we must needs bear room before the wind for the easing of the ship, and at all adventure seek some harbour wherein to dress her leaks. It was before night in an evening that we put roomer, where being the weather still terrible, one of our company kept aloof[1] still, who we saw not after; the ship was called the *William and John*.

The ancient *Jesus* had served Hawkins's purpose on the Spanish Main both as a vessel of majestic and powerful appearance and as a roomy warehouse for the stowage of his slaves and merchandise. The purpose was now achieved, and the great ship's usefulness was at an end. She was not needed to carry home the returns of the expedition, for they were of small bulk, the greatest value being in gold and pearls. She was nothing but a liability, and if she did reach England it would be with little prospect of ever making another voyage. Why then did Hawkins not take the first opportunity when the weather improved of abandoning her after transferring treasure and stores to the other ships? If she had been his own ship there can be little doubt that he would have done so, but she was not. A phrase in the passage quoted above explains his decision to stick to her: 'because she was the Queen's Majesty's ship and that she should not perish under his hand.' It was not romantic sentiment, but scrupulous financial integrity. By the charter-parties that have been preserved[2] we know that

[1] 'Kept aloof' means sailed on the wind; 'put roomer' means ran before the wind.
[2] For the charter-parties, see *Sir John Hawkins*, p. 182 n.

if the Queen's ships were lost on these expeditions the loss fell on her alone, but that if they came home, however damaged and decayed, the whole syndicate had to pay for them to be repaired and returned to her in good condition. The *Jesus* had cost £500 on that head after the second voyage, and it looks as though the charge would have been very much higher after the third. Hawkins, as a member of the syndicate, would have been in pocket by letting the *Jesus* sink. But he was something else, the Queen's servant, and he conceived the saving of her ship to be his duty. It was not an age of high standards in such matters, and the Queen's servants who would have taken his view were probably a minority. Hawkins's decision should be weighed by those who have doubted his good character. To profess high principles was easy; to take a heavy risk for them was the test of sincerity.

Running before the wind the fleet came diagonally upon the coast of Florida within the Gulf of Mexico. Neither the direction of the wind nor the locality of the landfall are recorded. It was, however, a useless coast for Hawkins's need. The water was shoal, and for two days he had to keep the great ships off while the pinnaces sought inshore for a harbour. They had no success, and then a three days' northerly blow carried the fleet across to the other side of the Gulf. Hawkins had never been in these waters, and had no pilot. He sighted the Triangles, islands north of the Yucatan peninsula, and there stopped a Spanish ship of which Francisco Maldonado was captain. It was now close on two months since leaving Cartagena, and victuals were running short. Maldonado was bound for New Spain with wines from Santo Domingo. He told Hawkins that the nearest port was Campeche, a rough, shoal place without facilities for the work to be done on the *Jesus*. The only alternative was San Juan de Ulua, the port of landing for the inland journey to the city of Mexico. At the end of September, he added, the *flota* or plate fleet was expected to arrive from Spain at San Juan, to lade the year's treasure output. Hawkins was anxious only to repair and revictual and sail for England. He had no desire to meet the *flota*. He thought he could do his business in ten or twelve days and be gone in time to avoid the complication. It was a gamble, but there was no other course. He therefore sailed for San Juan with Maldonado in company. On the way he fell in with two other small vessels and kept them with him, for he wished to arrive unannounced. A passenger in one of these ships was a resident of the city of Mexico named Agustin de Villa Nueva. Hortop seems to have learned something about him to which we have not the clue. He says that Villa Nueva 'was the man that betrayed all the noble men in the Indies, and caused them to be beheaded. . . . Our general made great account of him and used him like a noble man: howbeit, in the end he was one of those that betrayed us.' The first statement may conceivably relate to a conspiracy against the Viceroy of New Spain. Villa Nueva's part in the events at San Juan will appear.

On September 15, three days after meeting with Maldonado, Hawkins came in sight of San Juan de Ulua. He approached in line ahead with the *Jesus* leading, six ships of his and three Spaniards following. He gave orders to strike all the crosses of St. George and to display only the royal standard on the main topmast of the *Jesus* and the foretopmast of the *Minion*. As he drew near a boat came out with local officials. 'The Queen's arms', says the Cotton narrator, 'were so dim with their colours through the foul wearing in foul weather that they never perceived the lions and flower de luces till they were hard aboard the *Jesus*, who went in first as the general commanded, and the rest a good way astern one another.' This is the evidence that Hawkins sailed under the royal standard, a point of considerable importance in deductions about the policy underlying his voyages. The Spanish officials saw their mistake too late, having supposed that they were about to welcome the plate fleet. Hawkins ordered them on board and took them in with him.

The port of San Juan de Ulua was a wretched makeshift in relation to its function of being the sole approach from Spain to its great viceroyalty. A low shingle bank rising three feet above the highest water level and extending to a length of 240 yards lay roughly parallel to the main coast at a distance of four or five hundred yards from it.[1] The bank, dignified by the title of island, had on it some guns mounted to command the anchorage and some buildings to house a gang of slaves employed on the improvement of the port. The improvement consisted in scarping the inner shore of the island so that ships might be drawn in as closely as possible. They lay head-on, with their anchors carried ashore and with stern warps laid out in the deeper water to prevent them from swinging and colliding, for so small was the frontage that the ships rode abreast of one another with very little space between. The holders of the island were masters of the shipping, not only by having it under the fire of their guns but also by being able to cut the cables and throw all into confusion. San Juan de Ulua was active only during the season when the *flota* was expected or present. At other times there was hardly anyone there. The residential coast-town was fifteen miles up the coast at Vera Cruz, from which the main road led inland to the city of Mexico. Vera Cruz had no harbour.

Hawkins had acquired these facts before he approached. He knew that he must get possession of the island or lie at its mercy. Fortune favoured him. The minds of the San Juan officers ran in the single track of assuming that any incoming fleet must be the plate fleet. Antonio Delgadillo, the captain of the island, like his colleagues in the boat, saw the faded royal standards as the colours of Spain. As the *Jesus* led in, he fired a salute of unshotted guns. Then, as the ships brought up, he and his gunners realized their mistake. Whatever their captain may have done, the others simply bolted, tumbled into boats on the strand, and rowed across to the mainland. Thus Hawkins obtained the indispensable island with no trouble to himself. He found Delgadillo and told him to assure all men that his intentions were peaceful. When the panic subsided he came to an arrangement with the Spanish officials that he should have facilities for his repairs and a supply of

---

[1] The condition of the port is independently described by five English observers of the period 1555-68, whose writings are printed in Hakluyt. They are unanimous in saying that the island was a bowshot in length. A bowshot was reckoned as twelve score yards, or about a furlong. All but one agree that it was two bowshots from the main shore. The exception says two miles, an evident slip.

victuals, for which he would pay the proper prices. Hawkins and the officials combined to send word of this to Mexico, in order that the higher authorities should know that his appearance was not an act of war. The fact that there were already in San Juan eight Spanish merchantmen, which Hawkins believed to be laden with treasure and which he refrained from touching, emphasized the fairness of his intentions. It was now September 16, and the plate fleet was not expected until the end of the month. If he could get away before it arrived all would be well.

Next morning at sunrise the plate fleet was in sight. It had made the passage from Spain in a little over two months. It consisted of eleven large merchantmen escorted by two ships of war. Its admiral was Francisco de Luxan, and his second-in-command was Juan de Ubilla. They brought with them the incoming Viceroy of New Spain, Don Martin Enriquez, son of the Marquis of Alcanizes. The Viceroy, on learning that the English were in possession of the port, took over the command from Luxan and became responsible for the subsequent Spanish proceedings.

The arrival of the Spanish fleet placed Hawkins in a difficult position. If he behaved as a peaceful merchant and allowed the Spaniards to enter San Juan, he would then be at their mercy; for they would greatly outnumber him and could choose their own time to attack him. If he refused to let them enter, as he could with the island guns in his control, they would have to remain at anchor in the open and would probably be wrecked by an onshore gale before he was ready to go. He remembered how he had been reprimanded for refusing to allow de Wachen in the Cattewater. That offence would be nothing to the outcry that would arise over denying a Spanish port to a Spanish fleet, and most likely causing it to be wrecked in consequence. The immediately easy and profitable answer was to tell the Viceroy to keep out. The honourable course for the Queen's officer, pledged not to compromise his mistress, was to let him in to do his worst. 'Fearing the Queen's Majesty's indignation,' Hawkins decided that the *flota* must enter. The decision was again an expression of his character. What would Drake, Ralegh or Essex have done in his place?

On that day the wind was off the shore, unfavourable for entering, but innocuous to ships lying outside. The *flota* had accordingly anchored and there was time for negotiation. Hawkins sent out Delgadillo to explain the position, to give his promise to leave the port as soon as he had repaired and victualled, and to demand guarantees against being attacked when the Spaniards should come in; failing which, he would defend the port against them. Don Martin was indignant. He was no planter-governor, but a metropolitan grandee holding the highest office under the crown. It was bad enough that Hawkins should be trespassing in a forbidden port, but that he should occupy its defences and make terms for the Viceroy of New Spain to enter was intolerable. At first he said he would force an entry. The naval and military officers told him that it was impossible. He decided then to make terms with Hawkins, but to break them at the first possible moment after his ships should be within. He sent to Vera Cruz for all the soldiers it could furnish and took them on board by night while still anchored outside. Hawkins posted a force on the island and mounted some guns of his own in addition to the sixteen Spanish pieces already there. A firm hold of the island was a better guarantee than a Viceroy's word, but meanwhile he did not neglect to secure that.

The terms proposed by Hawkins were the minimum necessary for his safety, and the Viceroy, having no alternative, agreed to them. The English were to carry out unmolested the work for which they had entered the port, and were to occupy the island and its batteries until their departure. No armed Spaniards were to land on the island. Either side should hand over to the other ten gentlemen as hostages for the observance of the terms. Don Martin embodied his acceptance in a personal letter written to Hawkins on September 18. He began by expressing his belief that the arrival of the English was due to necessity and that they had traded honestly in the Indies, paying the King's dues and the price of the things they had received. 'Wherefore I am content', he continued, 'to accept the proposal which your honour makes in your letter, asking me to deliver hostages and to enter the port in peace, although I was determined to the contrary. Therefore I send ten principal persons and rely upon what your honour states, that those your honour sends me are similar persons. I well believe that although the people of this fleet enter without arms into the island, they will not be prevented from going about their affairs, nor harassed in any fashion. And I am very confident that when we meet friendship will increase between these fleets, since both are so well disciplined.'[1]

These words, written by a viceroy, the *alter ego* of a king, were treacherous. Before writing them, Don Martin had determined to attack the English unawares, he had begun his preparations, and he had even considered sending as hostages common men in gentlemen's clothing, since it appeared likely that the English would kill them when the treachery became evident. The substitution, however, was not proceeded with, because the proposed common men understood the position and would have saved their skins by warning the English. Ten Spanish gentlemen accordingly went as hostages, meriting high favour from the Viceroy for their risk. One of them was Agustin de Villa Nueva.

These things determined, the *flota* was ready to enter San Juan. The wind remained unfavourable until September 21, when at length the entry was accomplished. The next day was occupied in berthing the two fleets, prows overhanging the island, anchors ashore, stern warps laid out to anchors in the water between the island and the mainland. There was no room to spare. The island was not much more than 240 yards long. There were altogether twenty-eight ships. The average space per ship was thus twenty-five feet, if each had a place in the line abreast. Since the larger vessels were of greater beam than twenty-five feet, it seems that some of the less important must have been anchored off, especially as a space was left between the flanking ships of the English and Spanish fleets respectively. Fronting them all were the island guns in three batteries, ready to open a raking fire at close range, sixteen Spanish pieces and an unspecified number of English, in the hands of a strong English party under an officer whose name it would be interesting to know, but none has recorded it. It was necessary for Spaniards engaged on their mooring work to land

[1] *Caribbean Documents*, p. 128.

on the island. They were within speaking distance of the English, and fraternization soon began.

As soon as his fleet was berthed, Don Martin called a council to settle the details of the attack. This council was engaged in cold-blooded treachery which was to be remembered against the Spanish name for half a century. Yet neither its convener nor its members betrayed any consciousness of dishonour; they reported the proceedings objectively as though they had been describing the work of others. For Spaniards their allegiance and their religion were the arbiters of morality, just as among the English of that time there was a parallel tendency to invoke the letter of the law to cover any injustice. The Viceroy exerted his right of command, and dictated the plan, to the dissatisfaction at least of Ubilla, the vice-admiral, who had seen much service. Luxan and Ubilla, with the pick of their crews, were to go secretly on board a large merchantman, which had been so placed that she could be hauled alongside the *Minion*, the flanking ship of the English fleet. Having taken the *Minion* by boarding, the Spanish seamen were then to serve in the same manner the *Jesus*, which lay next, after which all would be over so far as the ships were concerned, for the remaining vessels were of little fighting power. This plan seriously disgruntled Ubilla, who held that his place was on board his own fighting galleon, and he did not hesitate to imply in a subsequent letter to the King that the Viceroy was a foolish amateur. The shipping being dominated by the island batteries, it was necessary to capture them. For this purpose the soldiers from Vera Cruz were stationed below decks in a number of the Spanish ships whose prows overhung the island shore. At a given signal they were to leap down and carry the guns with a rush. The officer appointed to lead them was Captain Delgadillo, who had so easily given up the same guns a week before. All other available men were to get into boats and take part in the attack on the English ships or in the landing on the island. The whole affair, timed for the morning of September 23, was to be set in motion when Luxan and Ubilla should be ready to haul alongside the *Minion*. They were to make a signal to the Viceroy, on board the Spanish flagship, and he would then press the button by means of a loud trumpet-call which would be the sign to everyone to begin.

From the outset Hawkins had been on his guard against treachery. On this Thursday morning he judged it to be imminent. He sent Robert Barrett, who spoke Spanish, to remonstrate with the Viceroy about the threatening activities which he could observe. Don Martin Enriquez answered 'that he in the faith of a Viceroy would be our defence from all villainies'. But the signs to the contrary continued, suspicious movements on board the nearest merchantman, opening of gun-ports bearing on the English ships, much more business by numbers of Spaniards than was occasioned by their ordinary work. Hawkins again sent Barrett to the Viceroy, and himself sat down to a hurried dinner in the cabin of the *Jesus*. According to Job Hortop the meal was interrupted by an ugly incident. An Englishman suddenly gripped the arm of the Spanish hostage Agustin de Villa Nueva and drew from his sleeve a dagger with which he was preparing to stab Hawkins. Hortop is the only witness to this story, which may be substantially true. His account is full of inaccuracies, natural when a man writes from memory of events of long ago, but it bears no sign of fabrication.

Hawkins ordered them to lock up the Spaniard and went on deck. He saw at once that the people in the merchantman were up to mischief, hauling on warps and preparing to close in. He recognized Vice-Admiral Ubilla on her deck, and told him that such trickery was not the work of a gentleman. Ubilla, according to his own account, replied that he was doing his duty as a fighting man, to which Hawkins answered that he was quite right[1] and shot an arrow at him. The Spanish ship was not yet in the requisite position, but Ubilla saw that the mask was off and made the signal to the Viceroy. At that moment Barrett was delivering his second protest. The Viceroy immediately made him a prisoner and sounded the trumpets.

Two factors should be considered in attempting to understand the battle that followed. It was a prolonged affair, lasting from ten in the morning to four in the afternoon, and it was fought out

[1] Hawkins was probably misunderstood.

in a very restricted space, all the guns being in action at ranges of not more than two hundred yards against stationary targets. That it could have endured for six hours is a testimony to the inaccuracy and slowness of the artillery of the period.

The vigilance of Hawkins had saved the *Minion* from being captured by surprise, and he at once gave orders to cut the headfasts which secured her to the island and haul off into the haven by the sternfasts. This was not so quickly done as said, and in the meantime it seems that the Spanish ship did come alongside and some of her 200 men boarded the *Minion*: 'whereat our General', says Hortop, 'with a loud and fierce voice called unto us, saying, "God and St. George! Upon those traitorous villains and rescue the *Minion*! I trust in God the day shall be ours!" And with that the mariners and soldiers leapt out of the *Jesus of Lubeck* into the *Minion*, and beat out the Spaniards.' As the *Minion* drew clear, the large merchantman fell aboard the *Jesus*, and two other vessels also grappled her. Hawkins says that she lost many men in repelling these boarders, and that some time elapsed before her headfasts could be cut and she could be hauled out clear of the island.

Meanwhile the decisive event was taking place on shore. At the sound of the trumpet Delgadillo and other officers led the attack upon the batteries. Spaniards on shore fraternizing with the English drew hidden weapons, soldiers poured down from the overhanging beakheads, more Spaniards in boats appeared from everywhere. Both sides agree that the English on the island were taken by surprise, gave ground, and collapsed. They were of course heavily outnumbered. Hortop says that only three escaped to the *Jesus*, all others being killed or captured. Ubilla remarks that if the English had fought as skilfully on shore as they did in their ships the result would have been different. It would seem that the officer in command had been at least careless. Hawkins does not mention his name, and it was no doubt a case of *de mortuis*; and since he was largely responsible for grievous loss the omission is generous. The loss of the island guns meant that in a matter of hours the English ships would have to evacuate San Juan. Hawkins foresaw it, although he wished to remain until nightfall. He concentrated the fire of the *Jesus* and the *Minion* upon the two Spanish fighting ships, determined that he would leave them in no condition to pursue him.

The Spanish ships made a poor response. Their commanding officers were not on board, and a Spanish witness remarks that as soon as the island was captured a large number of men repaired to it who had no business there. Francisco de Luxan established himself in command of the island artillery, Ubilla by his own account[1] roved about trying to get various people to do various things, and the Viceroy was left very much to his own devices on board the flagship. The fire of the two English ships was much heavier than that of their opponents. The English had hauled off for a distance of only two or three ships' lengths, sufficient to bring their guns to bear at point blank range. They sank the Spanish admiral, although the water was so shallow that she rested on the bottom without her upper works disappearing. The Viceroy was left on her deck with only five men, the others having withdrawn to defend the island, until Ubilla drove some of them back by main force. Ubilla disliked his superior but was a fair-minded man, and his evidence testifies equally to the Viceroy's coolness, courage and incompetence. The vice-flagship was set on fire and burnt out. She seems to have been a total loss, and thirty-five of her crew were killed. One of the merchantmen was also sunk, but it was less necessary to fire at them, and Hawkins left the rest unscathed. So, he says, 'within one hour ... the ships were little able to annoy us.'

That would have been before mid-day, with more than six hours of daylight in prospect. The island guns were now the determining factor. There was no hope of regaining them, for the English were outnumbered by three or four to one. It was a question of being able to stand up to them while certain arrangements were being carried out. Spanish accounts do not mention any shortage of ammunition, and so we must suppose that these

[1] Ubilla's letter is translated in *Fresh Light on San Juan de Ulua*, by M. Lewis, *Mariner's Mirror*, July, 1937, from the text furnished by Mr Conway from the Archives of the Indies. But some of the details given by Ubilla occur not in the letter but in his testimony at the enquiry, in *Caribbean Documents*, pp. 141-6.

guns maintained their fire hour after hour. Incredible as it may seem, they had not succeeded in sinking either the *Minion* or the *Jesus* until at four in the afternoon the action was ended by other means. The smaller vessels fared worse. The Spaniards sank the *Angel* and captured the *Swallow* and the Portuguese caravel from Cape Blanco. Captain Bland in his *Grace of God* made sail and turned to windward, meaning to run alongside the weathermost Spanish ship and set fire to his own. A shot from the island frustrated the intention by bringing down his mainmast, whereupon he fired his ship as she lay and brought his men on board the *Jesus*. Only the *Judith* under Francis Drake got clear and anchored at a distance until Hawkins should have need of her.

The reason why Hawkins himself did not quit the port at once was that the *Jesus* was immobile and that she contained the valuables acquired in the season's trading and the victuals that, scant as they were, would be indispensable for the voyage home. These things needed at all costs to be transhipped to the *Minion*. The task could not easily be performed under fire, and the best chance would come with darkness. The rigging of the *Jesus* was hopelessly cut up, her mainmast pierced by five shot, her foremast cut off below the hounds; and she had been unseaworthy at the outset. Hawkins moored her as a screen to the *Minion*, whose hull lay lower in the water, and hung on. It would be strange if during that time he did not carry the gold on board the smaller ship; but the matter is for later discussion. The cannonade continued, and not only in one direction. 'Our General', says Hortop, 'courageously cheered up his soldiers and gunners, and called to Samuel his page for a cup of beer, who brought it him in a silver cup, and he drinking to all men willed the gunners to stand by their ordnance lustily like men.' A shot carried away the cup as soon as he set it down, and Hawkins exclaimed, 'Fear nothing, for God, who hath preserved me from this shot, will also deliver us from these traitors and villains.' Hortop asserts that the gunners, thus encouraged, killed altogether 540 Spaniards, which sounds too many to be true.

Ubilla had already tried to set a fireship in motion against the English ships, but the fire had gone out after the vessel had been set adrift. The guns were failing to achieve victory, and a fireship was the obvious means of ending the situation. He tried again with 'a great ship', one of the large merchantmen, thoroughly set ablaze in four places and loosed down wind at the English. Hawkins was beginning to clear the *Jesus* and had sent some of her people outside on board the *Judith*. The *Minion* was alongside her great consort, with sails ready to set and anchor raised. The approaching fireship caused a panic among some of the *Minion's* men, who, in disregard of their captain's orders, made sail and cast off the warps connecting the two ships. As the *Minion* began to move, there was a rush from the *Jesus* to board her. The majority of the able-bodied got away, some following in a boat, the wounded presumably being left behind. Hawkins was one of the last to board the *Minion*. His duty was to bring home his men and his ship if it could be done, and he had intended to leave with her in any case. At a subsequent enquiry in the Admiralty Court, Jean Turren, his French trumpeter, deposed: 'the said John Hawkins, the captain and general, tarried so long upon board the said *Jesus*, for the better defence and safety thereof, that he was almost left behind, and hardly came to the *Minion*, which was then in shifting to loose and withdraw herself.'

A north wind was rising, and the *Minion* did not go far. She moved only a quarter of a mile, far enough to be out of effective range of the island guns. She was then anchored again close to the reefs of a lee shore on which she risked being driven during the night. There was no pursuit, the English guns having made sure of that. The *Judith* was anchored in the neighbourhood. Next morning she was gone. 'With the *Minion* only', wrote Hawkins next year, 'and the *Judith* (a small bark of 50 tons) we escaped, which bark the same night forsook us in our great misery.' It was a bitter thing to say of Drake, whose name he nowhere mentioned, and it was not a bitter man who said it; for Hawkins was not given to censuring his subordinates. Drake may have had his defence, but Hawkins had heard it, since they met again in England before the official account was written. The matter was allowed to drop, and there was no further public reference to it until twenty years had passed, when an enemy of Drake's raked it up against him. Hawkins and Drake were afterwards on good terms and collaborated in many enterprises, although they never sailed together until all England turned out in 1588.

Next day the *Minion* moved a mile away to a better anchorage, where she rode out a heavy blow from the northward. Battered and grim, with gold in her cabin, she was watched by those of San Juan, who could find neither ships nor men to follow. When the weather improved she sailed away.

X

THE END OF THE ADVENTURE

The departure of Hawkins from San Juan de Ulua left his enemies to engage in a recrimination. They had of his some fairly worthless ships and a small part of his valuables. They had seen him sail away with his only powerful fighting vessel and (as will be shown) with the bulk of the treasure which might have been balm for the wounds he had inflicted. Who was to blame? The Viceroy, whose plan had not proved infallible, and Luxan, who was obliquely aimed at in the criticisms against seamen who preferred to serve on the island, decided that the culprit was Ubilla. They held a court of enquiry, at which the witnesses stated that the vice-admiral had spoilt the scheme by giving the signal too soon. They disregarded his reasonable reply that since the English had discovered the purpose there was nothing for it but to fall on them at once. Ubilla felt that the Viceroy was treating him unjustly, and wrote to the King a variety of complaints and suggestions in the character of the bluff old soldier suffering under fools. There may have been something in his grievance. Don Martin Enriquez did in fact make a successful Viceroy of New Spain, but that required other qualities than those of a commander in an amphibious battle.

The ships remaining in Spanish hands were the *Jesus*, the *Swallow*, the *Grace of God* and the Portuguese caravel. The *Angel* had been destroyed, but Bland's ship, although he had set fire to her, was evidently salved. In the *Jesus* the Spaniards found their ten hostages unharmed, released in effect by Hawkins in the hope that the Viceroy would be moved to reciprocal generosity. They found also about fifty negro slaves, and linens, cloth, silver and gold to the value 'probably' of 3,000 ducats, which articles, however, were plundered by the soldiers and sailors who first got on board. Agustin de Villa Nueva had kept his eyes open. He not only carried off seventeen slaves, but he was observed by Ubilla's men to take away 'more than twenty thousand gold ducats contained in a coffer, which he smuggled out in some coverings ornamented with a coat-of-arms'. So says Ubilla, and if we believe him, the question of the treasure is to a large extent settled. But a rough arithmetical check arouses doubt. The gold ducat was worth about nine shillings, and more than twenty thousand of them would have equalled not much less than ten thousand English pounds. Their weight would have been well over a hundredweight, surely a little excessive for furtive smuggling out in the manner described. The matter was reported to Ubilla, who arrested Villa Nueva, but did not recover the swag. Presently the Viceroy sent a message ordering the unpleasant man's release. Ubilla complied, not without dark thoughts on his superior's probity. He had not seen the money himself, and did not learn what became of it, so that his story does not carry full conviction. Probably Villa Nueva did convey something, but the question is, how much?

We have other and better evidence about the treasure. When Hawkins at length reached home, he and the syndicate opened proceedings in the Admiralty Court to place the facts on record for complaint or reprisals against the Spanish government. William Clarke, a merchant who sailed in the *William and John*, declared that up to the departure from Cartagena the expedition had received 29,743 pesos of gold, or approximately £13,500, in exchange for its wares. Most of this was in actual gold, but some part in silver and pearls.[1] The statements made in the Admiralty Court show that it was not lost. They included detailed valuations of the ships and guns, of 57 negroes left in the *Jesus*, and of other articles on board. Under the heading of treasure they mention: gold and silver in the *Jesus*, £2,400; silver plate (Hawkins's table service), £200; silver called *coriente*, £500; total, £3,100. These were certainly not underestimates, since the syndicate was seeking to pile up the bill. It is therefore plain that not even the

---

[1] By this account the amount of gold was much the same as that which Ubilla declared Villa Nueva had stolen. Probably the captors of the *Jesus* found documents indicating the amount of the treasure, and this evidence suggested the figure given by Ubilla.

aggrieved parties alleged the loss of the bulk of the treasure, and that Hawkins must have brought it away with him. Obviously it is the first thing he would have transhipped while the *Minion* and the *Jesus* lay side by side. One small box of gold may have been overlooked and carried off by Villa Nueva; or alternatively the £2,400 may have been a liberal estimate of valuables in the hands of the men. They no doubt picked things up at the various places of trade; we hear casually of a seaman named Anthony Goddard who was 'given' a gold chain at Cartagena. The statements in the Admiralty Court are thus testimony that Hawkins brought home most of the treasure. Soon after his arrival on the English coast, Cecil wrote to a correspondent: 'Hawkins is arrived at Mount's Bay with the Queen's ship the *Minion*, having in her the treasure which he hath gotten by his trade in the Indies.' A fortnight later the Spanish ambassador wrote from London: 'Hawkins has come from the Indies and entered here with four horses loaded with gold and silver that he brings, which, however, I believe will not pay the costs.'

The loss of men was much more serious, and cannot be accurately determined. At Cartagena, according to the Cotton narrator, the expedition had 370 men. A small French ship then parted company, and afterwards the *William and John* did the same. Any figure for their crews must be a guess, but we may put it at fifty men, which would leave Hawkins with 320 before the battle at San Jüan. After it he sailed away with about 200 men in the *Minion*. Drake had already gone with the 50-ton *Judith*, whose company we may guess at not more than thirty. On this rather flimsy reckoning, the number killed and captured at San Juan de Ulua was about ninety. But the number of deaths resulting from the affair was to be considerably higher than that. Among the prisoners were the ten hostages, whom the Viceroy made no move to release, Robert Barrett, whom he had very treacherously seized, some of the men stationed on the island, and those left behind in the *Jesus*. The ten hostages, nineteen other Englishmen, and two Frenchmen were taken to Spain on board the *flota* which had fought Hawkins, and they arrived there in 1569. The Spanish government in its turn made no move to release any of them. On the contrary, it imprisoned them so harshly at Seville that some died of hunger and neglect. There for the present we leave the survivors, but they have yet a part to play in this story. Robert Barrett and six others, including Job Hortop, were sent to Spain in 1570. Barrett and one of his companions were burnt alive by the Inquisition at Seville. Four ended their days as galley slaves. Hortop alone escaped in 1590, after twenty-two years of it, a tough, cheerful man. Before leaving Mexico, Barrett was ordered to interpret for a Spanish friar who preached to the prisoners. He interpolated into the friar's sermon some remarks of his own, to the effect that the friar's doctrines were false and fraudulent and that the Pope was a Jewish knave. This was not detected at the moment, but afterwards it came out,[1] and may have been the reason for his execution at Seville. Robert Barrett might have been one of the great Elizabethans, courageous, competent, enterprising. Hawkins always gave him the command of parties and expeditions away from the main fleet. He was more prominent than his cousin Drake in the history of the voyage, and he was only twenty-five when the bars closed on him. A sad fate for such a man to be burnt in Seville market-place.

The *Jesus of Lubeck* was a disappointment to her captors. Not only did she contain little booty, but she was of small value, as the Viceroy found when he put the prizes up for auction. The bids were low, and after a survey at which the cost of repairing the *Jesus* was estimated at 4,000 ducats, the Viceroy accepted 600 ducats for her as she lay. If gold ducats are meant, the *Jesus of Lubeck* fetched £270; if silver, half of that sum. It was a breaking-up price, and nothing further is heard of her. The *Swallow* was sold for 300 ducats, and the Portuguese caravel for 400. Ubilla grumbled and insinuated corruption. He said that the *Jesus* could have done good service as an escort to the plate fleets. But there he was wrong.

Hawkins left San Juan with 200 men in the *Minion* and almost nothing wherewith to feed them. It is evident that he had transferred little food from the flagship before the collapse came. In the days that followed the *Minion's* company were stewing ox-hides out of the cargo, and finishing-up such cats, rats and parrots as

[1] Trial of Miles Phillips, pp. 20-1.

were to be found on board. Not only that, but the ship was leaking from her battle injuries and required hard labour to keep her afloat. The season of northerly winds in the Gulf of Mexico had set in, and it would not be easy to pass out through the Florida Channel and begin the Atlantic passage. The prospect was in short dreadful, and few could hope to reach home. Many of the men desired to save at least their lives by seeking the land and giving themselves up to the Spaniards, or taking their chance among the Indian tribes. After a fortnight's beating against contrary winds without making any progress out of the Gulf, Hawkins made a landfall in 23½ degrees, north of the region of Spanish settlement. The coast was all unknown to him, and he made it in the hope of watering, victualling and repairing the ship. There was a possibility of fresh water, but none of food, neither could the *Minion* be careened on a shoal and rocky shore devoid of shelter. 'We found neither people, victual, nor haven of relief, but a place where, having fair weather, with some peril we might land a boat. Our people, being forced with hunger, desired to be set on land, whereunto I consented.'

This was not Hawkins's story alone. Miles Phillips and Job Hortop give independent corroboration that those who were set ashore went by their own choice. Phillips says: 'there were a great many that did desire our General to set them on land, making their choice rather to submit themselves to the mercy of the savages or infidels than longer to hazard themselves at sea, where they very well saw that if they should remain together, if they perished not by drowning, yet hunger would enforce them in the end to eat one another.' Hortop says much the same in fewer words, and continues: 'He [Hawkins] asked them who would go on shore, and who would tarry on shipboard; those that would go on shore he willed to go on foremast, and those that would tarry, on baft mast: four score and sixteen of us were willing to depart.'

Hortop's figure was therefore ninety-six. Phillips says that there were a hundred and fourteen. He gives a more detailed reckoning than Hortop of their subsequent fates, and his number may be right. But we must remember that he was only a boy of fourteen at the time. Hortop was a man, with a capacity for vivid but inaccurate memory. Hawkins gave money to those who asked for it, and to each man six yards of cloth for barter. To propitiate the Spaniards they went almost unarmed and without any prayer books or other writings. When all were landed he went to them, took leave of every one personally, counselled them to serve God and love one another, and gave them a sorrowful farewell. He promised that if God sent him safe home he would do his utmost to get them back to England; and John Hawkins doing his utmost was capable of striking work, as will be shown at a later stage. This scene on the Mexican shore was no play-acting by a *faux bonhomme*. The situation was too grim for that. Hawkins knew that in sailing for England in the *Minion* he had less chance of survival than the poor men he had landed, and the farewell between them was the handclasp of parting friends. The voyage had ended in disaster, but he retained their affection. In Hortop's story 'our General' is his hero on every page.

The whole party set out along the coast southwards in search of a Spanish settlement. On the first day a band of Indians attacked them, and they were too weak to make much resistance. After eight had been killed they yielded. The Indians took their cloth and let them go. Some were now for going northwards into the unknown of North America. About half the party followed this course, but after losing more men to the Indians some of them turned south again and rejoined the others. Twenty-three men continued into the north, and of them the odd three, David Ingram, Richard Browne and Richard Twide, got home to England before the end of 1569. Ingram declared that they had tramped all through North America to the neighbourhood of Cape Breton where a French ship picked them up.[1] There are good grounds for thinking that the Frenchman must have found them much nearer to the Gulf of Mexico, but the fact is established that they were back in England within a year of their landing from the *Minion*. Nothing was ever heard of the other twenty in the north-bound party.

All the rest, seventy-eight men according to Phillips, chose

---

[1] Hakluyt printed Ingram's story in the 1589 *Principal Navigations*, but, having conceived doubts of its truthfulness, omitted it from the 1598–1600 edition.

Anthony Goddard as their leader and sought the Spaniards. After ten days they reached the settlement of Tampico and surrendered to the authorities. The next stage was the march under guard to the city of Mexico, in which several died from starvation and over-exertion. Many more would have died in the city but for the charity of the inhabitants, who found food for them. Hortop says that the Viceroy proposed to hang them all, but yielded to the protests of some men of quality. The Englishmen remained imprisoned for a year, during which time some were sent to Spain. The majority were kept in Mexico, and in the latter part of 1569 were discharged from prison to various employments. In the next two years some began to prosper and even to make money, and a good many were reconciled to marrying and settling for life in New Spain. Then their luck turned. There had long been an episcopal Inquisition in the country, a comparatively mild and innocuous institution. In 1571 a branch of the regular Inquisition, independent of all other authorities, was established in Mexico under two ruthless men, Moya de Contreras and Fernandez de Bonilla. The first action of the new court was to investigate the spiritual condition of all the Englishmen in the country.

The patient research of Mr. G. R. G. Conway has traced in the archives of Mexico the trials of thirty of these men. Eleven of them would have been boys of sixteen or under at the time of the battle of San Juan. Probably this does not indicate that thirty-five per cent of Hawkins's crews were so young, but that the youngsters were urged to choose the easier option of quitting the ship rather than that of trying to reach England on a diet of ox-hides. The inquisitors made a distinction according to the age of the prisoners. Those who had been small children when Elizabeth came to the throne, and had therefore never had any Catholic instruction, were for the most part sentenced to a period of menial service in a monastery, where they could be taught their new faith. Miles Phillips, for example, who was eighteen in 1572, was adjudged to serve three years in the house of the Company of Jesus in Mexico. The boys were not put to the torture in the course of their trials, but the proceedings lasted two years, during which they suffered rigorous imprisonment. The older prisoners, who would have been youths or men before 1558, were regarded more seriously, as Catholics who had lapsed into heresy. They were repeatedly and minutely examined, not only on their own beliefs and actions, but in order to make them incriminate others; and when a man was so incriminated, he was not confronted with the witness against him or allowed to know precisely what had been said. If the inquisitors thought that a man was keeping anything back, they applied the torture. It may be imagined that after two years of such proceedings ignorant men became extremely pliable in the hands of their manipulators.

The result was that at the first *auto de fe* held by the new Inquisition in February 1574 the following sentences were pronounced:[1] William Collins, of Oxford, age 40, seaman, ten years in the galleys; John Farenton (? Faringdon), of Windsor, 49, gunner, six years in the galleys; John Burton, of Bar Abbey, 22, seaman, 200 lashes and six years in the galleys; Paul de Leon, of Rotterdam, 22, seaman, 200 lashes and six years in the galleys; William Griffin, of Bristol, 24, seaman, 200 lashes and eight years in the galleys; George Ribley or Riveley, of Gravesend, 30, seaman, burnt at the stake, but first strangled; John Moon, of Looe, 26, seaman, 200 lashes and six years in the galleys; John Lee, of 'Sebria' in England, 20, seaman or gunner, 200 lashes and eight years in the galleys; William Brown, of London, 25, steward, 200 lashes and six years in the galleys; Thomas Goodal, of London, 30, soldier, 300 lashes and ten years in the galleys; John Gilbert, of London, 29, seaman, 300 lashes and ten years in the galleys; Roger Armar, of Gueldres (Netherlands), 24, armourer, 200 lashes and six years in the galleys; Michael Morgan (alias Morgan Tillert), of Cardiff, 40, seaman, 200 lashes and eight years in the galleys; John Brown, of Ireland, 28, seaman, 200 lashes and eight years in the galleys; John Williams, of Cornwall, 28, 200 lashes and eight years in the galleys; Robert Plinton, of Plymouth, 30, 200 lashes and eight years in the galleys; John Grey, Englishman, 22, gunner, 200 lashes and eight years in the galleys; George Dee or Day, Englishman, 30, seaman,

[1] Recorded in *An Englishman in theMexican Inquisition*, by G. R. G. Conway, Mexico City, 1927, pp. 155–62.

300 lashes and eight years in the galleys. At the *auto de fe* of March 1575, John Martin, of Cork, otherwise known as Cornelius the Irishman, age 22 or more, seaman, was condemned to be burnt at the stake, but was also first strangled. The more merciful death was the custom in the Mexican Inquisition, but not in that of Spain. All of Hawkins's men remaining in New Spain were tried by the Inquisition, although documents for only about half of the cases have been found. The only one of these, the main body of the prisoners, who is known to have returned to his native land was Miles Phillips, who sailed to Spain in the *flota* of 1582. He knew that he was to be consigned to the Inquisition of Seville, and made his escape as soon as his ship entered San Lucar, afterwards getting a passage to England. Hawkins's nephew Paul Horsewell, who is sometimes called Paul Hawkins in the Spanish records, had been captured at San Juan. As a youngster he got off lightly in the Inquisition.[1] He married and settled in New Spain, where his descendants were traceable a century later.

After landing the men whose fortunes have been indicated above, Hawkins watered the *Minion* with great danger and difficulty and sailed for England on October 16. The weather improved, and in a month he got clear of the Florida channel and out into the Atlantic. By this time of year the Newfoundland fishery was deserted, which was no doubt the reason that he steered direct for Europe instead of seeking victual on the bank as he had done in 1565. The east-bound passage was protracted: 'our men, being oppressed with famine, died continually, and they that were left grew into such weakness that we were scantly able to manage our ship.' With ordinary December weather the *Minion* should have found fair winds for England. But this year the luck was foul to the end. Malignant winds between north and east pressed the dying men off their course, and the best they could do was to fetch the north-west corner of Spain. Hawkins knew the peril, but to remain at sea meant death for all. On the last day of 1568 he entered Ponte Vedra, near Vigo, and afterwards Vigo itself. He did not lack money for victuals, and unhappily his men

---

[1] The Trial of Pablo Haquines, of which Mr. Conway kindly gave me particulars.

were too far gone to withstand the effects of sudden plenty: 'our men with excess of fresh meat grew into miserable diseases, and died, a great part of them.' Hawkins's published account gives no numbers, but a state paper, ambiguously worded, appears to assert that forty-five men died in Vigo Bay in addition to those lost on the passage. He allowed no one to go on shore, but the Spanish authorities divined his weakness. They knew who he was, and sought opportunity to seize the ship. Half dead of hunger, he faced them with all his flair and assurance. An erect, handsome, courteous man, one of them described him, looking younger than he really was. He wore breeches of crimson velvet, said another, a jacket of scarlet leather trimmed with silver braid, a silken cloak and a long gold chain. The rustic officials of Galicia could not stand up to such a man. King Philip, when he heard of it, was enraged at their pusillanimity, and ordered an enquiry why Haquines had been let out of the bag. From deponents of the usual verbosity we have the silken cloak, gold chain and the rest.[1]

After a terrible three weeks with his remnant dying around him, Hawkins got twelve new men from an English ship, and sailed from Vigo on January 20, 1569. On that day, as it turned out, Drake entered Plymouth in the *Judith*, after a long voyage of which no single detail is on record. The *Minion* reached Mount's Bay, the westernmost anchorage of the Channel, on January 25. Even with the reinforcement from Vigo her men could take her no farther. How many were left we do not certainly know. The Spanish ambassador wrote that there were not more than fifteen survivors of the hundred who had sailed from the coast of Mexico. It is very likely true, but there is no corroboration.

John Hawkins sent word from Mount's Bay to his brother at Plymouth. William Hawkins dispatched a fresh crew to bring the *Minion* home. Later in the year she went up Channel to the Medway, and passed out of history. Like the *Jesus* and the Anglo-Spanish alliance and the hope of a peaceful share in the expanding world, she belonged to an age that had closed.

[1] Arizmendi's article, see *ante*, p.105.

BOOK II
SEA POWER AND LIBERTY

I

THE NARROW SEAS

Times were changing while John Hawkins was away, the Anglo-Spanish alliance was breaking down, the diplomatic pattern of Europe dissolving in favour of a new grouping of Catholic versus Protestant. Scotland and England were Protestant with strong Catholic minorities, Portugal and Spain and the Italian states were Catholic without dissentients, the Netherlands and France were Catholic with determined minorities of the Calvinist type which were ready to fight for their freedom. The great Council of Trent had finished its sittings and published its decrees for the renaissance of the Catholic Church. The Counter-Reformation was setting in as a crusade to overcome Protestantism and compel every European to submit to the discipline of Rome. The Calvinists of Scotland, France and the Low Countries, and the milder Protestants of England, were threatened with conquest by a faith, a regimentation, a way of life, which they had rejected. In English history it was the first struggle of its kind, resistance against a universal authority; and since the English were only defending their own choice, and were not making any parallel claim to compel all Christendom to submit to the discipline of Canterbury, it was for them a struggle for freedom. Elizabeth and her people were to win their contest, and thus to lay the foundation of liberty for the centuries to come. The events of the late 1560's set the forces in motion.

The leading events may be briefly listed. In 1567 the second war of religion broke out in France, and after a brief stoppage continued as the third war. The Huguenots made the port of La Rochelle their capital, where the Prince of Condé and Admiral Coligny issued commissions to Protestant privateers to prey upon all Catholic shipping, and so created the nucleus of a Protestant sea power. In the same year '67 Philip of Spain sent the Duke of Alva with a Spanish army to the Netherlands, Alva's mission being to quell by martial law the Calvinist mutineers and also the constitutional opponents of Spanish rule, many of whom were Catholics. Alva's atrocities caused William of Orange and other Netherland nobles to take up arms in 1568; but the regular Spanish troops defeated them and chased them out of the country, after which the reign of terror continued.

In England the year 1568 witnessed two crucial events. The first was the arrival of Mary Stuart, Queen of Scots, expelled by her own people and claiming Elizabeth's aid and protection. Mary did not at the same time resign her claim to Elizabeth's throne, and remained for nineteen years a focus of plots and discontent and a tool for the enemies of English freedom. The second was the replacement of Guzman de Silva by Guerau de Spes. Its significance was that where de Silva had worked for peace, de Spes acted as the enemy of Elizabeth's government. He was for maintaining the Spanish alliance, but with a Catholic England. To urge the old Catholic families to revolt, to exploit the claims of injured Mary Stuart, to liquidate Cecil, to compel Elizabeth to conform or go, this was the policy that de Spes pursued. In general it was what his master approved, although in detail many of his moves embarrassed Philip by their premature rashness. For Guerau de Spes, luckily for England, was a headstrong fool who did not know his job.

Cecil was quietly summing up his new diplomatic guest, and probing skilfully into a transparent mind, when a crisis arose, unpremeditated by any. Alva's victorious army needed money, and its extortion from the victims of the reign of terror was disappointingly slow. The army was the keystone of government; discipline and efficiency depended upon pay; and Philip II, master of plate-fleets, had no ready cash. He raised a loan in silver coin from the bankers of Genoa. He despatched it from Spain up Channel for Antwerp in a few small vessels unarmed and unescorted; whereupon the Huguenots of La Rochelle gave him a lesson in sea power. In the days of the Anglo-Spanish alliance sea power had always been on its side, and Philip may have grown up to take for granted what now required consideration. Whatever the reason, he made an elementary blunder. Huguenot privateers chased the treasure carriers, which scattered and made for shelter in English ports, Fowey, Plymouth and Southampton. The pursuers waited without, their numbers growing towards the point where they would wait no longer but affront English sovereignty by cutting out the treasure as it lay. There was only one thing to be done, to unlade the treasure and get it behind battlements and guns. The Spanish officers reluctantly agreed, with misgivings about its future. One of them at Plymouth[1] has described his position; the port full of ships, some French, some English, discharging goods captured from Catholic vessels; the mayor (he probably means William Hawkins, who had just vacated the office) taking a leading part in the buying and selling; the same William Hawkins supervising the unloading of the treasure and its stowage in the castle; Sir Arthur Champernowne presiding, as vice-admiral of Devon, while his son Henry was at sea, cruising with a Condé commission; altogether a sinister port of refuge for the treasure of the King of Spain.

Elizabeth and Cecil mistrusted Philip's army in the Netherlands; for that army, having accomplished its mission there, might be used to strike at England in aid of the Catholic revolution. They were ready to welcome any means of preventing the money from reaching Alva, but as yet did not see their way clear. William Hawkins at Plymouth, joyfully lending a hand in unlading the treasure, was dismayed by a story that reached him by way of Spain and London, to the effect that his brother John had been attacked and killed by Spanish forces in the Indies. This was at the beginning of December, when nothing had been heard from John Hawkins and anxiety about him was beginning to grow.[2] The story of disaster came through the office of Benedict Spinola, the London agent of the Genoese financial house that was lending Philip the treasure. William Hawkins at once wrote to Cecil, urging him to examine Spinola about the attack, and if he found it substantiated, to seize the treasure in reprisal. Cecil had

[1] His ship was actually lying up the Hamoaze, near Saltash.
[2] Hawkins's previous expeditions had been home by the end of September. The rumour of his overthrow was fictitious, the time being too short to allow of news arriving from San Juan de Ulua.

his eye on the treasure, but would do nothing without legal justification. He did make inquiries from the Genoese, and could have learnt no real news about John Hawkins; but they let out casually a fact which altered the whole situation. It was that the money in the English ports did not legally belong to King Philip but to themselves. The transference of the treasure was to take place when it arrived at Antwerp, and not before.

The treasure situation was indeed delicate and demanded consummate ability from Philip's servants, he himself being too far away for the necessary day-to-day decisions. On Guerau de Spes fell the conduct of his master's case, and he plunged in and wrecked it with the abandon of the bull in the china shop. As soon as the treasure came into English ports, he asked that it should be sent on its way with the protection of a naval escort, and received answer that his request would be considered. The fact that it was not instantly granted aroused his deep suspicions, and when further news came that the treasure had been landed he made up his mind that its seizure had in fact taken place. He went again to the Queen, who still talked of naval escort, or even of carting the stuff through England and re-shipping it from the Thames. In fact the Queen was still perplexed and had not made a decision. Nevertheless de Spes wrote that day to Alva and told him that the English had seized the treasure, and urged him to arrest instantly all English goods in the Netherlands. Alva, whose talent was not diplomacy, complied; and they were jointly guilty of a mistake which lost them the game. For the question of arrest was governed by well-known and long-enduring treaties, going back to the *Magnus Intercursus* of 1495, which laid it down that no general arrest of goods must be effected until specific complaint of grievance had been made by the one party and redress denied by the other. The ambassador in England and the governor of the Netherlands might have been expected to know these treaties, but apparently neither did. It was sweet honey for Cecil and his Queen. Within a week of the arrest they had a proclamation out for public information. The arrest was a breach of treaty, it said, and an unwarranted act of aggression; there had been no seizure of the King's money; on the contrary, on the very day of the arrest the ambassador had requested the Queen to provide an escort, a request which she had promised to consider; therefore, being thus unreasonably attacked, and her subjects' persons and property being placed under restraint, she could only answer by ordering the arrest of Spaniards and Flemings and their goods in England. This was at once carried out, the enemy property seized in England being of much higher value than the English goods in Flanders.

As for the all-important military treasure, it naturally never reached Alva. Shortly after the proclamation the Queen, having learned as above that its owners were the Genoese bankers, borrowed it herself with their consent. The bankers must have consented with a sigh of relief, for there were always the Huguenot rovers in waiting. England's financial credit was higher than Spain's, and in fact the Queen repaid all the money when the debt fell due. King Philip had been badly stung, but he could not fight. The Netherlands were not conclusively subdued, and the army of occupation was weakening; for unpaid soldiers lost discipline and became robber bands. Philip therefore contented himself with extending the arrest to Spain, but did not declare war. For four years to come there was suspension of commercial but not of diplomatic intercourse between his dominions and Elizabeth's. A state of semi-war prevailed, in which Protestant sea power proved a punishing assailant to Spain and won the opening round in the fight for modern liberty. Such was the prospect that was opening out when John Hawkins at length came home in January, 1569.

On the 25th of that month, the day on which he anchored in Mount's Bay, he wrote to Cecil a brief statement that he had met with disaster and had returned with the *Minion* alone. He did not then know that Drake with the *Judith* had already come in, or that the *William and John* was shortly to do so. 'Our voyage', he said, 'was, although very hardly, well achieved and brought to reasonable pass, but now a great part of our treasure, merchandise, shipping and men devoured by the treason of the Spaniards.' He asked Cecil to report this to the Queen and the Council, and said that he would come speedily to London to declare more.

He saw his ship safe in Plymouth and went on to London at the beginning of February, taking with him, as Guerau de Spes reported, the treasure saved from the wreck of the voyage. The breach of intercourse with Spain had just begun, and the government thought it well to publish the story of Spanish perfidy. Hawkins accordingly wrote for the press the brief and pithy account of the voyage which is nowadays read in Hakluyt's reprint in the *Principal Navigations*, but which was first published as an independent pamphlet in 1569. Its tone did him credit, for he set forth the occurrences in direct and sober style, without exaggeration, railing or self-pity, and although he omitted much, he nowhere diverged from the truth. He and the syndicate then opened proceedings in the High Court of Admiralty in order to prove the wrongful action of the Spaniards and the damage sustained. The evidence bearing on the financial proceeds of the voyage has been quoted in the previous chapter. The fifty-seven negroes left in the *Jesus*, described as 'optimi generis et staturae', were valued at £9,120, or £160 each, which is a much higher price than could actually have been obtained. The poor old *Jesus* herself stood at £7,000, a contrast with the petty sum for which her remains were sold at the San Juan auction and with the £2,000 at which she had been rated in the syndicate's accounts for the second voyage. These inflations were to be expected from the nature of the case. Hawkins was moving for leave to make reprisals to the amount of the damage he had suffered, and his estimate was naturally liberal. The whole bill added up to £27,924 of which, as we have seen, a very small proportion was for treasure alleged to be lost. Proof of wrong was all that Hawkins was seeking to place on record. The accused parties were outside the jurisdiction, and no decision was pronounced against them.

It was not from the Admiralty Court but from the government that Hawkins hoped to get his letters of reprisal. In March he wrote to Cecil about them and asked for his influence, offering the minister one-fourth of the prospective spoil in recompense. Neither the sender nor the receiver of the proposition thought it dishonourable; it was the ordinary method by which administra-

HANDWRITING OF JOHN HAWKINS

This is part of the letter of March 6, 1569 (modern style), cited on
p. 164. It is all the autograph of Hawkins, although the subscription
is in a different style from the body of the letter.

From S.P. Domestic, Eliz., Vol. 49, No. 57

tion was then carried on. Hawkins did not obtain the letters of reprisal. The Queen on principle would never take an unnecessary step. The Prince of Condé's commissions were available to all enterprising seamen, and others issued by the Prince of Orange were now coming into play. If Hawkins would seek his remedy against Spaniards he could do so under those instruments without dragging the English government into a matter which might ultimately prove vexatious. He probably already had a Huguenot commission. Certainly his brother William had; and with that they did their best.

The Huguenots were already pouring captured goods into Plymouth, and the process continued through 1569. The English and French were more thoroughly commingled in the business than they could have been if regular forces of allied governments had acted in concert. At the end of 1568 there were fifty cruisers working under Condé's flag, and thirty of these were alleged to be English by La Mothe Fénelon, the Valois ambassador who complained to Elizabeth about them. Coligny's brother, the Cardinal Châtillon, a Huguenot in spite of his eminence, was in London distributing commissions 'to pass unto the seas in warlike sort to apprehend and take all the enemies of God otherwise called papists'.[1] The holders of these documents stopped every ship they met and took whatever they desired from all that did not pass their scrutiny as owned by good Protestants. They commonly released the ships themselves, sometimes with the less valuable parts of their cargo. It was for this reason that trade was able to struggle on in the ensuing years instead of being completely stopped in a few months. The Condé commissions, recognized by the English government, gave the legal cover which enabled men of position to take part. Sir Arthur Champernowne had cruisers at sea, and so had William Hawkins. One of Hawkins's ships bore the hereditary name of the *Paul*, and was commanded at the close of '68 by no less a captain than Jacques de Sores, who was in Plymouth in December discharging cargo from Flemish prizes. Another was the *New Bark*, in which Hawkins's partners were Champernowne and a Cornishman named Philip Budocushyde; and she captured a

[1] *Sir John Hawkins* (1927) p. 221.

cargo belonging to a Rouen merchant named Quintanadoine, evidently a connection of the Quintana Dueñas who had once got the better of old William Hawkins.

There are many cases relating to these captures noted in the records of the Admiralty Court. The impression they give is that Plymouth was rich with the sale of captured goods throughout 1569, and that most of the captures were by the Hawkins brothers and their partners. William Hawkins stands out as the organizer, almost the commander-in-chief, of the Protestant forces in the western Channel. Plymouth is equally their emporium and their base of supply. Farther east, in the central Channel, the Huguenots used the Solent as a similar base, and the anchorage then known as the Medehole, near Cowes, was the emporium to which buyers from Southampton and London resorted. Here the Huguenot Pourtault de Latour commanded in chief until he returned to La Rochelle in the spring of 1569 and was killed at the battle of Jarnac. Jacques de Sores then took his place and tightened the blockade of the Channel. He relentlessly took every 'papist' vessel, not even the Venetians escaping as neutrals. At the end of the year he captured a great Venetian off the Isle of Wight and converted her into *La Grande Huguenotte*, the most powerful ship in his command.

These actions amounted to a weighty counterstroke against Philip II and the advance of the Counter-Reformation, for they ensured that Alva's apparent conquest of the Netherlands should not endure. The interruption of the Channel highway, spectacular in the matter of the Genoese treasure, continued chronic and increasingly debilitating to Spanish interests. Catholic Flemings suffered from the blockade along with Catholic Frenchmen and Spaniards. These Flemings had never loved the Spanish overlordship, and resented being sacrificed for it. They were not yet ready to join hands with the Calvinists, but they were also not disposed to fight for Philip, whose hold on the provinces was growing less secure. It was one of the more recondite effects of sea power, less obvious but no less sure than the capture of treasure fleets. To Admiral Coligny belongs the credit of discerning this strategic force and setting it in operation. Sir William Cecil understood and co-operated as best he could, although hampered by a sovereign who was self-willed and less perceptive, and by colleagues in the Council who were, some of them, hostile to the Protestant cause. As 1569 drew on the coalition was completed by the Prince of Orange, who was technically a sovereign prince although also a subject of Philip, and who began under Coligny's inspiration to issue sea commissions to his Dutch supporters. The Dutch Sea Beggars, as history has named them, became in the end the most famous of the Channel rovers, but they came third into the business after the French and the English. In the autumn of 1569 they numbered about eighteen sail; in the following spring, over a hundred. The Lord of Dolhain was their first commander, and he made Dover his base, and there carried on the same operations as Latour in the Solent and Hawkins at Plymouth. Although these forces had three distinct national origins, they quickly became cosmopolitan. English, French and Dutch ships were to be found in all the fleets, the crews were international, and the vessels were owned by partners often of different countries. The genius of Coligny had called into being a Protestant navy, which was wielded by the international partnership of Coligny, Cecil and Orange.

The closing of Antwerp by the breach of intercourse was a blow to the English cloth industry and the merchants of London. English cloth found its greatest market in Germany, which it reached through the mart of Antwerp, and its second greatest in the Peninsula and the Mediterranean, which it reached mainly by way of Seville; for there was then little direct trade by English ships within the Straits of Gibraltar. Cecil had foreseen the possibility of a breach with Spain before the affair of the Genoese treasure. He had made preliminary moves towards the transference of the cloth market from Antwerp to a German port. In the summer of 1569 the arrangements took effect. William Winter in command of seven of the Queen's ships convoyed a great fleet of English merchantmen to Hamburg. They carried not only the cloth output but the spices, sugar, pepper, hides, dyestuffs and wines taken by the Channel rovers. So rich a trading fleet had seldom left English ports before. Alva knew of its crossing the

North Sea, but the naval escort prevented him from striking a blow. The great convoy returned in equal safety, and so lucrative had been the whole operation that it was repeated with like success in the autumn.

It is possible that Francis Drake served in the first convoy. We have no contemporary record of him from January 20, when he brought the *Judith* into Plymouth and was sent up to London to tell his story to the Council, until July 4, when he was married to Mary Newman at St. Budeaux. A late authority says that during this time he served in one of the Queen's ships, which would most likely be a ship of Winter's squadron. Miss I. A. Wright, on the other hand, has found Spanish evidence of operations in the West Indies in which someone who might have been Drake was concerned.[1] The dates make it difficult to accept this possibility. Early February to the end of June, four and a half months at the outside, are hardly enough for a West Indian raid. The course could have been sailed in the time, but only if the ship returned almost as soon as it arrived on the scene of action. However, it is a possibility which further evidence may amplify.

French trade and politics also demanded naval action. In December 1568, while the Spanish treasure was in Plymouth and Fowey, Winter was on that coast with the annual wine fleet bound for Bordeaux, and he was able to afford some protection to the treasure carriers. On his way south with the convoy he delivered in La Rochelle a present of guns, powder and ball from the English government. The Gascon wine trade was the most important business between England and France, and the Huguenots sought to divert it from Bordeaux to La Rochelle. De Sores began a blockade of the Gironde in the spring of 1569, but the Catholics were too strong for him and drove him off. As the year advanced La Rochelle itself was hard pressed. The defeat of Jarnac in the spring was tactically only a skirmish, but the Prince of Condé and some other eminent Huguenots were killed, and the moral effect was considerable. It was felt in the English Council, where Cecil's opponents were encouraged to denounce

[1] *Documents concerning English Voyages to the Spanish Main, 1569–80, Hakluyt Society,* 1932, pp. xxi–xxii.

his policy of aid to Calvinist rebels. The Queen, however, much as she hated Calvinists and rebels, at length decided for Cecil, and preparations began for a large expedition to go to the aid of La Rochelle.

The Hawkinses had much to do with this expedition, and it is almost certain that John Hawkins was its commander. The evidence, however, is nearly all French and not greatly concerned with the correctitude of English proper names, while in English records there is no mention of the commander. Two testimonies point to John Hawkins. John Prince the antiquary, who two centuries ago read manuscripts that are now lost, wrote in his *Worthies of Devon* that in 1567 Hawkins went to the relief of the distressed Huguenots at La Rochelle. The date is obviously wrong, for we know that Hawkins was not that year at La Rochelle, neither was it in particular distress. But if Prince or his printer made an error, the true date was in all likelihood 1569. The other witness is La Mothe Fénelon, then in London, who says[1] that the expedition was commanded by 'Sir John Basin'. Sir John Basin is not Master John Hawkins, but it is not impossible as a foreigner's corruption of the name, which the French generally called Haquin. Moreover, there is nobody named John Basin otherwise known at the time. We shall not be unjustified in assuming, with due reserve, that John Hawkins commanded the Rochelle relief.

In April the fleet began to gather in the Thames, and on the 23rd the forty-nine ships sailed down Channel. As they went westward they were joined by the west-countrymen, eight of them belonging to William Hawkins, who made up the total to more than sixty sail. The whole voyage was prosperous, and the fleet entered La Rochelle in the middle of May. There it landed grain and salt beef, arms, munitions and money, and English volunteers, including fifty engineers, perhaps Cornish miners, skilled in making trenches and batteries. Hawkins (or whoever it was) had important words from the English government for Coligny. It was in fact one of the infrequent occasions when Cecil could communicate at second hand with the kindred spirit whom

[1] Or, whose modern printers say. The present author has not seen the original manuscript.

he never saw; and what better intermediary could he have chosen than the John Hawkins he knew so well? The great crowd of shipping was not needed for the money and munitions it took out. On the homeward voyage it was fully laden, with salt from the Biscay marshes, wine from the western vineyards, popish bells from every church the Huguenots had sacked—invaluable for recasting into bronze ordnance—and all the tropical booty from the Caribbean, the sherry sack from Andalusia, the fine cloths from Bruges and Ghent, which the Huguenot sailors had piled upon the quays of La Rochelle. There was lading there for sixty sail and more. All went well, and the ships were home by the beginning of July.

La Mothe Fénelon in the Valois interest had some sharp things to say to the Queen on this affair. Disguised as trade, it was in fact a military operation of the first importance; for it may well have made all the difference to the fate of La Rochelle before the year was out. La Mothe's protests before the fleet sailed caused the Queen to abandon her intention of sending her own ships with it. She was half at war with Spain and had no wish to fight Catholic France. Yet Cecil assured her that the Huguenots must be helped or would perish, and after them might perish Protestant England and its Queen; and she believed him. So she dealt with the Valois in her own fashion, saying what they did not believe but found themselves accepting—normal trade, private merchants, nothing military—, and got finally away with it without permanent damage to her relations with her inferior in feminine diplomacy, Catherine de Medici.

Later in the year the private individuals who went to sea from Plymouth did something more for the Huguenot cause. Henry Champernowne raised a body of horse among the gentry of the south-west. One of its members was Walter Ralegh, who has left us a few recollections on the subject.[1] While they were landing at La Rochelle their friends suffered a heavy defeat at Moncontour, and young Ralegh's first experience of war was

---

[1] Further facts are recorded by the contemporary French writer La Popelinière, *Histoire de France*, I, pp. 140, 177. Ralegh was not present at Jarnac and Moncontour, as some of his biographers assert.

to meet a beaten army streaming back to its base. It was well
that the base was La Rochelle, fortified with English guns and
nourished from the sea. Coligny had a hard winter, but he
pulled his Huguenots together and retrieved the position next
year.

In England the chief public event of the close of 1569 was the
Rising of the North, in which some of the malcontents against
Cecil took the field while others did not, and the attempt collapsed as much by its own feebleness as by the strength of the
government. The Catholic earls, Northumberland and Westmore-
land, called out their followers, while the Duke of Norfolk, not
an avowed Catholic but a known sympathizer, made no move.
The objects were those of Guerau de Spes, to eliminate Cecil and
his Protestant policy, to restore Catholicism and friendship with
Spain, and to have Mary Stuart either made Queen at once or
recognized as heir to the throne and accorded the chief place in
England after a humiliated Elizabeth. The Spanish army in the
Netherlands impressed the rebels as it did the government, and
they seized a northern port and asked Alva to send troops. Alva
thought poorly of the rebels, and refused. They failed to carry off
Mary Stuart from her place of detention, and then disintegrated
without having suffered a serious defeat in the field. The Navy
turned out a force from the Medway in case of any movement
from the Netherland coast. The west was also alert, but we have
no details.

We have no information that John Hawkins was employed in
these defensive measures, although he is unlikely to have been
inactive during a crisis. The Spaniards believed that he was
engaged in some important operation in the Atlantic. A Seville
news-letter stated in early December that he had been seen off
Cape St. Vincent with twenty-five ships, and was thought to be
bound for the West Indies. Another Spanish document asserted
that he was near Teneriffe with a son of Jean Ribault in his
company.[1] He was supposed to be on his way to rescue the men he
had left in Mexico. Whatever John Hawkins may have been doing
—and we have no evidence of his presence in England from the

[1] Wright, *Spanish Main Documents*, p. xxvii.

middle of 1569 to February, 1570—it probably produced no decisive result, and we lack the facts for a clear statement.

William Hawkins is also stated by Spanish evidence to have been at sea in 1569–70.[1] Documents in the Archives of the Indies show that he had some vessels working between Spain and the Canaries. He was, by comparison with most contemporary captains, an old man, of about fifty years, an estimate by a Spanish prisoner which agrees closely with his birth date of 1519 assumed from English evidence. His subordinates showed him marked respect, and he treated his prisoners well. They gathered from what they heard that the expedition was going south of the equator, possibly to Brazil. The Spanish authorities suspected that it was for the Caribbean, but we have no evidence that it reached either destination. This voyage of William Hawkins is closely, while that of John is vaguely, attested. It is possible that the two were one, and that John was not concerned in it. His more likely post at a time of national danger was at Plymouth. The rescue of his men from the interior of New Spain was obviously not possible, and he did not yet know that some of them were being sent to Seville.

[1] Wright, *Spanish Main Documents*, p. xxvi.

ADVANCEMENT BY DILLIGE[NCE]

Sʳ Iohn Hawkins Knight

His shadow to the world brave Hawkins shewes,
Who was a Bulwark to his friends. to foes
Resistles Thunder: who for countries sake
    So many a hard attempt durst undertake
That Indian in their barbarous tongues do praise him,
    And vnto Heauen his very foes doe raise him,
He in his life whole Seas could boldly tame,
    Let not then lethes Reuer drowne his name. A.H.

SIR JOHN HAWKINS
From the engraving by Robert Boissard in *Bazileiωologia* (1618)
From the copy in Rawlinson MSS., 170; Bodleian Library, Oxford

II

JOHN HAWKINS AND GUERAU DE SPES

As we have seen, there is no clear evidence of the doings of John Hawkins in the latter part of 1569. We discern him with certainty in England in February 1570, when he received a commission to impress men for his *New Bark*, bound on 'a certain service', not specified, for the Queen. There is no clue to the nature of this service. He himself was meditating an important stroke, the capture of the homeward-bound plate fleets of 1570 in reprisal for San Juan de Ulua. Early in June he wrote about it to the Earl of Leicester. He expected to meet the treasure ships at the Azores about the middle of August, and would attack them with ten ships of his own and two which he asked Leicester to borrow from the Queen. He would also need guns and powder from the Tower; and nothing else but the Queen's consent. 'This whole fleet, with God's grace, shall be intercepted and taken within these three months, for the extreme injuries offered unto this realm; which wrongs being satisfied, with the costs, the great mass [of the booty] shall be at the courtesy of the Queen's Highness to restore or keep.' Not an act of war, merely of securing compensation, with an admission that the value of the capture might exceed that of the damages and costs: this was the established practice of the sixteenth century, in which sovereign powers would often put up with extreme insults without going to war.

Hawkins would no doubt have been happy to attack the plate fleet solely with his own ships, but that he needed those of the Queen to prove that he had official sanction for the act. As the Queen's officer he had been betrayed at San Juan, and only in that character would he seek a reparation that would make the world exclaim. The Queen would have been well within her rights in consenting. The men and the guns of the *flota* had destroyed her *Jesus of Lubeck*. Why should not her *Bull* and

Bonaventure shoot back? Those were the ships which Hawkins asked for, and for a time at least he had some sort of favourable promise. He worked hard at his preparations, riding to and fro between Plymouth, where he was fitting out, and London, where he had to be vigilant against a change of the royal mind. Guerau de Spes sent a spy to Plymouth, who reported that there were twelve ships and 1,500 men, and that they were going to plant a colony in the Straits of Magellan or Florida or New Spain. We may assume that the spy was spotted and that Plymouth was giving him something worth while to report.

Already there had been some objection in the Council, perhaps supported by Cecil, to letting Hawkins take a substantial force so far away during a time of danger at home. These Plymouth ships of his were a real fighting squadron and not a phantom of the tate papers, as the scantiness of English evidence about them might imply. They had a strategic function, and it was questionable to send them on a distant cruise unless the times were fair; for, just as the Queen's ships in the Medway had to be ready to turn out in defence against a stroke from the Netherlands, so Hawkins's western squadron was relied upon to parry a thrust from Spain or Catholic France. This is the first appearance of a western squadron in the plan of national defence. It marks also a stage in the development of Plymouth as a naval port. There are indications that shipping was already using the Hamoaze anchorage, more commodious than that close to Plymouth.

John Hawkins had only just formed this squadron during the exigencies of 1569, and may not yet have realized its permanent obligation. The Queen and her ministers were quite clear about it and had the advantage of using the force without paying for it. It was paid for primarily out of the winnings of the Plymouth privateers, mostly owned by the Hawkinses, in the war of religion which continued to be waged in the Channel. We have no English record of its composition; but a Spanish state paper of the next year, 1571, shows that it had then grown to sixteen ships, of which it specifies the names, tonnage, guns, and numbers of men required for service:[1]

[1] Add. MSS., 26056B, f. 251, a transcript made by Froude at Simancas.

Name	Tons	Men	Guns
Christopher	500	250	50
Saviour	500	250	50
New Bark	300	150	40
James	350	175	40
Edward	250	125	30
William	180	90	25
Unicorn	180	90	25
Paul	160	80	25
Great John	150	75	20
Angel	140	70	20
Swallow	120	60	20
Antelope	100	50	15
Pasco	80	40	12
Judith	60	30	12
Little John	60	30	12
Cleare	40	20	10
	3,170	1,585	406

The first two in the above list were larger vessels than private Englishmen were yet building, and were very likely foreign merchantmen captured in the Channel wars. We have English evidence that the *New Bark* was a Hawkins ship. The *William*, *Paul* and *John* were characteristic Hawkins names. The *Angel* may have been named in memory of her little predecessor lost at San Juan de Ulua. The *Swallow* was the ship of that name which John Hawkins used in his first slaving expedition. The *Judith* we know. The *Pasco* was taken to Nombre de Dios by Drake in 1572. Altogether we have sufficient independent corroboration to inspire confidence in the list of ships. The numbers of guns look like approximations; they are too nicely rounded to be exactly true. The numbers of men represent a scale which Hawkins believed to be correct for fighting service in home waters, that is to say, one man to two tons.[1] It is not necessary to believe that the men were on board in these numbers except during mobilization for imminent action. Neither need we suppose that all the ships were all the time lying in Plymouth. They would naturally be

[1] Hawkins's scale will appear again, see p. 280.

sent out to earn their keep, although within range of a fairly quick recall, cruising most likely in the western Channel.

These, or some of them, were the ships with which Hawkins intended to attack the plate fleets in 1570. He would easily have overcome the armed escort of from two to four fighting galleons, and would have captured the cargo carriers, if he had met them in favourable weather and far from a harbour of refuge. They were big ifs, as many another treasure hunter was to find, and on the great ocean the primary difficulty was to fall in with the *flotas* at all. In fact no one ever did capture a plate fleet for over half a century from this date. It was not until 1628 that the Dutch admiral Piet Hein took the entire year's silver output on the northern coast of Cuba. Hawkins was not allowed the chance. At the beginning of August the government told him that he must not leave the English coast. It was a test of his character as a public servant. There were some in those days who would have retorted angrily and impugned the motives of the Queen's advisers. There were some who would possibly have disobeyed and sailed without leave. Hawkins obeyed, and made no grumble that is on record. Years afterwards, in listing some of his financial claims on the government, he mentioned fitting out the ships and disclaimed any desire for reimbursement.

What had stopped him was the fear of a snap invasion. Early in 1570 the Regent Moray in Scotland was murdered. He had kept Scotland to the English alliance for the sake of religion, and his death encouraged Mary's partisans and brought on a civil war. In France the Huguenots made their peace with the Valois government before midsummer, and Charles IX (or rather, his mother) thought of turning a united France to intervention on behalf of Mary Stuart. In February, Pope Pius V excommunicated Elizabeth, and a copy of his bull was posted in London in May. It was a spur to Catholic resistance, inaugurating a fresh effort after the fiasco of the northern rising. It was very unwelcome to Philip II, who had already decided not to go to war with England in his own quarrel and now found himself cast as the leading crusader in the Pope's. He declined to publish the bull and continued to hope that the commercial quarrel with England might be patched up. Elizabeth was by no means sure that this was Philip's attitude. She and her Council knew that they had scored off him and feared a counterstroke. More than thirty years before, his father Charles V had seemed for a moment about to ally himself to the French in order to carry out a bull of excommunication against Henry VIII. Now it appeared that such a combination might really be effective. That summer Alva gathered a great collection of Flemish vessels in the Netherlands. The declared purpose was to escort a new Austrian bride for Philip down Channel to Spain. Ninety sail were engaged, with numerous nobles, knights and soldiers. The English took precautions against a landing on their southern coast. In July all shipping was stayed and held at the Queen's disposition. In August Hawkins was told that he could be no exception. The Lord Admiral took the sea in person with all the Queen's ships, and attended with courtesy and vigilance as the royal procession sailed down Channel. All passed off peacefully, and everyone was allowed to stand down; but it was then too late to attack the plate fleets.

It will be recalled that twenty-nine Englishmen and two Frenchmen from San Juan de Ulua, including the hostages, were sent from Mexico to Spain in 1569. They arrived towards the end of the year and were cast into a cold and insanitary dungeon in Seville, where they lay unprovided with food or clothing. Four died, and six more were said to be at the point of death when they wrote a letter to Sir William Cecil in February 1570. The letter, signed by George Fitzwilliam and two others, was carried to England by Hugh Tipton, the English merchant residing in Seville whom we have already seen acting as Hawkins's agent. The letter to Cecil is preserved. It was most likely accompanied by another to John Hawkins, but in any case Tipton would have seen Hawkins and told him all particulars. Tipton had already saved the lives of the survivors by pleading their case to the Spanish authorities, whom he shamed into providing food, pending which he provided it himself.

Hawkins lost no time. Before February was out he sought an interview with the Spanish ambassador and asked him to intercede for the release of the prisoners. There was a good enough case for it, since they were not prisoners of honourable war. Don Guerau reported the matter, but was not sympathetic. Hawkins probably hoped to achieve all by his plate-fleet stroke, which would have given him the wherewithal to extort everybody's liberation. Not until the hope had faded did he turn to Don Guerau again. In August, 1570, just after his sailing had been interdicted, he made another visit to the Spaniard and again pleaded for his comrades, at the same time expressing discontent and uttering seditious words about the English government. Don Guerau knew that Hawkins had been all the summer preparing some blow against Spain, and could not have regarded him *a priori* as a friend. But Hawkins had chosen the occasion well. He had just suffered a heavy disappointment, such as would have made the undisciplined sort of man feel seditious. Don Guerau was devoid of the higher intelligence which comprises the imagination to admit that some men act from unselfish motives. It seemed natural to him that in the circumstances Hawkins should be disloyal. He had persuaded himself that all the people of England were, except the little group round Cecil. So he believed the mutinous professions and wrote to Alva that here was a man who might be useful, and that the liberation of a few obscure prisoners might be a cheap price for his adherence.[1] Again nothing came of it, except perhaps this, that late in 1570 or early in the next year George Fitzwilliam was set free and came home to England. His good fortune may not have been due to Don Guerau at all. He was a kinsman of Jane Dormer, the English wife of the Duke of Feria. Feria had been with Philip in England and was still in his counsels. Undoubtedly the connection gave Fitzwilliam a pull in Spain, and it probably accounted for his liberation. None of the others seemed to have a chance of getting out.

Guerau de Spes thought the adhesion of a notable sea-captain worth having. The failure of the Rising of the North had not put an end to the conspiracy against Elizabeth and Cecil, the reason being that the rising was so feeble and ill managed that most of the conspirators took no part in it. Throughout 1570, with some

[1] Froude, *Elizabeth*, (Everyman edn.) III, p. 312.

encouragement from the Pope's bull, they were revolving their plan in half-hearted fashion but taking no steps to put it into execution. The elements were, a Catholic rising aided by a Spanish invasion, the release of Mary Stuart, and the overthrow of the Queen. The personnel comprised Mary, her ambassador the Bishop of Ross, Guerau de Spes, and a dozen English nobles more or less implicated, few or none ready to venture their lives, most of them merely indulging in a little verbal discontent. They looked to the Duke of Norfolk to take the lead, and he was very loath to do anything dangerous. He wished the Cecil regime to be ended, but hoped that someone else would do it. In spite of his reluctance, his position made him the leader, for the others would do nothing without him. Cecil was aware of the movement, and knew that external circumstances might suddenly make it dangerous. He could not convince the Queen of the need to lock up and isolate both Norfolk and Mary Stuart. The Queen always wished well to Mary and hoped that she would reciprocate. At the beginning of 1572 Elizabeth advanced Cecil to the office of Lord Treasurer, having already created him Lord Burghley, under which title he will henceforward be referred to.

The bull of excommunication had had no apparent effect, and Pius V was indisposed to accept failure. At this juncture he sent to England an agent of his own, Roberto Ridolfi, a Florentine banker. Ridolfi had been in England before and now reappeared in pursuit, as it seemed, of legitimate financial business arising from the arrests of trade. His true mission was not at once penetrated by Burghley, to whom he came from Paris with a recommendation from Francis Walsingham, the most anti-papal Englishman of the time. Ridolfi's task was to put life into the conspiracy and bring it into action. He was a persuasive but imprudent talker, a maker of large promises, and an unreasoning optimist. He made Norfolk promise to take the field as soon as Alva's troops should land. He made Mary promise to marry Norfolk and share the throne with him. He made Don Guerau promise Spanish aid to everyone, and himself told the Don that Mary's marriage should be at the King's disposition. Then he went off to Brussels to arrange for the Spanish aid and found that

Alva would not give it unless he first had news that Elizabeth was dead. Her assassination was therefore added to the programme, to the disquiet of Norfolk, who had a conscience. The feeble duke, in fact, had been led on from an original plan to force on the Queen a change of ministry and policy, to a plot to kill her and deliver England to foreign domination; and he was intelligent enough to perceive it. Most of his confederates must have shared his reluctance, leaving only the foreigners, Mary, Ross, and de Spes, really keen on the undertaking.

Guerau de Spes, who knew that Alva belittled the plot and despised the plotters, had in the meantime been pressing his views on Philip II direct. It was here that John Hawkins played a decisive part and did a service for which it was not possible to give him public credit. Burghley knew from his observation of various parties, Norfolk, de Spes, the Bishop of Ross and others, that something dangerous was going on, but he lacked the proof on which he could urge action on the Queen in face of hostile critics in the Council. Whether Burghley commissioned Hawkins to do what has now to be recorded, or whether Hawkins did it of his own motion and at the same time notified the minister of what he was doing, there is not evidence to decide. The established facts are that in March, 1571, Hawkins went to the Spanish ambassador and offered the services of his fleet at Plymouth for the furtherance of Spanish designs. The offer, transmitted to Madrid, was favourably received, together with Hawkins's profession of Catholicism. Fitzwilliam had by this time come home and may have brought important news by reason of his contact with the Duke of Feria.[1] The next move was that in April Fitzwilliam went back to Madrid as Hawkins's representative and in that character actually had an interview with Philip II. He asked for the release of the prisoners and offered the services of John Hawkins in the enthronement of Mary Stuart and the restoration of the Catholic religion. It was a queer turn of fortune whereby a

[1] The status and connections of George Fitzwilliam in Spain are the key to more than one passage in the career of John Hawkins, and unfortunately we know little about them. It is a matter upon which the student should be vigilant for new evidence.

man who had lain starving and facing death in the King's jail should in a few months discuss secret business with the King himself. Ridolfi was still in Brussels, and Philip did not yet know what arrangements had been made. He told Fitzwilliam that he would not release the prisoners at that stage and also demanded that Hawkins must produce a guarantee of his integrity from the Queen of Scots. The Duke of Feria gave Fitzwilliam a letter for Mary Stuart, written in invisible ink[1] and providing a general outline of the plot. Hawkins reported all this to Burghley on Fitzwilliam's return. Writing fluids which gave a script invisible until the paper was heated were well known, and Feria's procedure sounds rather childish, especially when we note that he was providing an introduction of Fitzwilliam to Mary in order that Mary might recommend Fitzwilliam's master to the King of Spain.

Guerau de Spes knew very well that no one was allowed to see the Queen of Scots without Burghley's permission. How then was Fitzwilliam to deliver the Feria letter to Mary, and obtain from her the testimonial for Hawkins, without arousing the Spaniard's suspicions? Hawkins had taken the measure of Don Guerau. With Burghley's consent he went to him and avowed that Burghley knew about the late visit of Fitzwilliam to Spain, but thought it concerned only the release of the English prisoners. Burghley, said Hawkins, did not connect it with any treasonable plot, and would forward Fitzwilliam to Mary on the same understanding, that he was working only for the release of his comrades. It was a thin explanation, but the Hawkins manner, after the testimony of that other choleric Spaniard Castellanos, was no doubt at its best, and Don Guerau was a gull who would swallow the most ancient piece of fish. He swallowed this one, and wrote to the King that Hawkins was dealing honestly and that Fitzwilliam was coming again to Madrid to complete the arrangements.

Fitzwilliam had little difficulty with the Queen of Scots. She always regarded imprisonment as worse than death, and never boggled at risks when there was a chance of getting Elizabeth's

[1] 'In a blank paper which was not to be read before it came to the fire.'

enemies to move. She accepted the good faith of this man who brought her a letter from the King's minister and a ring from the King himself. She at once vouched for the good faith of John Hawkins, whom she may scarcely have heard of until that moment. She embodied this in a letter to Philip which she entrusted to Fitzwilliam, together with a present for the Duchess of Feria. The letter was read by Burghley,[1] but it did not tell him what he wanted to know. What he wanted was evidence to justify the arrest of the Duke of Norfolk, who was in the position to start a revolution at any moment. He also wanted detailed evidence of Spanish military designs in order to take the proper steps against them. But Mary wrote only in general terms. The military details were the King's affair, and she would naturally not have mentioned the Norfolk marriage project to Philip, since she knew that he had other views for her future.

When Fitzwilliam reached Madrid for the second time, in July, Ridolfi had arrived and the plot had taken final shape: invasion of England by Alva from the Netherlands; invasion from Spain by the Duke of Medina Celi; rebellion led by Norfolk; attempt on Elizabeth's life: this last was to be the signal for all else and was to take place in September or October, when the Queen customarily travelled through the country and her person was more accessible than when the court was stationary in London. Philip, called the prudent king, had agreed to it all, despite the obvious truth that it was much more of a gamble than most conspiracies. Alva judged it more coolly. He did not believe it had a chance, and for that reason fixed a starting condition, the assassination, which he did not expect the irresolute English plotters to carry out. If they did not, he was absolved of any obligation to proceed.

However, in Spain they were keen for it, and Philip welcomed Hawkins as the man who could solve the naval difficulties. The Queen's ships in the Medway faced Alva, and Hawkins's squadron at Plymouth looked towards Spain. It was agreed that

---

[1] 'Fitzwilliam is returned and hath letters from the Queen of Scots to the King of Spain, which are enclosed with others in a parcel directed to your Lordship'—Hawkins to Burghley, June 7, 1571.

when the time came Hawkins should sail eastwards from Plymouth, leaving the Channel open, and should take his fleet to the Netherlands, there to join Alva's forces and convoy them across the narrow seas; while Medina Celi from Spain might land unopposed in the west. Then at length Hawkins won the stake for which he had played from the outset. For Philip ratified the bargain by releasing the prisoners at Seville. They were given money and sent as passengers to England. There had been thirty-one of them, and we know that four had died at an early stage, while others were very ill. Perhaps two dozen were set free, perhaps not so many. One of them was Anthony Goddard, who lived many years in Plymouth thereafter. Some writers of the past have implied that Hawkins acted discreditably in cheating the poor King so. There must be few in our time who will agree.

For, let there be no mistake, Hawkins was cheating the King from the very first word. The professions of loyalty to Mary Stuart, of love for Catholicism, of discontent with the Cecil regime, and the offer to desert in face of the invader, were all made with the cognizance of the Queen and her minister. Philip's ambassador, a man sent to maintain honourable communication between sovereigns, employed himself in inciting treason and murder. The prospective victims can hardly be blamed for seeking to detect such activities, and are entitled to praise for the very moderate reparation which they afterwards exacted.

Hawkins had got his men back, or as many of them as he knew to be in Spain. He evidently did not know that Barrett and Hortop and a few more had arrived subsequently from Mexico, for nothing was said about them. To keep up appearances he had to accept some other conditions. The King left it to the Duke of Feria to complete the negotiation, and he and Fitzwilliam signed the final agreement. By this the King granted John Hawkins a patent of Spanish nobility and a pardon for his offences in the Indies, together with a promise to pay for the upkeep of sixteen ships and 1,600 men for the two months, September and October, which the operations might be expected to cover. John Hawkins thus stood as what he had often claimed to be, heart and soul the servant of the King of Spain; not, as in the old days, of a King of Spain who was the friend and ally of his own mistress, but of a King who now sought her overthrow and death. The Catholic King, the fanatical Duke of Feria, and his no less fanatical English Duchess, honestly could not see that the murder of his Queen and subjugation of his country could be any matter of disquiet to an English sea officer. To them it appeared natural that if his own interests were suitably advanced he should serve in forwarding their designs. And so they believed quite easily in what seems preposterous to us of a different age and tradition.

George Fitzwilliam is an enigma. He was accepted in this Feria set as, we may almost say, a familiar friend; and through them was able to approach the King with something more than the freedom accorded to an English ambassador. He got right under Philip's guard, with results we have seen. We should like to know his antecedents, but they are unknown before his appearance as a gentleman adventurer of the second Hawkins expedition. One possibility may occur to some, namely, that he really was a genuine counter-revolutionary, doing his utmost for the overthrow of the new England and the restoration of the old; and that Hawkins made him a tool and a dupe as he did de Feria and de Spes. The present writer thinks this untenable. Hawkins liked and trusted the man long before these contingencies arose. It is probable that he was in Hawkins's service some time before we hear of him in September 1567, for he was then sufficiently a confidential servant to carry dispatches between his master and the government. No, there can be no doubt that Hawkins and Fitzwilliam were at one. We can say of Fitzwilliam that he had magnificent nerve and capacity, worthy of the high traditions of the English secret service. He left Madrid for the last time with a difficult task accomplished, and with friendly personal letters from the Duke of Feria and his half-English son to John Hawkins. The Duke died shortly afterwards.

Hawkins had detected the plan of the Spanish invasion, and had placed himself in the position to frustrate it with certainty; since both the moves, from Spain and the Netherlands, depended upon the action that he should take. As soon as Fitzwilliam reached Plymouth, Hawkins sent him on to London with the following letter to Burghley:

My very good Lord,

It may please your honour to be advertised that Fitzwilliams is returned from the court of Spain, where his message was acceptably received, both by the King himself, the Duke of Feria, and others of his privy council. His despatch and answer was with great expedition and with great countenance and favour of the King.

The articles [of agreement just signed in Spain] are sent to the ambassador [Guerau de Spes], with order also for the money to be paid to me by him for the enterprise to proceed with all diligence.

The pretence is that my power should join with the Duke of Alva's power which he doth shortly provide in Flanders, as well as with the power which cometh with the Duke of Medina out of Spain, and so all together to invade this realm and set up the Queen of Scots.

They have practised with us for the burning of Her Majesty's ships, wherefore there should be some good care had of them, but not as it may appear that anything is discovered, as your lordship's consideration can well provide.

The King hath sent a ruby of good price to the Queen of Scots, with letters also, which in my judgment were good to be delivered. The letters be of no importance, but his message by word is to comfort her and say that he hath now none other care than to place her in her own. It were good also that the ambassador did make request unto your lordship that Fitzwilliams may have access to the Queen of Scots, to render thanks for the delivery of our prisoners, which are now at liberty; it will be a very good colour for your lordship to confer with him [Fitzwilliams] more largely.

I have sent your lordship the copy of my pardon from the King of Spain in the very order and manner I have it. Also the Duke of Medina and the Duke of Alva have every of them one of the same pardons, more amplified, to present unto me (although this be large enough), with very great titles and honours from the King, from which God deliver me.

I send your lordship also the copy of my letter from the Duke of Feria in the very manner as it was written, with his wife and son's hand in the end.

Their practices be very mischievous, and they be never idle, but God, I hope, will confound them and turn their devices upon their own necks.

I will put my business in some order and give mine attendance upon Her Majesty, to do her that service that by your lordship shall be thought most convenient in this case.

I am not tedious with your lordship because Fitzwilliams cometh himself, and I mind not to be long after him, and thus I trouble your good lordship no further.

From Plymouth, the 4th day of September, 1571,

Your good lordship's most faithfully to my power,

JOHN HAWKYNS.

Burghley now knew what he wanted to know about the Spanish plans, and Hawkins would no doubt have been glad to see them put in operation in order that he might settle some part of the score for San Juan de Ulua. But the invasion was not proceeded with, because King Philip must soon afterwards have received the news that the Duke of Norfolk was in the Tower. It was during the second mission of Fitzwilliam to Spain that Burghley at length solved the domestic side of the problem by piecing together the evidence of Norfolk's guilt, and three days after Hawkins wrote his letter the Duke was arrested and sent to the Tower. At the same time the Bishop of Ross was told that he could no longer count on immunity as Mary Stuart's ambassador. In fear for his neck he confessed everything, sealing Norfolk's fate and providing deadly material against his own mistress if Elizabeth had cared to use it. Norfolk's minor fellow-conspirators were forgiven by the Queen, without any semblance of public disgrace. The Duke himself was executed next year, the only member of the great conspiracy to pay with his life. It was a mild winding-up, but it was decisive. For the arrest of the Duke meant that there would be no insurrection, no release of Mary Stuart or assassination of Elizabeth. Those were the conditions for Spanish action, which therefore did not take place. The King and Alva dropped the whole undertaking. One of them certainly was glad to do so.

Hawkins would no doubt have taken Philip's money with an easy mind, as the King had taken his; but the evidence is that he did not receive it. As the letter to Burghley indicates, it was to have been paid to him by Guerau de Spes. But almost as soon as that letter was written it began to grow evident that the plan was off, and on that account alone it may be inferred that the ambassador did not pay. In the early part of the next year, 1572, we have letters passing between Alva and de Spes which discuss a prospective payment to Hawkins in connection with future plans, and these imply that no payment had already been made. Again, in a recapitulation of the whole transaction, written by Hawkins, it is stated that the King gave money to the released prisoners, but there is no mention of payment to Hawkins himself. These circumstances are elaborated because Froude categorically stated that the King paid Hawkins from forty to fifty thousand pounds. He presumably had the figure from one of his own transcripts of documents in the Simancas archives, which speaks of a proposed payment of 45,000 ducats, a sum equivalent to about £11,000 in English money. If Hawkins bargained for this, he was allowing himself something for San Juan de Ulua, since the wages and victuals of 1,600 men for two months would have cost about £3,500 at the most. But Hawkins, knowing what he really meant to do, knew also that there was very little chance of touching the money, and must have regarded the negotiation as window-dressing. His reward would be to see his imprisoned comrades home and, as he hoped, to see Spanish invaders under his guns.

Although the King and the Duke of Alva gave up the invasion plan, they did so because they knew that without Norfolk the English plotters would not move, and not because they had any suspicion that their own intentions were known to the English government. Philip did not know that he had been taken in, and probably never knew. Guerau de Spes was so incensed against Burghley and so morbidly irritated by his English environment that he was all for going on with the invasion even though the English plot had failed. In October, and again in November, 1571, he wrote to the King and urged a decision for action, saying that Hawkins had his fleet ready and was eager to do his part. In December he reported that Fitzwilliam was prepared to set out for Spain again in order to make final arrangements. Philip was no longer prepared to receive him, which must have indicated to Burghley that an early invasion was not contemplated. It was mortifying to Don Guerau, who claimed to have done signal service in securing the adherence of Hawkins; but the unhappy ambassador was now to be released from a country which he hated. In mid-December the Privy Council summoned him to an interview and confronted him with the evidence implicating him in the Ridolfi Plot; and then commanded him to leave the country forthwith. It was a sore blow to one who considered himself the advanced guard of conquest. He still clung to a hope, for he had already bargained with two ruffians to creep into Burghley's garden and shoot him through his study window. But the luck continued foul. Ministers, then as now, made provision against such contingencies, and the two were arrested before they had done any harm. Guerau de Spes, who had lingered at Canterbury on pretence of illness, had then no option but to make for Dover and the Netherlands.

Hawkins, on Burghley's instructions, attended him to the coast. He and Fitzwilliam were continuously with their dupe for the last five weeks. Don Guerau continued to talk of the invasion and of Hawkins's share in it, and continued to press it upon Alva after reaching Brussels. The two cronies parted on the English shore in January, 1572, and Hawkins gave the Spaniard a cipher by means of which they might continue to communicate. Seldom can there have been such an embassage as that of Don Guerau de Spes.

Throughout these events the war in the Channel continued, and after 1569 the Dutch superseded the Huguenots as the most formidable group of privateers. Their leaders were the Count de la Marck and the Seigneur de Lumbres, operating from Dover and the Solent respectively. They captured all Catholic shipping that came in their way, including that of their own countrymen, the Catholics who were still in the majority in several of the Netherland provinces. This had a 'softening' effect on the Spanish position and prepared many hitherto acquiescent Flemings to turn against the king who was unable to defend them. Alva's conduct worked to the same end. The loss of the Genoese money had compelled him to impose crushing taxes for the support of his army; and economic oppression, falling on all alike, seemed a poor reward to the Catholics for their loyalty to the King. In short, the Netherlands were ready for revolt in 1572 as they had not been when Orange had tried to rouse them four years earlier. Orange himself expected the revolt to be an affair of armies under the command of himself and his brothers. The Sea Beggars were helping to finance the cause, but he seems at this stage to have expected nothing more from them.

The Sea Beggars played nevertheless the decisive part; and whether it was premeditated or incidental is still in doubt. By the opening of the year Burghley knew how he stood with Spain, which would invade England if the chance seemed good, but was for the present holding off until the good chance should arise. His answer was to draw England nearer to France, with talk of marriage between Elizabeth and a Valois, and of a military alliance. The French were difficult, because they also were suffering by the doings in the Channel, and knew that England abetted the privateers by opening her ports and markets. Elizabeth found herself expected to give proof of sincerity, and proceeded to do so.

Early in March, 1572, she issued a commission to John Hawkins and George Winter, Clerk of the Queen's Ships and brother of the more prominent William Winter. They were to go to the coasts of Kent, Sussex, Hampshire and the Isle of Wight and to order all the privateers to quit the harbours of England. They were also to command the Queen's subjects not to supply the rovers with food or munitions, nor to buy anything from them, nor to serve in their ships. The Court de la Marck, whose base was at Dover, was specifically mentioned and was to be 'presently commanded to depart'. These measures, it may be seen, were directed principally against the Dutch, and there was no parallel action for Plymouth and the Western Channel, where the Huguenots worked, and where Hawkins would have had the duty of warning himself not to connive at their doings. Coligny was at that moment reconciled to the Valois court, and his Rochellers were probably sparing Frenchmen although they were still active against Spaniards.

Hawkins and Winter carried out their instructions. At some sacrifice to English maritime interests they took action that was beneficial to France and could plausibly appear as a gesture of reconciliation to Spain. It was the more effective in that character since Hawkins was believed by the Spanish government to be anxious to do them a service. La Marck duly sailed from Dover, and his followers withdrew in his company. Their compliance is noteworthy, since Hawkins had no force at his disposal. He seems to have used no shipping, and his expenses amounted to only £100. La Marck had been in London and was well known in governing circles. Hawkins probably knew him personally, and we can hardly doubt that the two men conferred on future plans when the warning-off took place at Dover. La Marck was joined by de Lumbres and the Solent force, and all sailed for the Dutch coast. There on April 1st, 1572, they captured the port of Brille and decided to make it their base and headquarters. Shortly afterwards they took Flushing, the best harbour on the coast, and held it in permanence.

Historians have debated whether these moves were unpremeditated or part of a concerted plan consciously set in motion by Burghley when he sent Hawkins to Dover. There is no evidence, and it is not a matter of certainty but of the better probability. To the present writer the probability seems to lie with the assumption that Burghley was far-sighted rather than short-sighted; in other words, that he calculated what would happen when the Sea Beggars should be deprived of their English base. If he did not realize it himself, Hawkins would have told him that a cruising fleet must have a port for victualling and refitting; and, La Rochelle being too distant for their purposes, where else were they to get one but upon their own coast? Is it too much to imagine that La Marck may have been in collaboration with the English and may have had sound information of the possibilities at Brille? The further consequences may indeed have been a surprise to everyone, for the revolution spread like a fire all up the Dutch coast, and town after town declared for freedom and prepared for a desperate fight. It suited England's interest admirably, since Alva, with half-a-dozen sieges on his books, would obviously have nothing to spare for an invasion for some time to come.

The Protestant cause had been doing great things in France since the third civil war had ended in 1570. Coligny went to court, was respected by the young Charles IX, and tolerated by Catherine the queen-mother. Coligny worked in accord with William of Orange and his brother, Louis of Nassau, who was well known in La Rochelle and had fought hard at Moncontour. By the summer of 1572 a plan of campaign was matured for the expulsion of Spain from the Netherlands. The Dutch provinces were already rising, William of Orange was to invade from Germany, Louis of Nassau from France, aided by all the money and men the Huguenots could raise for them. The war indeed was to be an effort of all France, whose Protestants and Catholics were to end their quarrel and fight together against Spain. Coligny, as the ablest man, indeed the greatest man, in France, took the lead. Catherine de Medici, small and mean, grew troubled. She had turned to Coligny to deliver her from the pressure of the Duke of Guise and the ultra-Catholics. Now she began to think of turning back again.

In England also as the summer advanced the outlook grew alarming. The Spaniards entangled in an endless civil war might be regarded with equanimity. The Spaniards thrown right out of the Netherlands would be replaced by the French, by no means to the interest of England. Although France was for the moment friendly she was the age-long enemy, and her possession of the Netherlands would give her a grip upon England, both economic and strategic, a greater danger than Spain half-paralysed by Protestant sea power. Elizabeth sent over Sir Humphrey Gilbert with numerous levies. Ostensibly they were volunteers fighting for the Dutch against the Spaniards without countenance from the Queen. Secretly Gilbert had her orders to consolidate in the seaports and at all costs keep the French away from the coast. The volunteer effort was considerable. John Hawkins was preparing to lead a contingent, but was stopped by the Council, and afterwards was reported to be at Plymouth preparing a west-country force for the same purpose.[1]

Louis of Nassau had entered southern Belgium and seized Mons, and William of Orange had come over the south-eastern frontier with German mercenaries, when in August all was thrown into confusion by the massacre of St. Bartholomew. Catherine de Medici commissioned the Guise faction to kill Coligny and the Huguenot leaders, an action which the Catholic populace in Paris and the provinces extended to a general massacre of Protestants. At once the Orange campaign in the Netherlands ceased; and one brother surrendered at Mons, while the other retreated. The Dutch of the coast cities still held out, but with little hope of final success. England was staggered for a moment by the prospect of Catholic France uniting with Spain to enforce the bull of 1570 and overthrow Elizabeth. But soon it was seen that there was little chance of such a combination; for Catherine had not allowed the Guises to murder Coligny in order to be dominated by the murderers. Her object was a tranquillity incompatible with foreign adventures. Meanwhile the Huguenots were in a desperate case, many thousands of them killed, and their enemies resolved to make an end of all. La Rochelle and some inland fortresses saved them, but mainly La Rochelle. Early in 1573 the Duke of Anjou besieged the place with powerful forces.

As four years earlier, England organized a relief expedition, but this time it was not led by John Hawkins. Valois protests were so sharp, and the whole situation so critical, that the Queen had to disguise her aid. She would lend only second-class artillery—iron guns but not bronze—and she would not allow her first-class sea captain to appear in the business. The Hawkinses had a good deal to do with equipping the force, and some good officers of the second rank sailed with it. Henry Champernowne and the

---

[1] Spanish report of Sept. 16, 1572. Froude citing documents at Simancas, says that John Hawkins went on a cruise against the plate fleets. The *Calendar of Spanish State Papers* subsequently printed the sense of most of these documents, but contains no mention of the expedition. Neither does any English evidence.

Huguenot Comte de Montgomery were in command. They reached La Rochelle in April, and were beaten by the chains and batteries with which Anjou had sealed the harbour mouth. After some minor actions the force withdrew. It seemed that La Rochelle was left to its fate. It was saved by the departure of Anjou in May on his election to the crown of Poland, an event that altered the balance of French politics and allowed the moderates to patch up a peace.

Thus in 1573 the situation grew brighter for England. The Spaniards in the Netherlands were fully occupied with some dreadful sieges which cost the lives of a large proportion of their troops. The French were relapsing again into a state of compromise, yielding no prospect of strong external action. From the beginning of the year the Queen and Burghley thought it feasible to restore good relations with Spain. Hawkins's warning-off of the Sea Beggars in '72 had been window-dressing, and the rovers were soon rampant again throughout the Channel. In February, 1573, the government sent out William Holstocke, Comptroller of the Navy, with two heavily armed vessels. He captured the privateers, ships, men and booty, and in a few weeks made the Channel highway safer than it had been for years. Then the Queen turned to negotiations for ending the Spanish and Netherland arrests of trade. She had the higher hand in the matter, for she had suffered little while Philip had lost much. Philip was disposed to peace. The Netherland situation demanded that his shipping should pass freely through the Channel. It could do so only if he conquered England or if he made peace with her. He confessed himself unable to do the first, and so tried the second. By mutual agreement the arrests were declared at an end in April, 1573. Commissioners then met to assess claims and damages, and the final adjustment was made by the Convention of Bristol in 1574. For a brief period both governments pursued the path of peace, if not of good will.

III

PLYMOUTH AND THE OCEAN

In the period of the papal bull and the Ridolfi Plot, the Hawkins brothers were not solely concerned with the defence of England and the Channel blockade. They were also engaged in equipping tropical expeditions for trade and reprisal, and even in a plan for the discovery of the unknown southern continent. They worked in association with many others, a circle of progressive men who had ideas on the future of England as a world power and who staked their own fortunes on that future. The conception of a party, a solid connection of brains, courage and capital, a 'movement', to use the phraseology of our day, emerges with increasing clearness from the researches of the past half-century. In the 1890's, when Sir Julian Corbett gave his powerful impetus to such studies, the interpretation was rather in terms of individuals, isolated and unrelated: Drake did this, Hawkins that, Frobisher the other, with consequences which, somewhat astonishingly, added up to the foundation of the British Empire, accounted for as an unintended by-product of contempt for Spain and hatred of the Pope. Now, the emphasis is upon a movement with a large number of prime movers, upon efforts not rival but mutually assistant, upon concerted pressure by a body of striving men. By way of illustrating the argument we may briefly review some of the more prominent members of the movement and the connections that linked them.

John Hawkins was allied to the regular Navy as the son-in-law of Benjamin Gonson, its Treasurer. Two other members of the Navy Board were William and George Winter; and all of them invested in Guinea voyages and West Indian voyages. After 1569 we find the Winters acting with the Hawkinses in these ventures, and the two families (it may be inferred) jointly employing Drake until with his happy return in 1573 he became of position to stand on his own feet. The Winters were of Bristol origin, but long settled in official life in London. John Hawkins was a member for Plymouth in the Parliament of 1571, and his fellow-burgess was Sir Humphrey Gilbert. Hawkins's part is unrecorded, but we may suppose that he supported the Queen's ministers, who were having an awkward time with the religious enthusiasts; and while the Commons were sitting Hawkins was engaged with Burghley on the very secret business of the Ridolfi Plot and the bamboozling of Guerau de Spes. Richard Grenville (knighted in 1577) had a plan to discover and possess the unknown continent supposed to lie west of the Straits of Magellan. He formed a strong syndicate which included the county magnates and William Hawkins. He got some countenance from the Queen, conditional on his assisting the Irish plantation proposed by the Earl of Essex. John Hawkins, by his own account, 'adventured with' Essex, and Drake also entered the earl's service, where he met Thomas Doughty, his false friend of the voyage of circumnavigation. John Oxenham was one of Drake's company in 1572–3, and led his own venture to the Isthmus, and across it, in 1576. He knew about Grenville's plans, and Drake was privy to his, which were important. William Hawkins and Grenville were more than co-members of an exploring syndicate, they were joint owners of a ship named the *Castle of Comfort*, which appears in the records of the Admiralty Court more often than any other of the time. And so one might go on, expanding the connection to Ralegh, half-brother of Gilbert and firm friend of Grenville; Frobisher, a Yorkshireman with strong Cornish affiliations; Sir Francis Walsingham, who supported all of them and sought to forge them into one weapon to smite the King of Spain; and Burghley himself, who knew all and understood all far better than Walsingham, who regulated the movement of these active, thrusting men, and related it so ably to national policy and the international situation that the reign of his mistress, precarious at the outset, became the outstanding success of her age.

Plymouth and London were the bases of most of this enterprise, Plymouth for the commanders, the mariners, the fitting-out, and the management, London for the state support, the artillery and powder, the stocks of trade goods, and some of the finance. Why it should have been Plymouth instead of some other Channel port, Southampton or Dartmouth, or even Poole, is a question worth considering. The answer lies not in natural circumstances, as the geographers would probably have it, but in personal quality, the ability of the Hawkinses. The Hawkinses made sixteenth-century Plymouth. They made it an ocean port, a naval base, a privateers' mart, the western bastion of England's defences. If they had chanced to be Dartmouth men they might have made Dartmouth all that, for Dartmouth had natural advantages as good as Plymouth's. Geography had for some purposes given Southampton a better position than either, but its merchants and captains had fallen so sleepy in the later Tudor period that we hear little of them; yet in the previous century Southampton had been the second port in all the realm, second only to London. Natural science alone does not explain human affairs. Personality counts for much.

The ocean trade inaugurated by old William Hawkins under Henry VIII was contemporary with the advance of Plymouth as evidenced by its self-assertion against Saltash. In that time there was trade with Brazil, Guinea, Newfoundland and the Canaries, and buying and selling of dyewoods and ivory, salted cod, sugar and wines. Then came the privateering, begun by old William in the 1540's and continued by his sons through the century, pouring rich goods into Plymouth and stimulating the town and its hinterland to supply the victuals and drink, the clothes and the weapons, and all the chandlery for the upkeep of ships that were built from the forest and the forge and handled by stick and string. To the same end worked the ocean voyages of the 60's, and their successors, as will be shown, of the 70's, collecting men, multiplying wants, bringing home lavishly the means to pay for them. The Channel war of the 70's, with its plunder of England's would-be invaders, can be measured as an economic stimulant by the fact that it financed Hawkins's Plymouth squadron for the national defence, a force additional to the Queen's Navy and doing part of the Navy's work. Contemporary were Drake's Caribbean voyages and then his circumnavigation, all promoted and financed by the movement in which the Hawkins brothers were prominent, and

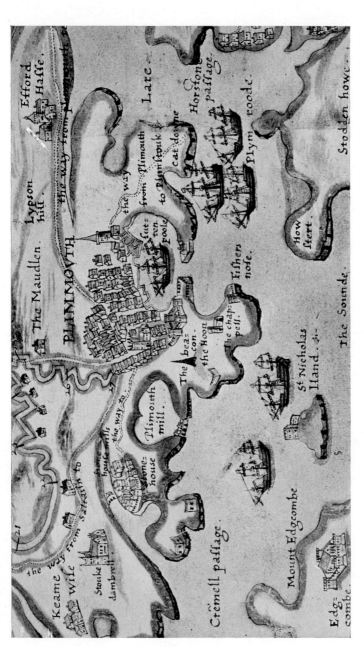

PLYMOUTH IN THE MID-ELIZABETHAN PERIOD

From Cotton MSS., Aug. I. i. 41

subscribed to by the brothers themselves. Drake's irregular ventures took few men and little shipping, but their returns to Plymouth were considerable. Finally the great regular expeditions of the Spanish War were to assemble at the Plymouth which the foregoing transactions had made a fit base for the purpose, bringing men in thousands to be equipped and fed, and in their turn making it necessary to improve upon the town's simple early defences with something more suitable to a great naval port. And so, in the last years of the century, we have the water-front more heavily gunned, and the land front moated and walled,[1] and Plymouth an epitome of Elizabethan England, rich by the sea, full of free men, strong for offence, and able to stand siege with the consciousness that no foe had much hope of breaking in.

Although the treachery at San Juan de Ulua provoked a desire for reprisals and inaugurated the period of English privateering in the Caribbean, it did not put an end to the period of irregular trade; and the same shipowners sometimes equipped the privateers and the traders simultaneously. We have details of a few Caribbean voyages of the 70's, and evidence that a great many more took place of which we have few or no particulars. The survival of evidence is a matter of chance, and it does not follow that the voyages of which little is known were unimportant, or that there were not a number of voyages, perhaps the majority, of which nothing whatever is now known. With these considerations we may review the record as it stands.

In 1569–70, according to a report by de Spes, a number of ships went to Guinea, and some of them proceeded with slaves to the West Indies. The gold trade had hitherto been a speciality of the Londoners, and the slave trade of Plymouth, so that possibly this is a record of some activity of the Hawkinses. William Hawkins, as we have seen, was personally at sea in 1569–70, and the Spaniards believed him to be bound for the Caribbean. Early in 1571, de Spes further declared, John Hawkins

[1] An older town wall had existed since the fifteenth century, but the town had grown beyond it, rendering a new line of fortifications necessary. See C. W. Bracken's *History of Plymouth*, p. 47–8.

and William Winter despatched seven or eight ships on the usual slaving voyage, but it was not made clear whether in a joint squadron or two independent ones. Some corroboration is supplied by Spanish reports from the Indies, discovered by Miss Wright, which show that Winter sent out three ships in March, 1571, that they were at Borburata in July, and that they made an unsuccessful attack on St. Augustine in Florida on their way home early in the next year.[1] But the Spanish documents do not say that the English were selling slaves, and indeed March was an inappropriate month in which to sail for Guinea. The likelihood is that Winter's ships were plundering, and that those of Hawkins were doing the like, following a different course of which no details have survived.

The French privateers were very active in the Caribbean in 1569, and we have already discussed the possibility that Drake was with them. The year 1570, on the contrary, was by Spanish reports unnaturally quiet, and hardly an incident was recorded in the Indies. If there was slave-trading it must have been of the clandestine kind that escaped the notice of authority. The open, confident manner of John Hawkins, servant of the King and friend of his colonial governors, was a thing of the past. That there may have been some trade is a possibility suggested by an English record that Drake went to the Indies in 1570 with two ships, the *Dragon* and the *Swan*, and made a reconnaissance in preparation for the stroke he launched two years later. Miss Wright points out that *Dragon* was more characteristically a French than an English ship-name, and that Drake afterwards put plans into operation which are known to have been evolved by the French. The suggestion is therefore that Drake may have made that year an illicit trading voyage in company with the French. There is no evidence that Drake was as yet a man of sufficient wealth to equip a ship from his own purse, and the probability is that he sailed as a captain employed by the Hawkinses. He may even have put to sea with William Hawkins at the close of 1569 and may then have been detached to trade in the West Indies. Drake was out again in 1571 with the *Swan* alone. It was a year in which the

[1] Wright, *Spanish Main Documents*, xxxvi, 36–9.

Spaniards complained of much plundering by French and English raiders, but their evidence does not allude to Drake by name, and his personal exploits cannot therefore be distinguished.

Drake indeed was not the only English captain in the Caribbean. There were others, how many we do not know. They had a harbour of their own, Port Pheasant on the Darien coast, about midway between Nombre de Dios and Tolu. When Drake came to Port Pheasant again in 1572 he found that an English ship under John Garrett had just left, while another, under James Ranse, came in shortly after him. John Garrett was a Plymouth man, perhaps in one of the Hawkinses' ships. Ranse had been in John Hawkins's third expedition, master of the *William and John*, although the ship in which he now appeared belonged to Sir Edward Horsey, Captain of Carisbrooke and military governor of the Isle of Wight. Horsey was deeply engaged with the Protestant rovers who frequented the Solent, playing much the same part there as William Hawkins at Plymouth; and here he is extending the war to the West Indies and employing a captain who had learnt his job under John Hawkins—one more instance of the homogeneity of the 'movement' already described. In 1572–3 Drake carried out his famous raid on the Isthmus of Panama, ending with the capture of a gold train after failures which would have broken up an expedition in less resolute hands.

Spanish documents indicate the gross value of Drake's gold as something over £20,000.[1] It was a handsome total for those days, and it all came back to Plymouth as a return for the investment on the equipment. Both his ships, the *Pasco* and the *Swan*, were Plymouth vessels, 'richly furnished with victuals and apparel for a whole year; and no less heedfully provided of all manner of munition, artillery, artificers' stuff, and tools, that were requisite for such a man of war in such an attempt; but especially having three dainty pinnaces, made in Plymouth, taken asunder all in pieces and stowed aboard, to be set up as occasion served.'[2] The

[1] An estimate based on various Spanish statements in Wright's *Spanish Main Documents*. The Spanish loss was higher, but Drake's French allies had half the proceeds of the greatest capture.

[2] *Sir Francis Drake Reviv'd*, reprint in *Spanish Main Documents*, p. 254.

employment, capital and economic stimulation accruing from such transactions were considerable. It is a pity that we have no figures for the growth of Tudor Plymouth in wealth and population. The careful fitting-out smacks of John Hawkins, and there is fair reason to believe that he and his brother were Drake's employers; for the *Pasco* was one of the ships sent out with Lovell in 1566, and one of those with which John Hawkins declared himself ready to aid the King of Spain in '71. We have no evidence of the *Swan's* ownership, save that she belonged to Plymouth. When Drake came home with the booty the quarrel with Spain was being settled, the damages assessed, and trade resumed. It was politic to hush him up, and he disappeared for two years. When he re-appeared it was in Ireland, in the service of the Earl of Essex, whom John Hawkins was supplying with ships and men.

John Hawkins sat for Plymouth again in the Parliament of 1572, his colleague being Edmund Tremayne, a man also deep in state affairs and at one time Clerk of the Privy Council. Hawkins, an experienced commander, had now a footing in the business of the Navy Board, to whose members he was allied by marriage and business partnership. He had even obtained in 1567 the reversion of the office of Clerk of the Ships, which carried a seat at the Board. The vacancy had not yet occurred, but Hawkins was consulted by Burghley and must have known much of the Board's business. He was often in London, and found it worth while to keep a house there. We hear little of his wife, Katherine Gonson, but the little is good. Her son Richard wrote of her with affection. There are indications that their real home at this period was in Plymouth rather than London.

It was in London that John Hawkins nearly met his death in 1573. Peter Burchet, a gentleman of the Middle Temple and a Puritan fanatic of unsound mind, suspected Sir Christopher Hatton of bringing Catholic influence to bear upon the Queen. On the morning of October 11 he determined to murder Hatton, and walked ready with his dagger in the Strand, where he expected his quarry to pass by. But first John Hawkins came along, riding in company with Sir William Winter, who had recently been knighted. Burchet mistook Hawkins for Hatton, sprang forward and stabbed him. The wound was severe, and recovery for some days uncertain. The Queen showed great concern, and sent her surgeons and her chaplain to minister to the victim. Hawkins was a tough man and survived it all, and was afterwards as fit as ever. To judge from portraits he had no great facial resemblance to Hatton. Most likely his taste for fine clothes had caused the mistake, for Hatton dressed magnificently. Burchet was sent to the Tower, where he succeeded in murdering a warder and was duly executed.

When Drake returned from his Nombre de Dios raid, Grenville was working on his project for discovering and exploiting that part of Terra Australis Incognita which was thought to form the southern shore of the Pacific Ocean. A few known facts, more supposed ones, and a great deal of arbitrary guesswork had caused this coast to be drawn in the current world-maps as stretching from the Straits of Magellan to the East Indian archipelago and including latitudes from temperate to tropical, while the continent behind it extended to the south pole. Interest had become acute when Englishmen heard of the voyage made by Mendaña in 1567-8. This Spanish explorer had set out from Peru, sailed far across the Pacific, and discovered the Solomon Islands, conferring upon them the Spanish names which some of them bear to-day. He thought that the natives were telling him of the continent not far beyond, and believed himself to be on the brink of the great discovery. The story of his voyage was brought to England by Englishmen dwelling in New Spain. Grenville expected great things of the project—the riches of the unknown southern continent, bases established on its coast for trade with Eastern Asia, and (though he did not avow it) the plunder of King Philip's treasure coast of Chile and Peru. This last is pure inference, but with our knowledge of Grenville it is a safe inference. The Queen evidently inferred it, for, after some preliminary encouragement, she revoked her consent to the enterprise. Her policy in 1574 was of peace with Spain. The prospect of a French conquest of the Netherlands had so alarmed her that she preferred the presence of the Spaniards as long as Dutch resistance precluded them from complete mastery. She had made up the old quarrel and did not wish to open a new one, which was just what Grenville and the Plymouth men in the Pacific would be certain to do. Grenville dispersed his ships and dropped his plan.

This enterprise of Grenville's was to have been a Plymouth and west country effort without any London element. The draft patent which was written out but not issued gives the names of the promoters, all landed gentry of the Plymouth region except William Hawkins, who, although *armiger* was his description also, stood for the mercantile interest. Others are alluded to, but not named, and their number probably included John Hawkins. Among the ships collected was the *Castle of Comfort*, of joint Hawkins-Grenville ownership. It was a might-have-been that is the less to be regretted since it came off three years later with a different personnel.

As Grenville and his friends intended the occupation of permanent sites in the continent they hoped to discover, the Queen's letters patent were essential to give them legal possession and government; and when the patent was refused they had to give up the whole idea. The Queen in fact never did issue letters patent for tropical enterprises until after she was at regular war with Spain and Portugal. So long as she was at nominal peace, however precarious, she would not take a step which would commit her to a firm line of policy and which she could revoke only with loss of prestige. So the Guinea traders and the Hawkins syndicates of the 60's, of which she was herself a member, never had the sanction of letters patent under the great seal, although that authority was granted to the Muscovy and Cathay Companies and to Humphrey Gilbert and Walter Ralegh, who all operated north of the tropics. But it is evident that there was no objection to private venturing in the West Indies even in these years of limited reconciliation with Spain. For we find the Hawkinses and Winters engaging in it, which as the Queen's servants they could hardly have done if the Queen's face had been set against it.

In May, 1575, a Spanish agent in London reported that three London ships and three from Plymouth, Sir Christopher Hatton being part owner, had been equipped by John Hawkins for the West Indies. Two months later he said that eight of Hawkins's ships had sailed for the same region. The inclusion of Hatton is interesting as showing that there was little risk of losing the Queen's favour by such speculations. Hatton was thenceforward a zealous member of the maritime movement.

In the same year 1575 a small vessel with fifteen men put into Plymouth after having made a voyage of remarkable audacity. She was the *John* of London, of 18 tons, commanded by Gilbert Horseley. He had sailed for the Caribbean in the previous November with a crew of twenty-five, ten of whom he had lost in encounters with the Spaniards. Horseley operated in the south-west angle of the Caribbean, where the Spanish Main merges through the Gulf of Darien into the coast of Central America. It was here that Drake, Garrett and Ranse had been active, and the French rovers also. The attraction was the plunder of the coastal shipping which concentrated valuable goods for the plate fleets to pick up at their few ports of call. Tiny armed vessels like Drake's *Swan* and Horseley's *John* could here make good captures if handled with luck and skill. Horseley had taken a considerable amount of gold and silver (the total unknown) when he came back to Plymouth after an eight months voyage. He bribed the Lord Admiral's officer at Plymouth to say nothing, and sent word of his return to the ship's owner in London. Then he went on up Channel to unlade his valuables at Arundel, a little Sussex river-port where authority was unlikely to be'vigilant. The whole adventure had been piratical and was best cloaked in obscurity. This story did not find its way into Hakluyt's *Voyages*. Our knowledge of it comes from the records of the Court of Admiralty.[1]

The year 1576 opens with a Spanish report in February of two ships sailing from Plymouth for the West Indies and of ten more gathering at Falmouth. Of these adventures there is no further record. The momentous event of the year was the departure of John Oxenham with fifty-seven men bound for the Isthmus of Panama. Oxenham was undoubtedly a Plymouth man, and must have been of some standing, although he has left little trace in the local records. He had been with Drake in the Nombre de Dios and Isthmus raid of 1572-3. At the time of his own voyage he was

[1] See *Sir John Hawkins* (1927), pp. 297-9.

described by the Spaniards as about forty years of age and much feared and respected by his men. With him went John Butler, who was very likely identical with a person described by a Spanish agent as 'an Irishman named Captain John', who had been many years in the Indies and was helping to prepare an expedition thither. The identity is not proved, and nothing is otherwise known of Butler's antecedents. The Spaniards at Panama seem to have known a good deal about him, and considered him a more formidable enemy than Oxenham himself.[1] There is an obscure notice in the Plymouth archives of the share of one John Willes in financing Oxenham's voyage; but apart from this we know nothing about its promoters. They may or may not have included the Hawkinses, although we may guess Drake to have been a likely subscriber. Drake certainly knew what Oxenham meant to do.

Oxenham's intention was to attack the Peruvian treasure-stream one stage nearer its source than Drake had done in capturing the gold-train on the Isthmus. Oxenham was to cross the Isthmus and cruise on the Pacific coast, to intercept the treasure ships that came up to Panama from the Peruvian and Chilean ports. He was to achieve his purpose by alliance with the Cimaroons, the negroes who had escaped from Spanish slavery and lived free in the wilds of Vallano, the southern base of the Darien isthmus. He had already made acquaintance with the Cimaroons in the course of his adventure with Drake. Oxenham carried out the plan, and by building a rowing pinnace on a river in the Cimaroon country was able to capture a larger quantity of treasure in the Gulf of Panama than Drake had taken in 1572-3. But there was more in the venture than this. Spanish documents show that the English intended to hold the Isthmus permanently and had a good chance of doing so; for the Cimaroons had been able to hold their part of it for many years, and the Spaniards had been unable to subdue them. The English plan, it appears, meant establishing what in later days would have been called a protectorate, and using it as a military base from which to dominate the treasure route. There was a basis of mutual interests between the negroes, who wanted English weapons and manufactures, and

[1] Important new evidence on Oxenham is in *Spanish Main Documents*, *passim*.

the English, who wanted treasure. Already English adventurers had been supplying arms and linens to the Cimaroons in exchange for gold captured from the Spaniards. On an authority which has now been superseded by recently discovered evidence, it used to be stated that Oxenham sailed in 1575. The date is now known to be 1576, and it was not until the latter half of 1577 that the adventure ended in disaster. Oxenham and Butler and all but a handful of their men were captured by the Spaniards, who recognized that their empire was in peril and made an unusual military effort.

The facts that Oxenham was one of Drake's men, that he sailed from Plymouth after discussing plans with Drake, and above all that he reached the Isthmus in '76 and was still holding out there in the following year—these facts provoke some legitimate speculations about Drake's great voyage of circumnavigation. Drake's crews were told that they were sailing for Alexandria to open a spice trade with the Turks. The inner circle of officers knew that the goal was very different, and supposed themselves to be going through the Straits of Magellan to discover Terra Australis Incognita, according to the Grenville proposals of three years before. Drake himself had an innermost secret intention, known only to himself and perhaps Thomas Doughty, which he imposed upon all the others when he turned northwards for the raid on Peru. By his own account it was on the Queen's command that he attacked the treasure ports; and Walsingham was privy to it, but Burghley was not. A brilliant raid, with transcendent luck in the lading of the *Cacafuego*, which yielded a profit of 1,400 per cent on the cost of the expedition, is all that we can say with certainty in explanation of the South American part of the voyage. But there is obviously room for speculation. There was a secret plan concocted between Drake, Walsingham and the Queen. What was it? Simply to capture a treasure-ship, which there could be no certainty of meeting, or something more? Perhaps Oxenham on the Isthmus supplies an answer. If Drake had found him there, at the head of a Cimaroon army with English officers, holding the portage between Atlantic and Pacific, inexpugnable by any Spanish effort, with Drake himself in the *Golden Hind*, the only armed ship in the Pacific, to supply the sea power domi-

nating the treasure ports, what a stranglehold would the Queen
have enjoyed upon King Philip, and how he would have had to
bend to her will in such matters as the Netherlands and the
Indies trade. There is no proof of any such plan, but we can say
that it was a possibility to Drake when he sailed from Plymouth in
December 1577; for he could not then have known that Oxenham
had been captured.[1] When he reached the treasure-coast he soon
did know it, for his first Spanish prisoner could have told him and
no doubt did. After that there was no reason for him to visit the
Isthmus of Panama, although many of the Spaniards still expected him to do so.

Whatever the truth about Drake's plans, the voyage was an
event in the history of Plymouth, and like most of its events at
that time owed something to the management of the Hawkinses.
John Hawkins invested about £500 in the expedition, although
he never touched the £7,000 which should have accrued, and
which seems to have stuck to the Queen's long fingers. The
Pelican, afterwards *Golden Hind*, occurs in a list of Plymouth ships
in February 1577. She may have belonged to John Hawkins and
been valued at the £500 of his investment. William Hawkins, as
we have seen, had been one of Grenville's syndicate for the voyage
to Terra Australis. The Hawkins brothers and Essex's Irish venture
supply the link between Grenville and Drake. But we have no
knowledge of the reasons why Grenville and his west-country
venturers were superseded by Drake with a backing which was
partly from Plymouth but mainly from London and the Court.
Not all of Drake's backers are known, but those that are suggest a
syndicate very like those that stood behind the Hawkins slaving
voyages—the Queen, her privy councillors, the Navy Board. The
Winters had a hand in it, and perhaps some City merchants. The
true story of those years 1573–7 would be interesting reading.

[1] According to a letter in the Foreign State Papers it was known in England
in August 1578 that Oxenham had taken treasure in Panama and was cut off by
lack of shipping to bring it home. It was not known, even at that date, that he
had been captured by the Spaniards. The relevant passage is printed in Quinn's
Gilbert, I, p. 169. Professor Quinn follows the *Foreign Calendar* in assigning the
letter to 1577, but a consideration of the other events and persons named in it
leads to the belief that it was written in 1578.

The Queen's change of front from prohibition to approval of attacking Peru is a reflection of the deterioration of Anglo-Spanish relations. By 1577 the hopes of permanent peace were fading and another period of semi-war was setting in.

Throughout this decade the Hawkins brothers were engaged in civic duties and interests, and in peaceful trade and such other business as came in the way of prominent shipowners. In 1568-9 William Hawkins built 'the new conduit' for the improvement of Plymouth's water supply. In 1573 the two brothers farmed the town mills, still, as in Henry VIII's reign, built across the mouth of the Mill Bay and worked by tide power.[1] As part of the bargain with the corporation the new farmers bought a house in which to weigh the corn before milling and provided a man and horse to fetch the sacks from the houses of the townsmen. William Hawkins was Mayor for the second time in 1578-9.

The check to the Protestant rovers in the Channel administered by the Queen in 1573 was not permanent, and the Dutch Sea Beggars, with the fine port of Flushing as their base, were soon active again, and played an essential part in securing the freedom of the seven provinces. William Hawkins and Grenville, operating their *Castle of Comfort*, were associated with them, and had to answer in 1576 for the capture of a ship of St. Malo. The Breton owners took action in the Admiralty Court, where Grenville attended to speak for himself and his partner. Their defence was twofold, that the Breton ship attacked the *Castle* and was by her 'apprehended'; and that they were not at the material time the owners of the *Castle*, having sold her to a Frenchman named Jolis, who had a commission from La Rochelle. Both pleas appear to have been farcical. The first speaks for itself. The second was accompanied by an admission that the vessel had been fitted out by Hawkins and Grenville, and her crew, all English, engaged by them. Captain Jolis, her alleged owner, was the only Frenchman on board. The sale to him was undoubtedly collusive, he being without the jurisdiction and, for the taking of a French ship, answerable only in a French court. It was the sort of quibble commonly used by the privateer owners, who were esteemed to have acted

[1] The mills are depicted in the view of Plymouth reproduced facing p. 196.

honourably so long as the law would allow them such ways out. Whether the High Court of Admiralty did so in this case is not on record. Most likely, on the statements sworn to, it had no option.

Another case, tried this time in the Court of Requests, shows John Hawkins using his maritime influence in a curious manner. It was a dispute between him and a London firm of underwriters, who had accepted the risk of a ship of Le Havre homeward bound from Barbary. A Huguenot rover captured the ship and brought her into Plymouth. Hawkins had a contract with the underwriters to act in such an event. He persuaded the ship's captors to accept a ransom much smaller than the sum for which the ship was insured, and so saved the underwriters from losing the full amount. At the trial he was claiming for his services a reward which they refused to pay. They said that he was in collusion with the rovers and encouraged them to bring their prizes into Plymouth—which was true. Again the division between honourable conduct and piracy lay solely in the existence of a commission signed by some technically sovereign prince, Orange or Condé, or later, the Portuguese Don Antonio, who enjoyed very little actual sovereignty but was recognized, for its own purposes, by the English government. There are other and similar cases which reveal John and William Hawkins 'redeeming' goods at reduced rates from their freebooting associates.

Lest the above incidents should give a one-sided picture of the brothers' activities—and those of the port of Plymouth—it should be emphasized that all the time they were the owners of a fleet of merchantmen, carrying on peaceful trade, and occasionally being captured and taken into Catholic ports by the opposite numbers of the doubtful characters who frequented Plymouth. The port books, which record the arrivals and sailings of merchantmen, have many entries testifying to this regular Hawkins trade. The legal records deal only with the voyages on which something went wrong, as when William Hawkins lost a ship to French rovers in the Narrow Seas, and when the two brothers sent four vessels on charter to lade alum at Genoa and were refused payment on the ground that the cargoes were spoilt.

IV

THE CRUCIAL YEARS

In the late seventies Anglo-Spanish relations deteriorated and never more than momentarily recovered before they broke down into admitted war. After Alva's recall from the Netherlands in 1573 there was a period of the balance that Elizabeth wished to see, with the Spanish government sufficiently in being to allow no vacuum for French occupation, but not so completely successful over its Dutch rebels as to permit of interference in the affairs of England. Such was the general position under Luis de Requesens, who succeeded Alva, and himself died early in 1576. His designated successor was Don John of Austria, illegitimate half-brother of Philip II, credited with great ambitions, and possessed of a brilliant military record. Don John delayed his journey to the Netherlands until the end of the year, and in the meantime the Spanish garrisons mutinied for want of pay and a strong commander. At Antwerp 'the Spanish Fury'—the excesses of the rebel soldiers—killed several thousands of the inhabitants, and there were many atrocities at other places. The seventeen Netherland provinces united to demand the withdrawal of all Spanish troops and the restoration of their ancient self-government, and they presented these demands to Don John when he arrived in November. After expostulation he consented, being at the moment powerless to do otherwise. But it was not to his autocratic taste, and he was only biding his time.

The English government looked doubtfully upon Don John, for it was no great secret that he intended to subjugate the Netherlands and then invade England. As a semi-royalty in search of a career he was prepared to reconcile himself to being the fourth husband of Mary Stuart or at least to use her as a stepping stone. In this he was exceeding the desires of his brother Philip, who still hoped to solve his problems without fighting England, and next year sent her a new ambassador, his fifth and last, Don Bernardino de Mendoza, to take up the mantle cast down by Guerau de Spes. But in this matter of preserving peace there was another Catholic power to be considered, that of Rome under Gregory XIII. He was not for peace, but for conquest. The *empresa*, the enterprise of England, filled his mind. An advance-party of missionary priests entered England in 1575, to make inert Catholics active and defiant of government; and the Jesuits were to follow in 1580. Elizabeth and her ministers could see the crisis of ten years earlier about to repeat itself. England was much stronger than then, but so also were her enemies. When therefore Don John repudiated his pledges in the summer of 1577, sent for new Spanish troops, and raised others from the Catholic Walloons, the Queen was persuaded that it was better to fight in the Netherlands than at home, and in September she agreed to give military and financial aid to the Prince of Orange. Such was the net effect of her decisions, but her intentions daily fluctu-ated and reversed themselves to the despair of the ministers in contact with her. Like Philip, she did not desire an Anglo-Spanish war.

Grenville had been forbidden to sail for the Pacific in the peace-ful optimism of 1574; Oxenham had sailed without the Queen's leave, or so he told the Spaniards, in 1576; Drake sailed with her secret instructions at the close of 1577. It was nearly two years before news of him began to reach Europe. In August 1578 Sir Humphrey Gilbert, John Hawkins's fellow-member for Plymouth in 1571, was preparing an expedition considerably larger than Drake's of the previous year. His intended destination has always been debatable. His well-known interests in North American colo-nization, the Newfoundland fishery and the North West Passage yield a presupposition that he was bound in those directions, but the date of his departure, November, precludes it. He told a French ambassador that he was going south on the quest of Terra Australis Incognita,[1] but the apparent frankness with which he discussed details arouses a suspicion that he was speaking to mislead. An English observer thought that he might be going out to make contact with Oxenham in the Isthmus. Whatever the

[1] Quinn, *Sir H. Gilbert*, I, p. 195.

truth it is interesting only as an intention, for he sailed in November and was back in February, 1579, having suffered damage in a fight with Spaniards of which no particulars are on record.

There was another expedition preparing to sail from Plymouth at the close of 1578, a squadron of five ships with 250 men, victualled for a year, under two leaders described as Captain Sharpham and Mr. Fortescue, bound on 'a like voyage' to that of Gilbert.[1] A chance allusion in a state paper tells us so much, and English records are otherwise silent. Something else, from a Spanish source, may link with it. After Drake had raided Peru, the Viceroy sent Pedro Sarmiento de Gamboa to survey the Straits of Magellan and then to sail to Spain to report to the King on the question of fortifying them. In the Straits early in 1580 Sarmiento met Indians in possession of European cloth, which they said they had recently obtained from two ships. These may have been Drake's, but some of the details are inconsistent with what is known of his passage of the Straits. At the Cape Verde Islands, later in his voyage, Sarmiento learned that in November 1579 some Portuguese on the Brazilian coast near Bahia captured five Englishmen who had landed from a boat. They said that they belonged to an English fleet of ten ships fitted out by a great lord in England. The fleet had been to the Straits of Magellan and had returned and cruised along the Brazilian coast seeking an advantageous port in which to make a settlement. For this purpose their flagship of 900 tons carried 1,000 prospective colonists. The great ship was wrecked on a lee shore, but her nine consorts got away. Finally, Sarmiento heard at the Azores that a large English ship had been wrecked on Terceira in November 1579, and that the authorities believed her to be one of the vessels seen on the Brazilian coast.[2]

---

[1] Document printed in Quinn's *Gilbert*, I, p. 210.

[2] C. R. Markham, *Voyages of Pedro Sarmiento de Gamboa*, Hakluyt Society, 1895, pp. 108–9, 191–4, 195. Owing to the omission of these references from the index of Markham's volume, the facts relating to this English voyage of 1579, although available for the past half-century, have been generally overlooked. They are of further interest as showing that the English were still entertaining the plans of Brazilian settlement about which the earlier evidence had ceased in 1542.

These are the elements of a story. They do stick together, loosely. Captain Sharpham, Mr. Fortescue, a great lord, five ships,—were they possibly a follow-up to Drake's expedition through the Straits, bound for the colonization of Terra Australis Incognita? The particulars supplied by the Brazilian Portuguese are evidently exaggerated. No ship as large as 900 tons sailed in a private expedition, and no ship even of that tonnage would have carried 1,000 men across the ocean. It may be then that the ten ships alleged by the Portuguese were really the five preparing to leave Plymouth at the end of 1578. In any case the voyage was a failure and at that we must leave it.

On August 3, 1579, London received important tidings from Seville. Reports were coming through that Drake had raided the West Coast and taken enormous booty. There was great indignation in Spain, and some trepidation in London at the possible consequences, perhaps war, almost certainly another arrest of trade. But Philip II was on the brink of an undertaking whose importance transcended even Drake's depredations, and he was not anxious to force an issue with England. Drake himself quitted the coast of Guatemala and was lost to view in the North Pacific, and not a word of him was to reach Europe during the following twelve months. By tacit mutual consent England and Spain postponed the awkward question until he should return.

Before this was apparent there was undoubtedly a war scare, more especially as a party of papal volunteers had reached Ireland in the previous month to excite rebellion there. It was supposed that Spain was the inspirer of this move, although in fact Philip had less to do with it than Elizabeth had with the English volunteers in the Netherlands. All things considered, Burghley thought it well to be prepared for war. A memorandum by John Hawkins for an opening naval campaign was probably drawn up in response to the minister's inquiries. It is dated August 12, 1579, and endorsed: 'A provision for the Indies fleet, drawn by Mr Hawkins. Admiralty.' By this date Hawkins was Treasurer of the Navy, the senior post on the Navy Board, as will be more fully recounted in a later chapter. His plan for the employment of the fleet is therefore that of the Queen's officer, and not the unsolicited proposal of a private individual.

Hawkins proposed to send westwards a squadron composed of four of the Queen's medium-sized ships, five armed merchantmen and eleven pinnaces, with 1,130 men. If we estimate the Queen's ships at 400 tons each, the merchantmen at 300, and the pinnaces at 50, we have a total tonnage of about 3,600, and a proportion of roughly one man to three tons. It shows what Hawkins thought to be the correct manning for a long-distance expedition. Drake, when he led an expedition of this sort six years later, took about the same tonnage as Hawkins proposed, but twice as many men, 2,300 or one man to one-and-a-half tons, and lost a great number by sickness, so that his effective strength on the Spanish Main was not much more than half that with which he set forth. To return to Hawkins's plan: he gave the primary object as the capture of the home-coming plate fleet, but knew that considerable luck would be needed to intercept it. In default, or in addition, the squadron was to carry out a systematic raid of Philip's Indies with the purpose of putting them out of business as the producers of his wealth: 'There is to be stricken with this company all the towns upon the coast of the Indies, and there need not be suffered one ship, bark, frigate or galley to survive untaken.' Hawkins had all this ready in 1579; but the need for action did not then arise.

Philip's reason for going gently with England in 1579 was that he was meditating the acquisition of Portugal. The young Portuguese King Sebastian had been killed in a rash invasion of Morocco in 1578. His successor Henry, an aged and childless relative, was on the brink of the grave; and he was the last legitimate male of the royal house. An illegitimate, Antonio, Prior of Crato, stood ready to claim the succession, but legal right was against him. Legal right was with Philip II, the proprietor of the best of several claims through female descent. Another such claim lay with the Valois of France, but Catherine de Medici saw little hope of enforcing it. In 1580 King Henry died, and Philip acted without hesitation. Alva led the Spanish army into Portugal and carried all before him in a brief campaign. Don Antonio attempted to make a stand but was given no chance to consolidate his position. He was quickly driven into exile, leaving the Portuguese nation to submit to the domination of a military conqueror, quite in the twentieth century fashion. For the credit of the sixteenth century it should be added that the conqueror behaved far better towards his new subjects than any such has done in our time.

To the world's view the conquest greatly strengthened Philip's position. He had acquired the monopolies of the Indian Ocean, the African coast and islands, and Brazil; the great ocean port of Lisbon, better situated than his own Seville; and the colonial experience, the shipping and the seamen of a small but intensely maritime people, between whom and himself there was no religious barrier and therefore a prospect that they would in time reconcile themselves to their position. It was the first outstanding success of a reign hitherto characterized by failure to control the Netherlands and deal with the general Protestant exuberance. It had a noticeable moral effect on Philip personally. He was thenceforward more self-confident and determined to grapple with his various opponents, in his heart more convinced that he was the appointed instrument of God and the Catholic Church. In those respects the conquest of Portugal made Philip and all he stood for a direr foe to the new England and all it stood for. All Europe thought so, and many in England were dismayed. But there were some among the Davids who discerned that the colossus in growing bulkier had grown more vulnerable. Administration was the weakness of the great powers of Christendom, and mere size was apt to induce flabbiness.

Into this situation Drake came sailing home in September 1580, with his first keen question to the Plymouth fishermen: Is the Queen alive and well? The answer meant much to him, for he might have found himself the subject of Mary Stuart or of James Stuart or some other 'rascal's son', and all his labour lost. His booty was so great that its disposal became an affair of state overriding the normal arrangements of a joint stock syndicate. The secrecy that enveloped the financial decisions is even now almost complete, and it is only from side winds that we know anything about them. It appears that the Queen took the distribution into her own hands, allowing Drake a sum sufficient to render him a rich man. His crew must also have done well in their several degrees. Among them were his young nephew John Drake and another young Plymouth man, William Hawkins (the third), son of William Hawkins the second and nephew of John Hawkins. On all counts the homecoming of the *Golden Hind* was a great day for Plymouth, not only for the immediate wealth but for the future possibilities opened up by Drake's visit to the Moluccas and his passage through the Far East and the Indian Ocean. Plymouth and the Hawkins interest developed their own views, different from those of London, about the exploitation of the achievement.

Don Antonio, exile in France and then in England, styled himself King of Portugal, and it was open to the English government to recognize him as such, and permit its subjects to act upon the commissions which he was entitled to grant. His importance at the outset was greater than that, for the Portuguese officers in the East were in sympathy with him, while most of the Azores declared openly for him and prepared to resist Philip by force of arms. The oceanic interest in England, strengthened by Drake's success, could hope for entry into the Eastern, African and Brazilian trades as a reward for promoting the claims of Antonio. In their different ways Drake and the Hawkinses acted under this influence in the ensuing years, and had they been successful Plymouth instead of London might have become the headquarters of English trade with the East.

Drake's great achievement, and the renown, the Queen's favour and the knighthood that rewarded it, altered the position of John Hawkins. Hitherto Hawkins had been regarded as the country's chief naval officer and the commander of any fleet short of a concentration of all the Queen's Navy. Had war come during the 1570's those would have been his employments, and there is no doubt that in submitting the plan for the Caribbean expedition in 1579 he expected to command it. Drake now stepped into his place, and Hawkins was regarded as second to Drake during the 1580's, in fact until the return of the 1589 expedition to Lisbon, at whose failure the Queen's displeasure was bitter and prolonged. After that the two were more or less on an equality. Hawkins was all those years doing administrative work of the highest importance, with results fundamental to the country's future; but no one placed administration on a level with active command, and Drake at sea gained all the laurels.

While in the Moluccas Drake had made an agreement with the Sultan of Ternate for an English trade in spices, but had then known nothing about events in Portugal. By 1581 the Portuguese developments rendered action desirable; and the sound decision for that year was to send a fleet and troops to the succour of Terceira and the other Azorean islands that were holding out for Don Antonio. The Azores were a dominating position on the ocean trade routes. Owing to the prevailing winds of the North Atlantic the carracks from the East and the plate fleets from the West necessarily passed near them, and in practice often stopped among them for refuge and instructions. The Azores held by a hostile sea power might mean ruin to Spain or Portugal and the control of the trade routes by the holding power. Don Antonio well rooted in Terceira would thus have been more formidable to Spain than if he had landed with an army in Portugal. The plan broke down on diplomacy. Elizabeth knew that Philip might declare war in retaliation for so serious a move on behalf of his enemy. She therefore insisted that France, which also favoured Antonio, should take part in the expedition and share the risk of its result. Catherine de Medici refused to commit herself, and Elizabeth would not act alone. The campaigning season passed with nothing done, and the money spent in preparations was wasted. This included the value of some rare diamonds contributed by Don Antonio from the Portuguese regalia. He was very angry at the loss, but the Queen, who was also out of pocket, refused to reimburse him. He withdrew to France and next year sailed to the Azores with a French expedition. It was of the semi-official, disavowable sort, led by an officer named Philip Strozzi. Spain sent in pursuit a force under the Marquis of Santa Cruz. At Terceira he annihilated Strozzi's fleet in a battle decided by boarding and hand-to-hand fighting. Don Antonio, who was near but not at the scene of action, escaped the Spaniards and returned to France.

These events were the prelude to others in which the Hawkinses were engaged. The first of them was Edward Fenton's expedition of 1582. It was designed to follow up Drake's contact with the Moluccas by establishing a regular trade and an English factory. The promoters were the set of influential men who commonly served as cover for what were really government enterprises—Leicester and four other leading noblemen, Burghley, Walsingham and Hatton, Drake himself, the Muscovy Company and other merchants. The Hawkins brothers were not investors in this voyage; John's name is omitted, and William's was included but struck out. The family was nevertheless represented, for the captain of one of the ships and second-in-command of the whole expedition was young William Hawkins the circumnavigator. Young John Drake, also of the *Golden Hind*, commanded a small vessel named the *Francis*, evidently his uncle's investment in the voyage. Edward Fenton himself was the brother-in-law of John Hawkins, having married Thomasine Gonson, the sister of Katherine Gonson. He had sailed with Frobisher to the North West and had quarrelled with him, and he was nominated to the present command by the influence of the Muscovy Company. Fenton was ordered to sail to the Moluccas by the Cape of Good Hope, and to conduct himself as the leader of a mercantile expedition, avoiding plunder and offence to the Queen's friends.

The instructions were the work of the party that desired to postpone the Spanish war, which most men by this time thought inevitable. Let Spain break her teeth on the Dutch, said this school of thought, while we grow stronger and improve our defences. To which the opposition answered, if we stand by and see the foreign Protestants conquered we shall fight without a friend when our turn comes. The fight-now party included Walsingham and Drake and generally Leicester; and they had money and ships and officers in the expedition. By the time Fenton crossed the equator a faction was urging him to make for the Straits of Magellan and reach the Moluccas by way of Peru. This party, needless to say, included John Drake and William Hawkins, who,

youngsters though they were, stood as veterans and heroes before
the crews dreaming of *Cacafuegos* full of gems and gold. Discipline dissolved in recriminations and intrigue, and the voyage
ended on the southern coast of Brazil, whence Fenton returned
to England patently unable to cope with his task. He brought
William Hawkins home in irons. What the family thought of it is
not on record, although it was in a sense a quarrel within the
family. John Hawkins was on good terms with Fenton in later years,
and recommended him to a post on the Navy Board in 1589.

The elder Hawkinses had stood aloof from Fenton's voyage
because they had in mind an undertaking of their own which
would need all their spare capital. A state paper,[1] unfortunately
without date, shows that William Hawkins was moving for a
patent to explore the coasts of Africa and America 'for the better
discovery of all trade of merchandises in the said coasts'. The
document is a sketch or outline of the terms of a grant which it is
proposed that the Crown shall make to Hawkins, and after having
been written out with space for interlineations it has been corrected
and amplified in a different handwriting. One of the additions so
made is more important and illuminating than the original
provisions. It runs as follows:

And further we do licence the said W. H. and his company to
serve Don Antony, K. of Port., against his enemies, and do hereby
allow anything that shall be done in the service of the said K. Don
Antony; and such pay, reward, wages, or both, either in money or
commodities, as shall be taken in and for the said service, the said
Wm. H. and deputies may hereby freely and lawfully sell and utter
in any place upon the coast of England or anywhere else within
our dominions, without anything to be said unto him for the same.

The above is only a proposal, and there is no trace of the issue
of a patent in its terms. It does however indicate the possibilities
conceived in forward minds in consequence of Philip's seizure of
Portugal. As it bears no date, we cannot say definitely that the

[1] S.P. Dom. Eliz., Vol. 142, No. 44, endorsed 'Draft of a letters patent for
Mr. W. Hawkins'. When commenting on this paper in *Sir John Hawkins*, I
expressed doubt whether the person was William Hawkins the second or the
third. I think now that there is no doubt that it was William Hawkins the second,
the brother of John Hawkins.

paper was written as a preliminary or a consequence of the voyage that has now to be recorded. On the whole it is more likely to be a preliminary, and there are independent suggestions that in 1582-3 the Hawkinses were working with Don Antonio as Drake had hoped to do if his Azores expedition had been sanctioned in 1581.

The Hawkins squadron of seven sail was equipped at Plymouth and ready to depart in November, 1582. It consisted of the *Primrose*, 300 tons, the *Minion*, 180, four other ships of about 100 tons each, and a pinnace of 80 tons. These details were reported by Mendoza, the Spanish ambassador. He further stated that two of the ships belonged to Drake and that William Hawkins was to be the commander. They were bound, he said, for the island of San Thome on the African coast and thence to Brazil, from which they would sail on to the Moluccas. Most of these statements are independently corroborated, but that of the Moluccas destination is not; and the voyage seems to have been limited to Atlantic objectives.

William Hawkins was well over sixty years of age. We have seen him at sea about the Spanish coast and the Islands in 1569, but apart from that voyage his known career is that of a landsman-shipowner. There are however unknown periods in which he may have gone to sea, particularly before his father's death, which took place when he was about thirty-four years old. For all we know, William Hawkins may have become by that date an experienced professional seaman. However, they were all able men, never too old to try something new, and here we have him in his old age leading a considerable squadron on a long tropical voyage. His son William being away with Fenton, he took with him as his vice-admiral his nephew Richard, the only son of John Hawkins.

Richard Hawkins was born in 1560,[1] and consequently twenty-two years old when he sailed with his uncle. To have been given command of a ship and the second place in the expedition he must surely have had some experience; but it cannot have been regular

[1] *The Observations of Sir Richard Hawkins*, ed. by J. A. Williamson, London, 1933, p. xli.

or extensive, for when writing in 1603 he used the phrase: 'In twenty years since that I have used the sea . . . ;' and he clearly considered the voyage of 1582–3 to have been his first service worth mentioning. He had grown up in a world of ships, but what he had been doing in adolescence we do not know. He was of an age to have sailed with Drake in the circumnavigation, but his father evidently did not think fit to claim a place for him in that venture.

Until recent times very little was known of this voyage of 1582–3. The present author printed what information could be collected twenty years ago, and since then Miss Wright's researches in the Spanish archives have revealed many further details.[1] One of her Spanish officials speaks of examining an English prisoner and obtaining a full account of the voyage; but unhappily the deposition cannot be found, and we are left with only an outline. On the English side, William Hawkins wrote no narrative and Richard Hakluyt, who knew the story, omitted it from his great collection of 1589, probably because it was then not politic to record offences between the English and the Portuguese.

The expedition sailed about November, 1582, and its first recorded destination was the Cape Verde Islands. Hawkins very likely had a commission from Don Antonio, as the draft patent suggests. To win over the colonies to the allegiance of Antonio, and at the same time to open them to English trade, were the objects of Drake and the Hawkinses. The policy was not successful at the time. Sixty years later it was substantially carried out when Portugal began her war of independence under the House of Braganza and achieved success with English assistance, after making treaties which opened the Portuguese empire to English commerce. In the 1580's the Portuguese had to choose between a foreign conqueror who was nevertheless a Catholic, and heretic allies who would prise open a national monopoly. The majority preferred the Catholic conqueror. This was what happened at Santiago, the capital of the Cape Verdes, where there was

---

[1] I am enabled to use these details by the kind permission of Miss Wright and the Hakluyt Society. The documents containing them are about to be published in a volume which the Society has now in the press.

considerable bloodshed between the Portuguese and the English. Our knowledge of it is derived only from an allusion made by a subsequent English visitor to the islands, who remarked on 'the great wrongs they had done to old Mr. William Hawkins of Plymouth, in the voyage he made four or five years before, when as they did both break their promise, and murdered many of his men'. The Spanish documents add a hint that others besides Hawkins's expedition were concerned in the affair, which included the 'sacking' of the Island of Fogo. It was evidently serious, but nothing more can be made out. Drake's ships and men were among the sufferers, and Drake's proceedings when he visited Santiago in 1585 seem to exhibit an element of vengeance. The Cape Verde Islands were an important, although not the only, key to the Guinea trade, and much might have resulted from their adhesion to Don Antonio.

William Hawkins sailed next to Brazil, as we know from the Spanish evidence, which does not, however, indicate the localities visited. Even as late as this date the Portuguese occupation of Brazil was extremely thin, and in the 1570's the English were as active as they had ever been. Their operations may never wholly have ceased since the first William Hawkins had led his ships there, perhaps accompanied by William Hawkins the second, who was now to revisit the scene. English records tell us little or nothing, and it is from Pedro Sarmiento that we learn some interesting facts. About 1572, he says, a great number of Englishmen entered the Bay of Paraiba, near Rio de Janeiro, in 21° 20′ S., and settled there. They were some time among the Tapuya Indians and 'they have a generation of the women of the land', which probably means that they have half-breed offspring. In 1577 the Portuguese of Rio de Janeiro attacked these English and killed a number of them. The rest took refuge with the natives, who were believed [in 1580] to have eaten them. Besides this, continues Sarmiento, other Englishmen settled north of Pernambuco in 5° 30′ S. in a bay also called Paraiba, from which they have not yet been driven out.[1]

[1] *Voyages of Sarmiento*, pp. 179, 182–3. There is a river mouth north of Pernambuco, still mapped as Parahyba del Norte, not to be confused with the Parnahyba farther north.

Certain merchants' letters printed by Hakluyt show that at Santos[1] there was a market for English manufactures and a supply of sugar and other tropical commodities, including parrots and monkeys and 'barrels of the leaf called petune', an early mention of the tobacco trade. Some Englishmen resident as merchants in southern Brazil were on good terms with the Portuguese until Philip's conquest of Portugal. What changes took place afterwards are not clear. William Hawkins evidently had scope to do good work in the interest of Don Antonio, and also to obtain cargoes which would make his voyage profitable. Whether he could also hope to make contact with an English colony we cannot tell.

It is not certain that he went as far south as Santos, but, wherever his port may have been, he sailed northwards round Cape San Roque and along the northern Brazil and Guiana coasts to the southern Caribbean, for he is next reported in June 1583 at Margarita. We do not know whether he kept in touch with the uncolonized parts of the coastline—the Amazon delta and Guiana as far as the Orinoco and Trinidad—but he can hardly have missed seeing parts of it, and he may well have been the first Elizabethan captain to do so. It was an interesting voyage, and we have lost every detail of it.

A Spanish report from Margarita records the arrival of William Hawkins on June 3, 'with the greatest force in men and ships ever seen in these parts.' He used a pinnace to dredge for oysters and obtained a number of pearls. Dredging, that is, dragging a net over the bottom, was the English method of bringing up oysters, although in tropical waters native divers were generally employed. Richard Hawkins, who embodied incidents from former voyages in his *Observations*, wrote: 'In anno 1583, in the island of Margarita, I was at the dredging of pearl oysters, after the manner we dredge oysters in England; and with mine own hands I opened many, and took out the pearls of them, some greater, some less, and in good quantity.'[2]

It would seem that the pearling at Margarita was only a means of filling in time until some more important business should be

1 In 20$\frac{1}{3}$° S., not the modern Santos in 24° S.   2 1933 edn., p. 156.

ripe, in other words, until the plate fleets should be moving. In the latter part of July Hawkins moved across the Caribbean and entered Port Vargas, at the western end of Puerto Rico. He had still his seven ships, but his people told the Spaniards on shore that they had come in to repair one which was damaged. The Spaniards asked who was in command and whether Don Antonio was with them. After some consultation the English answered that Mr. William Hawkins only was in command. Three other large ships appeared on the coast, and the two squadrons joined, but afterwards parted again. The outward-bound *flota* for New Spain was at the same time passing along the south coast of Puerto Rico.

A later report from the municipal authorities of Puerto Rico to the King continued the story. The arrival of Hawkins, it said, 'occasioned no little alarm in this city. The outcome was that this fleet departed from this island without doing damage, thanks to the activity, valour and efficiency of the captain named for this purpose. He is Diego Rodriguez Castellanos. . . .' Of course he was a Castellanos! Activity, valour, efficiency, carry us back to Rio de la Hacha twenty years before, and we turn to the end of the report and see that the first of its four signatories is the man himself, exactly as Miguel Castellanos of old had been wont to inspire his own eulogies. It seemed that the English sent a hundred and fifty men ashore to fill water casks. Then, according to his report, Castellanos went along, 'and with only seven men, whom he assembled on that coast, attacked the whole party the fleet had sent ashore. He lay in wait for them in the bush and fell upon them unexpectedly. Believing our force to be greater than it was, the enemy re-embarked in his boats and fled.' There is, however, another report to the King written two days later by the governor of Puerto Rico. He says of Castellanos: 'Being on watch with six men he saw about 150 English embark, and when he observed that few remained upon the beach, he attacked these with his six men, and came upon two English, alone. One of these was killed and the other taken prisoner. Although the ships . . . landed a large force of men who went into the bush against our six, they could not overtake them.' So the six fought two, and not a hundred and fifty.

The unhappy captive's name was Robert. The governor put him to the torture and extracted an account of the whole voyage, and then hanged him. His deposition, which would tell us where Hawkins went and why, in the Cape Verdes and Brazil, is missing. The Spanish officials at Puerto Rico believed that Don Antonio was with the expedition, but it is not clear what made them think so. They believed also that Hawkins was going to attack Havana, the port of assembly of the homeward-bound plate fleets.

Before he leaves Puerto Rico we may note an incident recorded by Richard Hawkins, which corroborates the Spanish statement that the expedition called at Port Vargas on account of damage to a ship. Richard says that one of the captains reported his ship, the *Bark Bonner*, to be leaking so badly that she was unseaworthy and ought to be abandoned. A council of captains met and decided on this course. Thereupon young Richard spoke up and said he would sail the ship home with a volunteer crew if they were given one-third of her value as salvage. This shamed the faint-hearted captain into saying that he would sail her home himself, which he did, and the ship served many years after. One phrase of Richard's preserves his uncle's dry humour, and it is almost the only personal touch recorded of William Hawkins: 'The General commended him for his resolution, and thanked me for my offer.'

In recounting the above incident Richard Hawkins stated that up to that point (the end of July) the expedition had made no profit.[1] Four months later, at the end of November, it came home rich. We have no narrative of what happened in the interim. But on November 26 Mendoza reported that William Hawkins and his ships had entered Plymouth, having captured great booty, whereof pearls and money had already reached John Hawkins in London. News from Seville was that the flagship of the homeward-bound fleet from Santo Domingo was missing, and she, said Mendoza, may have contained the pearls, treasure, hides and sugar which Hawkins had brought back. At the same time a Dutchman in London wrote home that Hawkins had taken booty worth 800,000 crowns. Next April, 1584, a Spanish report stated

[1] 'We had profited the adventurers nothing.'—*Observations*, p. 88.

that William Hawkins was preparing to leave secretly on another voyage. If the fact is true, nothing further is known about it. The reticence of William and John Hawkins is a trial to the historian. They were the least vainglorious of men and had no use for apologia, self-explanation or publicity of any sort. The mark they made in history, in the defeat of the counter-Reformation, has never been credited to them. Their father did not belong to a writing age; and John's son Richard, who did, was less taciturn, although he kept his *Observations* for twenty years after he wrote them before he sent them to the printer.

Drake, meanwhile, may have been troubled to see the years slip by with nothing done to follow up his pioneer work in the Spice Islands. He would undoubtedly have gone to sea had the Queen allowed it, but he was now suffering the penalty of eminence as John Hawkins had in the previous decade; he was too valuable a weapon of war to be let out of the Queen's reach. However, in the summer of 1584 he proposed a great expedition with himself as leader, and obtained sanction for the preparations to begin. By November some progress had been made, and a paper endorsed by Burghley, 'The charge of the navy to the Moluccas,' gives details. A state syndicate of the standard type was putting up the money: the Queen, £17,000; Drake, £7,000; Leicester, £3,000; John Hawkins, £2,500; William Hawkins, £1,000; Hatton, £1,000; Ralegh, £400; and minor adventurers made up the total to £40,000, which was to be spent on ships, victuals, wages and munitions, without allowance for merchandise. The fleet was to comprise eleven ships, four barks, and twenty pinnaces, manned by 1,000 mariners, 100 gunners and 500 soldiers. The general purpose undoubtedly was to gain control of the Moluccas, but the detailed plan is unknown, whether by approaching the Portuguese settlements in the name of Don Antonio, or attacking them outright, or establishing English factories with the independent princes such as the Sultan of Ternate. The expedition never sailed East, and this is all we know about it.

While it was taking shape in the winter of 1584-5 the situation in the Netherlands grew critical. The Prince of Parma, successor to Don John of Austria, proved to be a statesman and a soldier. In 1583 he drove out the Duke of Anjou, the brother of Henry III of France, who had tried to found a kingdom for himself by taking the leadership of the rebels. In the following year Parma captured most of the cities of the southern Netherlands, leaving Antwerp to be taken, as it duly was, in 1585. The turn of the Dutch would follow, and without help they were expected to fall. In France also a decision was threatened. The Catholic League took the field as allies of Philip II, led by the Guise princes, to achieve the destruction of Protestantism. No reasonable man in England could any longer advise the postponement of the war. Burghley and Walsingham agreed that the Dutch must be aided with money and men. Leicester also agreed, for he was to command the men and spend the money. The Queen agreed, unwilling as ever, and clinging to the diplomatic fiction that she was not at war with Spain, but acting only as an auxiliary to its enemies. Drake's preparations marked time until the decisions were taken. Then, with two powerful ships of the Queen's at the head of his fleet and his force made up with additional soldiers to 2,300 men, he sailed not for the Moluccas but for the Caribbean, to carry out the opening campaign of the war at sea by attempting to destroy Philip's wealth in the West Indies, as Hawkins had recommended six years before. Drake's commission was dated July 1st, but his action was stayed. The Queen pledged her aid to the Dutch in August, and Drake left Plymouth in September. Most people realized that it was war. The Queen shrank from admitting it until the Armada sailed three years later. There was no formal declaration by either side.

A year earlier, in July 1584, John Hawkins had addressed a memorial to Burghley. He said that, although a man of peace, he believed that war was inevitable, and accordingly suggested the best means of annoying the King of Spain without charge to the Queen and with great profit to her subjects. An agreement should be made with Don Antonio for Englishmen to fight under his flag. The Queen should give them the right to victual, refit and sell their booty at some west-country port, on payment of a percentage to her. English gentlemen and merchants would take a prominent part, as would the Dutch and French Protestants. Revolts against Spain would be raised in the Portuguese colonies. The Spanish fisheries, which would supply victuals for a force to invade England, could be destroyed. The Atlantic islands might be sacked and their defences broken up, the coast of Spain itself being kept in constant alarm. Drake's East Indian voyage may be incorporated in the plan, and kept secret until all is ready. Even in peace time, says Hawkins, it costs three times as much to equip shipping in Spain as it does in England, and under the naval pressure here proposed, it will be impossible for Spain to create a fleet strong enough to fight that of England. All this, Hawkins points out, is not equivalent to beginning war. The Queen may make it matter of diplomacy for years to come.

The above is the second of John Hawkins's written statements of policy for the conduct of hostilities. It is more developed than the first (of 1579). It will be followed by another evolved in subsequent years, the whole forming an interesting series, such as we have from no other Elizabethan leader. The 1584 statement must be read in the light of the attendant circumstances, the chief of which was the Queen's aversion from a formal and irrevocable declaration. Hawkins had to propose, not the best of all courses, but the course that had a chance of acceptance. He did not deceive himself about what constituted war, but he had to leave to Elizabeth the possibility of deceiving herself.

BOOK III
THE QUEEN'S SHIPS

I

THE TUDOR NAVY

The history of the Royal Navy as a force continuous in existence and development begins substantially with the Tudors. Mediaeval fleets rose and declined and perished out of being; but the fleet which took shape in the late fifteenth century had a history which has lasted unbroken to the present day, generation interlocking with generation, of ships and men, so that it was never possible to say of any given date: here the whole thing ended and something else began. Such a statement is possible of the early fifteenth century, when the ministers of Henry VI's minority terminated the existence of the royal fleet built up by Henry V. There indeed the whole thing did end, although it was not until after the Wars of the Roses that something else began, the Navy whose Tudor century is the subject of these chapters. The events of the half-century of troubles illustrated the need for a strong regular Navy. The lack of it caused three main disadvantages: English merchants and their shipping were attacked and maltreated without redress; English governments were repeatedly challenged by adventurers who could land unopposed and build up a following; and the recovery of Normandy and Brittany by the French crown gave France a northern coast rich in ships and men from which a full-dress invasion of the English realm was possible, as it had not been while northern France was occupied by the English.

If England was to thrive as a modern state it must have a modern navy. But apprehension was tardy and money scarce, and the new fleet was of slow growth. Henry VII took over a few small ships from his Yorkist predecessors, but no organization for making proper use of them, nothing that could dignify them with the name of a service as the word is now used. Their principal use indeed was most likely that of making trading voyages to increase the royal revenue. Henry himself built half-a-dozen genuine fighting ships, of which the *Regent* and the *Sovereign* were among the first-class vessels of their time. Records of his naval activity are scanty, but the existence of his little fleet may help to account for the contrast between the earlier and later parts of his reign. In the earlier he was frequently invaded or threatened by his foreign enemies. In the later he was strong and immune and able to threaten others. His finance and diplomacy had much to do with the advance; but perhaps his Navy assisted.

Henry VIII was imbued from the outset with the importance of the fighting Navy, and so were his ministers and people. The wars of their time were against France and Scotland. The functions of the Navy were to facilitate invasion of France and prevent invasion by France; to keep open the Channel highway in the interests of our continental allies; and to transport or accompany English forces up the east coast to the Firth of Forth. Henry VIII's Navy was thus a home-waters force. Its most distant southerly reach was to the Bay of Biscay; northerly, half way up the east coast of Scotland; and easterly, to the shores of the Low Countries: westwards, it never cruised beyond the Land's End. The same continued to be substantially true under Edward VI and Mary, and during the first half of Elizabeth's reign. In the 1580's the Navy suddenly and immensely increased its range of action and became an oceanic force, in answer to a demand for new applications of sea power made by officers with ocean experience, chief among whom were Hawkins and Drake. The change of employment necessitated many other changes, and should be borne in mind as the key to the transactions of John Hawkins's later years.

At the beginning of his reign Henry VIII rapidly increased the numbers of his fleet by purchases from foreign merchants as well as by building in English yards. A varied assortment was the result, from which a few standard types evolved as building progressed and the misfits were eliminated. Henry's greatest ships were of the high-charged type of which the *Jesus of Lubeck*, illustrated in this book, was an example. They were broad in proportion to their length, sometimes in the ratio of one to two-and-a-half, and needed to be in order to carry their high superstructures. These, from a broadside view, present the ship as hopelessly top-heavy; they were made possible only by the fact that the sides tumbled in above the waterline, and poop and fore-castle were very much narrower than the main portion of the hull. The overhanging forecastle illustrated in the *Minion* and the *Jesus of Lubeck* was characteristic of the type, which is sometimes described as carrack-built, from its resemblance to the large sailing merchantmen employed in the Mediterranean. The carrack-built ships were the main fighting strength of Henry VIII's Navy, headed by the *Great Harry* of 1,500 tons and de-scending to small and useful sizes like the *Minion* of 300, and others smaller.

Henry also built some large flush-decked vessels of four or five hundred tons, devoid of superstructures, driven mainly by sails, but provided also with oars for quick manoeuvring in battle. These ships were not intended to risk boarding and fighting hand-to-hand with the castellated carracks, but rather to keep their distance and batter the enemy with their great guns. They were known as galleasses, another Italian word which signified a large vessel with oars and sails and a proportion, beam to length, of one to four-and-a-half. As the word galleass was applied in England the arithmetical proportion was not strictly intended, and a galleass meant any long ship without high superstructures. Henry VIII's galleasses were not an enduring type, and seem for the most part to have died out of the fleet or to have been modified in rebuilding before the accession of Elizabeth. They had, however, an influence on the ideas of the succeeding generation. Smaller vessels, again with oar-power as auxiliary to sails, were known as rowbarges. Not much is certainly known of them, but they appear to have been shorter and more seaworthy than the pure galleys of the Mediterranean, a fragile and delicate type which never flourished in northern Europe. The early Tudor rowbarge was more nearly the progenitor of the Elizabethan pinnace which, in the Navy, was a small sailing vessel of 50 to 80 tons, provided with auxiliary oars, and used for scouting and despatch-carrying. Among the private adventurers the word pinnace was applied to almost any small craft down to an open rowing-boat.

In the armament of his ships Henry effected a radical improvement. Before his time the fighting vessels even of the first class had been provided only with little guns firing light projectiles at close range, stones or iron balls of two or three pounds weight, or showers of 'hail-shot'. These weapons were intended to kill the enemy's men but hardly to sink his ship, and were in effect small-arms. Their lightness and small size is attested by their numbers: Henry VII's *Regent* of about 600 tons had 225 of them. A fight between vessels so armed was decided by grappling and close conflict across the decks. Outside Brest in 1512 the *Regent* fought in this way with the *Cordelière* of France. The English were gaining the upper hand when in an instant the French ship was 'a flaming fire', probably by the explosion of her powder. The English could not get clear in time and the *Regent* took fire also; and both were lost with nearly all on board. Fire was the deadliest peril, and it induced a new policy of lying off and battering instead of closing and boarding. This in its turn demanded the use of heavy guns which would sink the opponent from a distance. Such appears to have been the origin of the change which Henry VIII personally introduced into his fleet. In the high-charged carrack-built ships he retained the little pieces in the superstructures for defence against boarding, but lower down in the hull he placed a few heavy battering guns. His galleasses relied exclusively on such guns and on oars to keep them in motion to avoid being grappled. But naval battles were not so numerous as naval wars, and it is a curious fact that all through the fighting sixteenth century from the battle of Brest in 1512 to Drake's attack on Cadiz in 1587 the English Navy was never engaged in an action decisive enough to entail the loss of a first-class ship by itself or its opponents.[1] Such an action might have occurred half-a-dozen times, but never did; and English admirals had to judge the validity of their gunnery and constructional policy by reference to foreign battles like Lepanto and Terceira and the irregular commerce-destruction by the privateers in the Channel wars.

[1] The *Mary Rose* was lost when preparing to engage the French in 1545. This was not due to enemy action but to water pouring through open gun-ports as the ship heeled to the wind.

As the reign of Henry VIII progressed, the national perils and the need for a strong navy increased. His dissolution of the monasteries and repudiation of Rome imperilled the alliance with Spain and the Empire without terminating the ancient quarrel with France. On two occasions, in 1539 and in 1545, Charles V and Francis I seemed about to combine against him. The reign of Francis I was one of great progress in French sea power. The full possession of the northern coast strengthened the royal naval policy; the development of the new port of Havre de Grace provided France with a Channel harbour and dockyard equivalent to a combination of Portsmouth and Southampton; and the enterprise of all the coastline from Dieppe to St. Malo bred numbers of captains and seamen with fighting experience gained on the coasts of Guinea, Brazil and the Caribbean, and with the character that comes from facing difficulties without support. In the war of 1544-6 the resulting French navy was a fine force fit to enterprise the invasion of England, and it required all England's naval strength to parry the blow.

Henry's Reformation intensified the danger but also increased the force with which he could meet it. The confiscation of Church property provided a fund wherewith the coast was fortified and the Navy strengthened. In the years before and after 1540 the Navy was in fact replaced, with new ships for old. The extent of the change has been obscured by the retention of the ships' names. There was a *Great Harry* in 1515 and in 1545, a *Mary Rose,* a *Minion* and other names throughout the reign. But the ships themselves were different vessels in the earlier and later periods. The first *Great Harry* was of 1,500 tons and was broken up at Portsmouth in the late 30's. The second *Great Harry* was of 1,000 tons and was burnt by accident at Woolwich in 1553. The *Mary Rose* also was a name that covered two different ships, with a replacement date about 1536. The explanation of a very deceiving practice is that the King's ships were properties regarded in the same way as the King's houses. If the King's palace of Greenwich had been destroyed by fire or suffered to decay, an entirely new one might have been built and would still have been the palace of Greenwich. In the same way the *Great Harry* or the *Mary Rose* might become obsolete and be replaced by vessels different in every timber and dimension, but these new ships would occupy the same relative positions in the establishment of the fleet and would still be the *Great Harry* and the *Mary Rose*. The process was called 'new building' and has often been erroneously equated with rebuilding in the sense of a thorough overhaul. New building was much more than that, and the sense of the words is to be taken literally. It has been necessary to be explicit on this matter, because new building was still going on in John Hawkins's time and still meant the building of a new ship, although she might contain some of the fittings and materials of an old one.

Dockyards were necessary for the building, repair and laying-up of the growing fleet. Henry VII chose Portsmouth for his chief dockyard, and Robert Brigandine, his Clerk of the Ships, constructed there the first dry dock recorded in England. Southampton, close at hand, was then the second port in the kingdom, with plenty of materials and craftsmen available for the King's service. Henry VIII maintained Portsmouth as the chief fighting base of his fleet, well placed for offence against France, the town itself fortified, a spacious natural harbour within, and the sheltered anchorage of Spithead without, where fleets could assemble in readiness for speedy action. For these purposes Portsmouth was good, but for laying-up and winter work between campaigns it was not so good. Unless protected by a large standing force it was open to raids by the French, who might mobilize early and take the sea before their adversaries should be ready. Henry therefore developed building and repairing yards within the Thames estuary, where the shoals and sands and the distance from France were reckoned a sufficient deterrent to the sudden raid. Early in the reign royal dockyards were established at Woolwich and Deptford, immune from attack and more convenient for government supervision, and these places diminished the need to lay up valuable ships at Portsmouth. Three years after Henry's death the government of Protector Somerset laid the foundations of the yard at Gillingham on the Medway, subsequently known as Chatham Dockyard, which became the chief home port of the Navy in the Elizabethan period.

While the King's ships numbered no more than half-a-dozen, a single official sufficed for their administration. He was the Clerk of the Ships, traceable as early as the reign of King John. With the Tudors the office began to grow, and Robert Brigandine, who served from 1495 to 1526, was a man of many talents, able not only to keep the accounts but to supervise if not to design the construction of the first *Great Harry*.[1] Brigandine, however, was not left to carry on alone. The early growth of the fleet and the business of the first French war caused the appointment of a Keeper of the King's Storehouses for supplying the King's Ships, and this office took a financial bias and developed successively into Paymaster and then Treasurer of the Navy. Its second holder was William Gonson, a merchant and sea captain, who was favoured by Henry VIII but died by suicide in 1544, leaving a son to carry on the succession in the naval service. When the Keeper of the Storehouses was transforming himself into Treasurer, there was need for a new officer to supervise materials and to check waste and fraud in their purchase and disposal. In 1524 the first Comptroller of the King's Ships was appointed for these duties. This was at the close of the second French war, which had doubtless revealed abuses.

The third war was a much more serious affair, waged by a new and stronger Navy fighting against a stronger and more determined enemy. It led to several developments in 1545, its most dangerous year. Three new officers were appointed, the Lieutenant of the Admiralty, the Master of the Ordnance for the Ships, and the Surveyor of the Ships, whose primary duty seems to have been that of seeing that they were properly rigged. The King's artillery and weapons for land as well as sea were stored in the Tower of London, and the Master of the Ordnance represented a separate naval department for their supervision. In 1545 also we have the first mention of these officers in joint consultation as a council or board, the Navy Board, which may be dated from that year and was to last for nearly three centuries to its abolition in 1832. It was

[1] In this account of the origins of the Navy Board I am indebted to *The Principal Officers of the Navy*, by A. W. Johns, an article in *The Mariner's Mirror*, January, 1928, which supersedes previous work on the subject.

formerly thought that the Board and all its members, except the Clerk, were created at one stroke in 1545–6. The above account shows that it was of more gradual growth. The 'at one stroke' impression ought to have aroused our scepticism, for it was not the way in which administrative machinery was produced in England before the age of the planners.

The Lord Admiral or Lord High Admiral[1] has not yet been mentioned in this survey of the early Tudor navy because he was not at the outset a naval officer in the true sense of the word. His main responsibility was the operation of the legal system as it applied to shipping, in other words, the jurisdiction of the High Court of Admiralty, over which he presided by a deputy of his appointment, the Judge of the Admiralty. Until the reign of Henry VIII the Lord Admiral might be, and generally was, an individual who never went to sea. Henry VIII made him a naval officer by appointing to the position men who were capable of leading fleets. Sir Edward Howard, the first Lord Admiral appointed by Henry, was killed in action with the French in 1513. His successors were active leaders, the last of the reign being Lord Lisle, who commanded the fleet in 1545, and became successively Earl of Warwick and Duke of Northumberland in the reign of Edward VI. The Lord Admiral was always one of the great officers of state, a member of the Privy Council, and occupied with the highest affairs. As such, he did not give regular attention to the administration of the Navy, whose routine was conducted by the officers already described. The appointment of the Lieutenant of the Admiralty in 1545 was an attempt to bring the Lord Admiral by deputy into the work of administration, for it was intended that the Lieutenant of the Admiralty should be the head of the Navy Board. The arrangement did not take root, and Elizabeth did not fill the office of Lieutenant when it became vacant in 1562. Thenceforward the Lord Admiral, although he did not commonly attend the Navy Board, received its reports, and the Treasurer of the Navy became the working head of the Board and more responsible than anyone else for the administration of the fleet.

[1] Lord High Admiral was the official title in Elizabeth's time, but its holder was almost invariably referred to as the Lord Admiral.

The Royal Navy possessed fifty-three ships at the time of Henry's death. Six of them were of 500 tons or more, nineteen between 200 and 500 tons. The total tonnage was 11,268. The greater part of it was in new vessels, built since the dissolution of the monasteries. This fleet had justified the wealth and care bestowed on it by foiling a French invasion in 1545, by enabling England to hold the balance between the Hapsburg and Valois combinations at other times, by applying pressure to the Scots on the shores of the Firth of Forth, and by helping to discourage a general continental movement to restore the Roman jurisdiction in England in 1539.

There followed a period of eleven years which may almost be called the interregnum of the Tudor period, the reigns of Edward VI and Mary, in which naval power declined. In the six years of Edward VI the decline, although real, was not immediately evident, for Northumberland, the former Lord Admiral, was first influential and then supreme, and he understood sea power in principle and detail. In this time the Chatham yard was founded, a choice of location that was almost prophetic in its relation to the Elizabethan problems of defence, and the administrative machine was rounded off by the creation of one more office, that of Surveyor of the Victuals for the Seas. Its first holder, Edward Baeshe, was honest and devoted, and carried on the work until the opening of Elizabeth's Spanish War. He was not a member of the Navy Board, as one would naturally expect him to be.

The decline in the Navy was for the most part in such matters as did not show on paper and could be disguised in the public view. These wooden ships, constructed often of doubtful timber by men with only rudimentary ideas of the causes of dry rot, required constant vigilance to keep them in good condition. When rot appeared , as inevitably it did, the only remedy was to cut out and replace the affected part, a process that was always going on when the laid-up ships were properly looked after. To neglect or conceal the trouble was sometimes to involve the whole ship. In the minority of Edward VI the state fell into the control of self-seekers who cared less for the public interest than Henry VIII had done. They busied themselves in making their fortunes, and their example spread downwards. It is evident that it affected the administration of the Navy. Expenditure in the dockyards continued, but they became less capable of turning out fleets for service. Ships were unfit and materials lacking. The results were seen in the reign of Mary, but the process must have begun before. In 1555 ten decayed ships were sold out of the service, and how decayed they were may be judged from the prices realized, £8 and £10 apiece for the small craft, £35 for the *Grand Mistress* of 450 tons, built ten years before at a cost at at least £1,500.[1] The *Great Harry* was lost by fire at the opening of the reign, and not replaced; while other ships silently disappear from the lists. War with France began again in 1557, and in the winter of 1557-8 England had no adequate squadron afloat. Henry VIII had been used to lay up his great ships, but always to keep a winter guard of the medium sort on duty in the Channel. This time there were only five 'ships and barks', with 400 men, and Calais fell to an attack which would not have been attempted if the English had commanded the sea.

It must be admitted that direct evidence is lacking for much of the naval administration of the decade between Henry VIII and Elizabeth, and that adverse judgement is mainly inferential. But the inferences are made from the results, and they are clear enough. Ships decayed beyond repair form one; the failure to save Calais, another; and the final figures of naval strength in Mary's reign are a third. When the Queen died in 1558 there were twenty-six royal ships, or fifty per cent fewer than Henry's total. The total tonnage was 7,110 tons, or thirty-six per cent less. Some of this surviving tonnage was in fact unserviceable. We have seen the *Jesus of Lubeck*, whose 700 tons are included in it, condemned as beyond repair at the opening of Elizabeth's reign. The French war had led to some new buying and building, some of which was completed in time to be included in the above total. If the figures of 1557 were fully available they would show an even greater decline.

[1] A 450-ton ship, honestly built, cost £5 a ton in 1575 (see below p. 261). In 1545 the cost would have been lower, but at least £3-£4 a ton.

A HIGH-CHARGED SHIP

From the painting *The Fall of Icarus*, by P. Brueghel the elder

Making allowance for the poor condition of the ships and their unreadiness due to the depletion of the stores, we may assess the strength of Mary's Navy at no more than half that of her father's. Under Elizabeth there was an improvement. The Queen was not, like her father, a lover of the sea with a lively practical interest in the fleet. She had, however, a habit of promoting efficiency and discouraging the more flagrant forms of corruption. Burghley understood the importance of sea power and its more immediate uses in the defence of England and the support of her foreign allies. He made himself sufficiently acquainted with naval affairs to have a good general idea of the country's requirements and the condition of the fleet, but he was not a master of the details which could only be learnt by lifelong experience with shipping. Burghley was a good non-specialist minister of marine, and the Queen seems to have left naval matters mainly to him. This is evident from many circumstances and not least from the fact that, as we shall see, John Hawkins as head of the Navy Board addressed nearly all his official correspondence to the Lord Treasurer. In their first years the Queen and her minister stopped the rot in the Navy and stabilized its strength at something considerably more than Mary's standard, if less than Henry's. They did not greatly increase the number of the ships which they took over in 1558, but they did convert paper strength into reality. They built or bought almost immediately four or five new ships of the largest sort, and these replaced the decayed wrecks in Mary's list without expanding the total. The fleet's numbers of vessels large and small remained at from twenty-five to thirty, with some the individual vessels kept in reasonable repair, although others were left in poor state. Strength in those years was still measured in relation to France; and the French fleet under the sons of Catherine de Medici was less formidable than under Francis I and Henry II.

The personnel of Elizabeth's Navy Board demands attention. Its senior member was Benjamin Gonson, a son of 'old Master William Gonson' who had served as Henry's chief naval official for twenty years. Benjamin Gonson seems, unless there has been a confusion of identities, to have been a clergyman, recorded in

1542 as rector of St. Mary Colechurch in London.[1] Whether he retained the benefice does not appear, but his appointment as Clerk of the Ships in 1545 was the beginning of a service on the Navy Board which lasted the rest of his life. From Clerk he became Surveyor in 1546, and in 1549 was promoted to Treasurer, an office which he held for twenty-eight years. During that time there are indications that he was engaged in commerce. He was an investor in Guinea and West Indian ventures. He never went to sea in command of any of the royal ships, as did all the other members of the Navy Board, and it is evident that he was strictly a landsman. John Hawkins married his daughter Katherine in 1559.

On the death of old William Gonson in 1544 his office of Paymaster (which was evolving into Treasurer) was filled by the Bristol merchant and seaman John Winter. He served at sea as captain of one of the King's ships in the campaign of 1545, contracted a burning fever, and died at the end of the year. Two of his sons, William and George Winter, entered the royal service. William Winter became Surveyor of the Ships—his Elizabethan designation was Surveyor of the Marine Causes—in 1549; and in 1557 he was also appointed Master of the Ordnance of the Ships. He held the two offices concurrently until his death in 1589. George Winter was made Clerk of the Ships about 1560 and held the post until he died in 1582. William Holstocke, an old servant of Henry, who had been granted a small annuity in 1546 for 'services in our marine causes', was made Comptroller of the Ships in 1562 and likewise retained office until his death in 1589. He must then have been an old man, for he had been at sea as early as 1534, when he made a voyage to the Levant in one of William Gonson's ships. All these men had junior service in the Navy behind them before they became Principal Officers, as the members of the Navy Board were later designated. While they were Principal Officers they all (except Benjamin Gonson) took their turns in command

[1] A. W. Johns in *Mariner's Mirror, ut supra*, p. 34. The doubt is mine and is only a doubt. It arises from the fact that the marriage of the clergy was not authorized until 1547, while Gonson had a legitimate daughter of marriageable age in 1559. It is possible that he was married in spite of prohibition.

of such squadrons of the royal ships as were sent on service. It was a practice of the Board that each of the officers should take over the work of any of the others when necessary, and so release them for the sea service which maintained touch between the office and the companies afloat.

To sum up, the Navy Board, for approximately the first twenty years of Elizabeth's reign, consisted of Benjamin Gonson, Treasurer; William Winter, Surveyor and Master of the Ordnance; William Holstocke, Comptroller; and George Winter, Clerk of the Ships. The Lord Admiral during this period was Lord Clinton, afterwards Earl of Lincoln, who held office from 1557 to 1585. He appears to have had less practical contact with the Navy than did some of his predecessors under Henry VIII.

All these men had been brought up in the service of a Navy that fought only in home waters. The high light of their experience was the campaign of 1545, when two great fleets had faced each other and the fighting had been at Spithead and off Brighton. Since that time there had been more engagements with the French in the Channel, expeditions against eastern Scotland, convoying of the Bordeaux wine-ships, partial mobilizations at Chatham on alarms from the Netherlands, convoying of the Hamburg fleets in 1569, roundings-up of Channel rovers, and one general turn-out of the whole Navy under the Lord Admiral to see the Spaniards and Flemings down Channel in 1570. In spite of widening horizons and of adventures, in which they themselves invested, in distant parts of the world, not one of these men had personally sailed beyond the seas of Europe, and not a squadron of the Navy which they administered had ever been more than a few days' sail from Portsmouth or the Thames. These circumstances governed their ideas and practice more inevitably than they would do now, when there are professional books and organized instruction to widen a man's view beyond the scope of his own experience. For them, the Navy would always have to fight in the Channel and the North Sea, and no other scenes of action were conceivable. The carrack-built floating castle was their ideal man-of-war. No doubt its swarms of men consumed the victuals at inordinate speed and themselves died off rapidly of burning fevers and other penalties upon dirt and overcrowding. It did not greatly matter; they were always close to England, whence new beef, beer and sailors could be had. The Navy Board had never seen what Hawkins had seen, their heavy superstructures wrenching themselves asunder in a violent sea, far out between the continents away from shelter and aid. Any attempt to convert them to the view that a Navy fit to serve thousands of miles from home was now needed, and that it would be a different Navy from that which they had known all their lives, was pretty certain to encounter their incredulity, scorn and opposition; such being the nature of practical men who never open a book.

When John Hawkins, with his ocean experience of ships and men, his expectation of war with Spain, and his views upon the employment of the Navy in such a war, undertook the conversion of the fleet and its officers to new purposes, he was asking for trouble on that ground alone. There were other grounds also on which the advent of a new man with new standards was unwelcome to the Navy Board. Public servants, chosen as first-class men at their jobs, were extremely ill paid if they pocketed only the halfpence prescribed in their patents of appointment. They always took perquisites which stuck to their fingers in the course of their transaction of the Crown's business; and since everyone knew it and no one objected, there was nothing immoral in their doing so. The perquisites were part of their remuneration. But there was no hard and fast line to be drawn between such pickings and what may be called financial irregularities, transactions to which the Queen and her ministers would have objected had they known of them. These again shaded imperceptibly into the sort of corruption so flagrant that only a weak and corrupt government would wink at it or fail to know that it was going on. The Navy Board had known this last stage in the days of Edward VI and Mary. In the early years of Elizabeth it grew more respectable and moved back into stage two, the sort of peculation that could be concealed from reasonably efficient employers. That was possible because it could be shrouded in the technicalities of an art and mystery not understood by those who did not practise it. The Queen and Cecil were not fools, but neither were they dealers in timber and rope, and they could not themselves distinguish between a ship in fit condition and one full of hidden defects. They had to trust their experts. The experts were moderate and sensible men. They kept the Navy fairly but not superlatively fit for the duties that fell to it in a time of petty campaigns that were short of serious war; and the Queen and her people paid about twice as much as they should have done for the service rendered. That, as will appear, is a fair statement of the conduct and efficiency of the Navy Board in the sixties and seventies.

A glance at personalities may round off the delineation. We know nothing of Benjamin Gonson in his best days, when he must have displayed good ability to have earned promotion in spite of his lack of experience at sea. We have light on him only in his closing stage. Then he was well intentioned but weak, worn out and sick in spirit at the corruption which he saw but could not stop. He was glad to resign at last, and told his successor that it would be a thankless job: 'I shall pluck out a thorn from my foot and set it in yours.' The master spirit in the Navy Board was the elder Winter, Sir William as he became in 1573. Filling two important offices, which enabled him to deal more directly with goods and with men than did the Treasurer, he was able to organize thoroughly for his personal profit and at the same time to achieve a standard of efficiency. He did it in the character of a masterful man, greedy for wealth and power, careful of his reputation, intolerant of any rival. With all his covetousness he was not mean. He did promote the public service after his own, and to that end displayed a magnanimity which must modify judgements that would otherwise be harsh; a big man, who had to be fought and beaten before reform and progress could win their way in the Navy. His brother George was less prominent, less obviously masterful, but, so far as we can see, his ally and assistant. Between them they enjoyed control, whose continuance they would seek to ensure by a suitable filling of the approaching vacancy in the treasurership. No doubt Sir William considered himself the candidate with the best claim. There remains William Holstocke the Comptroller. About him there is little to be said. Whatever he may really have been, the surviving evidence gives an impression that his character was neutral and colourless. We know he was there in the office and the dockyards, for his signature appears on the routine papers; but neither praise nor blame of him as an individual is on record. He shares only in the common accusation that was to be launched against the aims and methods of the Navy Board. This is a negative impression resulting from lack of evidence, and it may be quite wrong. Holstocke must have had ability, to stand where he did, and to be sent out in independent commands as he sometimes was.

II

HAWKINS AND THE NAVY BOARD

In the years after San Juan de Ulua, John Hawkins had no doubt that Spain was the enemy and that England's freedom and religion were in danger. We have seen him fooling the Spanish king and his ambassador, assisting in the Channel blockade, organizing his western squadron, taking part in the defence of La Rochelle, and asking leave to attack the plate fleets. He was thinking out a new naval policy, and there are indications that in the mid-seventies he was talking to Burghley about it and beginning to influence the Navy Board. That he already had his eye on the Board is evident from the fact that he had secured the reversion of George Winter's office of Clerk of the Ships. The vacancy did not occur till 1582, before which time Hawkins had entered the Board at the top and not at the bottom.

The French wars had imbued on the minds of English statesmen some fixed doctrines about the employment of the Navy. Its use when strong and offensive was to drive the enemy off the sea and cover the transit of English armies to his shores. When the enemy was in a position to invade England, the Navy was expected to cruise along the coasts—'to ply up and down' was the phrase in use—and intercept the assailants. After the Reformation England grew more susceptible to invasion, since it was calculated that the religious dissidents would form a serious force in favour of the enemy. Whether they would really have done so is not known, for they were never put to the test, but Spanish ambassadors and English exiles had great hopes of them. The defensive value of the Navy was therefore emphasized in Elizabeth's reign, and in due course circumstances changed its duty from defence against France to defence against Spain. The regular parry to a Spanish threat was mobilization at Chatham to guard against a landing from the Netherlands, and at Plymouth against a direct blow from Spain. Since neither the Queen nor anyone else entertained the possibility of invading Spain, as English kings in the past had invaded France, this defensive policy was unlikely to win the war, and by itself could only result in successive guards against successive thrusts until at length a thrust got home. Yet this was all that could be looked for from the old Navy and the old Navy Board, whose strategy and organization derived from the French wars of Henry VIII. The ships could not go far from their home waters because they could not carry sufficient stores for the purpose, quite apart from the fact that they were unsuitable in design. Sir William Winter's Navy Board were men of experience in the old sort of service, and they were unwilling to think beyond the bounds of their experience.

John Hawkins, whose wide-ranging mind had generated the political-commercial schemes of the sixties, was quite unsatisfied with the above as the pattern of an Anglo-Spanish war. The ocean offered something better. Philip II was chronically at war in Europe with his Netherland rebels and the Turks in the Mediterranean. He had besides to maintain garrisons in his Italian provinces, which would not have remained his without them. His armies were so expensive and his financial system so wasteful that his European revenues did not nearly meet his expenditure, and his military power rested on the treasure received from his American empire. Even with that, he could only just carry on, pledging future assets for present loans, hovering on the verge of bankruptcy, his credit standing at twelve per cent while Elizabeth could raise money at eight. That Philip's power depended upon the treasure, without which it would quickly fall, was the opinion of financiers and statesmen throughout Europe, and undoubtedly of Philip himself. Professor R. B. Merriman, Philip's modern historian, calls for caution in estimating the proportionate amount of the American treasure.[1] It naturally varied; for the 1570's it was about ten per cent or more of the revenues due to the crown from European sources. But the American treasure was the profit from the American empire after all its expenses of government had been paid: while the European

[1] *The Rise of the Spanish Empire*, Vol. IV, New York, 1934: compare pp. 207 sqq. and 436 sqq.

revenues were offset by the European expenditure, which was greater than they were. The American treasure alone staved off collapse. The detailed figures were not known to Philip's contemporaries, but their general effect was no secret and may even have been exaggerated. 'It is his Indian gold', wrote Ralegh in after years, 'that endangereth and disturbeth all the nations of Europe;' and John Hawkins appreciated the fact when Ralegh was a youth. Hawkins's ideas on a Spanish war were that Philip depended for his life upon the plate fleets and that sea power applied upon the Atlantic trade routes would bring him down. A surprise attack, such as he had proposed in 1570, might capture one plate fleet as a promising beginning, but there was no great certainty of it and still less of its continuance. A real effort would demand an ocean-going Navy to maintain the pressure. In order to provide it, he brought his energies to bear upon the Navy Board. From 1577 onwards we have clear evidence of his ideas. Before that date they rest upon inference and must be discussed with caution.

We may bear in mind that from the period of the slaving voyages Hawkins was known to the Queen and on such terms of free speech with Burghley as must have resulted from the secret business on which they were jointly engaged. He was elected a member of two successive Parliaments, the second of which remained in existence for some years. He was therefore in a position to speak to the government as a man of weight on the subjects of which he had special knowledge. He had facilities for knowing what went on in the dockyards and what was the policy of the Navy Board, for his father-in-law was head of the Board and he himself was formally promised a seat on it. Sir William Winter, its most active member, was his business associate in many ventures. There is therefore a case for believing that Hawkins's advice may have had influence with the government and the Navy Board from the moment that he began to tender it.

When was that? It may well have been in 1569, when he was hot from the misfortunes that would never have befallen him but for the unseaworthy qualities of the *Jesus of Lubeck*. Her faults were the rottenness which neglect entailed in any ship, but also the inherent weakness of structure unavoidable in the high-charged ship. It was plain mechanics that such a ship was unfit for an ocean voyage. Men may not have had that from textbooks, but they had it all the more in their senses and their brains. Hawkins had visions of fighting Spain in the Atlantic and the Caribbean, and he had no wish to do it with high-charged ships. In 1570 the *Foresight* of 300 tons was launched for the Queen, presumably laid down in that or the previous year. She was of a new type that came to be known as galleon-built, with a proportion of beam to length on water line of about one to three-and-a-half. Whether her poop and forecastle were high or low we cannot say, for there is no drawing or detail; but in after years, when the galleon type was established, the poop was much lower than of old and the forecastle even more markedly reduced and set back aft of the stemhead, instead of overhanging it. The high overhanging weights of the carrack, which loosened the stoutest fastenings in a plunging and rolling ship, were reduced in the galleon to a quarter or less of their dynamic effect, with the result that Hawkins's galleons could defy any weather and stay at sea for months without harm. It is possible that the *Foresight* of 1570 was the first of them.

If the innovation was not due to Hawkins it is difficult to suggest anyone else who may have urged it. The new ships of the previous decade had been of the more ancient type, and the personnel of the Navy Board which produced them remained unchanged. In the next two new ships, the *Swiftsure* and *Dreadnought* of 1573, the length was somewhat lessened in proportion to the beam, a partial but not complete return to earlier practice. Then came the *Revenge* of 1575–7, 450 tons, very moderate in size, yet a hard hitter, as her end in '91 was to prove. Drake thought her the perfect galleon of his time, and chose her of all the fleet as his ship for the Armada fight. She became the type on which all the new battleships were built after Hawkins took charge in 1577. Was she his child in 1575? We cannot be positive, but it is very likely. Either the Navy Board taught Hawkins how to build ocean-going fighting ships, or he taught them. And if the Board, where did they learn it?

From inference we pass to facts. They are drawn from a report made by Hawkins to Burghley.[1] The copy we have is not dated, but internal evidence fixes its date as 1578 or late in 1577, just after Hawkins had taken office as Treasurer of the Navy. Internal evidence also shows that it is a formal presentation of matters that had already been discussed with the minister. Ten years later a detractor of Hawkins asserted that he had gained his appointment 'by way of accusation',[2] an evident reference to the substance of this report. We are entitled to say therefore that in substance the report was made before he took office. He wanted the Navy to be made as strong as possible before the outbreak of war. He knew that finance was the greatest obstacle. The Queen ruled a nation which objected to being taxed and was free to say so. Increased expenditure in time of peace would arouse discontent. Extravagance would foment revolution. The only way to strengthen the Queen's fleet was to secure greater value for the money already being spent.

Here it is necessary to explain two technical terms, the 'ordinary' and the 'extraordinary' expenditure. The ordinary comprised the cost of moorings, repairs to the ships while afloat or grounded but not in dry dock, upkeep of wharves and storehouses, wages of shipkeepers and dockyard staffs, and purchase of all victuals and materials incident to these services. The extraordinary was the expenditure on 'new building' and heavy repairs in dry dock. Additional new ships which were not replacements of old ones were an extra charge not included in either category, and so also were the expenses of mobilization and sea service, for which the stores, munitions and wages were defrayed by special payments from the Treasury upon the requisition of the Navy Board. The ordinary and extraordinary together therefore represented the cost of maintaining the Navy at a fixed establishment in its laid-up or peacetime condition.

Hawkins's report begins with broad considerations for economy. The ordinary, it states, is now costing nearly £6,000 a year. It may be done for £4,000, better than now, the number of ship-

[1] Lansdowne MSS. 113, ff. 45–7, endorsed, 'Abuses in the Admiralty touching Her Majesty's Navy, exhibited by Mr. Hawkins'.
[2] Lansdowne MSS. 52, art. 43.

keepers augmented, and all things better performed. Under the extraordinary heading the heavy repairs are being done in great disorder, and the Queen is monstrously overcharged. The last repair of six ships and their boats may serve as an example. A warrant was granted for £4,845, which would have done the work royally and left something over. Instead of that Her Majesty is already £600 in debt, and another £1,000 will not finish the task, 'which proceeds of the wilful covetousness of one man, and to set forth his glory.' In the same way the cost of building new ships has been unwarrantably raised, so that vessels that ought to have cost £2,200 have come to £4,000, and in general the Queen has paid for 900 loads of timber where 500 would have sufficed. The ships' boatswains were formerly obliged to indent for tackle and cordage, and the indents were filed in the Navy Office. Now the Surveyor (W. Winter) keeps all such business in his private books, and the Office knows nothing of what is supplied to the ships.

In the purchase and disposal of timber and plank, the report proceeds, great abuses prevail. Since 1570 the Queen has paid £9,000 for these materials, and not £4,000 worth has been used in her service. The purveyors of timber, using the royal prerogative of compulsory purchase at fixed prices, make great profits, for they sell the best of the material for private use and make the state pay extremely for the refuse. When the quality is considered, the Queen does not get one-third of the value she pays for. The master-shipwrights corroborate these statements, which have already been discussed at length with Lord Burghley and the Chancellor of the Exchequer.[1] Although this fraud is done in the name of another, 'we[2] say that it is for Sir William Winter's commodity.'

Detailed statements follow, headed: 'Matters that touch Sir William Winter particularly.' The *Mary Fortune*, a ship of his, was built in great part with the Queen's material. The *Edward*, another of his ships, was built entirely of royal timber. The timber for the Queen's *Foresight* was already for the most part in Her Majesty's possession, yet she paid for it all again, as Matthew Baker the shipwright will prove. Many of the ships are decayed

[1] Evidence that the substance of the report predated its existing form.
[2] 'We' may stand for Hawkins and Benjamin Gonson.

and not repaired. Winter uses the Queen's timber to build wharves for private use. The ship which Francis Drake had was built with much of the Queen's timber, and so also were his four pinnaces made at Her Majesty's charge, but Winter took of him £120 for them.[1] He also sold to Mr. Frobisher two pinnaces for £24, but they were built of the Queen's stuff and at her charge. Masts are sold, but nothing is paid into the Treasury. All the decayed great cables are likewise sold for the benefit of Winter and his confederates.[2] Thirty loads of knees (oak naturally bent) were entered in the books and paid for by the Queen, but none of them came to her use. She paid £45 for a specified consignment of timber which was already her own, and £209 for some plank not worth £50. The fittings of the *Jennett*, a worn-out ship, were wholly taken away, although they would have served for other new ships of 300 tons. Brass sheaves are removed from the blocks and iron ones substituted. Many of the clerks are paid double wages and then have unreasonably great allowances. All the boatswains, gunners and pursers are appointed by Winter, 'and so all reduced to his profit.'

Here then was Hawkins's proposal for increasing the strength of the Navy. Stop all this knavery, and you may have a better fleet for less money, or a much better one for the same money. It was perfectly true, as the next ten years were to prove. But what was Hawkins's motive? A vision of how a war was to be won, zeal for his country, greed of power, determination to rob rogues of their plunder in order to pocket it himself? The reader must take his choice after hearing the story, which will contain plenty of accusations of the latter sort, even to taking Spanish pay for the ruination of England's defences. Hawkins names Winter as the culprit, but in other statements he included the whole Navy

[1] Drake did not get finally away till December 1577. The ship is not the *Golden Hind*, which is known to have been French built. It is more probably the *Elizabeth*, commanded by John Winter, nephew of Sir William.

[2] Cables, cordage, tar and masts were collectively known as Baltic stores, and an officer known as the Queen's Merchant was employed to purchase them at Danzig. Thomas Allen had filled this office and was afterwards a virulent enemy of Hawkins. It is possible that he participated in the frauds here alleged, and was incensed by Hawkins's stopping them.

Board. Their responsibility indeed was collective, and if William Winter was the dominant personality, the others were guilty at least as accessories. Gonson himself comes out poorly. The abuses had been going on for years, and he had never had the courage to speak out until his son-in-law's equally dominant personality led him to it. In making the exposure Hawkins was not doing something easy and pleasant. Winter had long been his ally, perhaps his friend; and Hawkins made him an unsparing enemy, an influential man, too, who could pull many strings. The details remained confidential, and the public, who had not seen the report, were left to conclude that Hawkins was using his family influence to get a snug job, and playing a dirty trick on a friend with a much better claim to it.

For the report did its work, and Hawkins became Treasurer of the Navy. In November, 1577, a patent appointed him to act jointly with his father-in-law, and ten days afterwards Benjamin Gonson died.[1] Hawkins then became the sole Treasurer. His charges had been accepted by Burghley, in council with other ministers; and they had obviously better means of testing the matter than we have. We may be satisfied that in the main Burghley held the case proved. He had known both Hawkins and Winter for many years and had had occasion to assess the integrity of each. It was he who in effect appointed Hawkins to office, and it was to him rather than to any other minister that Hawkins held himself accountable.

So far as we know, the Treasurer was not given any formal authority over the rest of the Board. They were all theoretically equal in subordination to the Lord Admiral. Until 1577 it would have been more accurate to regard Winter as the head than Gonson. It was mainly a question of personal qualities. Hawkins behaved from the outset as one having authority not only to overlook but to give orders to the others, and it is clear that he would not have accepted office on any lower terms. It was probably an informal understanding with Burghley, conveyed informally to the other officers. In one important respect the affair took a course that would be unusual or impossible to-day. One would expect the acceptance of such charges to have entailed the dismissal of

---

[1] A. W. Johns, in *Mariner's Mirror, ut supra*, p. 46.

every one of the culprits. In fact not one was dismissed. They all three stayed on as the assistants of the man who had exposed them, his instruments in making good his undertaking that he would do the work more honestly and efficiently than they had. The continued employment of men who were known to have been unfaithful or disloyal was a foible of Elizabeth's administration. Vindictive as she could be when her personal feelings were touched, she was reluctant to punish for plain knavery. It may have been her cynical admission of the fact that there were not enough honest men to go round.

By this date nearly all the Navy was kept at Chatham. There, below Rochester bridge, the Medway made a U-shaped bend, in the first arm of which were the moorings of the smaller ships, and in the second, nearer the sea, of the greater. Throughout the year the routine work went on, rummaging, cleaning, renewal of timbers and plank, careening or 'casting over' for examination below water, making of sails, spars and rigging, radical reconstruction jobs in dry dock. All movables, except the lower masts which passed through the deck to the keel, were normally kept in storehouses ashore. Some of the ships may have had a few guns on board, but most of the armament was at the Tower of London, where there were workshops for its maintenance. The stripped hulls were unballasted and floated high. Shipwrights, seamen and clerks were busy, probably not more than two or three hundred all told, a small enough number for the directing officer to know them all individually. Two master-shipwrights, Peter Pett and Matthew Baker, were his chief lieutenants in the brainiest part of the work. A fleet of twenty-five sail, large and small, was a big responsibility but within the compass of a skilled and able man. John Hawkins settled down to manage and supervise, improve and economize, for the Queen as he would have done for himself. It was work which on a smaller scale he had been born to, and he knew he could do it. He probably had quarters at the dockyard, but lived chiefly in the City. For there was a London side to his duties, and the Navy Office was on Tower Hill. There, once a week or oftener, the Board met, and every month reported on its doings to the Lord Admiral.

III

THE FIRST BARGAIN

Hawkins did not take long to decide that the existing method of carrying on the dockyard work was unsuitable for the reforms which he had promised. The Surveyor, the Comptroller and the Clerk, in other words Sir William Winter, still had primary control of the work done and of the men who did it, and of the purchase of materials and stores. However vigilant the Treasurer might be, and however relentlessly he might probe and question, there must have been ways and means whereby the old hands could still contrive to steal. They were on their mettle to do it and prove their accuser wrong in his claim that he could show large economies and better work. Hawkins, it may be recalled, had not been vague. He had said that the ordinary cost nearly £6,000 a year and could be done more efficiently for £4,000. For five years out of the seven from 1571 to 1577 the amount of the ordinary expenditure is available from the Declared Accounts in the Exchequer. The average for those five years is £5,822, which shows that Hawkins had studied his case and was not talking wildly. About his promised reduction we shall have some figures to quote from the same source at a later stage. He had also said that many of the ships were worn and decayed and not repaired, with the implication that he was pledged to make them fit for service. There will be details to quote in support of either statement.

Some eighteen months after taking office he proposed to Burghley a new system of control. He may have had it in mind from the outset. All we know is that it came into force at Michaelmas 1579. Such matters were not hastily decided; for Burghley always took his time to consider them. The new system of 1579 is known as the First Bargain and is embodied in two agreements, one between the Queen and John Hawkins, the other between the Queen and the master-shipwrights Peter Pett and Matthew Baker.

Qui Vicit toties ins Fructis classibus Hostes
Jlle Vagis HAWKINS Vitam relliquit in Vndis

SIR JOHN HAWKINS
From the engraving in *Heroologia* (1620)

In his agreement Hawkins undertook to provide at his own cost all the cables necessary for mooring the ships, reserve cables of specified numbers and sizes, hawsers for grounding the ships and drawing them off again, cordage of various kinds all specified, and other gear. The old cables and junk were to be at his disposal for conversion into smaller gear. For all this he was to receive a lump sum of £1,200 yearly without being obliged to account in detail for its expenditure. The condition was that the gear so provided was to be sufficient for the work to be properly performed, and the Surveyor, Comptroller and Clerk were jointly and severally empowered to oversee his proceedings and report upon them to Lord Burghley and the Lord Admiral. In addition a commission of four persons, two named by those ministers and two by Hawkins, was to make an annual survey and report. It is to be noted that the cables and other mooring gear were the most expensive and perishable of all the materials necessary for the good keeping of laid-up ships. Chain, which is used nowadays, was not then available, and rope submerged in water rapidly deteriorated and became rotten, lasting probably no more than a year at most. It was also liable to chafe in spite of precautions, and it is obvious that a dishonest official might totally condemn a cable that was still good in parts and make it his perquisite, while an honest one would cut out the bad bits and splice the remainder to get more use from it. By placing the whole of this service on a contract duly supervised, Hawkins was ensuring that he would suffer in his own pocket if the work were wastefully done. It was no doubt this contract that aroused the wrath of Thomas Allen, the Queen's Merchant who had been supplying these goods. At any rate we shall find him angry enough, and may guess the reason.

The agreement with Pett and Baker dealt with the repair of the ships. The master-shipwrights undertook to ground the five largest vessels at least once in three years, or more often if necessary to stop leaks; and every year to 'cast them over' and renew three or four strakes on each side below the waterline.[1] They were to ground every two years the next five in order of size, and the

[1] 'The swimming mark.'

remainder every year, with the same provisions about casting over and renewing strakes. All the ships were once a year to be ransacked, caulked, and perfected above water within board and without. Pett and Baker were to provide at their own cost all the masts and spars needed by the ships while in harbour, except that trees for the lower masts and yards of the medium and large ships were to be supplied free by the Queen. In addition they were to find wages, victuals and lodging for their workmen and all necessaries for their work, to repair all boats, cocks and skiffs, and to supply specified carpenter's stores to ships ordered to sea. For this they were to receive £1,000 a year and the use of all storehouses, their performance being supervised in like manner to that of Hawkins.

By these instruments £2,200 of the ordinary was placed on contract. The ordinary expenditure still remaining on the old footing included the wages of shipkeepers, clerks and watchmen, and of the gunners at Upnor Castle; and the repair and upkeep of storehouses and wharves. With Hawkins as Treasurer there would be less opportunity for fraud over the wages than over the work which involved the purchase and use of materials. The extraordinary, that is, the dry-docking and heavy repairs, remained outside either contract, and was to be conducted as before, by the Board as a whole. But the intention was to conduct it more economically. Hawkins accompanied the Bargain with a definite promise to Burghley to save £4,000 every year, not all of which could come from the ordinary.

The documents contain a list of the fleet as it stood, twenty years after the beginning of the Queen's reign, ten before the fight with the Spanish Armada. The vessels, given in descending order of magnitude, are as follows: the five greatest ships, *Triumph*, *Elizabeth Jonas*, *White Bear*, *Victory*, *Mary Rose*; five middle-sized ships, *Hope*, *Philip and Mary*, *Elizabeth Bonaventure*, *Golden Lion*, *Revenge*; fifteen ships from about 400 tons downwards, *Dreadnought*, *Swiftsure*, *Antelope*, *Swallow*, *Foresight*, *Aid*, *Bull*, *Tiger*, *Scout*, *Achates*, *Handmaid*, a small bark probably the *Merlin*, *Galley Elenor*, *George Hoy*, and a great lighter. This makes twenty-five in all, but the last three were not sea-going fighting ships. The galley had been captured from the French in 1563, and in the Armada year was used only as a guardship in the Thames Estuary. A hoy was a small vessel of fishing or coaster type. The lighter was for harbour work only. The Queen thus possessed a sea-going fleet of twenty-two combatant vessels, some of which were pinnaces.

The ships, as Hawkins found them, were a mixed lot.[1] Of the five greatest, of about 600–800 tons, the *Mary Rose* was a pre-Elizabethan ship, built to replace her namesake lost in 1545. She was the third of that name in the Tudor service. The *Triumph* and *Elizabeth Jonas* were launched in 1559–60, part of the revulsion from neglect of the Navy occasioned by the disgrace of Calais. The *Victory* was bought at the same time from merchants and may have been a 'hulk' of the kind used for cargo-carrying by the Hanseatic League. Such a vessel, broad and capacious, was capable of receiving the high superstructures required to convert her into a high-charged fighting ship. Henry VIII had bought several, including the *Jesus of Lubeck*. The *White Bear*, of the same old-fashioned type, was built a few years later and was the last of her size and kind constructed for the Elizabethan Navy. Among the five middle-sized ships, from about 600 tons down to 450, the *Philip and Mary* and the *Golden Lion* were pre-Elizabethan, the *Hope* was one of the post-Calais programme of 1558–9, and the *Elizabeth Bonaventure* was built a little later. The *Revenge* alone was, in Hawkins's view, of a modern and desirable design, low-built and of galleon proportion, fast and weatherly, with a broadside of heavy guns but not many of the light close-range pieces, economical in crew, and therefore able to carry victuals for a long voyage.

All of these ten ships survived to fight the Armada. Or rather, in justice to Hawkins, we should say of some of them that the names survived but the vessels were different. The *Revenge* needed no treatment so far as her design was concerned, although

---

[1] A most valuable general list of the Elizabethan ships is on pp. 120–1 of M. Oppenheim's *History of the Administration of the Royal Navy*, Vol. I, London, 1896. This work although corrected in some details, remains the foundation of research on the subject.

under Winter's care her building had not been of the best material. Three of the greatest of the high-charged ships, the *Triumph, Elizabeth Jonas* and *Bear*, were kept substantially in that form, of which they remained the only examples in the English fleet. The *Victory* was cut down and remodelled into a more modern shape. We owe this information, not to administrative records, but to the remarks of Richard Hawkins on the Armada campaign, in which he served. He brackets the *Victory* with the brand-new *Ark Royal* as ships of one type, low-built and strong, in contrast with the other three great ships, to which he attributes more 'majesty' and moral effect on the enemy.[1] But John Hawkins preferred material advantages and chose the *Victory* as his own flagship. The *Mary Rose* was treated in the same manner, and others in the above list were drastically reconstructed. We have some details of the work, but the record of every ship is not complete. To assess the achievement of Hawkins some inference is justifiable. We shall find it true to say that he substantially rebuilt the fleet in the years before the Armada and converted it from archaic to modern.

The fifteen smaller vessels were also a mixture. The *Dreadnought, Swiftsure* and *Foresight* were fairly modern. The *Scout*, a pinnace, was new, having been built with the *Revenge* in 1575. The rest were old, of pre-Elizabethan or early Elizabethan build; and we have record of the new building or alteration of some of them.

Hawkins's fellow officers of the Navy Board cannot have regarded the First Bargain with favour, since its meaning was so obviously that he and the government continued to believe them untrustworthy. In 1580 Sir William Winter was given an opportunity of withdrawing for some time from a scene that must have been trying to his temper. He was made the commander of a squadron of ten ships which lay for six months on the Irish coast to intercept forces expected from Spain. A few hundred Spanish and Italian papal volunteers got past him and landed at Smerwick. He took part with the Lord Deputy in besieging their fort and wiping them out.

The master-shipwrights were not included in the condem-

---

[1] Sir R. Hawkins, *Observations*, 1933 edn., p. 138.

nation. Hawkins had not accused them, and had cited them as witnesses against Winter. He relied upon them as his assistants in the reformation he intended to carry out. Possibly they misunderstood its extent and nature, for we shall find them lukewarm and under some censure from the Treasurer at a later stage. It certainly looks as though they were undertaking a great deal for their thousand a year, and one may guess that they counted on additional gains. Pett was an elderly man, a veteran of Henry VIII's later years. Baker was younger, having been appointed in 1572 after service in junior ranks. Some drafts of his of the lines of Elizabethan ships, preserved in a manuscript at Cambridge, are the earliest examples of English ship designing now known to exist.

Turning now to such details as can be collected of Hawkins's work under the First Bargain, we may pause on the question of prices. The value of Tudor pounds, shillings and pence is so different from that of our own that the statement of money totals is meaningless (except for comparison) unless we have some idea of what the money would buy. Any general factor, such as counting the Elizabethan pound as ten times the value of our own, is entirely misleading, not only because some things have altered in price more than others, but also because a great number of things in common use now were unknown and unpriced then. For the Navy costs, however, we have a useful measure of what the contemporary money may mean, in a statement that a fair price for building a ship of 450 tons and a pinnace of 50 was £2,600, or approximately £5 a ton.[1] It will help to understand the sums mentioned in the records if we translate them into tons of new shipping.

The following particulars are drawn from various sources, some from Hawkins's own statements, others from the Declared Accounts in the Exchequer, which were the final figures submitted by the Navy Treasurer, always two or three years in arrear. The *Mary Rose* was reconstructed at Woolwich in 1580, and for the work done upon her the master-shipwrights were allowed £600 additional to their contract money 'by agreement of all the officers'. This was evidently not the building of a new ship, but it represents

[1] The statement is in Hawkins's 'Abuses' report already cited.

some heavy work, probably much replacement of decayed timber, the cutting down of the superstructures, and possibly the lengthening of the hull to the galleon proportion. The lengthening of a wooden ship by cutting her in two and inserting an additional portion amidships was a recognized operation and was frequently carried out in the nineteenth century with no greater mechanical resources than those available in the Tudor dockyards.

Some other tasks are not precisely dated, but were done between 1579 and the beginning of 1585, that is, in the period of the First Bargain. The *White Bear* had £240 worth of work done on her beyond the ordinary routine. The *Elizabeth Bonaventure* was drastically reconstructed for £1,200. The *Foresight*, although a new ship in 1570, was found to be 'in great decay' and required an expenditure of £600 in 1581, which suggests rotten work by the Winter régime. The *Golden Lion*, a pre-1559 ship, was new built at a cost of £1,400. This may represent the making of a virtually new ship, for the cost, although less than that of a 500 ton galleon at £5 a ton, would have been lightened by the use of some of the timber, ironwork, masts and gear of the broken-up vessel. The *Golden Lion* was at least lengthened, for her tonnage was increased from 450 to 500. Similarly the *Nonpareil* (the old *Philip and Mary*) was 'new built' for £1,600. Her tonnage was 350, and the cost was that of an entirely new vessel with some fittings from the old one. The *Antelope* of 350 tons, another pre-Elizabethan, was also rebuilt, although to an extent of which the evidence is not clear. Some dimensions of later date show that she was a true galleon after the rebuilding, as also were the *Golden Lion* and the *Nonpareil*. The *Bull*, *Tiger* and *Hope* were 'reformed' in 1584. This seems to mean that along with the heavy repairs a change was made in their form or shape, since it is stated that the *Hope* was converted into a galleass. In English usage the word galleass meant a long, low-built ship, and the statement is in accord with the general policy of lengthening and lowering. An entry in the Declared Accounts of 1585 definitely says that the *Achates* had been lengthened. The same may perhaps be inferred of the *Aid*, another of the smaller ships, which was listed up to 1579 as of 200 tons, but after reconstruction became a 250-ton

vessel. Finally, Hawkins rebuilt the *Galley Elenor* at a cost of £600.
A single galley was not of much combatant value in a fleet
otherwise composed of broadside sailing ships, but she may have
been used as a tug for getting the great ships in and out of the
Medway and other narrow channels. The Spaniards habitually
used galleys to aid in getting their fleets to sea from Cadiz, as
Pedro Sarmiento notes in the narrative of his voyage to the
Straits of Magellan.

It must be emphasized that these records are incomplete.
Students know that it is unusual to find system, uniformity or
exactness in Tudor accounts, in which it is common even for a
column of figures to be added up incorrectly. We have here only
some samples of what Hawkins did, and not the full story. Yet in
the period of the First Bargain we have mention of just over half
of the ships in the fleet more or less completely reconstructed. It
may be repeated that his policy had three objects, to save the
Queen £4,000 a year out of the pockets of peculators, to convert
decayed ships into sound ones, and to make the whole force fit for
distant service in oceanic expeditions. There was during this
period no question of expanding the Navy, much as the international situation would have justified it. English government
had to be economically conducted, and the Queen took risks. At
this stage she was no more inclined to build additional galleons
than to take precautions against her personal assassination.

Although a small establishment remained at Portsmouth, and
repairs and building were actively carried on at Woolwich and
Deptford, Chatham was now the principal dockyard of the Navy.
Foreign invasion plans are known to have included, more than
once, plots for the burning of the fleet at its moorings. This was a
matter for vigilance of the police kind, but there was also the
possibility of a sudden armed raid from the Netherlands. At
Sheerness, where the Medway opened into the Thames Estuary,
there was an old fort that had fallen into decay. In 1579 Hawkins
reconstructed it on orders from the Council, which empowered
him to impress men and material for the purpose. Farther up the
Medway, just below the berths of the great ships, the guns of
Upnor Castle commanded the channel. But the slow-firing pieces

of the period were not a perfect defence against a resolute push
with a favouring tide. An effective supplement was available, as
had been demonstrated when a strong boom had foiled the
attempt to relieve La Rochelle in 1573. The Council and the
Navy Board therefore devised such a precaution at Upnor. It
consisted of a great iron chain made in London at a cost of £250.
It was secured to piles on one bank and led over two wheels in a
winding-house on the other, so as to allow for slackening to
permit the passage of the Queen's ships. The winding machinery
and lighters for supporting the chain across the channel cost a
further £360, and the whole was completed in 1585. At the same
time a narrow bye-channel called St. Mary's Creek, which gave
another possible access to the moorings, was blocked with piles.[1]
Driving heavy piles involved the use of a machine, and it would
be interesting to know its details.

Dover also was important to the patrol of the Narrow Seas, the
more so since Calais had been lost. We have to imagine it as
devoid of its great modern harbour works and consisting only of
the little haven which still exists embedded within them. It was
formed by the outfall of the Dover river and prolonged and protected by wooden jetties at either side. Its defect was that the
entrance was liable to be choked by the eastward drift of shingle
along the Kentish coast, a drift due principally to the action of
waves driven by the prevailing winds. Every year it shifted eastwards masses of material furnished by the erosion of cliffs and
headlands farther west. The Dover river was of small volume,
and left to itself the balance of natural forces allowed the shingle
to form a bar across the harbour entrance so shallow that only
small vessels could enter at the top of the tide. Even then a south-
westerly gale might leave an obstruction that virtually sealed the
place for weeks. The remedy had long been understood, and in
the growing urgency of national defence it was determined to
apply it.

In 1583-4 the Navy Board and the town of Dover jointly
carried out an effective task of sixteenth century engineering.
Where the river broadened into the port they dug a basin or

[1] See plan reproduced on p. 267.

reservoir called a pent, and closed its seaward end with a timber barrier furnished with sluice-gates. The river water was allowed to fill the pent, and at low tide, when there was a fall of nearly twenty feet, the sluices were opened and the torrent rushed through the haven, scouring a passage through the bar at the entrance. So long as the works were maintained, the action was effective. The Pent is still there, forming one of the docks of modern Dover, although the great new harbour walls have altered the conditions of the problem. The town and the local gentry provided the labour for digging the Pent, which was done with great enthusiasm on the part of the onlookers, who came in numbers from the countryside to view the work. The Navy's master-shipwrights designed and constructed the sluices at Chatham, and supervised their erection, after which Hawkins inspected and reported to the Council. A few months later, when the scourings had had time to deepen the passage over the bar, it was declared that Dover harbour was fit for the largest of the Queen's ships to enter.

So far this account of the First Bargain has appeared smooth and constructive, but there was another side to it. The Treasurer's fellow officers were resolutely obstructive. In his own words, their policy was 'to weary Hawkins of his bargain'. They unceasingly alleged that Hawkins was corrupt and the ships were rotten, that he was filling his purse by imperilling the nation, that his apparent economy was obtained by neglecting necessary work and leaving what should have been ordinary expenditure to accumulate until it passed into heavy work under the extraordinary heading. They said that he did this partly by being 'an invisible partner' in the bargain with the master-shipwrights, and so influencing them to neglect their repairs. Sir William Winter was recognized as an able man, and he had powerful friends. Statements like the above, oft repeated, were bound to have an effect. Hawkins was of Burghley's appointment, and some of the Council and many of the courtiers were no friends of Burghley. If Winter kept up the pressure he had a hope of ousting his supplanter and securing his own reinstatement. By the autumn of 1583 he had made such progress that the Privy Council decided to appoint a commission to inquire into the state of the Navy. The decision was not necessarily taken in a hostile spirit towards Hawkins. He may have courted an inquiry, knowing that it would vindicate him.

Five principal commissioners were appointed: Burghley, Walsingham, the Lord Admiral (Earl of Lincoln), the Lord Chamberlain (Lord Hunsdon), and the Chancellor of the Exchequer (Sir Walter Mildmay). Of these, any three were to act; and it appears that the Lord Chamberlain in fact presided, since the proceedings were afterwards referred to as 'my Lord Chamberlain's survey'. The Lord Admiral was one of the three, and the third is unknown. Very likely he was the Chancellor of the Exchequer, since financial matters were involved. Burghley, it seems, stood back and watched. The commissioners were to select sub-commissioners, who were to play the part of a jury of experts, from a list comprising the principal sea captains of the time: Sir Thomas Cotton, Sir William Gorges, Sir Francis Drake, Richard Bingham, Martin Frobisher, Fulke Greville, Carew Ralegh, Walter Ralegh, Henry Palmer, George Beeston and Thomas Ellis. Cotton and Gorges were old sea officers. The others were all on the active list, and most of them received knighthood in the course of the wars. We do not know which of them were selected to serve on the commission, but the verdict of any selection would carry weight. Drake's biographers, by the way, are given to asserting positively that he was one of those selected. Very likely he was, but there is no evidence to prove it.

A first draft of instructions[1] to the commission ordered it to inquire into the work done since Hawkins had taken charge, but not into any previous transactions. This was not proceeded with. It would have been unfair to Hawkins, since his case was that he had found great decay and arrears of work which the four years since 1579 had not been long enough to remedy completely. The final instructions were wider. Their preamble states that the Queen is informed 'by rumour' that her ships are in such decay that few of them are fit for service. The commissioners are therefore to survey them, using all expert assistance, and to report truly on

[1] The instructions are given in *Sir John Hawkins* (1927) p. 348.

their condition. This was the main purpose of the commission, but three other matters were also to be particularly examined, all belonging to the period before the beginning of the Bargain: the allegation that since the opening of the Queen's reign the officers of the Admiralty had been embezzling and conveying timber and plank; the dry-docking of three ships at Deptford in 1578, for

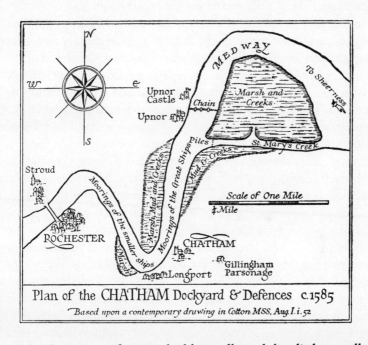

Plan of the CHATHAM Dockyard & Defences c.1585

Based upon a contemporary drawing in Cotton MSS, Aug. I. i. 52

which a large sum of money had been allowed, but little actually spent; and the building of the *Revenge* and the *Scout* (pinnace) in 1575, for which the Queen had paid £4,400 although the work should have been perfectly done for £2,600. The first and last of the above are evidently charges by Hawkins against Winter. The alleged fraud at Deptford took place immediately after he became Treasurer, and may have been his main reason for seeking the control of such work in the subsequent Bargain. It is interesting to note that the famous *Revenge* had not only cost far too much, but was alleged to have been built with 'unseasoned plank of no continuance', a defect which Hawkins repaired as need arose.

The record of Tudor maritime history is in general fragmentary, and it is so here. Hardly a word has been preserved of the personnel, the proceedings, or the report of this commission on the Navy. One paper alone exists on its proceedings, a set of questions to be put to the master-shipwrights, without any indication of their answers. The questions asked whether they had truly spent the £1,000 yearly on the repair of the ships, whether they thought it sufficient, whether they had any partners in their bargain, and how many of the ships were immediately fit for six months' service at sea. Such is the gist of the interrogation, but it is considerably elaborated, and conveys an implication that Pett and Baker thought themselves hardly treated and regretted entering into the bargain. No doubt they had expected more irregular gains than they had received under Winter, but Hawkins allowed none. The question of his alleged partnership with them is obscure. If, as they complained, there was no profit, the partnership was not corrupt. It may have been that he recognized that their contract was too harsh and relieved them of some of the loss.

The all-important report to the Council is missing. We know that it vindicated Hawkins by two circumstances, first that it was followed by a new arrangement which extended his control to cover all the Board's operations, ordinary and extraordinary; and second, that in a letter to Burghley in 1585 he alluded to the survey as having declared the ships to be in an efficient state. Whether the vindication was quite unqualified we do not know, but it must have been substantially so, or his powers would not have been increased. In losing these things we have lost much. To have followed those famous captains round the fleet, to have heard their comments and criticisms, to have read the answers they made to the lords commissioners, and their statement on the ships they were to command in the crisis of their century, would have been an education in the history of the Tudor Navy which no man will now attain.

In April, 1584, Hawkins wrote to Burghley on the work achieved and proceeding. Although long, the letter is worth reading and is here given in full, the first for thirteen years since he had written to the minister about the detection of the Ridolfi plot. In some ways it is a different Hawkins, now fifty-two years old, who writes:

My duty in right humble manner remembered unto your good Lordship.

After it had pleased Her Majesty to commit this office of Treasurer of the Navy unto me, I have endeavoured with all fidelity and painful travail to reduce the whole course of this office into such order as the same might be safe, sure, and bountifully provided, and performed with an easy and convenient charge, so that Her Majesty thereby should not be discouraged to maintain so necessary a defence for her royal state and country, considering that the force and puissance of these small number of ships are a bridle to daunt the malice of the adversaries of Christ's church, Her Majesty and our country.

It pleased your Lordship about five years past to take consideration for the reforming of the ordinary, which by your lordship's singular judgment at the second hearing was with great facility set in order, and so after that time your lordship proceeded to other of the extraordinary points, which hath greatly availed[1] Her Majesty.

In the passing of these great things the adversaries of the work have continually opposed themselves against me and the service so far as they durst be seen in it, so that among a number of trifling crossings and slanders the very walls of the realm have been brought in question; and their slander hath gone very far and general, to the encouragement of the enemies of God and our country, only to be avenged of me and this service, which doth discover the corruption and ignorance of the time past.

Considering, my very good lord, what a froward and untoward company I have been matched with (even as a sheep among wolves) the business which I have brought about hath been doubled in tediousness and very cumbersome for me to accomplish. Yet much more had been done if I had had a quiet passage in the business; and although by their contrary and politic dealings some trifles have been brought behindhand, whereby they have taken occasion to raise slanders, the same have been of so small moment that our Lord God hath made it a special mean to make my service the better known and to open the

---

[1] profited.

unprofitable and careless order of the time past, which otherwise might have passed in silence; so as always our good God doth never forsake nor leave his children destitute, but causeth the pit prepared by the adversaries that themselves fall into it.[1]

I did your lordship lately a book which doth plainly show that £3,000 yearly is availed to Her Majesty, beside the lessening of the charge of cordage and canvas, which was before the reformation *communibus annis* £2,000, and is now and may be hereafter done for £1,000 yearly. So that now I have performed that which I promised to your lordship at the passage of my first accompt at Greenwich, which was that Her Majesty was availed £4,000 by this service.

I have set down in a note which I send herewith[2] the particulars of such services as have been overcome since the reformation determined by your lordship.

It may please your lordship to remember that lately in your chamber amongst other of the Council there was urged a dubbing and other reformation of the ships, whereof Peter Pett was willed by your lordship to make an estimate, which amounted to £1,480, all which is now performed (saving the dubbing of the four great ships), which shall be likewise done as their time of grounding cometh on; the *Bull* and the *Tiger* being parcel of that demand, which are now made strong and perfect ships for six or seven years, also finished, and the service very well performed; yet the charge is diminished, as it will be under £500 extra ordinary. So far as I doubt not but your lordship will have good liking of the service and commend the same as no doubt it deserveth; for now I thank God the Navy (before Bartholomewtide next) will be in that state that the very adversaries shall be afraid to find a fault in any of the ships.

I have been bold to be a little tedious to your lordship, for although some of mine adversaries have given out that your lordship had an ill opinion of me, I have always seen the singular understanding wherewith God hath indued your lordship, with your continual integrity of life and your dexterity in justice, so that I was always glad and ever desirous to come before such a judge.

[1] It may be gathered from the above that the commission had not only justified Hawkins but had pitched pretty heavily into Winter and the others.
[2] Not found.

Now I do most humbly pray your good lordship to take knowledge of this my careful and painful service, and finding at your lordship's leisure some understanding that you have good liking of the same, which exceptacy of your lordship I shall not only take as a great recompence of my pains, but thereby be greatly encouraged to travail both carefully and uprightly in the said service.

If your lordship have liking in that last course (whereof I did a book and your lordship perused it) there would fall a great benefit and quietness to the service, and avoid occasion of strife. The Navy would always be in most ready order and very perfectly built, and Her Majesty never troubled with warrants extra ordinary.

When your honour's good pleasure shall be, I will give mine attendance, etc.

Here is John Hawkins growing Puritan, with a different emphasis from that of the Hawkins who made Philip II believe him a good Catholic and addressed the Bishop of Valencia as 'right reverend father in God'. The trend of the age helped the development in many of them, Burghley and Walsingham included, to the annoyance of the Queen, who could not see that it made them her stouter servants. The bull of deposition, the struggles of the continental Calvinists, the fifth column work of the missionary priests, the threat of Catholic conquest when the Queen should die, all pushed in one direction Englishmen who would be free. They found spiritual peace in a creed that braced them to physical war: the enemies of their country were the enemies of God. With Hawkins the theme grows insistent, and he becomes a Church of England Puritan of the generation that gave birth to the Cromwellians.

Sir William Winter was a stubborn fighter and did not yet acknowledge defeat. The controversy, as carried before the Queen's ministers, had been on the alleged decay of the ships and corrupt dealings of Hawkins. The findings of the commission had answered the one, and the reduction in expenditure substantially the other. It was obvious that if Hawkins was keeping the ships well and saving four thousand a year his corruption was pure integrity in comparison with that of the Winter régime. Never-

theless, with work involving the handling of so much expendable
and wasting material by an officer who naturally did not show
his books to all and sundry, there was still the possibility of
accusations of fraud based on current dockyard gossip. There was,
however, another grievance that Winter and the old hands may
have entertained sincerely, that of Hawkins's alteration of the
design of the ships with a view to strategic uses unthought of by
the old Navy Board. This comes up in the next attack upon
him, promoted by Winter, but advanced in the name of William
Borough.

Borough was a new recruit to the Navy Board, having been
appointed Clerk of the Ships when George Winter died in 1582.[1]
Hawkins had once held the reversion of the office, and Martin
Frobisher possessed it when the vacancy arose. He did not elect
to take it up, and Borough was brought in. He was an old servant
of the Muscovy Company, an accomplished navigator and
surveyor,[2] and a captain in many voyages to the White Sea and
the Baltic, but he had no oceanic experience like that of Drake
and Hawkins. As some later transactions were to show, he was
hidebound and resistant to new ideas, but withal an honest man.
His ideal fighting ship was naturally the ancient type which
Hawkins was abolishing. Winter must have primed him judici-
ously; but it is an extraordinary circumstance that Borough, as his
own statements reveal, did not know how Hawkins had denounced the old Navy Board in 1577-8, and did not know that
Hawkins was a man of comfortable private fortune who was not
managing the dockyards for his living. Borough indeed seems to
have been a very innocent tool. So Hawkins considered him, and
never bore him any malice. In after years they were on excellent
terms.

First, however, came the attack, in the form of a memorial
written by Borough to Burghley in February 1585 and endorsed
'A Dutiful Declaration.' The Queen, says the writer in evident
ignorance of the financial results of Hawkins's work, has lost, not

[1] The date given by Mr. A. W. Johns in *Mariner's Mirror*, 1928, p. 51.
[2] His 'Chart of Northern Navigation' (Royal MSS. 18D, iii, 124) is the
earliest guide to the White Sea and its approaches.

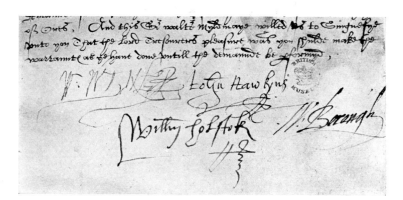

SIGNATURES OF THE NAVY BOARD, 1583

From Lansdowne MSS., 37

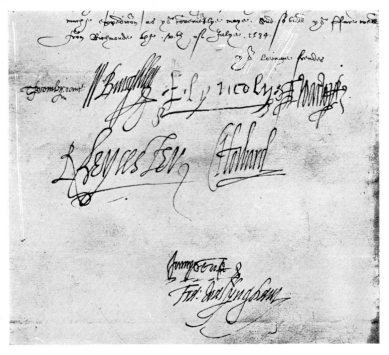

SIGNATURES OF THE PRIVY COUNCIL, 1584

From H.C.A., Exemplifications, 7/22, No. 57

gained, by the Bargain. Hawkins carries matters with a high hand and speaks of his reliance on powerful friends to cover his ill deeds and maintain him in his place. He spends far more than his salary and fees of £300 a year; his household alone costs him £800, besides other lavish expenditure. Peter Pett also is dishonest, but Baker is more upright. The great evil is that the design of the ships is being altered. Hawkins has cut down 'the romthes and commodious fights', so that they look like galleasses; without their superstructures these majestic ships of the Queen's may be taken for merchantmen. It is not right that one man's will should prevail in these matters. All things should be done jointly by the whole Board, and Hawkins ought to specify the faults he found in 1579.

That last is rich indeed, and the whole effusion must have made Burghley smile. He had no doubt talked with Hawkins, and with Drake also and other progressive sailors, about the form of a fighting ship. But the diehards clung to their 'fights', the high overhanging forecastle and the higher poop, walled in with heavy timber and bristling with man-killing swivels, murderers, port-pieces, and hailshot pieces. These things had decided the tragic fight between the *Regent* and the great Frenchman seventy years before, and Borough and his like could not see that their time had passed; nor also, it is fair to add, could Santa Cruz in Spain, another man of long experience and closed mind. The 'romthes' or rooms within the fights were wanted also for the crowd of fighters. There they huddled in damp heaps, and typhus and dysentery raged through them, so that six weeks was the utmost service to be expected from a squadron of the old-fashioned sort. Scurvy might kill off the ill-provided ocean voyager, but it had not much chance with the seaman in the royal fleet 'plying up and down' in the Channel: jail fever got him first. Hawkins was alive to these things and striving against them, and wicked fools were trying to thwart him. But Burghley was on his side, one in fact of the powerful friends mentioned in the memorial, and the 'dutiful declaration' came to nothing. Perhaps the minister never showed it to Hawkins. At least, no reply of his is on record.

Far from Hawkins's position being weakened, it was about to be consolidated.

IV

THE SECOND BARGAIN

War was near at the opening of 1585. The Queen was loath to acknowledge it, but her councillors had no doubt. Burghley himself believed that the time had come, and Walsingham had long been saying so. The Prince of Parma had almost reconquered the Belgian provinces and was about to round off the work by the capture of Antwerp. Then would come the turn of the Dutch, who had lost more than an army by the assassination of William of Orange in the previous year. The Dutch held Flushing and the mouth of the Scheldt, without which Antwerp was neutralized as an invasion port. But the Dutch, after thirteen years of torment, were on the point of collapse, and England was bound in honour and policy to aid them. If she did not, she would still have to fight, and fight alone. It did not need a higher statesman to understand these things, which were patent to all. Hawkins understood them and saw salvation on the sea. It was not enough to keep a static Navy fit by patching new timbers into old ships. He wanted additional galleons and pinnaces of his own clean design and honest building. He must somehow find the money for them. He had been a member of Parliament[1] since the days of the Ridolfi Plot, and knew the Queen's difficulties in that direction. The money must come from an extension of his own economical control. The master-shipwrights' part of the Bargain had not been working well, and he and they were ready to end it.

He had already suggested a new arrangement to Burghley, as appears from the last paragraph of the long letter quoted in the previous chapter, and Burghley, it seems, took just a year to consider and approve it. In March or April, 1585, the minister called a meeting of the Navy Board and himself discussed the matter with them. We have no record of 'the confusion of

---

[1] The Parliament of 1572 continued undissolved for some years, although its sessions were infrequent.

speeches', no doubt angry, at the meeting; but afterwards both Winter and Hawkins wrote to Burghley on the same day, April 8.

Winter was full of hearty hate. Hawkins's new proposal, he said, made a show of good service, 'but I am sorry to speak it (as I desire comfort at God's hands), there is nothing in it but cunning and craft to maintain his pride and ambition, and for the better filling of his purse, and to keep back from discovering the faults that are left in Her Majesty's ships at this day, which should have been perfected by the bargain made between Her Majesty and the two shipwrights Pett and Baker, wherein Hawkins was an invisible partner.' The Queen, he went on, has 'disbursed in the clouds' as much as £1,500 a year over and above the £1,000 allowed for the ordinary repairs,[1] and still there are faults remaining. I went on board the *Hope* with Mr. Borough at Deptford yesterday and we found three timbers rotten, although Hawkins and Pett had declared that there were none. The great chain, also, at Upnor will be another costly and useless undertaking. I perceive your lordship withstands this Hawkins as much as possible, but he has charmed the Queen, your equals and your inferiors, 'for he careth not to whom he speaketh nor what he saith; blush he will not.' After which testimonial to the Hawkins manner, still unimpaired by supervening Puritanism, Winter concluded by protesting his own sense of duty to the Queen and declaring that he was tired of these quarrels.

Hawkins's letter might almost have been an answer to Winter's. If there are faults remaining, he said, they are trivial and 'not such as have been reported, or any cause in them to disable the ships, contrary to my Lord Chamberlain's survey'. Under the old order the Navy Board had £5,714 yearly for the ordinary and nearly £4,000 a year extra to build new ships, all of which they consumed and left many of the ships in ruin. In the time of the First Bargain, he continued, he had done the whole business for less than the former ordinary alone, rebuilding some ships and repairing past neglect in the others. The faults of which these men

---

[1] The £1,500 was the cost of the extraordinary under Hawkins. On that very day, had Winter known it, Hawkins was writing in detail of the work done for that money and providing a crushing answer to the innuendo.

talk so loudly cannot be less than fifteen years old, 'which no man can take from the officers themselves.' They neither did the work nor will suffer others to do it, and so they should be compelled to answer for their foul and negligent consumption of the Queen's treasure, 'for I am persuaded that God in justice doth harden their hearts to that end as he did Pharaoh's, who never left the resisting of God until he was drowned in the Red Sea.' Matthew Baker takes charge one quarter at Chatham and Peter Pett the other, and because Pett and I have found fault with the wastefulness of Baker's proceedings, he has joined the ill-speakers, 'and they have thought it the best mean to make the slander of the Navy to be the pathway to their purpose.' With a last invocation of God, 'the righteous judge,' the main letter ends.[1]

But Hawkins unlike his opponents, did not content himself with heated generalities. He appended a note of the way he had spent the money in the five years and a half since the Bargain had begun, the work which we have already mentioned on the *Bear, Mary Rose, Bonaventure, Foresight, Galley Elenor, Golden Lion, Nonpareil,* and various smaller ships. This amounted to £8,470 or an average of £1,540 a year, while the ordinary had been reduced to £4,000. The whole list forms a contrast to the *Hope's* three rotten timbers, the only specific fact which Winter could adduce. Burghley believed Hawkins and could at least verify his financial claims. He held that the opposition had failed to prove its case, and proceeded to the new arrangement, which is known as the Second Bargain.

By the Second Bargain the contract with the master-ship-wrights was rescinded, and they reverted to their previous status of salaried servants of the Crown. Hawkins undertook to do at his own charge the whole of the ordinary work for a payment of £4,000 a year. This included repairing ships afloat or grounded, paying all shipkeepers, clerks, watchmen and gunners in the harbour services (including some forts at Portsmouth), paying the garrison of Upnor Castle, finding all moorings for ships in harbour, repairing wharves and storehouses at Portsmouth, Deptford, Woolwich and Chatham, and finding all materials, wages,

---

[1] The letter is printed in full in *Sir John Hawkins* (1927), pp. 357–9.

victuals and lodgings incident to these services. He also undertook for £1,714 2s. 2d. a year to do the extraordinary, which meant the heavy repairs in dry dock, and find the material, wages etc., incident. Thus the whole maintenance of the Navy was made his sole responsibility at a charge formerly fixed for the ordinary alone. The agreement for the extraordinary seems to have included a provision that Hawkins was to provide a new ship in place of one that should be condemned as useless, the old one being sold for his benefit.[1] The Second Bargain was concluded in the summer of 1585, but antedated to January 1st for the purposes of the accounts.

In one respect the arrangement, which had been a year under consideration, was a little out of date when it was signed. War was coming nearer, and some expansion of the Navy was in prospect, an expansion which Hawkins desired. But the fixed sum for which he had contracted would turn to his disadvantage with a growing fleet, and a time would come when he would be out of pocket. Regular war would also modify his position, for he hoped to take part in commanding the fleet he was creating. Any prolonged employment at sea would be incompatible with sole responsibility for the dockyard work. On these grounds it may be supposed that Hawkins did not expect the Second Bargain to be of long duration. It may be regarded as the final stage of preparation before going into action, in which the supreme administrator was to have a free hand and bring his forces into service at the top of their form. And this is just what Hawkins did in 1588, as will be shown on the testimony of the Lord Admiral and other officers.

Sir William Winter had spoken truth when he said that he was tired of the quarrel. That venomous letter was his last flutter in the struggle to evict Hawkins. When the Second Bargain was concluded in spite of it, he gave up the attempt. Borough also gave it up, and so did Holstocke, if indeed he had been actively concerned. From the commencement of the Second Bargain they all worked in amity, and there is specific evidence that Winter and Hawkins were at one. It is not easy to interpret. Hawkins had taken office under conditions which, however

[1] No full text of the Second Bargain has been found, but only two summaries or digests. See *Sir John Hawkins* (1927) pp. 361-2.

impossible now, were the custom of the country, of the Elizabethan England in which known traitors were the confidential servants of the Crown, and noblemen who had forfeited their heads were allowed opportunities to forfeit them again, and even murderous fanatics were free to come to court and approach the Queen's person. Hawkins had made the best of it in working with these men whose knavery he had exposed. Now they were his loyal colleagues. If the common run of Elizabethans were unprincipled and untrustworthy, they had good qualities not usual now. Winter and Hawkins shook hands on it. They could not have been petty-minded men.

The numerical strength of the Navy had been almost stationary since 1579, but that was a condition that was now to pass away. A 'Book of the whole Navy' drawn up in December, 1585, shows that there were then twenty-one ships at home in addition to two serving with Drake in the Caribbean. These were ships above 50 tons; and there were ten pinnaces below that limit, for the most part additional building and not replacements. It was a feature of Hawkins's policy that he built plenty of pinnaces, and it became the practice to construct one with every new ship of the larger sort. He was thinking of fleets operating on little-known coasts such as those of the West Indies, and remembered how necessary he had found small craft for the inshore work. A new building not previously mentioned occurs in this list, that of the *George*, formerly a hoy, now a ship of 100 tons.

With the campaigns of Drake in the West and of Leicester in the Netherlands, both begun in the latter half of 1585, war was substantially in progress, although the Queen clung to hopes of arresting it by diplomacy. In her realistic moments she admitted that they were hopes, and consented to spending some of Hawkins's savings on new ships. His annual savings amounted in terms of tonnage to 800 tons or very nearly two new *Revenges*. In 1586 came the first of the additional ships, a small one named the *Tremontana* of 150 tons. Next year, 1587, when the Armada was known to be assembling, saw a greater effort. Sir Walter Ralegh had built for himself a large galleon of 600 tons called the *Ark Ralegh*. The Queen purchased her and renamed her the

Ark Royal, a vessel beautiful to behold, which became the Lord Admiral's flagship and the galleon-type successor to the carrack-type *Great Harry* as the pride of the fleet. At the same time Pett and Baker built the *Vanguard* and the *Rainbow*, respectively a little larger and a little smaller than the *Revenge*, and modelled upon her design. Together these two and the two 50-ton pinnaces which accompanied them amounted to 1,000 tons and cost £5,200. By the end of 1587 there were twenty-five fighting ships of over 100 tons and eighteen ocean-going pinnaces. This was the Queen's Navy that fought the Armada.

The armament of the ships was not Hawkins's business and was unaffected by the Bargains. It was under the direction of Sir William Winter as Master of the Ordnance of the Ships. The guns were allotted on a 'proportion', drawn up by Winter and based on tonnage and design. They were in two main classes, the man-killing weapons throwing small shot and generally breech-loading, and the battering weapons firing roundshot at longer range and always (by Elizabeth's time) muzzle-loading. In the early sixteenth century the heavier guns had been loaded by removable chambers wedged into the breech, but the mechanism, if it can be so called, was slow and inefficient and offered no advantage over muzzle-loading for the larger sizes. It was retained only for the light pieces of the 'hailshot' type, generally mounted on swivels. The battering guns were themselves divided into two classes, one with large bore and short barrel, of which the 30-pounder demi-cannon was most common at sea; and the other with longer barrel and smaller bore, comprising 18-pounder culverins, 10-pounder demi-culverins, and sakers, minions and falcons of smaller sizes. By the time of the Armada the demi-cannon was giving place to the culverin, which was less violent in recoil, longer in range,[1] and more accurate in fire. The *Revenge* on Winter's proportion, had 10 man-killing guns and 34 battering guns, of which 22 were culverins, demi-culverins and sakers. The guns were mostly kept at the Tower in time of peace. On the order for mobilization, the issue of guns, the victualling, and the

---

[1] The extreme range of the culverin was said to be a mile and a half, and of the demi-cannon a mile.

collection of crews went on simultaneously, and it probably took less time to ferry the guns round to Chatham than it did to find beef and bread for the gunners to eat.

In 1585 Hawkins accomplished what may well have been his greatest reform, that of the manning of the Queen's ships. As we have seen, the old Navy of the Narrow Seas had grossly overcrowded its crews. In the reign of Henry VIII the proportion had been one man to $1\frac{1}{3}$ tons. In 1582 one man to $1\frac{2}{3}$ tons was still thought necessary. Hawkins believed in one man to 2 tons for the Queen's ships, and in far fewer men for the armed merchantmen. He wished to prevent sickness and mortality, but such motives would have aroused little interest at that time; and he therefore rested his argument mainly on the prospect of obtaining better work for the same expenditure.

He suggested that the pay of officers and men should be increased by one-third, so that the common mariner would have ten shillings a month instead of the existing 6s. 8d., and at the same time the crew should be proportionately reduced. He gave as an example the *Golden Lion* of 500 tons, existing crew 300 officers and men at a cost of 23s. 4d. a month each for pay and victuals; proposed crew 250, at 28s. a month for pay and victuals; total cost for the ship, in either case, £350 a month. Here it is evident that the proposed new proportion was one man to two tons, and that the reduction in consumption of victuals would help to counterbalance the increase of pay. There was no experienced captain, he urged, but would rather have 250 good men than 300 of tag and rag. These were inevitable with the existing inadequate pay, which caused the best men to desert or bribe their way out of the service, and 'insufficient, unable and unskilful persons' to take their places. 'By this means,' he asserts, and here we have John Hawkins as a shining light to his time, 'by this means Her Majesty's ships would be furnished with able men, such as can shift for themselves, keep themselves clean without vermin and noisomeness, which breedeth sickness and mortality, all which could be avoided. The ships would be able to continue longer in the service that they should be appointed unto, and would be able to carry victuals for a longer time.'

So John Hawkins in 1585. He was working towards a fleet with an endurance of from four to six months on ocean service, away from all supply and succour. His manning reform was one of the steps to obtaining it, and was carried by his advocacy at the end of 1585. The Queen's ships which fought the Armada were manned at the rate of one man to two tons.

There had been no full mobilization of the fleet since 1570, on which occasion, if we may trust a chance remark of Lord Howard's, considerable defects had revealed themselves. From 1585 onwards Hawkins and the other officials made detailed preparations for turning out the whole of the Navy and supporting it with twenty-two armed merchantmen of a burden of 140 to 300 tons. The ships of the Turkey Company, or such of them as might be available, were to be taken seriously for war service, since they had habitually to fight their way from the Straits of Gibraltar to the Levant, and were built and armed to that end. There were a few other good fighting ships in private hands, although the majority of the privateers were too small and belonged rather to the pinnace class. The preparations of the Navy Board included working out the quantities and prices of the materials and supplies that would be needed, and the wages of all the men to be engaged. The Queen's ministers thus knew in advance what a full-scale war would cost. Hawkins saw to it that all the canvas, cordage, pitch and spars were provided. In one respect he had an easier task than Edward Baeshe, the Surveyor of the Victuals, since the dockyard stores were not so perishable as the foodstuffs. With them the difficulty was that large supplies could not be had at short notice, while the keeping of large stocks in anticipation of crisis involved continual waste and replacement. Meat in casks would not keep as it will in tins, and there was a limit to the putridity at which salt fish could be served out, while beer was equally unstable. The alternatives were a running expense in anticipation of a call that might not come, or unreadiness when it should come. The government chose the second, and seriously hampered the action of their fine fleet. The undervictualling of 1588 was not the fault of the victualling department or the Navy Board, but of a decision taken 'at the highest levels'.

It may have been the hard necessity of finances that would not stand the strain. Froude declares that it was perverse meanness, and that the Queen had an ample reserve of treasure; but his evidences are not precise, and he is sometimes guilty of exaggeration in recording money matters.

The reconciliation with his fellow officers of the Board, perhaps even more than the increase of his powers by the Second Bargain, enabled Hawkins to complete his reforms and preparations without a hitch. In the latter part of 1586 he was able to be spared, for the first time for many a year, for a period of leave in the shape of a cruise in command at sea. Its particulars will appear in the next chapter. William Borough went with him, leaving Winter and Holstocke to carry on the dockyard work. That they did so with honesty and efficiency is attested not only by the absence of recriminations but by some good words from Hawkins subsequently.

In 1587 there came the first large expansion of the Navy by the addition of the *Ark Royal*, *Vanguard* and *Rainbow* already mentioned. More building was in prospect, and a third master-shipwright was appointed in the person of Richard Chapman, hitherto a private shipbuilder, who had already turned out the *Tremontana* for the Queen. The Armada preparations were unmistakeable, and Drake sailed that spring to impeach them. He was back at the end of June, having inflicted enormous damage and ascertained that there would still be a serious attempt at invasion. In the earlier days of such threats the position of John Hawkins had been in command of the western squadron at Plymouth. He wanted to be free to serve the Queen at sea and in council. The Navy was now in a good state and could hardly decline before the clash. Preparation was merging into action, and Hawkins was bent on going with it. On June 27 he wrote to Burghley suggesting that the Second Bargain should be terminated.

He pointed out that with the expansion of the fleet and the more frequent service of ships at sea, the terms of the contract were ceasing to be applicable. The work of supervision was also growing, 'so as it is impossible for any one man to answer the

office of Treasurer and to take this care.' He was able to vouch for
the good conduct of Winter and the other officers, who 'do and
will endeavour themselves, and are most desirous, to ease Her
Majesty's charge . . . and withal to take such substantial care as
Her Majesty be not overcharged'. He believed in the contract
system in time of peace, but thought it unsuitable for the hurly-
burly of war. Presumably he did not expect the war to last long,
for he recommended that the Bargain should be suspended for
the duration, but that a commission should be appointed to fix
fair terms for a new contract to begin with the coming of peace.
He did not desire to monopolize the new contract, but suggested
that a number of persons should jointly undertake it.

The above was tentative and not a formal request for the
termination of the Bargain. As usual, Burghley was in no hurry.
His character in these naval transactions appears so often as that of
one who never hurries but always arrives in time. In this case it is
more than three months before we hear of the next step, an order
to Pett and Baker to report on the present state of the ships. They
did so on October 12, 1587. The *Elizabeth Jonas*, *Triumph*, *White
Bear* and *Victory*, they said, are very old ships, are decaying, and
will not last long; but they have had work done on them of late,
and are good for a summer campaign. The *Mary Rose* is so very
old and decayed that little can be done for her; she ought to be
condemned. The *Bonaventure*, *Dreadnought* and *Swiftsure* are due
for dry-dock repair, but may serve without it. The *Antelope*, *Aid*
and *Swallow* are very old, although lately rebuilt; they are good
for present service. The *Bull* is greatly decayed but still serviceable.
The *Revenge* has lately had a thorough overhaul. The *Golden
Lion*, *Ark Royal*, *Vanguard*, *Rainbow* and *Merlin* are in good order.
The *Hope* is very old, but still serviceable. The *Nonpareil* and *Tiger*
have lately had much done to them and are in good state. The
Foresight, *Scout* and *Achates* are serviceable, but will soon need
repair. The *Galley Elenor* is decayed and will not last long.

In reading the shipwrights' report we should remember that they
were not enthusiasts for Hawkins. They had aided him to overthrow the corruption of the past, but they had received no
financial reward. His ruthless suppression of peculation had fallen

like a blight on all the snug jobs in the dockyards, and Pett and
Baker must have found living harder than before 1579. They give
the impression that the older ships were nearly done for, although
they do not suggest neglect by Hawkins. That their view was too
pessimistic may be inferred from the record of 1588; while the
aged ships were still serving several years after. The *Mary Rose*
went to sea with Hawkins in 1590, and cruised for six months in
the Atlantic without revealing defects. Hawkins in fact made her
his flagship, although there were newer ships in the squadron. It
was perhaps his silent answer to the report of the shipwrights.

In November he wrote to Burghley and asked definitely for
the Bargain to be terminated. Freedom from it, he said, would
enable him to serve the Queen better. The service he desired was
the command of the western squadron based on Plymouth. After
reviewing the chief things done in the dockyards under his rule, he
said:

For my own part, I have lived in a very mean estate since I came
to be an officer, neither have I vainly or superfluously consumed
Her Majesty's treasure or mine own substance, but ever been
diligently and carefully occupied to prepare for the danger to
come. And whatsoever hath been or is maliciously spoken of me, I
doubt not but your lordship's wisdom is such that ye may discern
and judge of my fidelity, of which Her Majesty and your lordship
have had long trial. And hereafter I will speak little in mine own
behalf, but endeavour myself with my ability and knowledge to
prevent the malice of our enemies, and lay aside the vanity of the
defending of every malicious report. . . . And so, wishing your
good lordship health and happiness, I humbly take my leave.
From London, the 13th of November, 1587.
Your honourable lordship's humbly to command,
JOHN HAWKYNS.

An undated paper in Burghley's hand may bear reference to
the termination of the Bargain and the reinstatement of the
officers of the Navy Board in their several responsibilities. The
paper is one of the partly burnt documents saved from the fire
in the Cotton Library two centuries ago. The heading and upper
lines are burnt off, but the intact portion shows that the minister

was drafting a set of rules for the conduct of the Board. The entries that are complete run as follows:

That no officers of the Admiralty be builders of ships nor [partners] with any other in building of ships. That no officer be a merchant of things to serve usually as provisions for the Queen's ships. That no other officer alone make the prices of the provisions. That no payments be made for any provisions or other charges by the Treasurer without the warrant of the rest of the officers. That all provisions do come first into Her Majesty's storehouse, and none be issued without warrant from all the officers. . . . That none that make ships for the Queen should keep timber yards for [supplying] merchant ships, for by colour thereof they take up timber.

'Provisions,' as the word is here used, does not mean victuals but anything provided for the equipment of the ships. The rules read like an answer to the report with which John Hawkins began his Treasurership, the 'Abuses in the Admiralty touching Her Majesty's Navy', of 1578. The Bargains had shelved the question of ensuring honest conduct by the Navy Board, but now it was recurring. There is no evidence that Burghley promulgated these rules. Some time after writing them, he picked up the paper again, as if to refresh his memory, and jotted at the foot of it:

Remembrances of abuses past. John Hawkins was half in the bargain with Peter Pett and Matthew Baker.

The absence of dates renders interpretation open to doubt; but the footnote was certainly written on a different occasion from the main body of the paper. Its handwriting is less firm and its alignment less regular, and it is in a different ink. The best guess may be that the regulations were drafted when Burghley was first considering the 'Abuses' report, and laid aside when the Bargains rendered them unnecessary. Then, years afterwards, Burghley took up the document again and identified it as 'Remembrances of abuses past'. The second jotting, about Hawkins's share in the Bargain, is independent of the first. It may refer to the 'invisible partnership' which has already been recorded, and carries no implication of censure upon Hawkins. It may simply express the fact that the First Bargain was in two divisions, one with Hawkins, the other with the shipwrights.

Before terminating the Second Bargain, Burghley obtained formal testimonies from the master-shipwrights and the officers of the Board about the manner in which Hawkins had performed it. The shipwrights said that during their contract under the First Bargain Hawkins, and not they, was responsible, for he deprived them of the benefit they had expected from it. Of the Second Bargain, they said that the ships were not so well repaired as when they were in control, and that Hawkins had not done so much rebuilding as he ought to have done; and that now that heavy work was due he thought it a good time to terminate. He had been using the right of purveyance for timber not only for the Queen's yards but for a private yard at Deptford, 'which breedeth ill speeches in the country.' The new ships had not been built at his charges.

Pett and Baker, it is evident, had been deceived in Hawkins. They had hoped much from him and perhaps believed what was said about him. And now, after all these years, they were poorer men than they would have been if he had played the game in true official style. No wonder it rankled. The new ships had not been built at his charges. No, they had been built with money saved out of all the dockyard's pockets, their own included. Their insinuation about the Queen's timber going to the private yard at Deptford was a poor effort, because, as Burghley well knew, the yard was Chapman's, and he had been building for the Queen. But Richard Chapman was another grievance. He had been made a master-shipwright, and now there were three instead of two to share the miserable perquisites that remained.

Winter and Holstocke answered for the Navy Board, William Borough being under arrest on charges brought against him by Drake. The two said that they had been careful to see that Hawkins had performed the conditions of the Bargain, and had advised impartially about the allowances under it which in equity he should have; 'certifying your lordship hereby, that he hath carefully performed the conditions of that offer in such sort that we have no cause to complain of him, but are thoroughly persuaded in our conscience that he hath, for the time since he took that bargain, expended a far greater sum in carpentry upon Her Majesty's ships than he hath had any way allowance for.' They appended a statement of the detailed work done, so that Burghley might judge that the Queen's money had been well employed. In all other matters, moorings, wages, upkeep of buildings 'we find no want'; and everything had been sufficiently done. The date of this certificate was December 9, 1587. From the end of that month the Second Bargain ceased, and the old pre-1579 constitution of the Navy Board returned. How the Board was changed since eight years past is shown by the terms and tone of their document.

Attacks from within the Navy Office had ceased since 1585, but Hawkins was still worried by ill-speaking from other directions. It was the common lot of public servants in a time when preferment, whether of good men or bad, went by influence, and when the Queen's ministers, not a united body like a modern cabinet, were competitors for her favour, their success depending much upon the pressure they could exert at court and in the City. A recognized method of attacking a minister was to discredit the men who were known to depend on him. A man ousted from office would seek his revenge by slander, or would rely on his nuisance-value to regain his place. Outrageous libels were so common as to be accepted as normal and pass unpunished. They were, moreover, the instrument not only of domestic intrigue but of international politics. As war set in they merged into the propaganda of the fifth column and the fellow-travellers with the enemy. Such things were not within the experience of the historians of Victorian England, and they found it difficult to assign to the circumstantial lie and libel its true zero value. We know more.

When it became known that Hawkins was moving for the termination of the Second Bargain, the accusation-mongers scented a chance. His demotion could be represented as the evidence of a grave scandal. Someone therefore wrote a paper entitled 'Articles wherein may appear Her Majesty to be abused and Mr. Hawkins greatly enriched'. It asserts that Hawkins has not maintained the Queen's ships 'so that they are brought to their last end and dangerous state'. He wishes to revoke the Bargain so that he may quit with great profits, while the Queen is left to pay again for the work he ought to have done. He has charged extra money for repairs that should have come under the contract. The master-shipwrights are his instruments and abet his frauds. He sells timber and builds ships privately at Chapman's yard. He overcharges the Queen for gear supplied to ships on service. The ships are unsafe by reason of leaks caused by caulking with rotten oakum. He sells cordage and canvas at excessive prices and under false descriptions to the Queen's storehouses. Great supplies go to sea with the fleets, and little is returned, all to his gain. He should be required to put the fleet in good order, and even then will not be out of pocket.

The foregoing may have been by Thomas Allen, the Queen's Merchant for Danzig stores. The following is certainly by him, being so endorsed in Burghley's hand. The Treasurer of the Navy, it says, and the other officers of the Board ought not to supply commodities or build or own ships for themselves. They ought not to buy materials for the Queen's use but to have them supplied by accredited merchants. Hawkins grasps all business, great and small. Mrs. Hawkins and her maids even make the flags and pendants, and so deprive poor artificers of employment. Hawkins is now very friendly with Sir William Winter, who allows him to pass into the storehouse inferior English-made rope, falsely described as Danzig. Hawkins took half the profits of the shipwrights in the First Bargain and then persuaded the other officers to agree to excessive allowances for extra work. His accounts are in arrear. Private ships ought not to lie at Deptford, neither ought the Queen's shipwrights to keep their own timber yards or build for private owners. Finally, Allen suggests that he himself should be appointed to supply to the Navy the stores that have been the occasion of these practices.

The 'ought nots' in the above are plausible and are certainly the established rule to-day. But they were not in the sixteenth century, when all the state's servants from Burghley downwards made their own profits while serving the state. Hawkins sent privateers to sea in all these years, and so did Leicester, Hatton,

A LATE SIXTEENTH-CENTURY SHIP-OF-WAR
From the title-page of *De Const der Zee-vaerdt*, Amsterdam, 1599

Ralegh and Drake. What they gained in that way they spent in another, by subscribing to the joint-stock expeditions that carried on the state's warfare and usually resulted in financial loss. Had that not been the method the Queen, for all her care, would have been broke and bankrupt as the Stuarts were in time of peace. It is not fair to elaborate one side of the account and suppress the other. The test of the man's probity is the final result. The courtiers gained excessively, Burghley kept level, Walsingham died poor, Hawkins was worth little more at the end than when he entered the Queen's service as a well-to-do young merchant from Plymouth.

The longest of the effusions against Hawkins is in an anonymous paper entitled 'Articles exhibited against Mr. John Hawkins, 1587'. Its writer appears to have been one of Leicester's servants, who had been on familiar terms with Hawkins's household. In 1583, he says, he had much talk with Sir William Winter, who was then an enemy of Hawkins, all of which made evident 'the baseness of the said Mr. Hawkins in birth, mind and manners'. He tried to pump Hawkins on the matters then in dispute, 'but say I what I could, or object what I would, he would seem to make such a sound answer or avoidance of the matter, that he made me some-times think I had mistaken that which now I know I perfectly knew.' Hawkins used to invite the informant to his table, where there was talk of the botching of the ships, the frauds over the cordage, the use of the Queen's timber in private building, and the profits on the moorings; and Hawkins once showed him a paper proving that the other officers shared these gains with him. Winter protested that he never dealt in such matters, but did not answer for Borough and Holstocke. Hawkins once remarked that when he and his brother parted at Plymouth his share was £10,000, and Winter commented: 'What a dissembling knave is that! When he was hurt in the Strand and made his will, he was not able to give £500.' Much tattle follows, picked up in the dockyards, and a statement that Winter is still the enemy of Hawkins but is seeking to lull him into security. They have nevertheless shared a pretty prize of £5,000, taken by a pinnace sailing in the Queen's service. Hawkins has also grown great friends with Borough, and each supports the other. Now is the time, when the enemy are upon us, to make an example of Hawkins. His former familiarity with Spain and the present decay of the Navy make it manifest that he is false.

The statements in such documents as these were not kept confidential. They were circulated as widely as their authors could contrive. The purpose of some was to serve private ends, of others, the enemy. 'The decay of the Navy' was played as an inducement to the invasion of England. That very year, when Cardinal Allen, the prince of the renegades, was urging the Pope to finance the enterprise, he was able to assure him that the dreaded English fleet was so consumed with rot that only four ships were fit for sea.

V

THE FIRST YEARS OF THE WAR

If the Spanish War may be reckoned to have begun with Drake's West Indian expedition of 1585-6, Richard Hawkins served in its first campaign, for he accompanied Drake in command of a minor vessel named the *Duck*, of 20 tons. His personal adventures are unknown, save that he had a bad attack of fever, but he must have learnt much in this his second tour of the Caribbean. For Drake had a formidable force both by sea and by land, and used it to strike a resounding blow at the economic foundations of Spanish strength.

It would be out of place and out of proportion in this book to attempt a history of the Spanish War. Its general story is sufficiently well known, and here we shall concern ourselves with the part played by the Hawkinses. Richard Hawkins was a young man of twenty-five, and had the advantage of seeing Drake's methods at first hand. Drake and John Hawkins both believed that Philip II could be beaten by an oceanic offensive against the sources of his wealth; but in their methods of applying the pressure they were beginning to differ. Drake thought first of the plate fleets, as Hawkins had done, but missed them in 1585, and then used his strength against the ports of call and concentration of Philip's Atlantic trade. He sacked and disarmed Santiago in the Cape Verde Islands, a focus for the trade of the African coast, and Santo Domingo and Cartagena in the Caribbean. He found himself with insufficient men to attempt the old design of capturing Panama and placing there a garrison to throttle the communication between Spain and Peru. He passed out of the western end of the Caribbean and did not seriously attack Havana, and then sacked the Spanish settlement of St. Augustine in Florida before going on to visit Ralegh's new colony in Virginia. The booty was not enough to pay the cost of the expedition, which was financially a disappointment to the joint-stock syndicate that equipped it.

But the 240 guns which Drake carried off were hard to replace, and the demonstration of what could be done by a squadron which comprised no more than one-tenth of the Queen's regular Navy was a moral blow to Spanish prestige and a very material one to Philip's credit with the European money-lenders. Philip had to spend money on fortifying his colonies, and this diversion, coupled with the enhanced difficulty of obtaining loans, slowed the Prince of Parma and rendered more aid to the Dutch than did Leicester's English auxiliaries.

The raid had brilliantly demonstrated the possibilities of the oceanic offensive, but it needed to be followed up without a pause. It was on this point, the incapacity of the Queen as a director of war and the inability of Burghley to overcome her weakness, that the plans of both Drake and John Hawkins were to come to grief. There was no real follow-up in the season of 1586-7, and Philip obtained the respite which enabled him to continue the Armada preparations. Meanwhile Richard Hawkins could meditate on the fact that the Panama stroke had been impracticable because Drake had half his force dead or sick at Cartagena. Richard had his father's interest in hygiene and pride in keeping his men fit. He had learnt something useful about the Cape Verde Islands. 'In two times that I have been in them,' he wrote subsequently, 'either [time] cost us the one half of our people with fevers and fluxes of sundry kinds.' The two times were in 1582 with his uncle William and in 1585 with Drake. The island fevers accompanied Drake across to the West and so depleted his force, coupled no doubt with original overcrowding to the extent of one man to 1½ tons of shipping, that he had to sail home from Cartagena leaving much undone. When Richard Hawkins himself came to lead an Atlantic expedition, although he was near the Cape Verdes, he refrained from landing there.[1]

The plans earlier submitted by John Hawkins for a war against Spain had included blockading operations on the Spanish coast in addition to the offensive in the West. In 1586, just as Drake was returning, Hawkins was given command of a squadron for the nearer operations. It comprised five of the Queen's ships, four

[1] *Observations*, p. 33.

middle-sized and one small, together with thirteen armed merchantmen and pinnaces. Hawkins made the *Nonpareil* (the former *Philip and Mary*) his flagship, and William Borough, who went as his vice-admiral, had the *Golden Lion*. Both were old pre-1558 ships rebuilt by Hawkins. He usually sailed in an old ship which he had cut down and perhaps lengthened to galleon form; and this was no doubt of policy, to demonstrate what his treatment of these ships was worth. The *Hope*, another old ship, in which Winter had detected rotten timbers a year before, was also of the squadron, as were the *Revenge* and the little, brand-new *Tremontana*.

It was said above that Hawkins's mission was to operate on the Spanish coast, but that is only an assumption based on what took place. His instructions have not been preserved, and it may be that he had originally hoped to make another sweep of the Caribbean just as the Drake wave was receding. Nothing of the sort proved to be possible, owing to the difficulties and the fears of the Queen's government. In 1586 the *empresa* or enterprise of England was coming to the stage of action. Philip II had determined on invasion, and some of the early plans allotted considerable scope to his satellites in France, the Catholic League led by the Duke of Guise. In the summer Walsingham was completing the detection of the Babington conspiracy for the assassination of the Queen and the enthronement of Mary Stuart. The Catholic party in France were known to be interested, and Guise had stationed troops in Normandy. In August the English government arrested Babington and his gang, and in so doing were uncertain whether they would checkmate the plot or touch it off; for it comprised much weightier elements than the would-be assassins. England was in a frenzy of excitement and a prey to rumours, such as that the Duke of Guise had landed and the Catholics had risen to join him. The Queen believed that he might try it. And so John Hawkins, whose fleet must have been fitted out for quite other purposes, found himself involved in the panic and directed by the Council 'to ply up and down' in the Channel and intercept the invaders. This 'plying up and down' and waiting for something to turn up was the type of naval operation that was always uppermost in the Queen's mind.

Hawkins was kept in the Channel until the latter part of September, when the alarm subsided and he was allowed to proceed to the Spanish coast. He arrived there too late to fall in with the silver fleets from the West, which contrived to make their voyage in spite of what Drake had done. It is not certain whether he would have had a chance of taking them if he had not been delayed, but it is undoubted that he could have met the returning carracks from the East Indies, which were now bringing rich cargoes home for the benefit of Philip's treasury. The carracks slipped into Lisbon in the nick of time. Hawkins cruised along the western coast of Spain and Portugal, no doubt gathering information of what was going on in the ports, the invasion ports, as they were soon to become. He then turned westwards towards the Azores and was home by the end of October. He captured several minor prizes, but nothing of great value. This account is combined from brief references in the Spanish state papers summarized in their *Calendar* for 1580–6. There is no narrative by Hawkins or anyone else who took part. If there were, the expedition might appear in a different light. If nothing brilliant had been achieved, Hawkins knew that he was not to blame, and would have had no difficulty in saying who was. But he was a loyal man, and said nothing, and everyone else was equally silent.

William Borough, vice-admiral of the expedition, had been a detractor of Hawkins and became his adherent. Hawkins was understanding and sympathetic, and his leadership won over Borough as it did others. Borough had a different experience as vice-admiral to Drake in the Cadiz expedition of the following year. He was so perturbed by Drake's unorthodox methods and daring decisions that he made formal protests and was placed under arrest on board his own ship, which was again the *Golden Lion*. The crew mutinied for lack of food and sailed home in advance of Drake, with Borough on board. Drake assumed the worst, and convened a court-martial which condemned Borough to death in his absence for incitement to mutiny. The case was eventually quashed when all came home, and Borough was reinstated in his seat on the Navy Board. So much was the ostensible side of the affair, but it evidently covered tensions between Drake and other highly placed persons. It was to the credit of all of them that they subordinated their resentments to the public good in 1588.

Before leaving the expedition of John Hawkins in 1586, the report of one of his prisoners may be noted. This man was the master of a ship taken by the *Nonpareil* on September 30, thirty leagues from the mouth of the Tagus. Hawkins questioned him and treated him kindly, allowing him to keep his personal effects. Hawkins showed him over the flagship, which carried 44 bronze guns and 300 men. There were three other galleons in the fleet, excellently found, the hulls clean and the sails new. The victualling was beyond the ordinary sea standard, for there were live sheep and pigs on board, and quantities of apples and pears. These things may well have been extras provided by Hawkins out of the economies so detested in the dockyards. Another prisoner on board the *Golden Lion* told much the same story. Hawkins in fact, as we shall see, was studying the question of how long such a squadron could remain at sea with its crews in good health. His apples and sheep and general cleanliness were a contribution to the answer.

Fifteen eighty-seven was Drake's year, the year in which his strategical genius and tactical skill combined to mystify, baffle, insult and despoil the enemy, to deprive the gathering Armada of part of its shipping, and to cause the rest to waste its time in unnecessary movements. The events at Cadiz, Cape St. Vincent, Lisbon and the Azores raised English confidence and depressed Spanish, and weakened Philip not only by loss of material but by hardening the attitude of the Pope and the moneylenders towards him.

These were the obvious results of the campaign. Their brilliance tended to obscure the fact that Elizabeth had yielded the initiative to Philip, and that Drake had postponed but not prevented the invasion. The initiative had passed to Spain when the Queen failed to keep up the oceanic pressure by another West Indian expedition in 1586. Philip had then been able to begin the collection of money and material for the invasion, and he went steadily on with his preparations until the moment came for the

Armada to sail. The English counter-blows delayed but did not stop him; and until the Armada fled from Gravelines into the North Sea all English movements revolved around its growth and greatness. Elizabeth had not put forth her strength at the right moment. In 1586 with Hawkins, and in 1587 with Drake, she had sent out only four of her fighting galleons, the rest being pinnaces and merchantmen. The propagandists seized upon the weakness, and it was not a coincidence that Allen told the Pope that there were only four ships fit for service in the Navy, while the fifth-columnists were spreading the like reports in London.

With the commencement of the war there had come a revival of the activity and importance of the Lord Admiral. Lord Lincoln, who had held the office for most of the reign, died in 1585. His successor was Lord Charles Howard of Effingham, the fourth of his house to be Lord Admiral in the Tudor period. He was fifty years of age, a Protestant and a devoted servant of the Queen, an ally of Burghley, and an exponent of the view that war was inevitable and that Spain should be struck with the utmost force that the Navy could exert. Howard admired and supported John Hawkins and believed that he had rescued the fleet from decay. His accession to office coincided with the negotiation of the Second Bargain, and it may well be that the reconciliation between Hawkins and Winter was of his contriving; but of that there is no evidence. Howard, with an inherited knowledge of naval affairs, was determined to be no merely titular chief. He knew that when the whole Navy should be mobilized he would be in command, and he prepared himself by learning as much as possible about his ships and his officers. He had no training of the modern sort for the responsibility he would have to bear, but neither had anyone else in the English service. Not one of them—Howard, Drake, Hawkins, Frobisher—had ever seen a large fleet in action with another fleet, or had taken part in any manoeuvres designed to evolve or practise the tactics of such an occasion. Training of that sort was not yet thought of and would have been vetoed on the ground of expense. There was not even any proper instruction of the gunner in the use of his culverin. Drake, greatly innovating, fired a few rounds of practice ammunition, but since a gun burst and a man was killed and there was no powder to spare, Howard gave him a hint to desist.

The customary disposition against a Spanish threat in the 1570's had been that the Queen's ships at Chatham should guard against a move from the Netherlands, while John Hawkins looked westwards with his own squadron at Plymouth. Until the early part of 1588 the government maintained the same distribution of the main fleet in the Thames and the subsidiary force at Plymouth, with the difference that the Plymouth squadron now included a growing number of the Queen's galleons. In the 1580's we hear no more of a Plymouth force belonging especially to John Hawkins. Times had changed since he had maintained a dozen fighting ships for the Queen on the proceeds of Channel privateering. There had been a quasi-peace for several years in France, rendering the Huguenots less active than of yore; while Hawkins himself was tied to London by his Navy duties. He still considered, as we have seen, that he had a claim to the western command. But Drake had shown in 1587 how he could beat up the Armada in its own ports, and Plymouth was the base for such an enterprise. Drake was placed in command at Plymouth in the winter of 1587-8, while Hawkins remained at Chatham at the elbow of the Lord Admiral. At the stage of mobilization his presence there was indispensable. The Lord Admiral and the whole Navy Board, his particular henchmen, were therefore together at the eastern base, while Drake, ranking higher in public estimation than any of them, but holding no formal position in the hierarchy, was in the west. In some aspects it was an unstable situation.

Drake had destroyed only a minor part of the Armada shipping, and when he left the Spanish coast for the Azores, where he captured a carrack that more than paid for his expedition, Santa Cruz at Lisbon sent in pursuit all the ships he could get ready. They were too late to interfere with Drake and were not back until October. It was then, in the autumn of 1587, that Philip desired the Armada to sail without further delay. Parma in the Netherlands was eager to receive it, for his army was ready, and he had intelligence that the English were in no great force in the Narrow

Seas. Santa Cruz was the obstacle. His ships needed refitting and his crews were under strength, and he had no faith in out-of-season campaigns. On his advice Philip reluctantly postponed the invasion to the following spring.

The English were indeed in no great force, for the Queen had not yet given the order to mobilize the fleet. She ran a risk, for if Santa Cruz had moved in the autumn he might not have found much opposition. It depended on the 'security silence' which the Spaniards would be able to maintain. If the news that the Armada was coming out preceded it by more than a fortnight, then the whole English Navy could be at sea to meet it; for Hawkins had so ordered his preparations that he could get men, food and guns on board and the ships to sea in a fortnight or little more. The English secret service was superior to the Spanish, but neither could furnish dependable information about intentions that varied daily in the minds of their own framers. So it can be seen in the retrospect that Elizabeth's postponement of mobilization exposed her country to peril in the autumn of '87, while the Spaniards' postponement of action threw away their only chance of winning the war.

In December, when Philip had in fact agreed to postpone, the Queen became impressed with the danger and at length gave the order to turn out the whole fleet. Everything was done according to the plans that had long been perfected, and by the end of the year the Lord Admiral had the whole Navy afloat, with men, guns and stores in readiness to carry out any operations that could secure sanction. Drake's force at Plymouth was to be made up to thirty sail, including seven of the Queen's galleons. Small vessels based on Dover, aided by the Dutchmen from Flushing, maintained the close blockade of the Flemish coast. Howard himself, with Hawkins and Frobisher, remained in the Medway. No sooner was all complete than the prospect and the policy changed. The Queen saw a chance of negotiating for peace under colour of mediating between Spain and the Dutch, which she might do with diplomatic correctness since she was not formally at war with Philip. English representatives went over to Flushing to confer with Dutch and Spaniards, and English naval activity was stayed.

Drake with his western force had hoped to make another stroke at the invasion ports, but it was not allowed. Howard in January was ordered to discharge half his men, although not to lay up his ships. Philip was resolved on the invasion and never meant the negotiations to lead to peace. He gained from them three months' respite from Drake's enterprises, during which the Armada creaked into the ramshackle readiness which represented its highest efficiency.

If nothing was to be done for several weeks, the dismissal of half the crews had the advantage of sparing the victuals, of which it was so difficult to collect adequate stocks. Howard wrote to Walsingham on January 28, protesting against the step. He was convinced that the negotiations were insincere and that the war would go on, and foresaw that at any moment he would be commanded to recruit the very men he was now to send away. As for the ships, they gave him no anxiety. 'The ships', he said, 'shall prove some persons notable liars, and if cause fall out, do a better day of service for England than ever ships did for it yet.' Howard was a generous man, indignant at the attacks upon Hawkins. He knew also why the notable liars had been set to work, to shake English confidence and play the enemy's game, and he returned more than once to the question of the ships, determined that the Queen's ministers at least should be under no illusion about them. On February 21 he wrote to Burghley: 'I have been aboard of every ship that goeth out with me, and in every place where any may creep, and I do thank God that they be in the estate they be in; and there is never a one of them that knows what a leak means. . . . [They] shall prove them arrant liars that have reported the contrary.' A week later he repeated: 'I protest before God, and as my soul shall answer for it, that I think there were never in any place of the world worthier ships than these are.' If Howard did not show these sentences to John Hawkins he must at least have told him their purport; and Hawkins, we may believe, went about his business in those days of preparation for battle with more peace in his heart than he had known for many a year.

Winter, Holstocke and Borough were also at Chatham, all assiduous in putting the final touches to efficiency and maintaining perfection when it had been reached. Borough's court-martial had by this time been quashed and himself reinstated in his duties. The Lord Admiral thought that the accusation had been excessive, and took care to give the lame ending the appearance of an acquittal by replacing Borough in command of the *Golden Lion*. It was a post, however, which he could not retain, for it might have brought him into personal contact with Drake when the fleet was concentrated; and an explosion would have resulted. Borough was therefore transferred to command the *Galley Elenor*, which remained in the Thames throughout the campaign. So was justice substantially done; for though Borough may not have instigated a mutiny, he had certainly cut a very poor figure as a captain at Cadiz and Cape St. Vincent. The Navy Board had long ceased to be numbered among the detractors of the Navy, and Winter added his testimony to that of Howard: 'Our ships doth show themselves like gallants here. I assure you it will do a man's heart good to behold them; and would to God the Prince of Parma were upon the seas with all his forces, and we in view of them.'

The full list of the captains who sailed with Drake in 1587 has not been preserved, and it is possible that Richard Hawkins was one of them. There is no record of his doings during the period of the expedition, but later in the year he was in Plymouth, where he sold the corporation some guns for the defences.[1] Although his service in 1587 is uncertain, he is accounted for in 1588. He was made captain of the Queen's *Swallow*, of 350 tons, and in her fought the Armada. He was himself a private shipowner, and records that two of the merchantmen used as fireships at Calais belonged to him. His uncle William Hawkins, brother of John, was Mayor of Plymouth in 1587-8, and it was fitting that a Hawkins should hold the office in that year of all the century. William Hawkins was nearly seventy, but active as ever. In January and February, when Drake was hoping for another change of policy and leave to sail for Spain, old Hawkins was keeping his ships fit, grounding, scrubbing and tallowing, and working the shipwrights night and day by the light of cressets

[1] R. N. Worth, *Cal. of Plymouth Municipal Records*, p. 128.

and torches. The ships, he said, were as staunch as if they had been carved from solid timber.

John Hawkins, like Howard and Drake, disapproved of the halt in naval action and considered the negotiations a trap. On February 1st he wrote to Walsingham. The right way to peace, he said, was not by hesitation and negotiation. Delay was disadvantageous because it consumed England's resources. Trade was suspended, merchant shipping idle, and the poor unemployed; and while we waited, the enemy was increasing his power. 'We have to choose,' he asserted, and the words have a familiar ring in our ears, 'we have to choose either a dishonourable and uncertain peace, or to put on virtuous and valiant minds, to make a way through with such a settled war as may bring forth and command a quiet peace.' To hinder the concentration of food and stores for the Armada and to prevent Philip from receiving money from the West, he asked that six good ships of the Queen's and six smaller ones should be sent to cruise on the coast of Spain or between it and the Azores. They would be able to keep the station for four months and might then be relieved by a similar force. Meanwhile the main strength of the Navy would be sufficient to defend the country.

This advanced force proposed by Hawkins was essentially for the same purposes as Drake's, for Drake had also operated on the Spanish coast and round the Azores. But Hawkins's force was to be of very different composition. Drake's fleet in 1587 had been equipped by a joint-stock syndicate, and very badly victualled by the same. It had consisted of four of the Queen's galleons and a mixed lot of privately owned ships of war and armed merchantmen. It had achieved heart-lifting victories, but had lasted only two months as a coherent force before beginning to disintegrate by hunger and sickness; whereupon its commander had followed rather than led it home. No continuous pressure upon Spain could be exerted by expeditions of this sort. Hawkins had been thinking of something better. He considered that a disciplined squadron of the Queen's ships, not of mixed privateers and merchantmen, could be adequately victualled and stored for a service of four months. His own cruise in 1586 had given him experience in the matter and, as subsequent events were to show, his estimate was within the mark, for a squadron organized on his lines could endure at a pinch for six months. After its term of duty the squadron would be replaced by another and could go home to refit, to come out again in its turn. Thus the pressure of blockade could be kept up continuously. Hawkins's insistence on continuous blockade and the war-winning effects of it was novel at the time and has been justified by the subsequent history of naval warfare. We shall find him elaborating these ideas at a later date; at the moment they had no effect.

It was about the end of March, 1588, that the peace negotiations broke down and the Queen had to face unqualified war. Drake became ever more insistent that the proper place to fight the Armada was on its own coast or in its own ports. He urged that the bulk of the fleet should be sent down Channel to Plymouth, leaving in the Narrow Seas only a force sufficient to blockade Parma's flotillas, and that then the great main armament should sail for Spain to seek the enemy. So far the officers at Chatham agreed with him, for the intelligence was that the Armada was ready and would shortly move; it was no longer a question of preventing its preparation by blockade. But Drake assumed that he would be in chief command and that the Lord Admiral would remain at Dover or Chatham. He even implied that he was doubtful of receiving loyal support from the officers of the Navy Board. The Borough incident, Howard's evident kindliness towards the culprit, and Hawkins's known friendship with him, had cut deep, and Drake scented a combination against himself. He desired a free hand, with subordinates of his own choice and connection. The Lord Admiral could not agree. When the Queen's Navy served entire, his place was at the head of it. Its prestige, in that age of pomp so much more important than to-day, would have suffered if he had remained at home, and the senior officers, men of their time and not of ours, would not have yielded willing obedience to one whom they viewed as no more than their equal.[1] It needed a man of rank, a great officer of

----

[1] The rough-tongued Frobisher was no admirer of Drake, and did not hesitate to say so when an incident in the Channel fighting displeased him.

state and a member of the Queen's Council, to command their unquestioning allegiance. The government took this view and solved the difficulty by sending Howard to Plymouth with the main fleet, there to join with Drake and take over the command. A might-have-been, perhaps a great passage of sea history, but also certainly a gamble, was lost when Drake was relegated to vice-admiral under Howard, with Hawkins as rear-admiral and third. But together they were to make some history in compensation.

Howard reached Plymouth towards the end of May, and Drake received him with fitting ceremony and obedience. In this Drake made no mental reservation. His duty was to England, and he performed it with complete vigour and cheerfulness. Knowing what he had hoped, and what he believed of his own powers, we may regard his self-conquest as the greatest act of his life. Hawkins, detained by business, did not reach Plymouth till June, and then they all set to work in concert. Winter remained in the Straits of Dover, with Lord Henry Seymour as his superior in command of the blockade. Holstocke, now an aged man, carried on single-handed at the Chatham dockyard.

The despatch of the entire fleet on active service, coupled with the enlistment of multitudes of private vessels and their crews, threw upon the Navy Treasurer an unprecedented load of business. He would have had more chance of coping with it if he had not gone to sea himself, but to that he could not consent. He had spent ten bitter years in making the Navy ready to fight the King of Spain, and he claimed as his reward a share in its leadership. A letter which he wrote to Burghley in March discusses some of the extraordinary business of the year:

My bounden duty humbly remembered unto your good lordship,

I have been very ill since I was with your lordship, but am now better, I thank God.

I do daily hear good report of the good estate of the ships abroad, as it may appear to your lordship by the letters I send herewith enclosed; so do I hear many of good judgment that have served now in them report, wondering how these lewd bruits could have been cast abroad, and the ships in that efficient and strong estate.

. . . .

I would to God Her Majesty were so well provided of all furniture that belongeth to the ships, which indeed is the least matter I fear. But the provisions that come from foreign countries, and such as require long time to provide, do most trouble me—as great cables, anchors, cordage, canvas, great masts, and such like; waste and spoil of boats and pinnaces by this winter weather, as Sir William Winter doth well note.

I am now about to gather together the great issuing that hath been in this year of *anno* 1587 of cordage, canvas, and other provisions out of Her Majesty's store, which I think will be 12,000 or 13,000 pound, which must be cared for and supplied in time, without the which the ships cannot serve. There hath been great service abroad these two years past, and the ships mightily supplied from time to time with many provisions, and now call daily in such sort as I am both afraid and sorry to present it to your lordship. Howbeit, it must be done, and care had to do it in time. The expenses extraordinary have been great, and such as before this time have seldom come in use; for the navy is great, and men more unruly and chargeable than in time past, so as it doth not only amaze me to answer everything, but I do grieve at the charge as much as it were to proceed from myself.

I have been careful to replenish the store, for I found it not worth £5,000; and now I think with this years issuing it is worth 16,000 pound. So likewise the ships I found in weak estate, and now they are as your lordship doth see; and this is done in effect upon the sparing out of the ordinary warrant of £5,719, yet I am daily backbited and slandered. But your lordship doth know what a place this is to hold that I am in. Many are to receive out of this office, and among a multitude there are some bad and unreasonable; and although I endeavour myself to pay and satisfy all men with order and equity yet some be displeased.

The matters in the office are great and infinite. My men are sick and dispersed. The trust I am forced to commit abroad and at home is very much; and with great difficulty I keep things in that order as I can give reason for the things that are paid; and many losses I receive by negligence of servants, by such as I put in trust, and by prests[1] which be without number.

Therefore, my good lord, consider in your wisdom the burden I bear. My service to Her Majesty I grudge not, but all my ability and life is ready to be employed in her service. When it shall be your lordship's pleasure, I will give mine attendance to inform your lordship substantially what is to be done touching the provisions that are to be provided for the navy, and the debt that the office doth and will daily grow into. And so, wishing your lordship health and prosperity, I humbly take my leave.

From London, the 3rd of March, 1587,[2]

Your lordship's humbly to command,

JOHN HAWKYNS.

In June, as we have seen, Hawkins was at length able to leave all this and join the fleet at Plymouth. There he took command of the *Victory*, one of the old ships which he had rebuilt and re-shaped as modern galleons. Howard sailed in the *Ark Royal*, Drake in the *Revenge*, and Frobisher in the *Triumph*. The move westwards had been made none too soon, for at the end of May, just as Howard reached Plymouth, the Armada sailed from Lisbon. But the Duke of Medina Sidonia, who had succeeded Santa Cruz in command, was unable to press forward. Adverse winds pinned him to his own coast, and then a gale inflicted damage and dispersal. On June 9 he put into Corunna to rally and refit. The Armada had already passed its best and was deteriorating. Medina Sidonia advised the King that it would be better not to proceed, but it was obvious that Philip could not draw back; the downfall of prestige in the eyes of all Christendom would have equalled the worst material defeat. Parma also no longer thought as he had done. Winter sickness and lack of money had diminished his army to little more than half its autumn strength. He had no harbour in which to receive the Armada. The blockade of his own flotillas in their minor ports

[1] Prests were payments in advance, usually of wages to sailors. Rascals made a practice of taking their money and then deserting. See Richard Hawkins's *Observations*, p. 20.

[2] i.e. by modern usage, 1588.

was tighter than ever. He would have been glad to hear that the attempt was off. But it had to go on.

Meanwhile Howard and his officers did not learn for some time that the Armada had been out. They agreed that they ought to attack it on its own coast and at first had difficulty in securing the Queen's consent. She was afraid that it might slip past them and find England undefended, and her mind was still running on plying up and down in the Channel approaches. Howard had to tell her that this would not do, and at last got his way. He was foiled by two factors acting successively, first, that he was short of victuals and that the vessels bringing them were slow in making their way down Channel; and second, that up to mid-July it was a summer of wild weather, depression following depression from from the Atlantic, with strong winds between south and west. The English fleet was twice driven back, the second time when almost in sight of the Spanish coast. It put into Plymouth on this occasion on July 12, again short of food and with many sick. Then the weather changed, and a settled period with the lightest of westerly breezes set in. The English had now heard of the Armada's false start, and perhaps had received exaggerated news of the damage it had sustained. They were considering blockading it with part of their strength while the rest cruised for the plate fleets and the East Indian carracks. They were hard at work refitting and taking in a scanty supply of victuals when they were surprised by the Armada's appearance off the Lizard on July 19. Medina Sidonia had sailed from Corunna as the last gale died out, and was then favoured with twelve days of the most perfect weather he could have desired for his enterprise.

For John Hawkins the state of the ships was the especial concern, and on it he wrote his last report to Burghley on July 17:

My bounden duty remembered unto your good lordship,

By the letter and estimate enclosed, your lordship may see how charges doth grow here daily. My Lord Admiral doth endeavour by all means to shorten it, and yet to keep the navy in strength.

In this demand is the ships serving under the Lord Henry Seymour included: and I do write to Mr. Hussey to stay so much money as may clear them.

The four great ships—the *Triumph*, the *Elizabeth Jonas*, the *Bear*, and the *Victory*—are in most royal and perfect state; and it is not seen by them, neither do they feel that they have been at sea, more than if they had ridden at Chatham. Yet there be some in them that have no good will to see the coast of Spain with them but cast many doubts how they will do in that seas. But, my good lord, I see no more danger in them, I thank God, than in others. The *Bear* one day had a leak, upon which there grew much ado; and when it was determined that she should be lighted of her ordnance, her ballast taken out, and so grounded and searched, and that my Lord Admiral would not consent to send her home, the leak was presently stopped of itself; and so the ship proceedeth with her fellows in good and royal estate, God be thanked. I was bold to trouble your lordship with these few words touching these four ships, because I know there will be reports as men are affected; but this is the truth.

The strength of the ships generally is well tried; for they [the captains] stick not to ground often to tallow, to wash, or any such small cause, which is a most sure trial of the goodness of the ships when they are able to abide the ground. My Lord Admiral doth not ground with his ship, but showeth a good example, and doth shun charges as much as his lordship may possible. And so I leave to trouble your good lordship. From Plymouth, the 17th of July, 1588.

> Your honourable lordship's humbly to command,
> JOHN HAWKYNS.

The captain of the *Bear* was Lord Sheffield, Howard's son-in-law, who owed his command to his rank rather than to his experience; and there were evidently some with him who would have liked to be sent back to Chatham to excuse their shirking by saying that Hawkins had given them a rotten ship. Howard saw through them and prescribed the hard labour of taking out the guns and ballast, whereupon the leak vanished. He himself had already written that the ships had come creditably out of a hard trial by the weather, and that their detractors should be ashamed.

Hawkins wrote no more until two days after Gravelines, when he sent Burghley a modest summary of the events in the Channel.

In the first fight on July 21 near the Eddystone, he was hotly engaged with a group of the enemy's ships, but he did not mention it himself. All he said was : 'We met with this fleet somewhat to the westward of Plymouth upon Sunday in the morning, being the 21st of July, where we had some small fight with them in the afternoon.' Here the Spaniards left behind two of their great ships, crippled, the one by a collision, the other by an explosion; and both were taken by the English. That night and through the next day the Armada slowly sailed eastwards with the English following but not engaging, and so they all came just east of Portland Bill on the Monday evening. 'The Tuesday following,' says Hawkins, 'we had a sharp and long fight with them, wherein we spent a great part of our powder and shot, so it was not thought good to deal with them any more till that was relieved.' This was the Battle off Portland, important, but so ill recorded that Hawkins's sentence gives almost all that is validly known of it. The essence was that there was heavy firing, but no loss of ships on either side, and that thenceforward ammunition was short with both.

From Portland to St. Katherine's Point in the Isle of Wight the fleets drifted rather than sailed at an average speed of little more than one knot. During that time Howard divided his great array into four squadrons each with a proportion of the Queen's ships and the merchant auxiliaries, commanded respectively by himself, Drake, Hawkins and Frobisher. Off St. Katherine's in a calm on the morning of the 25th a battle was begun almost unintentionally when Hawkins's squadron got out their boats and towed into action to cut off a Spaniard separated from the rest. Other ships on either side joined in, and the battle became general as the breeze arose. The English tried to drive the enemy on the Owers shoals, east of the Isle of Wight, but failed to do so, and the procession moved slowly up Channel as before. It was by no means a race or a brisk chase. The average speed was under two knots, and the English could join battle whenever they chose. They preferred to wait until the lack of a friendly port on the Netherlands coast should place the Armada in difficulties. Richard Hawkins says that Howard insisted on careful handling of the fleet, against

AN ENGLISH SHIP-OF-WAR OF THE ARMADA CAMPAIGN
From the engraving by J. Remius in the British Museum

the advice of some who wished to board and risk all in a hand-to-hand fight. John Hawkins says of the Isle of Wight action only that 'by the occasion of the scattering of one of the great ships from the [Spanish] fleet, which we hoped to have cut off, there grew a hot fray, wherein some store of powder was spent; and after that, little done till we came near to Calais'.

Little done between St. Katherine's and Calais; it is a characteristic omission by one who held everything little but the service of England. In that unmentioned interval fell one of the great days of John Hawkins's life. On Friday, July 26, drifting in the morning calm, Howard called his officers on board the *Ark Royal* and there conferred knighthoods, of which the most important recipient was John Hawkins. The Lord Admiral on active service with the fleet had the right to create knights. Howard was discriminating, for he made only six, most of them no doubt for conspicuous gallantry. For all we know, Hawkins may have come within that category; but if not, we know that he had well earned his honour. His ships were proved. Not one had fallen out for sea damage or the enemy's shot. Ten years of battle with lies and corruption were justified in ten days' fighting with the great Armada, then in sight as he knelt to receive the accolade. It was better there on the flagship's deck than at Greenwich even in the Queen's presence. What he felt, we guess; he said nothing, not even a word to his old friend Burghley.

Of the doings at Calais and Gravelines Hawkins tells us more than of the previous encounters:

We came near to Calais, where the fleet of Spain anchored, and our fleet by them; and because they should not be in peace there, to refresh their water or to have conference with those of the Duke of Parma's party, my Lord Admiral, with firing of ships, determined to remove them; as he did, and put them to the seas: in which broil the chief galleasse spoiled her rudder, and so rode ashore near the town of Calais, where she was possessed of our men, but so aground as she could not be brought away.

That morning, being Monday the 29th of July, we followed the Spaniards; and all that day had with them a long and great fight, wherein there was great valour showed generally of our company. In this battle there was spent very much of our powder and shot;

and so the wind began to blow westerly a fresh gale, and the Spaniards put themselves somewhat to the northward, where we follow and keep company with them. In this fight there was some hurt done among the Spaniards. A great ship of the galleons of Portugal [had] her rudder spoiled, and so the fleet left her in the sea. I doubt not but all these things are written more at large to your lordship than I can do; but this is the substance and material matter that hath passed.

Our ships, God be thanked, have received little hurt and are of great force to accompany them, and of such advantage that with some continuance at the seas, and sufficiently provided of shot and powder, we shall be able with God's favour to weary them out of the sea and confound them. . . . Now this fleet is here and very forcible, and must be waited upon with all our force, which is little enough. There should be an infinite quantity of powder and shot provided, and continually sent abroad, without the which great hazard may grow to our country; for this is the greatest and strongest combination, to my understanding, that ever was gathered in Christendom. Therefore I wish it of all hands to be mightily and diligently looked unto and cared for.

The men have been long unpaid and need relief. I pray your lordship that the money that should have gone to Plymouth may now be sent to Dover. August now cometh in, and this coast will spend ground tackle, cordage, canvas and victuals, all of which should be sent to Dover in good plenty. With these things and God's blessing our kingdom may be preserved, which being neglected great hazard may come. . . .

The Spaniards take their course for Scotland; my lord doth follow them. I doubt not, with God's favour, we shall impeach their landing. There must be order for victual and money, powder and shot, to be sent after us.

Hawkins was in no mood for self-congratulation and did not allude to a matter which his statistical mind must have considered. Victuals were very low, and only the worst of food and drink remained. They were just enough to see the Spaniards past the Firth of Forth and then Howard was obliged to turn back. If the fleet had been manned on the old crowded proportion, these victuals would not have lasted beyond Gravelines, if as far. Hawkins's reduction of the numbers in the crews had saved the situation, one more of those commonly unnoticed factors by which his industry and wisdom served his country. His account shows that he was not elated, and if his mind had needed sobering the previous ten days would have had that effect. The Armada had proved itself a greater fighting force than he had expected, with his expert knowledge of ways and means and his estimation of the poor work to be looked for in a Spanish equipment. He had underestimated the moral factor, the intense religion and patriotism of all the Spaniards, and the high discipline and chivalry of their officers, so different from the demoralized colonials he had once known. It was a lesson for those who could learn, and so he wrote coolly of the victory of Gravelines, in fact he understated the results achieved. 'This is a matter', he said, 'far passing all that hath been seen in our time or long before.' Howard was of the same mind. 'All the world', he wrote, 'never saw such a force as theirs was.'

The Armada sailed into the northern sea, from which not half its ships were destined to return. Parma laid up his flotillas and sent his troops about their normal duties. The Catholic world swallowed tales of extraordinary victory until credulity was bankrupt and had to face the truth. The English fleet turned back to look for food and land its sick. Of them there were many, for victualling had been not only scanty but scandalous. Edward Baeshe, old and faithful, had died the year before, and rogues had found their moment. Hundreds of English seamen, running into thousands, were almost literally poisoned, and their wreckage had to be set on shore without delay. By August 8 Howard was in the Downs with part of the fleet, while Hawkins had the remainder at Harwich. His ships were soon moved to the southern side of the Estuary and anchored off Margate, between the North Kent shore and the outlying sands. Then, as the month progressed, the news became clear that the Armada had accepted defeat and that Parma could do nothing. It became then a question of paying-off the men and getting the ships to Chatham to refit for the next stage of the war. Only skeleton crews were to be kept for the purpose, and the great majority to be dismissed from Margate, the Downs and Dover. It was Hawkins's task as

Treasurer of the Navy, but Howard stood by till it was done. He was called to court to tell his story, but got away almost at once to his men, whose sufferings haunted him. Howard was a noble man, a pioneer in some of the qualities which England now looks for in a great commander.

The paying-off was a slow business, although Burghley seemed to think it could be done in a moment. He was at his wits' end to find the money, and every day's delay increased the bill. At the end of August Hawkins wrote from Dover that the fleet was still divided and the weather prevented movement, while at Margate it was so bad that communication by boat was almost severed. It was difficult to visit the ships and impossible to get large numbers of men ashore. Howard wrote by the same post that Hawkins was doing as much as possible and that he himself was standing by: 'howsoever it fall out, I must see them paid and will.' This letter was crossed by another from Burghley which has not been preserved, but which evidently contained reproaches for wasting money by keeping men in pay. Its quality can be inferred from Hawkins's answer:

My honourable good lord,
  I am sorry I do live so long to receive so sharp a letter from your lordship, considering how carefully I take care to do all for the best and ease charge. The ships that be in Her Majesty's pay, such as I have to do for, your lordship hath many particulars of them and their numbers; notwithstanding, I do send your lordship all these again. I had but one day to travail in, and then I discharged many after the rate that I thought my money would reach; but after that day I could hardly row from ship to ship, the weather hath been continually so frightful. . . . Some are discharged with fair words;[1] some are so miserable and needy that they are holpen with tickets to the victuallers for some victual to help them home; and some with a portion of money such as my Lord Admiral will appoint to relieve their sick men and to relieve some of the needy sort, to avoid exclamation.[2] The sick men are paid and discharged that are in Her Majesty's pays; the

---

[1] i.e. without money.
[2] These sentences refer to the crews of the hired merchantmen, who should have been paid by their owners.

soldiers also, for the most part, we discharge here; the retinues, some have leave to go to London, and are to be paid there; and thus there is left but convenient companies of mariners and gunners to bring home the ships to Chatham. . . . It shall hereafter be none offence to your lordship that I do so much alone; for with God's favour I will and must leave all.[1] I pray God I may end this account to Her Majesty's and your lordship's liking, and avoid my own undoing; and I trust God will so provide for me as I shall never meddle with such intricate matters more, for they be importable for any man to please and overcome it. If I had any enemy, I should wish him no more harm than the course of my troublesome and painful life; but hereunto and to God's good providence we are born.

Rejoicings were still going on in London, bell-ringing, Te Deums, and bonfires, while the sailors were dying of dysentery, the little Kentish towns were so crammed with the sick that there were not roofs to cover them, the Queen's finances were wellnigh bankrupt, and old friends like Burghley and Hawkins were tormented into hard thoughts of one another. 'I know I shall never please his lordship two months together,' wrote Hawkins to Walsingham, 'for which I am very sorry. . . . My pain and misery in this service is infinite. . . . God, I trust, will deliver me of it ere it be long, for there is no other hell.'

Perhaps as the tension eased he reflected that such things are not uncommon after a famous victory.

[1] i.e. resign.

VI

AFTER THE ARMADA

Sir John Hawkins sought and was granted a year's leave from duties as Navy Treasurer, to date from January 1st, 1589. This was to enable him to reduce to order the muddle in the accounts left by the Armada campaign. When we think of the suddenly enlarged scale of operations, the extension of business from Chatham to Plymouth, Portsmouth, Dover and other ports, the recruitment of numbers of untrained clerks and officials, local and temporary, and unknown to the Chatham staff, the vast number of payments, receipts and issues of material, and all this complicated by the deaths of many of the men concerned, we can understand that to straighten things was a terrifying task. Nevertheless it had to be done, and was done, as the Exchequer documents entitled 'Declared Accounts' bear witness. In requesting a year's leave Hawkins was not asking too much. Although it was granted, he did not in fact enjoy it, for administrative work forced itself upon him from which he could not escape. He proposed as his substitute for the year his brother-in-law Edward Fenton, who was accepted. Hawkins, who wished to resign the office, may have thought that he was easing the entry of a successor, but it did not turn out so. The Queen soon found that no one but Hawkins would do, and as long as he lived he was indispensable.

In 1589 Sir William Winter and William Holstocke both died. It would have been an opportunity, if the government had believed the tales against Hawkins, to introduce two new men to keep an eye on him. What it did do was to allot to Hawkins the post of Comptroller in addition to the Treasurership, to promote William Borough to be Surveyor, and to appoint a younger Benjamin Gonson,[1] Hawkins's brother-in-law, to be Clerk of the

[1] Son of old Benjamin Gonson, the Treasurer. The post of Master of the Ordnance (naval) was not continued.

Ships. Thus the new Navy Board consisted of Hawkins, holding two offices, his relative Gonson, and his devoted adherent Borough. Nothing could more forcibly show what the Queen and Burghley really thought. Indeed it was what all now thought. After the Armada there are no more vilifications, not even anonymous ones. The integrity of John Hawkins was unassailable, and enemy propaganda turned to more promising themes.

In the same year died William Hawkins the second at the age of seventy. His had been a full career, active to the end, the life of one of those numerous able men of high secondary standing who made the new England and laid the foundations of its future. His brother John placed a monument to his memory in the church of St. Nicholas at Deptford. It described him as a practiser of true religion, beneficent to the poor, most learned in maritime affairs, a promoter of distant voyages, a just judge in difficult causes, and of singular faith, probity and prudence, twice married and the father of eleven children. *Johannes Havkyns, eques auratus, classis regiae quaestor, frater moestissimus, posuit. Obiit spe certa resurgendi 7 die mensis Octobris anno domini* 1589. The eulogy is supported by all that is known of him and not denied by any transaction of which record now remains.

Two years later came another loss, when Katherine Hawkins died in July, 1591. She and John had been married for thirty-two years, and she had been, we may imagine, the haven of peace amid all the storms, doubts and malignancies that had assailed him. Not long before he had written: 'Touching mine own worldly contentation, in my wife, my friends, or any other worldly matter, I am as well pleased and contented as I desire.' Her son Richard spoke of her as 'a religious and most virtuous lady'. John Hawkins was not a man who could live without a home. He took a second wife, Margaret Vaughan, daughter of a Herefordshire gentleman. They had no children, and she outlived him by twenty-four years. That is all that is known of her, save that she behaved meanly to her stepson Richard by withholding the money (his money) which would have ransomed him from Spanish captivity after her husband's death.

In 1590 Drake and Hawkins took the lead in founding the Chest at Chatham, a fund for the relief of sick and aged mariners. Sixpence a month, or five per cent, was deducted from the wages of seamen in the Queen's ships, and in default of banking facilities the money was lodged in coin in a large chest provided for the purpose. Under the decent administration of its founders the institution did good work, but in the periods of corruption that followed there were grave frauds upon the seamen. Not only did needy governments raid the chest, but persons with no sea service were allowed to draw pensions from the fund. That was not a Tudor development; it belonged to the following two centuries. In 1592 Hawkins alone founded an almshouse at Chatham for aged mariners and shipwrights. It was called Sir John Hawkins's Hospital, and the Archbishop of Canterbury was the head of its governing body. This foundation had a better history than that of the Chest and survives to this day.

Drake had been denied the command in 1588, but he had it in 1589, when the counterstroke to the Armada was planned and led by him, without the participation of the Navy Board. The plan was to make use of Don Antonio, and to restore him to his throne by landing an English army to take Lisbon. The method was that of the joint-stock syndicate, to which the Queen contributed, while the greater part of the expense was borne by other members. Her finances would not allow her to continue the war in 1589, or so she believed, with the full strength of the Navy; and this explains the absence of the Lord Admiral. Six of the Queen's ships took part, with a hundred other vessels carrying about 20,000 men, most of them soldiers. Drake was hampered by unpractical instructions from the Queen which prevented the landing near Lisbon from being the surprise it ought to have been, and the result was failure. Joint-stock fleets had done brilliant work in Drake's hands, but a joint-stock army to hold Lisbon had little chance of success; for the method implied seeking a financial profit, which could have been obtained only by plundering its Portuguese allies. In fact there was poor co-ordination between army and fleet, and Lisbon was not taken. Many thousands of the men died, and all the money was lost, and the wrecks of the

THE CHATHAM PORTRAIT
Now in the National Maritime Museum, Greenwich
For discussion of authenticity, see Note on Portraits, pp. vii-viii

expedition straggled home little more than two months after it had started. If Philip could not invade England, England could not invade him.

Hawkins firmly believed that there was no need to invade him. Hawkins was no enemy of Drake, and he and his brother had helped to collect supplies for the large and disorderly force, probably more than twice the permanent population of Plymouth, gathered there in the spring of 1589. But the whole idea was contrary to his own, which distrusted military expeditions to the continent of Europe. In July, soon after Drake had returned, Hawkins placed before Burghley the plan for the conduct of the war about which he had written to Walsingham in the previous year. In the covering letter he explained that he had drawn it up while lying at Queenborough with the Lord Admiral in December, 1587. The original exists among the state papers, endorsed 'A discourse for obtaining a good peace, December, 1587'.

The explanation of the plan opens with a clear condemnation of military adventures: 'In the continuance of this war, I wish it to be ordered in this sort, that first we have as little to do in foreign countries as may be (but of mere necessity), for that breedeth great charge and no profit at all.' This, it must be emphasized, was dated before the Armada and was not a reflection on Drake written after the event. The alternative, to which allusion has already been made, was the continuous patrolling of the seas between Spain and the Azores by successive squadrons of the Queen's ships, each to consist of six fighting galleons and six pinnaces victualled for four months. Each squadron would need 1,800 men, and the monthly cost for wages and victuals would be £2,730; 'and it will be a very bad and unlucky month that they will not bring in treble that charge, for they can see nothing but it will hardly escape them.' The charge, continues Hawkins, may be met by private investment, the Queen paying only the cost of equipping the ships and taking one-third of the prize-money, the other two-thirds going to the account of the victuals and the wages. Spain will not be able to drive such squadrons from the seas, for she will not be able to turn out a force with the necessary sea-endurance. Hawkins was here counting on the superior administration of the English Navy, giving a sea-endurance double that of the mixed expeditions of regulars and merchantmen, and of the Armada itself. It seems that his experience of the Armada's powers did not move him to revise the estimate of 1587. The effect, he concludes, will be that the East Indian carracks and the West Indian plate-fleets will not reach port, 'which [fleets] if we might once strike, our peace were made with honour, safety and profit.' He appended schedules showing that sufficient force was available. The cruising squadrons would absorb twelve ships and twelve pinnaces. There would be left twelve ships and six pinnaces for the defence of the Channel; while most of the time one of the cruising squadrons would also be at home for refitting.

For his own part, Hawkins offered to take the command at the outset and inaugurate the oceanic blockade, 'by which example I doubt not but other more than myself in ability and knowledge will, for the like good, endeavour to continue this good purpose.' His years, he said, were beginning to tell upon him, and he was no longer inspired by feelings of revenge for the injury the Spaniards had done him. Although not rich, he was out of debt, without children depending on him, and content with what he had. Yet, 'forasmuch as I shall never be able to end my days in a more godly cause for the Church of God, a more dutiful service to Her Majesty, or a more profitable service for our country, I . . . offer myself and my ability to execute it.'

John Hawkins was ageing, but ripening like the fruit of a good tree. With the vindication of his great work for the Navy the bitterness departed from his Puritanism. His life was to be 'painful' to the end, but he began to meet misfortune and endure folly with a milder temper than in the bad time of the Bargains. The present letter shows that he was no longer estranged from Burghley, to whom he writes in a tone implying sure friendship and almost affection.

His ideas on the conduct of the war need comment. It was the first of the prolonged modern wars against a continental military power. England was a strong sea power. There were two ways of using her command of the sea, to land armies on the continent and challenge the enemy on his own ground, and to blockade his ocean approaches and cut off the wealth which maintained his armies. With variations of emphasis, proportion and detail, this choice has existed in all modern wars. It does not follow that the right answer would always have been the same, for the critical factors have varied in importance. Sometimes the purely naval answer to the problem has been the right one, sometimes the military, and sometimes the first merging into the second as the war proceeds. For Hawkins there were three considerations yielding the conclusion that an oceanic blockade without military expeditions was the best means of winning the war: first, his certainty that Philip's armies and hold upon the continent depended absolutely on the receipt of the western treasure; second, his realization of the financial poverty of the English government, making it unable to support decisive military forces, while naval warfare was much cheaper and might to some extent pay its own cost; third, that for military operations an army is needed, and England had none. The last point was emphasized by the events of 1589, the disorderly rabble embarking at Plymouth, destroying itself by its own indiscipline on the enemy's coast, its remnants returning sick and inglorious after two months' service.

Hawkins was therefore in favour of a purely naval effort, the continuous interruption of the Spanish and Portuguese trade routes with America and the East Indies. Sir Julian Corbett described this as commerce destruction without gaining command of the sea, which shows misunderstanding of what Hawkins proposed, and said further that it was attempted and failed, which is a complete misinterpretation of what took place. Hawkins's plan, of which continuous pressure was the essence, never was attempted, not even for a single year. What failed was the succession of isolated cruises with wide intervening gaps, upon which Hawkins tried vainly to obtain an improvement.

Events in the Atlantic in 1589 illustrated Hawkins's argument. The Earl of Cumberland sailed to the Azores with one ship of the Queen's and several of his own. The treasure fleet from New Spain arrived from the west while he was there, eluded him, and slipped into the fortified harbour of Angra. There it simply waited until hunger drove him away, which it did after he had been three months about the islands. The treasure was then conveyed to Spain. If Hawkins's continuous blockade had been in operation, this treasure might have been sunk by the Spaniards themselves, but none of it would have got through to its destination. In the autumn Sir Martin Frobisher was at sea with a naval squadron. He was instructed, not to take over the Azores blockade from Cumberland, but to cruise on the coast of Spain. He took four ships of the *flota* as it continued its voyage after Cumberland's withdrawal, and, although two were wrecked, the other two more than paid for his voyage. Substantially, however, the year's Mexican treasure and rich trade got through. Philip, who had been unable to turn out a fleet to escort it, received money enough to begin a programme of naval revival which was to make good the Armada losses and more.

The *galeones* from the Spanish Main with the usually larger treasure output of Peru had not been in question in the above proceedings. Their voyage had been delayed, but they were expected to come home in the spring of 1590. Hawkins got leave to prepare to meet them in good time and so to inaugurate his ocean blockade with the chance of a weighty blow. In December and January, 1589–90, he was fitting out six of the Queen's galleons at Chatham. In February the Queen became worried by reports of Spanish ships collecting at Corunna and of an intention of Philip to occupy Brittany and make it a base for the invasion of England. Behind Hawkins's squadron she had ample force to deal with such a threat, as his plan had expressly allowed; but she lost sense of proportion and decided that he must stay in port. A note of Privy Council business dated February 23 gives the question: 'Whether it be convenient that Sir John Hawkins shall proceed in his voyage?' and the answer: 'Thought unmeet for him to go.' Next month the *galeones* came home to Spain with five million ducats, a sum which would have much more than paid for the whole of the Queen's Navy for the whole of the Queen's reign. Well might Hawkins write of 'the overthrow of this journey which I had with great care and cost brought to pass' as placing him 'out of hope that ever I shall perform any royal thing'.

The opportunity would not remain for ever. King Philip was slowly beginning to create an ocean navy such as the Armada had not been. He was also reforming the transport of his treasure. The great fleets of 1589-90 were the last that carried the bulk of it. Thenceforward they brought rich merchandise in plenty, but the bullion was mainly shipped in fast, armed vessels of 200 tons which sailed independently. They were fast enough to run and strong enough to fight according to the quality of their pursuers, and added greatly to the difficulties of treasure-hunters. Spanish records name them *gallizabras*. The English described them as the King's treasure-frigates.

The threat to Brittany caused the government to fit out six galleons under Frobisher in addition to the six under Hawkins, but the two squadrons were contemporaneous and not successive, as Hawkins would have desired. At the end of May the concern had subsided, and both commanders were allowed to sail, Frobisher for the Azores, and Hawkins for the Spanish coast. Frobisher was victualled for the stipulated four months, but Hawkins, with his 'great care and cost', had provided for six months on a more liberal daily scale than the Queen allowed. He was seeking to demonstrate that a new advance in sea-endurance was possible. Just before Frobisher reached the islands an early consignment of 1590 treasure in the new *gallizabras* had passed through and reached Spain, another proof of the need for continuity. When the King heard of the mission of the English fleets he countermanded all further dispatch of treasure for the year, which showed the immediate effectiveness of the blockade. Meanwhile Hawkins had the duty of watching the expedition gathering in Corunna, which precluded him from watching Lisbon for home-coming trade. He did, however, capture some prizes, as did Frobisher at the Azores. Together they made a useful contribution towards their own expenses and threw the Spanish maritime world into consternation; for at last it appeared that English sea-power was going to take the action that Spain dreaded as fatal.

Hawkins sighted some of the Spanish ships making for Brittany, but did not cut them off. Early in October they reached their destination, where they landed less than 3,000 men. These troops did not find themselves in an entirely friendly country. The Catholic League were their allies, but Henry of Navarre, the Huguenot leader, had a considerable hold on Brest and its district. The Spaniards had so much to do in maintaining themselves that they were not an immediate danger to England. Knowing that Frobisher's stores would be exhausted in September, Hawkins sailed to the Azores to replace him. There was little chance that anyone would come to replace Hawkins, and another long interval was to be expected in the blockade. In fact one vessel did come from England, a pinnace at the end of October to order Hawkins home on account of new fears about Brittany. Before this, Philip had been able to get a squadron to sea, twenty ships of all sorts under Alonzo de Bazan. The force was intended to tackle Hawkins at the islands, but was driven back by a gale before reaching him. When Hawkins returned to England he had been at sea for a full five months without suffering excessive casualties. His son Richard, who was with him, says that there were sick in the other ships, but not in his own; and it is fairly evident that there was no great mortality. This was an advance on what Hawkins had claimed that the Navy could do, five months instead of four. It was an example of what he called doing things 'by good order', that is, by methodical preparation and careful administration, in contrast with the scrambling, ill supplied expeditions that had reduced their ships to floating pesthouses in six or eight weeks.

Although Spain had suffered some immediate loss, and a disruption of commerce that was to cost her dear next year, and the English had taken some valuable prizes, John Hawkins was disappointed. In comparison with the 'royal thing' that he had looked for at the opening of the year, the campaign had been a failure. He wrote to Burghley in his later tolerant Puritan style, quoting scripture and ending: 'but seeing this hath been the good pleasure of God, I do content myself and hold all to come for the best.' Upon this the Queen, who had no use for Puritans, mild or bitter, made comment: 'God's death! This fool went out a soldier and is come home a divine.' It was her only recorded tantrum against Hawkins, less than the common ration of those who served her. There is no doubt that she liked and respected him.

After this there was no pretence of following Hawkins's plan. The ocean routes were left open till the following May, 1591, when Lord Thomas Howard led the Queen's squadron to the Azores. He hung on, awaiting the *flota* and the *galeones*, two seasons' shipping sailing in one great fleet, until at the end of August he was at the limit of his resources. To the rescue of the great prize Philip was able to send out Bazan with fifty-five sail, a significant increase on previous strength. Howard, taken at his weakest, lost Grenville and the *Revenge* and had to withdraw. But a great gale smote the western shipping as it made the Azores a few days later, and less than half the ships and goods survived to reach Spain. The ships were many of them unsound from long exposure to the worm of tropical waters; and this was due to the delay imposed by Hawkins and Frobisher in the previous year. In justice to Hawkins it should be noted that if his plan had been punctually followed, Howard's relief would have arrived before the battle, and Bazan would have faced an English squadron fighting-fit instead of one with its victuals finished and most of its men sick. Moreover, the treasure, which came through in two consignments before and after Howard's cruise, would also have been stopped. No relief, early or late, was sent to Howard, and even the summer blockade thenceforward dwindled to little but privateering. In 1592 the Queen sent only two ships into the Atlantic, in 1593 two, and in 1594 none. The treasure regularly came through, as did the bulk of general trade, although the privateers took heavy toll. Philip increased his naval forces and just kept his head above the rising tide of insolvency. A relatively small effort, well within England's power, would have sub-merged him. It is not generally recognized that the finest navy then existing was virtually laid-up instead of carrying on the war during these crucial years, while the English government spent its money on military efforts in France and the Netherlands.

Drake also was laid-up, and Hawkins as a leader of fleets, although he continued to do good work at the Navy office. The Queen was willing to strengthen the Navy and unwilling to send it to sea, both for the same reason, that she was dominated by the fear of invasion. She wanted her ships under her hand in Chatham yard, and would not let them out of her sight in case a Spanish army should slip past them and land in England. One speculates on the use her father would have made of the ocean fleet and the enemy treasure trade. After the Armada the fighting fleet was increased by the construction of four new galleons of the standard design, of which the *Revenge* had been the prototype. These were launched in 1590 and the following years, and more were added as the war lengthened. In the 1590's the Elizabethan galleon reached the peak of its development, fast, weatherly, heavily armed, and able to keep the sea for periods that had been impossible to its predecessors. The administration under Hawkins worked ever more efficiently and handed on a tradition whose force continued for some years after his death. The deaths on service, even in distant expeditions, seem to have been fewer as time went on, and in the whole course of the war there was no large ship of the Queen's lost by leakage or any defect of hull or gear. The only ship lost from any cause was the *Revenge*, in the hopeless odds of the fight at Flores.

The fleet was in a very true sense Hawkins's fleet. He worked for it as though every ship had been his own property and engaged in bringing home for his personal fortune the treasures of the West and the spices of the East. He was jealous of its good name and smarted under unjust criticism of its value. Its expenses weighed as heavily upon him as if they came from his pocket: 'I do grieve at the charge as much as it were to proceed from myself,' he had written as the costs mounted in the Armada year. His personal and even family proprietorship is charmingly illustrated by a passage, a gem in a dunghill, in the attack made upon him in 1587, wherein the author complains that even the flags and pendants are made by Mrs. Hawkins and her maids. They would have kept her busy, twenty-five great ships and their pinnaces, with the lavish spread of bunting those times required. It is a snapshot of Katherine Hawkins that we are glad to have. Take this again, from a letter to Burghley in 1592: 'When the *Swiftsure* was launched at Deptford, the ship sitting very hard, we were

forced to use great violence upon the tackles, whereof one gave
way and brake, so as one end of a cable ran by my leg and hurt me
in vi places.' The ruler of the Queen's Navy is here not an office
dignitary after the later pattern, but the working head, who
knows every job in the yard, and takes charge when there is
something difficult to be done. In spite of the cuts and bruises and
the *Swiftsure's* reluctance, he launched her that day and went
home content.

But he felt at sixty that he had earned a rest. He made two more
attempts to resign, the first in July, 1592: 'I do most humbly pray
your good lordship to be a mean to Her Majesty that some dis-
creet and able man may be thought upon to supply my place . . .
and will nevertheless ever during my life attend Her Majesty's
service any other way that I shall be appointed, wherein my
experience and skill will serve; for with good favour of Her
Majesty's and your lordship's I shall ever acknowledge myself
more bounden than if I had received in gift great treasure.' This by
its date and its reference to 'service any other way' is probably
connected with a project that Richard Hawkins tells us was then
afoot, for an expedition to capture Nombre de Dios and Panama.[1]
The conquest had been an ambition with the English leaders for
twenty years and, if it could have been maintained, would have
been a mortal blow at the Spanish treasure trade. Presumably
Drake or John Hawkins or both would have led the attempt. But
the business 'waxed cold' and was dropped, most likely by reason
of the Queen's agony of defensiveness, and both leaders remained
on the shelf. Hawkins's last request for release was made in
February, 1594, in a letter which shows him to be depressed and
out of health and begs 'your lordship to favour me to be delivered
from this continual thralldom, which I mind to procure by all the
means I can'. It was of no use. They would not let him go.

While John Hawkins was bound, Richard was free, and his
proceedings form a remarkable passage in the Elizabethan record.
At the close of the Armada year Richard Hawkins laid down a fine
galleon of about 350 tons for a private venture of his own. He
intended to pass the Straits of Magellan, pay expenses by plun-

[1] *Observations*, p. 10.

dering the treasure coast of Peru, refit in California, and then sail across the Pacific to achieve his main purpose, a thorough reconnaissance of eastern Asia with a view to establishing English trade and empire. When the new ship was launched, 'pleasing to the eye, profitable for stowage, good of sail, and well conditioned' (a characteristic Hawkins portmanteau carrying a chapter of meaning), Richard asked his mother to christen her. Katherine Hawkins named the ship the *Repentance*, saying that for those who would reach the port of Heaven repentance was the best ship to sail in. But the Queen, when she saw the ship, disliked the name and commanded that she should be known as the *Dainty*. For various reasons Richard Hawkins had to postpone his South Sea voyage. He sailed with his father in the Atlantic cruise of 1590, and expected to go with him in the projected Panama expedition of 1592, which came to nothing. The *Dainty*, under another captain, helped to capture the great carrack *Madre de Dios* in 1592, an event which stimulated Asiatic projects.

After the collapse of the Panama design Richard Hawkins began to prepare in earnest for the South Sea. In April, 1593, he sailed the *Dainty* from the Thames to Plymouth, where he provided also a pinnace and a storeship, the latter to carry additional victuals and to be abandoned when the two fighting ships had room for the goods. At the end of May he was almost ready, when a gale drove the pinnace on the rocks beneath the Hoe and cost the *Dainty* her mainmast, cut away to avert a similar disaster. After a fortnight spent in repairing the damage he set sail on June 12, 1593:

I set sail . . . about three of the clock in the afternoon, and made a board or two off and in, waiting the return of my boat, which I had sent ashore for dispatch of some business; which being come aboard and all put in order, I luffed near the shore to give my farewell to all the inhabitants of the town, whereof the most part were gathered together upon the Hoe to show their grateful correspondency to the love and zeal which I, my father, and predecessors have ever borne to that place, as to our natural and mother town. And first with my noise of trumpets, after with my waits, and then with my other music, and lastly with the artillery of my ships, I made the best signification I could of a kind farewell.

This they answered with the waits of the town and ordnance on the shore, and with shouting of voices; which with the fair evening and silence of the night were heard a great distance off.

It was to be ten years before Richard Hawkins came back to Plymouth. He had taken leave of his father in London, and never saw him again.

The expedition sailed south through the Atlantic, touching at none of the island groups. At the Cape Verdes, at least, Hawkins knew by experience that there were deadly fevers to be picked up. He avoided this, but suffered heavy loss by an outbreak of scurvy which carried off many men in spite of his precautions. After long delay in the equatorial calms he got through and refreshed his crews on the southern coast of Brazil. He cleared the storeship and destroyed her, and sailed for the Straits. At sea he was deserted by the pinnace, whose master parted company without cause and returned to England. Hawkins confesses that he was a fool to trust this man, who had played the same trick on another commander. The loss of the pinnace left the *Dainty* without the assistance of a light draught vessel, which was necessary for many purposes.

As Hawkins drew southwards near the latitude of the Straits at the beginning of 1594, he sighted a strange coast of which he believed himself to be the discoverer. It appeared to him to be continental, and he considered that it was the Atlantic part of Terra Australis Incognita, which was then thought to encircle the world. He called it Hawkins Maidenland, and we can hardly be sorry that the name did not become established, for it is a rather obvious imitation of Ralegh's Virginia. It was in fact the coast of the Falkland Islands, and he had been forestalled by John Davis, who had sighted it eighteen months before. Davis returned to an Irish port on the day before Richard Hawkins quitted Plymouth, so there had been no communication. The lack of a pinnace prevented Hawkins from making a proper examination, for he could not risk his large ship close to an uncharted coast. A fair wind for the Straits caused him to turn away.

Richard Hawkins was the third English commander to make the successful passage of the Straits of Magellan, the first and

second having been Drake and Thomas Cavendish. Others had
failed, as Cavendish himself had done on a second voyage. It was
on that occasion that Davis, who commanded one of his ships,
sighted the Falklands. The passage needed a good ship, crew and
commander, and was then very much a matter of luck. For the
prevalent winds were from the west, the channel was not wide
enough for ships to turn to windward, and anchorages were so
few that it was a common experience for an adverse wind to
cause much loss of distance painfully won. The bottom was nearly
everywhere so foul with rocks that anchoring meant the loss of
the anchor by chafing of the hempen cable. The lucky and competent commander was he who got one of the infrequent easterly
winds and lost no time in using it. Magellan, the discoverer of
the Strait, took thirty-seven days to pass its three hundred miles.
Drake did it in sixteen days, and Cavendish in fifty-one. Richard
Hawkins got through in forty-six days. He nearly lost the *Dainty* by
striking an unknown rock. Great exertion saved the ship, but her
stem and bottom were damaged, with detriment to her speed, a fact
of the utmost importance when he had to fight in the South Sea.

Drake, the pioneer in the plunder of Peru, had found the
Spaniards unarmed by land and by sea. Cavendish, who came next,
found them armed and alert in the seaports and passing on
warning of his approach by a system of couriers. Richard Hawkins
was not long in discovering that they had good fighting ships,
bigger and more heavily armed than the *Dainty*, ready to turn
out against a would-be raider of the treasure coast. No doubt he
had some information of the progress in the Spanish armaments,
and he had not purposed to close with the coast and show himself
until he should be north of Callao, the chief seaport of Peru. But
his men were insubordinate and clamorous for treasure. He
yielded, and attacked the shipping in Valparaiso, far to the southward of his intended point of contact. He gained some quantity
of gold and became thenceforward the quarry in a hunt of
increasing seriousness. The news sped northwards, and the
Viceroy of Peru sent out Don Beltran de Castro with six ships and
about two thousand men against the *Dainty* and her seventy-five.

At the first encounter Hawkins made a disconcerting discovery and had all the day's luck. He found that the South Sea ships, built for a coast on which really heavy weather was unknown, had a fineness of lines, lightness of spars, and spread of canvas that not only enabled them to sail faster than the damaged *Dainty*, but also to get to windward of her, although they were six miles to leeward when first sighted. The luck consisted in the fact that the wind freshened to an unusual degree as the Spaniards came up with him, and one after another they split sails, lost masts or broke spars. Night fell just in time, and in the darkness he altered course and sailed clear. Don Beltran went back to Callao to refit, and was soon at sea again with a more efficient force, thirteen hundred men in two good ships. Hawkins says that one of them was equal to his father's *Victory* in the Armada campaign, while the other was equal to the *Dainty* herself. This was to speak of size and armament. The odds in men were more than fifteen to one. There was also a large fighting galleon farther north at Panama, whose services were not called for.

Richard Hawkins had been impressed by the weatherliness of the Spanish ships and the large numbers of men that they carried. The first of these factors meant that they could force him to close action if they chose, and the second that they would have an enormous advantage in doing so. It was his purpose therefore to rest content with the gold he had captured, water his ship, and sail northwards out of danger as soon as possible. It must be remembered that China, not Peru, was the main objective of his voyage. But he lacked his father's mastership of men. His crew were out of hand, full of unreasonable contempt for the Spaniards, and greedy for more treasure. They forced him to waste time in chasing ships that he could not catch, and these vessels reported his movements to the government on shore. The result was that just as the *Dainty* was weighing anchor in the Bay of Atacames, north of the equator, to leave for good the coast of Peru, Don Beltran de Castro came in sight for the second time, determined that on this occasion there should be no mistake about fighting to a finish. The result, short of extraordinary luck, was inevitable, and this time the English had no luck. The *Dainty* was battered by superior fire at close range and her small crew depleted by heavy casualties. With the slow and feeble artillery of the time the action took three days, at the end of which the ship was sinking and fewer than twenty of her seventy-five men remained unhurt. Hawkins was dangerously wounded and carried below. Surrender was talked of, and his flaming spirit prevented it. But in the end it had to be, for the ship, with nineteen killed and forty wounded, was filling with water. Don Beltran promised that all the survivors should be sent home to England, and on those terms Hawkins surrendered on June 22, 1594.

Beltran de Castro was a man of honour who did his utmost to secure that his word should be fulfilled. The Viceroy of Peru, his superior, had other views. After some delay he sent the men to Spain, and after some further delay, about three years in all, they were released. But for Richard Hawkins there was no release. He knew too much and fought too hard. He was detained for some time in Peru, where he was admired and beloved for his valour and good temper. Southey, who had access to Spanish documents, gathered that Hawkins became a permanent convert to Catholicism. It is highly probable that he conformed while in Peru, with the Inquisition as the alternative, but it was not from conviction; for he was no sooner home than he was pursuing popish recusants with vigour.[1] After three years in Peru he was transferred to Spain. He attempted escape and was strictly imprisoned at Madrid. Highly placed Spaniards protested at the breach of faith by which he was detained. Their government at length gave way, and it became a matter of ransom, a ransom of £3,000. Here his stepmother played a sinister part, for she had in her hands money of his which would have covered the liability, and she would not let go. Richard Hawkins got a letter through to Sir Robert Cecil, begging his intervention. It was evidently successful, for the money was paid over and Hawkins set free at the close of 1602. He was home before Christmas and at once took up the employments usual to his family, of which he was now the head. Before he sailed on this voyage he had married Judith Heale of Plymouth.

The Queen died in March, 1603, and the war was ending. The Hawkins fortunes had long been linked with the Cecil and

[1] Worth's *Plymouth Calendar*, p. 143.

Howard interests, and they were ascendant with the new King. In the summer of 1603 James I knighted Richard Hawkins and made him Vice-Admiral of Devon. In 1603-4 Sir Richard was both Mayor of Plymouth and one of its members of Parliament, that happy Parliament which escaped being blown up by Guy Fawkes. But the great days were over. He had hopes and projects, which came to nothing. His last employment was as second-in-command of a mismanaged Jacobean expedition to attack the Barbary pirates. After twenty years of James I the Navy had forgotten how to do such things, and nothing was accomplished. The men were unpaid and badly treated on their return, in 1622, and Sir Richard Hawkins died suddenly of vexation, as a contemporary declared. His *Observations*, written in 1602-3, were being printed at the time of his death, and the book bears date 1622. His widow Judith Hawkins, outlived him by seven years.[1]

[1] The career of Richard Hawkins is treated at greater length in the Introduction to the present author's edition of *The Observations of Sir Richard Hawkins*, Argonaut Press, 1933.

VII

THE LAST VOYAGE OF SIR JOHN HAWKINS

From 1590 the Spanish troops in Brittany had played a considerable part in immobilizing the English Navy during the critical years in which a new Spanish navy was being built. The Spaniards at first occupied only a position of minor utility on the Blavet river in southern Brittany. Its possible extension was a threat always active in Elizabeth's mind and one of the factors which moved her to send expensive military expeditions to support Henry of Navarre. In 1594 the Blavet Spaniards made a move northwards against Brest, held by King Henry. They occupied the peninsula which forms the southern side of Brest water and built a fort at Crozon to secure their hold. With the prospect of gaining possession of the huge anchorage, fit for the assembly of any invasion fleet, they became dangerous, and Elizabeth's military advisers were quick to warn her of the fact. The Queen sent Sir Martin Frobisher and Sir John Norreys with ships and troops to remove the menace. In November the English stormed Crozon, with the loss of Frobisher, and the Spaniards were thenceforward restricted to their Blavet position.

These events had their effect on the Queen's policy, and for a while she appreciated the Spaniards at Blavet at their true value, and allowed preparations for a West Indian expedition to go forward.

As at first conceived, the plan was that which had been dropped in 1592–3, to land an English force at Nombre de Dios, march across the Isthmus, and capture Panama. Success in such an undertaking appears so improbable, and all later experience of English troops fighting in fever-stricken tropical countries has been so adverse (omitting the twentieth century with its very different medical resources), that commentators have regarded the project as visionary, and have wondered how Drake and Hawkins could have entertained it. Yet we now know that John Oxenham in

1576–7 was in sight of making it a success and was defeated only by exceptional efforts on the part of his opponents. Since his time the Cimaroons, upon whom he relied, had been subdued by the Spaniards; they themselves had become more numerous, so that Panama was better defended; and a fighting force of Spanish ships had been built for service on the Pacific coast. On the other hand Drake and Hawkins were not going to the attack with fifty men, as Oxenham did; they were to take a force that would seem adequate. Success promised not only plunder but the winning of the war. If Panama could be taken and held, the Peruvian treasure-stream would cease to flow to Spain, and Philip would have to come to terms. It was for this great stake that the two English leaders were preparing to play.

Why there were two of them has never been explained. The Queen was ordinarily a shrewd judge of character and human qualities, and she ought to have known that Drake and Hawkins with equal authority could not pull together. Their natures and approach to their work were different to the bottom. Hawkins believed in doing things 'by good order', by which he meant foresight, the accurate working out of requirements and careful provision for them, thorough planning of the campaign and sticking to the plan when made, refusal to be diverted by new issues. Drake declined to think ahead, he would act according to circumstances and make new decisions and rapid changes in his plans, which was the best of reasons why his opponents never knew what he would do; and he was careless of administration, with consequences such as faulty victualling and needless misunderstandings with others. Drake was the supreme opportunist, who could do nothing wrong when his genius burned bright, but could fail when he was not at his best. His campaigns of 1587 and 1589 were respectively the high and the low levels of his performance. What good end could be expected from yoking these two men together? Why did they not see clearly and refuse to be yoked? To us who know the outcome it is unanswerable. They saw only the opportunity and swallowed its ominous limitation, the one an ageing man grasping the last chance to do 'a royal thing', the other conscious of the years passing fruitless, and eager to repeat the glories of his prime. Neither could draw back when the Queen called on both. On her rests the responsibility.

The first months of '95 saw the fitting-out of the Queen's ships, which was mainly Hawkins's work. In fact, an indenture for this purpose expresses terms only between Hawkins and the Queen, without mention of Drake. The Queen paid the expenses of fitting out six of her ships, for which she was to receive one-third of any booty taken. Hawkins (his name standing for that of Drake as well, and possibly some sub-partners of each) was to victual the squadron for four months and take one-third. The remaining third was to go to the crews, or Hawkins could pay them fixed wages and take it himself. There was most likely another indenture, which has not been preserved, between Hawkins and Drake, for there is no doubt that each had administrative control of half the fleet, each separately engaging his officers and men and providing his victuals and other supplies. There were thus three of the Queen's galleons under Drake and three under Hawkins, and divided between them there were twenty-one privately owned ships of various sizes, some quite small. These presumably came in on the same terms, of 'adventuring on thirds', their owners standing instead of the Queen in the financial arrangements.

By the end of April the Queen's ships had reached Plymouth, and the private ships were joining them there. The exact number of the men is not known, but seems to have been from 2,500 to 3,000, half of whom were soldiers. There was an agreed scale of men to tonnage, and it is clear that Hawkins kept to it. It is also clear that Drake exceeded it. He may not have known even at the date of sailing how many men he had. The same uncertainty had prevailed in the Portugal expedition of 1589. His name attracted many volunteers, and it was not in his administrative nature to turn them away. Hawkins appears to have provided much of his victualling in London, while Drake was still completing his from the Plymouth countryside in July. A correspondent wrote to Robert Cecil on the 16th that the ships were in good order, for which Hawkins deserved the credit, and that Drake was little in Plymouth, being busy about provision in the country. Of this phase of the preparations the remark of Thomas Maynarde, a land captain, has often been quoted, that Hawkins was 'a man old and wary, entering into matters with so laden a foot that the other's [Drake's] meat would be eaten before his spit could come to the fire': which was one view of the contrast between deliberate method and brisk improvisation. Maynarde, who disliked both the admirals, considered that the victualling was meanly done in order to fill their pockets, but as he was a landsman on his first long voyage his judgement may not be more weighty than that of a boy at a boarding-school.

The long delay at Plymouth is unexplained, unless the need to complete victualling accounts for it. Probably it does not, and there was something else of which record is missing. It was unfortunate, for it allowed news of the preparations to be sent to Spain. They were sent quite early, and in June an English spy reported back from Lisbon that a Spanish fleet was to be prepared for the Caribbean. In August another spy in Spain wrote that the King had been assured that he need not fear Drake and Hawkins, for their voyage should be overthrown at the outset. This came very near to being true. There was a cloud over the whole project, bad for loyalty and morale. The two commanders at Plymouth kept up a show of co-operation, but the acid pen of Maynarde wrote that 'whom the one loved, the other smally esteemed'. The procrastination was apparently not due to the Queen. At least she and the Lord Admiral both blamed the commanders for not getting away as the months passed.

Here it should be explained that John Hawkins entered into the project without knowing that his son Richard had come to grief in the previous summer. No news came of that disaster until a year after it had taken place. In May, 1595, Sir John was anticipating his son's return with information from the Far East, and wrote to Robert Cecil about a new commission for Richard, with allusions to a project which would concern the Queen and the West Country. What they had in mind may have been a Plymouth East India Company, to exploit the discoveries of Richard Hawkins. Then, on June 9, came the bad tidings from Lisbon of ships entering there with the report that 'in the South

Seas the *Dainty* is taken, with Captain Hawkins, who had taken great treasure'. The story was true, and John Hawkins had now to regard his own voyage as one to provide the wherewithal to obtain his son's release.

Towards the end of July he and Drake were ready, and then the Blavet Spaniards demonstrated their nuisance value. They sent out 400 soldiers in four galleys, which appeared at sunrise on July 23 at Mousehole in south-western Cornwall. The Spaniards landed half their men and burnt the place, then landed the whole 400 at Newlyn and burnt it, thence going on to serve Penzance in the same fashion. The local people, thin on the ground, were taken by surprise and at first made little stand, but afterwards they began to concentrate from a wider area, and the Spaniards re-embarked. The call for help reached Plymouth, whence Drake and Hawkins sent men by land, and ships to cut off the retreat of the galleys. But a north-west wind carried them away just in time, and they returned to Brittany, having made a successful and valuable raid.[1] On the way back indeed they got into an irrelevant action with a convoy of merchantmen, and one of the galleys was lost, but this made no difference to the serious effects of their Cornish proceedings. The timing of the raid was no accident, and it was clearly intended to interfere with the expedition preparing to sail from Plymouth. It marked a new and surprising stage in the Spanish renascence.

The affair was really significant in the sphere of militia and local defences, but the Queen took it seriously and worried herself into imaginations of an invasion intended that year. She ordered Drake and Hawkins to sail from Plymouth and take station off the Irish coast. Then she allotted a separate squadron to that duty, and ordered them to cruise on the Spanish coast and counter any aggressive movements there, and afterwards to spend not more than one month in cruising for the plate fleet expected from Havana. She appeared not to realize that their armament and equipment were unsuited for these duties or that they had spent their money in preparation for something quite different. It is in this connection that we must read the warning from Spain that the

[1] A. L. Rowse, *Tudor Cornwall*, London, 1941, pp. 404–6.

voyage would be overthrown at the start; for the Queen was so perturbed by the Cornish raid that she may have listened to persons giving her treacherous advice. On August 13 the leaders at Plymouth replied that they could not undertake a blockade with their expedition, which comprised a force of soldiers who would do nothing but consume the victuals. The Queen dictated a furious answer ending with a veto on their sailing anywhere, but did not send it. Burghley was regaining some control and persuaded her to send instead her permission to sail westward on promise to be home within six months, to encounter an invasion supposed, on second thoughts, to be due in 1596.

Six months was not much for the conquest of Panama and settlement of a garrison there in addition to the voyage out and home. If the commanders had agreed to do it in the time they would have risked deceiving the Queen. At that juncture (mid-August) a privateer came into Plymouth with some Spanish prisoners, who were immediately questioned about the movements of the plate fleets. They revealed that the *galeones* from the Spanish Main and Nombre de Dios had sailed in March from Havana and had arrived in Spain with the exception of their flagship. She had been severely damaged in a gale in the Florida Channel and had taken refuge at San Juan de Puerto Rico, where she lay without a mainmast, leaking badly, and unable to continue the voyage. This crippled vessel, the information continued, had treasure worth two million ducats on board. Here was the solution. Here was a task that could be accomplished in six months. Drake and Hawkins wrote to the Queen offering to sail straight to Puerto Rico, cut out the treasure, and sail home. She approved heartily and told them to be off. They sailed out of Plymouth on August 28.

In spite, then, of all previous discussions, the last expedition of Drake and Hawkins sailed with one limited purpose only, the capture of two million ducats in San Juan de Puerto Rico, to be achieved by speed and surprise on the directest course available. The fact is emphasized, because on it depends appreciation of what followed.

The twenty-seven ships sailed out of Plymouth under two

joint commanders with absolutely equal authority. If the two had sailed together in the same ship there might have been a chance for goodwill and forbearance to yield a tolerable outcome. But they sailed in different ships, Hawkins in the *Garland*, Drake in the *Defiance*, both new post-Armada galleons, and days passed without their having speech together; and with their different types of mind producing different trains of thought, they were at at complete misunderstanding when they did meet. The arrangement was that councils were to be held as weather permitted alternately on board the *Garland* and the *Defiance*.

Four days out from Plymouth the first council met on board the *Garland*, chiefly for the purpose of appointing a rendezvous in case of separation. This was usually not done until a fleet was well away from the English coast in case its movements should be revealed by any vessel that might put back. At the meeting Drake told Hawkins that he had 300 men in excess of his proper numbers and that his victuals would not suffice for all of them, and he suggested that Hawkins should take over and feed the surplus. This casual handling of what Hawkins had always regarded as a primary duty, that of seeing that the crews were properly victualled, revealed the incompatibility between them. Hawkins saw that to take over Drake's men would mean that his own would go short. He would not hear of it, 'and this drew them to some choleric speeches,' according to the testimony of Maynarde. Another witness, Captain John Troughton, said 'there passed many unkind speeches, and such as Sir John Hawkins never put off till death.' The wrangle continued as the officers came on deck to return to their ships, Hawkins shaken out of his customary wariness and, says Maynarde again, 'revealing the places whither we were bound in the hearing of the basest mariner, observing therein no warlike or provident advice; nor was it ever amended till the time of their deaths.'

For a week they separately nursed their resentments, and then Drake called a second council on board the *Defiance*. He had always hated this business of councils, preferring to give orders rather than to deliberate, and we may picture him awaiting his visitors in no affable mood. But necessity compelled him to resume the argument. The deficiency of supplies was even worse than he had at first supposed. His meat was indeed eaten before the other's spit had come to the fire. When the council assembled he declared that he would be unable to take his squadron across the Atlantic without an increased supply of victuals. He proposed therefore to attack Madeira or the Canary Islands, preferably Grand Canary, and levy a ransom in foodstuffs, before continuing with the main purpose of the voyage. Hawkins answered that this would waste time which could never be made up, and that it would entail serious fighting which would hazard a depletion of strength when they came to Puerto Rico. Drake had won over Sir Thomas Baskerville, the commander of the soldiers, who airily promised that he would capture Las Palmas in four hours and that within four days they could collect the victuals and depart. Faced with this irresponsible stuff, Hawkins declared that he would sail straight to Puerto Rico, and Drake replied that he would attack the Canaries with such as would follow him. Here the council seems to have broken into two groups, while inter-mediaries sought to patch up an agreement. Hawkins knew that the Canary diversion, with its almost certain sacrifice of surprise at Puerto Rico, meant the probable ruin of the voyage. Yet the split into two commands meant certain ruin. How could senior commanders face the Queen with that to their account, that they had disintegrated her fleet by quarrelling like children? He decided that he must give way, and the formula-finders did their best. Drake 'confessed need', and Hawkins 'was content to assist them'. Next day they all dined together on board the Garland, 'when it was resolved that we should put for the Grand Canary, though, in my [Maynarde's] conscience, whatsoever his tongue said, Sir John's heart was against.'

Meanwhile Spain was taking measures. The English com-manders knew that a substantial fleet was being turned out to pursue them. They did not know when it would be ready, and the possibility that it might at any time be crossing the Atlantic was a factor in their decisions. It did not leave Spain until the late autumn, but they had no means of knowing that it would be so long delayed. In addition to preparing this fleet, Philip ordered out five of his *gallizabras* or treasure carriers, to sail to Puerto Rico and bring away the lading of the crippled galleon. These vessels were ready long in advance of the main fleet. They sailed from Spain shortly after the English had left Plymouth. The English commanders had no information of them, although they could guess that two million ducats in peril would stimulate the King to all possible measures of rescue.

On September 27, after a very slow passage, the English fleet anchored off Las Palmas. Baskerville got his soldiers into the boats, while Drake selected a landing-place. It was an open beach with the surf running high upon it, entrenchments commanding it, and Spanish foot and artillery taking post. Baskerville's four hours vanished as a dream. The attack would be that of the most forlorn hope conceivable. He sought the admirals and asked them 'if they would put their voyage thereon or no', evidently meaning that he expected a repulse and the loss of nearly all engaged. It was a folly to which there was only one answer. All re-embarked and the ships weighed anchor as soon as possible. The fleet coasted round to the western side of Grand Canary, where watering parties landed, but there was no further attempt at capturing the island. Some of those who landed were captured by the inhabitants and interrogated by the governor, who immediately despatched a swift caravel to warn Puerto Rico. The English did not know this, but could legitimately imagine it, for the efficiency of the Spanish despatch service was well known to them. It was a sufficient justification of Hawkins's protest against the Canary diversion. He himself had used the Canaries as his post-office in the old days when he had sent word to the West while he collected slaves in Guinea.

From Grand Canary, without any further attempt and without capturing an ounce of foodstuffs, the expedition sailed across the Atlantic in the trade wind track to the Lesser Antilles. No further representations from Drake about a shortage are recorded. Probably Hawkins let him have some victuals, but whether he did or not it is evident that the visit to the Canaries was as unnecessary as Hawkins said it was. It was also as ruinous, as events shortly made clear. The West Indian rendezvous was Guadeloupe, where most of the fleet arrived on October 28-29. Some strag-glers were a day or two late; and of these a small bark named the *Francis* was captured by the five *gallizabras*, which, starting late, had made a non-stop passage from Spain and had overtaken the English. The captain of the *Francis* possessed written instructions which he failed to destroy, and these revealed that Puerto Rico was the objective, while interrogation of the prisoners established the strength of the expedition. Don Pedro Tello de Guzman, the Spanish commander, turned immediately for Puerto Rico, where his men and his guns formed a substantial reinforcement to the defences.

A small consort of the *Francis* escaped capture and told the news to the English admirals at Guadeloupe. She reported eight or nine *gallizabras*, although in fact there were five. Drake was for an immediate general chase, although the enemy, built for speed, had a good start. He wished to prevent the *gallizabras* from warning Puerto Rico, but would have had to capture every one of them to that end, and his own fleet would have been scattered in the process. Meanwhile the main Spanish fleet might be approaching. Hawkins therefore insisted on a sufficient halt 'to trim his ships, mouni his ordnance, take in water, set by some new pinnaces, and to make things in that readiness that he cared not to meet with the King's whole fleet'. Lord Thomas Howard and Grenville had been caught at a disadvantage by a fleet fresh from Spain in 1591, and Hawkins had taken the lesson to heart. It made no difference at Puerto Rico, which had by this time received its warning from the Canaries.

So to the end had continued the fret between opportunism and order, improvisation and method. For this was the end of the joint command. On October 31 Hawkins became ill, and Troughton says that he was struck down by grief at the failure of the voyage. Two days later he was unable to leave his bed, and never did so again. The nature of the disease is not recorded. That he 'sickened' is all that we know. He had remained active and driven himself hard for many a year in spite of the ill-health of which we have various notices, and now that hope gave place to disappointment, irremediable and final, there was not much of his constitution left to keep him going. A small ill was enough to sicken him to death.

The remainder of the voyage is not his story. It was Drake who led the fleet to attack San Juan de Puerto Rico and was repulsed by a fortress which he found alert and well defended. He made no second attempt, but stood over to the Main, where he took Rio de la Hacha and Santa Marta, but found Cartagena too strong for him. It was ten years since he had seen these places, and they were more heavily armed and better garrisoned than he had expected. Last of all he returned to the Panama plan, the masterstroke postponed during twenty years. He landed Baskerville and the troops at Nombre de Dios and saw them march for Panama. In four days they were back, defeated by a well-posted Spanish force. After that there was nothing effective to be done. Drake died, and Baskerville brought the depleted expedition home.

All that was not in the story of John Hawkins. At three in the afternoon of November 12, 1595, as the fleet was anchoring for the attempt on Puerto Rico, he died in the cabin of the *Garland*. He was lamented by many, says Captain Troughton, his chief attendant during the last days. His thoughts were mainly on his duty and the public service, the service of the Queen to whom from the beginning he had been as devoted as had been old Burghley, his superior officer, now also nearing the end. He charged Troughton with his last message to her, and Troughton wrote it when he came home:

Sir John Hawkins upon his deathbed willed me to use the best means I could to acquaint Your Highness with his loyal service and good meaning towards Your Majesty, even to his last breathing; and forasmuch as, through the perverse and cross dealings of some in that journey, who preferring their own fancy before his skill, would never yield, but rather overrule him, whereby he was so discouraged, and as himself then said his heart even broken, that he saw no other but danger of ruin of the whole voyage, wherein in some sort he had been a persuader of Your Majesty to hazard as well some of your good ships as also a good quantity of treasure, in regard of the good opinion he thought to be held of his sufficiency, judgement and experience in such actions; willing to make Your Majesty the best amends his poor ability could then stretch unto, in a codicil as a piece of his last will and testament did bequeath unto Your Highness two thousand pounds, if Your Majesty will take it; for that, as he said, Your Highness had in your possession a far greater sum of his, which he then did also release; which £2,000, if Your Majesty should accept thereof, his will is, should be deducted out of his lady's portion and out of all such legacies and bequests as he left to any of his servants and friends or kinsfolk whosoever, as by the said codicil appeareth.

What kind of man he was, how he grew from youth to age, and what service he did his country, this book has tried to convey. As a true epitaph it may stand that loyalty was the golden thread of his career, and that he was a worker, a manager, a seaman, and a great Englishman. He was modest too, without itch for self-advertisement, and no monument in his native Plymouth bears his name.

INDEX

Africa, West, *see* Guinea
Alas, Martin de las, 130–1
Allen, Cardinal, 290, 296
Allen, Thomas, 257, 288
Alva, Duke of, 159–60, 162–3, 171, 177, 182, 213
Ango, Jean, 11
Antonio, Don, 213–14, 215, 216–17, 218, 219, 220, 223, 226, 316
Armada campaign, 302–13
Arrest, Anglo-Spanish, 162–3, 193
Austria, Don John of, 209
Azores, 16, 216–17; battle, 1591, 323

Babington plot, 293
Baeshe, Edward, 239, 311
Baker, Matthew, 252, 255, 256–8, 260–1, 268, 273, 275, 276, 283–4, 286
Barlow, Roger, 9
Barrett, Robert, 105, 116, 117, 122, 125, 128, 141, 150, 183
Baskerville, Sir Thomas, 339, 340, 342
Bazan, Alonzo de, 322, 323
Benin, 5
Bernaldez, Alonzo, 76–80, 88–9, 120
Bernaldez, Lorenzo, 52–3
Bland, Captain, 115, 144
Bontemps, Jean, 46, 80, 96
Borburata, 76–80, 96, 120–3
Borough, William, 272–3, 282, 286, 293, 294–5, 299–300, 314–15
Brazil, 8, 25–33; brazil wood, 8, 26, 30–1; English in, 26–33, 211–12, 221–2
Brigandine, Robert, 236–7
Brille, 190
Bristol, Convention of, 193
Brittany, Spaniards in, 320, 321–2, 332, 336
Bull, Thomas, 21
Burchet, Peter, 200–1
Burghley, Lord (Sir W. Cecil), to

1568, 45, 62, 63, 88, 102, 110; 1568–77, 160, 161–3, 164, 166–7, 168–9, 177–90, 195, 241; 1577 to end, 227, 265–6, 273, 274–5, 276, 312, 313, 337; paper on Navy Board, 284–6
Butler, John, 203

Cabot, Sebastian, 9, 12
Canary Islands, 16–17, 24, 340
Cape Verde Islands, 4, 16, 280–1
Caribs, 10, 14, 75, 76, 80
Cartagena, 130–1
Castellanos, Diego Rodriguez, 223
Castellanos, Miguel de, 80–3, 89, 98, 123–9
Castro, Beltran de, 328–30
Cecil, Sir William, *see* Burghley
Challoner, Sir Thomas, 57, 71
Champernowne, Sir Arthur, 161, 165
Champernowne, Henry, 161, 170, 192–3
Chapman, Richard, 282, 286
Charles V, colonial policy, 9, 66
Charter-parties, 133–4
Chatham dockyard, 236, 239, 255, 263–4, 267
Châtillon, Cardinal de, 165
Cimaroons, 204–5
Clarke, William, 105, 148
Clinton, Lord, 63, 102, 110, 243, 266, 296
Cockeram, Martin, 29–30
Coligny, Admiral, 89, 101, 159, 166–7, 190, 191
Collins, William, 113, 154
Condé, Prince of, 159, 168
Cornwall, Spanish raid on, 336
Cromwell, Thomas, 20, 21, 22, 30–1
Cumberland, Earl of, 319–20

Delgadillo, Antonio, 136, 138, 140
Dolhain, Lord of, 167

344

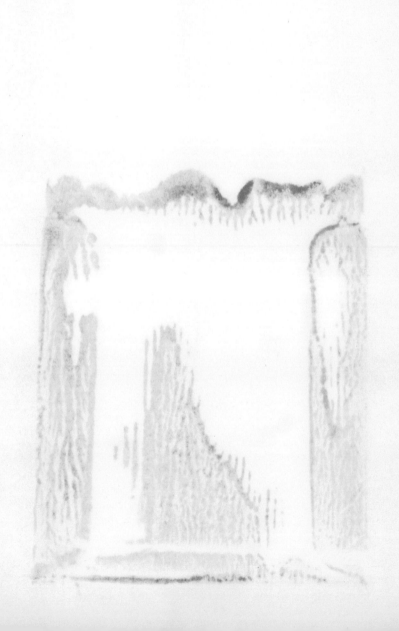